Lecture Notes in Computer Science　14241

Founding Editors

Gerhard Goos
Juris Hartmanis

Editorial Board Members

The series Lecture Notes in Computer Science (LNCS), including its subseries Lecture Notes in Artificial Intelligence (LNAI) and Lecture Notes in Bioinformatics (LNBI), has established itself as a medium for the publication of new developments in computer science and information technology research, teaching, and education.

LNCS enjoys close cooperation with the computer science R & D community, the series counts many renowned academics among its volume editors and paper authors, and collaborates with prestigious societies. Its mission is to serve this international community by providing an invaluable service, mainly focused on the publication of conference and workshop proceedings and postproceedings. LNCS commenced publication in 1973.

Omar Alonso · Helena Cousijn ·
Gianmaria Silvello · Mónica Marrero ·
Carla Teixeira Lopes · Stefano Marchesin
Editors

Linking Theory and Practice of Digital Libraries

27th International Conference on Theory and Practice
of Digital Libraries, TPDL 2023
Zadar, Croatia, September 26–29, 2023
Proceedings

 Springer

Editors
Omar Alonso 🆔
Amazon
Santa Clara, CA, USA

Helena Cousijn 🆔
DataCite
Hannover, Germany

Gianmaria Silvello 🆔
University of Padua
Padua, Italy

Mónica Marrero 🆔
Europeana Foundation
BE Den Haag, The Netherlands

Carla Teixeira Lopes 🆔
University of Porto
Porto, Portugal

Stefano Marchesin 🆔
University of Padua
Padua, Italy

ISSN 0302-9743   ISSN 1611-3349 (electronic)
Lecture Notes in Computer Science
ISBN 978-3-031-43848-6   ISBN 978-3-031-43849-3 (eBook)
https://doi.org/10.1007/978-3-031-43849-3

This Springer imprint is published by the registered company Springer Nature Switzerland AG
The registered company address is: Gewerbestrasse 11, 6330 Cham, Switzerland

Paper in this product is recyclable.

Preface

These proceedings contain the full papers and short papers selected for presentation at the 27th International Conference on Theory and Practice of Digital Libraries (TPDL 2023).[1] The event was organized by the University of Zadar, Croatia. The conference was held on September 26–29, 2023, in Zadar, Croatia.

Over the years, TPDL has established itself as an important international forum focused on digital libraries and associated technical, practical, and social issues. TPDL encompasses the many meanings of the term "digital libraries," including new forms of information institutions; operational information systems with all manner of digital content; new means of selecting, collecting, organizing, and distributing digital content; and theoretical models of information media, including document genres and electronic publishing.

A selection of the best papers accepted to TPDL 2023 will be invited to submit an extended version to the *International Journal of Digital Libraries* (IJDL). Three of the best papers published by IJDL in 2022 have been invited to present at TPDL 2023.

TPDL 2023 received 64 submissions in two categories: 39 full and 25 short papers. Full and short papers present high-quality, original research relevant to the TPDL community. The accepted full papers are published in these conference proceedings (12+ pages) and presented as long conference talks. In contrast, short papers are published in these conference proceedings (6+ pages) and presented as short conference talks at the conference.

All submissions were reviewed by at least three members of an international Program Committee and by one senior meta-reviewer. Of the full papers submitted to the conference, 13 were accepted for oral presentation (33% of the submitted ones), 7 full papers (18%) were accepted as short papers. Of the short papers, 10 were accepted for oral presentation (40% of the submitted ones).

We thank all Program Committee members for their time and effort in ensuring the high quality of the TPDL 2023 program.

We would like to thank our keynote speakers for their contributions to the program: Laura Hollink (CWI - Centrum Wiskunde & Informatica, The Netherlands) presenting "Responsible AI & GLAM: challenges and opportunities" and Beatrice Alex (University of Edinburgh, UK) presenting "AI language technologies and digital collections: the need for interdisciplinary communication and co-design".

The Coalition for Networked Information supported TPDL 2023.

August 2023

Drahomira Cupar
Omar Alonso
Helena Cousijn
Gianmaria Silvello

---

[1] http://tpdl2023.dei.unipd.it/.

Organization

General Chair

Drahomira Cupar University of Zadar, Croatia

Program Chairs

Omar Alonso Amazon, USA
Helena Cousijn DataCite, Germany
Gianmaria Silvello University of Padua, Italy

Short Program Chairs

Mónica Marrero Europeana Foundation, The Netherlands
Carla Teixeira Lopes University of Porto, Portugal

Proceedings Chair

Stefano Marchesin University of Padua, Italy

Publicity Chair

Fabio Giachelle University of Padua, Italy

Organization Committee

Drahomira Cupar University of Zadar, Croatia
Zrinka Džoić University of Zadar, Croatia
Laura Grzunov University of Zadar, Croatia
Marijana Tomić University of Zadar, Croatia

Senior Program Committee

Trond Aalberg	Norwegian University of Science and Technology, Norway
Maristella Agosti	University of Padua, Italy
José Borbinha	Universidade de Lisboa, Portugal
Fabien Duchateau	Université Claude Bernard Lyon 1, France
Edward Fox	Virginia Tech, USA
Mark Hall	Open University, UK
Martin Klein	Los Alamos National Laboratory, USA
Michael Nelson	Old Dominion University, USA
Christos Papatheodorou	University of Athens, Greece
Gabriella Pasi	University of Milano-Bicocca, Italy
Thomas Risse	University of Frankfurt, Germany

Program Committee

Sawood Alam	Internet Archive, USA
Daniel Alemneh	University of North Texas, USA
Marco Angelini	University of Rome "La Sapienza", Italy
Miriam Baglioni	CNR-ISTI, Italy
Wolf-Tilo Balke	TU Braunschweig, Germany
Eleonora Bernasconi	University of Bari, Italy
Carlos Bobed Lisbona	University of Zaragoza, Spain
Zeyd Boukhers	University of Koblenz, Germany
Ricardo Campos	University of Beira Interior, Portugal
Yinlin Chen	Virginia Tech, USA
Giorgio Maria Di Nunzio	University of Padua, Italy
Boris Dobrov	Moscow State University, Russia
Guglielmo Faggioli	University of Padua, Italy
Stefano Ferilli	University of Bari, Italy
Anderson Ferreira	Universidade Federal de Ouro Preto, Brasil
Yannis Foufoulas	University of Athens, Greece
Nuno Freire	Europeana Foundation, The Netherlands
Fabio Giachelle	University of Padua, Italy
William A. Ingram	Virginia Tech, USA
Antoine Isaac	Vrije Universiteit Amsterdam, The Netherlands
Adam Jatowt	University of Innsbruck, Austria
Jaap Kamps	University of Amsterdam, The Netherlands
Johannes Kiesel	Bauhaus-Universität Weimar, Germany
Claus-Peter Klas	GESIS, Germany

Andrea Mannocci	CNR-ISTI, Italy
Stefano Marchesin	University of Padua, Italy
Nicola Orio	University of Padua, Italy
Edie Rasmussen	University of British Columbia, Canada
Andreas Rauber	TU Wien, Austria
Irene Rodrigues	Universidade de Évora, Portugal
Andrea Scharnhorst	Royal Netherlands Academy of Arts and Sciences, The Netherlands
Heiko Schuldt	University of Basel, Switzerland
Martin Schäler	University of Salzburg, Austria
Giuseppe Serra	University of Udine, Italy
Hussein Suleman	University of Cape Town, South Africa
Anna Maria Tammaro	University of Parma, Italy
Carla Teixeira Lopes	University of Porto, Portugal
Francesca Tomasi	University of Bologna, Italy
Ricardo Torres	Wageningen University & Research, The Netherlands, and Norwegian University of Science and Technology, Norway
Thanasis Vergoulis	Athena Research Center, Greece
David Walsh	Edge Hill University, UK
Michele Weigle	Old Dominion University, USA
Peter Williams	Center for Astrophysics – Harvard & Smithsonian, USA

Short and Accelerating Innovation Program Committee

Vangelis Banos	Aristotle University of Thessaloniki, Greece
Gerd Berget	Oslo Metropolitan University, Norway
José Borbinha	Universidade de Lisboa, Portugal
Ricardo Campos	University of Beira Interior, Portugal
Vittore Casarosa	CNR-ISTI, Italy
Florence Clavaud	Archives nationales, France
Mickael Coustaty	La Rochelle Université, France
Theodore Dalamagas	Athena Research Center, Greece
Giorgio Maria Di Nunzio	University of Padua, Italy
Boris Dobrov	Moscow State University, Russia
Fabien Duchateau	Université Claude Bernard Lyon 1, France
Ralph Ewerth	University of Hannover, Germany
Edward Fox	Virginia Tech, USA
Nuno Freire	Europeana Foundation, The Netherlands
Daniel Garijo	Universidad Politécnica de Madrid, Spain

Additional Reviewers

Serafeim Chatzopoulos
Laura Menotti
Andrea Pasin

Human-in-the-Loop Latent Space Learning for Bibrecord-Based Literature Management (Keynote)

Shingo Watanabe, Hiroyoshi Ito, Masaki Matsubara, and Atsuyuki Morishima

University of Tsukuba, Tsukuba, Japan
{watanmabe.shingo.ss@alumni,ito@slis,
masaki@slis,mori@slis}@tsukuba.ac.jp

Abstract. Every researcher must conduct a literature review, and the document management needs of researchers working on various research topics vary. However, there are two significant challenges today. First, traditional methods like the tree hierarchy of document folders and tag-based management are no longer effective with the enormous volume of publications. Second, although their bib information is available to everyone, many papers can be accessed only through paid services. This study attempts to develop an interactive tool for personal literature management solely based on their bibliographic records[2].

Figure 1 illustrates how it works. First, since the relationships among bibliographic records are naturally modeled as a graph, the set of bib records is represented as a heterogeneous graph of bib records whose nodes correspond to papers, authors, conference names, years, etc. (Fig. 1(1)). Then, the machine learner, which implements our human-in-the-loop latent space learning method, computes and visualizes the positions in a *two-dimensional space on the screen* that corresponds to the space for papers that exists in the researcher's mind (Fig. 1(2)). Next, the researcher gives feedback on the suggested positions by *moving papers in incorrect positions in her criteria to the correct position*. In the feedback phase, the researchers are given details about the literature, including the title, authors, publication place, and year. Then, the learner takes the feedback and updates the criteria in the space so that it can correctly predict the positions of newly arrived papers. Since a set of bibliographic records forms a graph, our model is naturally designed as a graph-based encoder-decoder model that connects the graph and the space. The experiments with ten researchers from humanities, science, and engineering domains show that the proposed framework gives superior results to a typical graph convolutional encoder-decoder model.

Challenges and Contributions. (1) We show a *principled* framework for interactive latent space learning for literature management. It is based on a common graph convolutional encoder-decoder model, in which the criteria for individual literature management are represented by the weights of a set of *meta-paths* (i.e., sequences of attributes at the schema of bib-records data), which are a popular means to capture the semantics of heterogeneous graph [1].

---

[2] This abstract is a summarization of our ICADL and IJDL papers [3, 4]

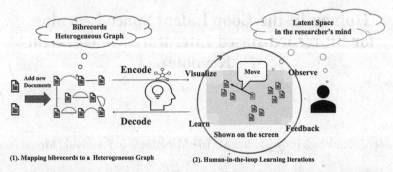

Fig. 1. Overview of the framework. (1) A graph of bib records is constructed for the arrived documents; documents are connected if they mention the same terms, are written by the same author, etc. (2) Next, we have a human-in-the-loop learning iteration for learning the latent space in the user's mind. Then, the learner predicts the positions of newly arrived papers in the space.

Our model is unique in that it is based on the following two assumptions. First, the user's criteria in the latent space are consistent *only locally*. This is inspired by the results in psychology such as [2]. Thus, our first research question (**RQ1**) is whether each researcher has different criteria at different sub-spaces in the latent space or not. Second, two papers are connected through paths on the graph if they are close to each other in the latent space. Therefore, unlike other popular graph convolutional encoder-decoder models, our decoder is based on the Euclidean distance of latent vectors. Thus, our second question (**RQ2**) is whether our decoder is effective or not. (2) We show experimental results where the subjects are ten academic researchers from *science, engineering, and the humanities domains*. The results answer the two research questions positively and show that the approach is much superior to a typical graph convolutional model, and the resulting quality is practically good in that it can put the new paper in a position close to the correct one. This implies that our tool can help researchers manage relevant publications with their own criteria.

References

1. Ma, X., Wang, R.: Personalized scientific paper recommendation based on heterogeneous graph representation. IEEE Access **7**, 79887–79894 (2019)
2. Vlaev, I.: Local choices: rationality and the contextuality of decision-making. Brain Sci. **8**(1), 8 (2018)
3. Watanabe, S., Ito, H., Matsubara, M., Morishima, A.: Human-in-the-loop latent space learning for bibrecord-based literature management. Int. J. Digital Libr. (to appear)
4. Watanabe, S., Ito, H., Matsubara, M., Morishima, A.: Bibrecord-based literature management with interactive latent space learning. In: Tseng, YH., Katsurai, M., Nguyen, H.N. (eds.) ICADL 2022. LNCS, vol 13636. Springer, Cham (2022). https://doi.org/10.1007/978-3-031-21756-2_13

Contents

Knowledge Creation

Human-Computer Interaction

Digital Humanities

Digital Cultural Heritage

Invited Papers from IJDL

Holistic Graph-Based Document Representation and Management for Open Science

Stefano Ferilli[✉][iD], Davide Di Pierro, and Domenico Redavid

University of Bari, 70125 Bari, BA, Italy
stefano.ferilli@uniba.it

Abstract. (Extended Abstract) While most previous research focused only on the textual content of documents, advanced support for document management in Digital Libraries, for Open Science, requires handling all aspects of a document: from structure, to content, to context. These different but inter-related aspects cannot be handled separately, and were traditionally ignored in Digital Libraries. We propose a graph-based unifying representation and handling model based on the definition of an ontology that integrates all the different perspectives and drives the document description in order to boost the effectiveness of document management. We also show how even simple algorithms can profitably use our proposed approach to return relevant and personalized outcomes in different document management tasks.

Keywords: Document Representation · Knowledge Graphs · Document Management · Open Science

1 Introduction

Open Science (OS) is an approach to the scientific process that focuses on making all research knowledge available, so as to build a more replicable and robust science using new technologies, altering incentives, and changing attitudes [11]. Fundamental to OS are the FAIR (Findability, Accessibility, Interoperability, Reusability) principles for data and metadata [10]. The obvious infrastructure to support OS are Digital Libraries (DLs). However, to handle OS issues, the standard realm of DLs must be expanded, in order to describe and/or store the content of the documents (textual or conceptual content, physical, layout and logic structure, semantics), additional information and materials that are external to the publications (datasets, systems, tools, etc.), and their *context*. This expansion requires advanced knowledge handling approaches, but also enables new, high-level functions that support scholars and researchers in their activities.

The solution we propose is to leverage approaches and methods developed in the field of AI, and specifically knowledge representation and handling models based on Knowledge Graphs (KGs). In this direction, a few works have tried

O. Alonso et al. (Eds.): TPDL 2023, LNCS 14241, pp. 3–7, 2023.
https://doi.org/10.1007/978-3-031-43849-3_1

to go beyond simple metadata schemas and proposed the use of ontologies for DLs. Still, there is a lack of infrastructure to support the practices of OS [6]. Some existing taxonomies to describe OS are just organizations of concepts, but cannot be used as schemes of a DL database. Even the data model proposed in OpenAIRE [8] does not fully grasp our idea of context.

The objectives of our work are:

1. crafting an ontology for DLs that: (i) moves from traditional record-based description to a graph-based representation of knowledge; (ii) expands the area of description to both content and context; (iii) can describe concepts that are typical of OS; (iv) may support the FAIR principles on both standard and additional materials;
2. implementing a prototype with an initial set of functions that this ontology may enable, and that may improve the practice.

The core ontology we defined can be extended by each community based on its needs, and that would act as a schema for the knowledge base.

A novel contribution of our approach is the *contextual* perspective. It can establish additional, direct or indirect, non-trivial connections between documents, document components, or pieces of content, based on domain-specific or common-sense knowledge, automatically extracted from, or manually contributed by, external sources.

2   Proposed Representation

The top-level classes (i.e., the immediate subclasses of the universal class) in our ontology are the following: Artifact, Collection, ContentDescription, **Dataset**, **Device**, Document, DocumentDescription, Environment, Event, Intellectual-Work, InternetComponent, Item, Organization, Person, Place, **ProcessComponent**, **Project**, **Setting**, **Software**, **System**, TemporalSpecification, **Tool**, User. In bold are those specifically connected to OS and sufficiently general; any specific branch of science may develop, if needed, its own subclasses for these classes. Relationships are also provided to connect items within each of the above classes or across classes. More technically, we adopt an LPG-based approach to ontologies and knowledge graphs, as described in [3], and thus we may also define properties on nodes and arcs.

The portion of ontology dealing with DL concepts is compliant with the Dublin Core Metadata Initiative (DCMI), the IFLA Functional Requirements for Bibliographic Records (FRBR) [7] and the Open Archives Initiative Object Reuse and Exchange (OAI-ORE) standards[1]. The portion of ontology dealing with OS is aligned to OpenAIRE [8]. We expanded this core in several directions: while [5] discusses the DL-related extensions, we considered that the following different but complementary aspects must be considered in DLs to provide a real support to OS:

---

[1] https://www.openarchives.org/ore/.

- *Textual*, related to the lexical and grammatical features;
- *Layout*, concerning the geometrical structure of documents;
- *Logical*, dealing with the roles played by the document's components;
- *Conceptual*, interested in the meaning conveyed by the documents, both explicitly (e.g., the terms appearing in the text) and implicitly (e.g., the subject dealt with in the document);
- *Contextual*, adding information and creating connections outside what is expressed in each document, or even in the entire collection.

We call our ontology-based approach a 'holistic' one, because it considers and brings to cooperation all these aspects.

The Textual, Layout, Logical and Conceptual aspects concern the content, and may describe the documents as a whole or their single (layout, logical, or grammatical) components. Concepts are typically organized in taxonomies. E.g., the WordNet ontology [9], the Dewey Decimal Classification (DDC) system [1], and the ACM Computing Classification System (CCS)[2]. Several taxonomies can be stored, inter-connected and expanded with additional user-defined and/or domain-specific items. Any instance of these classes can be used to tag individuals of other classes, possibly with different weights. Instances of the various relationships enable forms of associative reasoning, such as graph traversal, that leveraging textual, semantic and contextual information allow finding non-trivial paths between the documents and their contents.

Contextual description of documents relies on general and domain-specific classes provided by the ontology, and not strictly related to document structure, content or management. It may also involve DL-related classes in the ontology, but using them in additional and different relationships than in bibliographic records. Even classes to express users and their profiles, useful for personalization purposes, may be included. Together with the textual-semantic portion of the ontology, the contextual portion acts as a hub to interconnect pieces of information that would otherwise be disconnected, e.g. two documents using the same dataset that do not explicitly mention each other. This can help in carrying out some research tasks: in scholarly research, supporting or even suggesting investigation directions not explicitly present in any of the single documents, but emerging from their direct or indirect relationships; in document clustering, improving the quality of similarity computation, by leveraging information that is, again, not present in any of the available documents; in document classification, improving performance by expanding and integrating the information present in the document with related information coming from the background knowledge or from other documents; in document indexing, allowing to retrieve documents that do not explicitly contain the search parameters set by the user; in query answering, allowing to find more source documents, indirectly related to the question posed by the user but relevant to answer it.

---

[2] https://dl.acm.org/ccs.

3 Prototype Implementation

For a first implementation of our proposal, we leveraged a number of previous works and systems from our past research, as described in [2], and specifically GraphBRAIN [4] for knowledge storage and management.

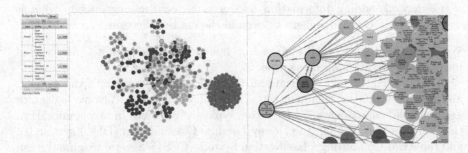

Fig. 1. Overall and zoomed portion of GraphBRAIN's knowledge base

The prototype included a few demonstrative functions:

Subgraph Extraction Starting from a set of nodes provided as input, returns a selected portion of the knowledge graph which is more relevant to these nodes (see Fig. 1, where the starting items are dragged on the side).

Information Retrieval based on both (lexical or conceptual) content and on context, for extending the set of results compared to traditional approaches.

Question Answering based on identifying a subgraph including the answer and translating it into natural language.

Instance Clustering where clusters are emerging aggregations of related items that may involve instances of any kind (see Fig. 1).

Recommendation based on both closeness in the graph and compatibility with the user's profile.

Support for Scholarly Research through automatic extraction (by applying network analysis algorithms) or manual browsing (by expanding portions of the graph at need, and exploring the properties of the nodes and arcs).

The prototype was tested in various domains: history of Computer Science, Cultural Heritage, LAM (Libraries/Archives/Museums), Tourism and Food, but also including linguistic, ontological and contextual information. Each of these sub-domains is organized according to its specific ontology, and these ontologies are connected to each other.

Our proposal responds to the five 'schools of thought' of OS. For democracy, we guarantee access to all types of users and provide functions for searching and question answering. From a pragmatic point of view, we bring different people together through links between works and authors. Concerning infrastructure, the information we store about the structures, tools and technologies used in a given context allow to share and reuse ideas on how to build infrastructure. For integration with the public, our system does not pose any technological barrier to entry. The interface is simple, secure and does not distinguish users with specific knowledge from others. Through cooperation and the amount of data available, different metrics can be shared to evaluate any solution from several viewpoints and a more accurate overview can be obtained.

References

1. Dewey, M.: A classification and subject index for cataloguing and arranging the books and pamphlets of a library. Amherst, Massachusetts (1876)
2. Ferilli, S.: An automatic intelligent system for document processing and fruition. Trans. Mach. Learn. Data Min. **11**, 43–62 (2018)
3. Ferilli, S.: Integration strategy and tool between formal ontology and graph database technology. Electronics **10**(2616) (2021)
4. Ferilli, S., Redavid, D.: The GraphBRAIN system for knowledge graph management and advanced fruition. In: Helic, D., Leitner, G., Stettinger, M., Felfernig, A., Raś, Z.W. (eds.) ISMIS 2020. LNCS (LNAI), vol. 12117, pp. 308–317. Springer, Cham (2020). https://doi.org/10.1007/978-3-030-59491-6_29
5. Ferilli, S., Redavid, D.: An ontology and knowledge graph infrastructure for digital library knowledge representation. In: Ceci, M., Ferilli, S., Poggi, A. (eds.) IRCDL 2020. CCIS, vol. 1177, pp. 47–61. Springer, Cham (2020). https://doi.org/10.1007/978-3-030-39905-4_6
6. Hocker, J., Schindler, C., Rittberger, M.: Participatory design for ontologies: a case study of an open science ontology for qualitative coding schemas. Aslib J. Inf. Manage. **72**, 671–685 (2020)
7. IFLA Study Group on the FRBR: Functional requirements for bibliographic records - final report. Tech. rep., International Federation of Library Associations and Institutions (2009)
8. Manghi, P., et al.: The openaire research graph data model (2019). https://doi.org/10.5281/zenodo.2643199
9. Miller, G.: WordNet: a lexical database for English. Commun. ACM **38**, 39–41 (1995)
10. Mons, B., et al.: Cloudy, increasingly fair; revisiting the fair data guiding principles for the European open science cloud. Inf. Serv. Us **37**, 49–56 (2017)
11. Spellman, B.A., Gilbert, E.A., Corker, K.S.: Open Science, pp. 1–47. John Wiley & Sons, Ltd (2018). https://doi.org/10.1002/9781119170174.epcn519

A Multilingual Dashboard to Analyse Intercultural Knowledge Circulation

Amel Fraisse[(✉)] [ID]

GERiiCO - Université de Lille, 4073 Lille, France
`amel.fraisse@univ-lille.fr`

Abstract. This paper presents the multilingual Rosetta Dashboard, an NLP-based, data-driven visualization tool for points of divergence between translated texts and their original source. While the NLP algorithms that power this dashboard are modest, this project nonetheless stands as an example of an NLP application that has been shaped by the needs of an adjacent scholarly community.

Keywords: Digital Humanities · Multilingual Data Visualization · Multilingual and Parallel Texts

1 Introduction

From a global perspective, human knowledge of culture and heritage has been shared, explored, and preserved for nearly centuries through translation. The art of translating texts is largely to thank for our ability to learn about and from other cultures, and vice versa. It is crucial to recognize that every person is shaped by their culture and identity. Hence, every body of knowledge, regardless of type of classification, is similarly impacted by specific historical, geopolitical, and sociocultural factors. TL- Explorer is created not only with this diversity in mind, but also as a tool to explore these nuances as they are reflected in translated literature.

The Rosetta Dashboard is designed as an adjunctive tool for researchers and scholars in human sciences for analyzing the multilingual circulation of texts. The algorithms underpinning this tool are modest compared to the current cutting-edge of NLP, but the tool is nonetheless significant as an example of how to apply "just enough" NLP in the service of research priorities shaped by another field.

2 Background

Over 98% of the world's languages lack most or all of the linguistic resources of the Basic Language Resource Kit (BLARK) [8], such as monolingual and bilingual corpora, machine-readable dictionaries, thesauri, part-of-speech taggers, morphological analyzers, parsers, etc. [14]. Consequently, these languages

O. Alonso et al. (Eds.): TPDL 2023, LNCS 14241, pp. 8–14, 2023.
https://doi.org/10.1007/978-3-031-43849-3_2

are cut off from the potential value of NLP for enhancing digital information access and retrieval, or for providing new insight into linguistic, literary and cultural research questions. Parallel corpora are of particular value for bootstrapping the development of NLP tools for under-resourced languages, e.g. using Statistical Machine Translation to learn word alignment models between two languages [12].

Researchers have drawn on a diverse set of sources for building parallel corpora that include endangered languages, as well as languages that have attracted little commercial interest in NLP, such as the Bible, Wikipedia, and European parliamentary proceedings. While the interpretive nature of literary translations has caused a lag in their adoption as a source for NLP development, multiple recent projects have developed parallel corpora based on texts including the *Harry Potter* series and *Le Petit Prince*. The Translation Dashboard was developed in service of the Rosetta Project: ResOurces for Endangered languages Through TranslAted texts[1].

Rosetta has created a parallel corpus containing over 90 Huckleberry Finn translations in over 50 languages as a basis for developing NLP resources for under-resourced and endangered languages [4,5]. The Slavic (Bulgarian, Polish, Russian, Ukrainian) and Finno-Ugric (Hungarian and Finnish) translations have served as the initial data sets for testing the project's text alignment algorithms.

While there already exist alignment visualization tools such as ANNIS [2], SWIFT Aligner [6], Cario [15], VisualTCA [7] and MkAlign [3], most of them focus on word alignment. Even some of these tools provide sentence alignment visualization, it just serves as an intermediate step before lexicon level. There does not exist a tool that leads users explore data in a chapter-paragraph-sentence-word, coarse-to-fine fashion. Moreover, nearly all tools are not literary texts oriented, which is more challenging for alignment approaches because the entire corpora must be aligned and alignment should be as confident as possible [17].

As translation studies scholars worked with this corpus of Slavic translations, they expressed the need for a parallel reading environment and visualizations that would allow them to easily see patterns of structural divergence between the source text and translations, at different levels of granularity. The Translation Dashboard aims to help translation scholars to easily see patterns of structural divergence between the source text and translations, at different levels of granularity. The visualizations and parallel reading environment have been designed as a direct response to the kinds of questions raised by translation studies scholars as they have worked with this corpus of Slavic translations.

3 The Rosetta Translation Dashboard

3.1 Functionality and Application

The default view of the Rosetta Translation Dashboard displays a per-chapter paragraph count (based on newlines and whitespace), which also determines the

---

[1] https://francestanford.stanford.edu/projects/rosetta-resources-endangered-languag es-through-translated-texts.

color variation in the heat map within the table (Fig. 1). An exceedingly high divergence from the source paragraph count alerts the scholar that there may be data cleaning issues (e.g. one instance where each line in a poem embedded in a narrative was treated as a new paragraph), but a moderate divergence can reflect the translator's deliberate stylistic choices about how the flow of the narrative should be rendered. A translation studies scholar in the literary tradition may use this information to select chapters for a close-reading analysis.

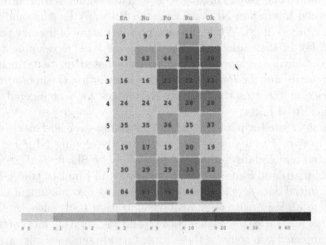

Fig. 1. Paragraph counts from Chap. 1 to Chap. 8 in English, Bulgarian, Polish, Russian and Ukrainian of the novel *Adventures of Huckleberry Finn*. Heat map color varies with the difference of paragraph counts in the corresponding chapter.

By selecting an individual language in the table header, the scholar can view a pie chart breakdown of the chapter-level divergence in paragraph numbers for the entire novel.

Also from the table overview page, a user can select an individual chapter for a particular language, and view a parallel reading display that juxtaposes the original English with a particular translation.

As an example, a scholar may notice when consulting the table that Polish, Russian, and Ukrainian all have 22- or 23-paragraph Chap. 3, whereas the original only has 16. Selecting Chap. 3 for a particular language would allow the scholar to consult the texts side-by-side. This close reading may surface the cause (e.g. differences in how to split up quotations). After reaching an understanding about the phenomena that lead to this divergence, the scholar may consult the pie chart to better understand how widely occurring these phenomena may be throughout the entire translation.

3.2   Text Sources and Copyright

Mark Twain died in 1910, meaning that under the Berne convention, his works have been in the public domain since 1960, with local laws expanding the window of protection up to 70 years. Even when the original text is in the public domain, translations are treated as new works that receive their own copyright. As a result, recent translations of *Huck Finn* remain in copyright, even though copyright has expired on the original work. However, because Mark Twain was immensely popular during and after his lifetime, many of the translations are largely contemporaneous with the original work, and therefore likewise outside of copyright protection.

The corpus was compiled through a combination of an open call to the Mark Twain literary community to identify translations, in addition to a bibliographical survey carried out by [13], consulting the UNESCO-funded "Index Translationum", and finally, incorporating input from people online via a paid crowdsourcing tasks.

3.3 Algorithms of Paragraph Aligner

We divided chapters into 3 major categories based on their differences in paragraph counts compared to the original English version: *exact-match*, *large-difference*, and *regular-difference*. Different paragraph aligners may apply to different categories.

For *exact-match* chapters, our hypothesis is that their paragraphs were translated one to one. No further paragraph alignment methods are needed. This hypothesis has been confirmed for most of the *exact-match* cases by the human validation experiment.

As we have discussed in Sect. 3.1, *large-difference* cases are normally caused by different ways of splitting quotations. So we provide a text preprocessing option before paragraph alignment when long quotations have been found under *large-difference* cases. This preprocessing option splits quotations into paragraphs according to the same standard in all translations. Experiments have shown that it can largely reduce differences in paragraph counts and sometimes move a chapter from the *large-difference* category to the *regular* category.

For the majority *regular-difference* cases, we started with applying frequently used open-source sentence alignment packages such as GMA[2] [10], BMA[3] [11], Hunalign[4] [16], Gargantua[5] [1] and Yasa[6] [9]. Here we treat paragraphs as sentences so as to feed them into sentence aligners.

4   Experiments

In this section, we show an example for the user side of the Rosetta translation dashboard tool.

---

[2] http://nlp.cs.nyu.edu/GMA/.

[3] http://research.microsoft.com/en-us/downloads/aafd5dcf-4dcc-49b2-8a22-f7055113 e656/.

[4] http://mokk.bme.hu/en/resources/hunalign/.

[5] http://sourceforge.net/projects/gargantua/.

[6] http://rali.iro.umontreal.ca/rali/?q=en/yasa.

Starting with the main heat map page as shown in Fig. 1, each cell value corresponds to the number of paragraphs in its chapter (row) and language version (column). Cell's color varies with the difference of the paragraph count compared with the original English version. By referring the legend below, we can have some instant general impressions of the paragraph count such as: Bulgarian translation has a better paragraph count matching with the English version compared with other languages (columns); The number of paragraphs of Chap. 5 and Chap. 6 are close over all 4 translations.

By clicking any target language label at the top of the heat map, a user can jump to the corresponding translation page as shown in Fig. 2. On this page, all 43 chapters are categorized into several groups by their paragraph count difference. For instance, in the Polish translation, we see that there are 18 chapters whose paragraph count difference is equal or less than 2, including 4 chapters which are exact match to the original version.

We may apply different prepossessing and paragraph alignment algorithms to different type of chapters. This pie chart also provides useful information for algorithms selection.

Fig. 2. Pie chart of the chapter categories of Polish translation compared with the original English version.

A user can jump back to the main page by clicking the "43 chapters" label at in center of the pie chart. Selecting the target language and chapter number takes the user to the paragraph alignment page of the selected language and chapter as shown in Fig. 3. The paragraph alignment page contains re-organized paragraphs from two languages. The aligned ones are shown close to each other in horizontal position. Mousing over one paragraph will highlight the related aligned paragraphs.

A deeper aligned paragraph visualization is also supported just by clicking the desired paragraph. This is similar to the yellow highlighting part from Fig. 3 but with more detailed analysis information.

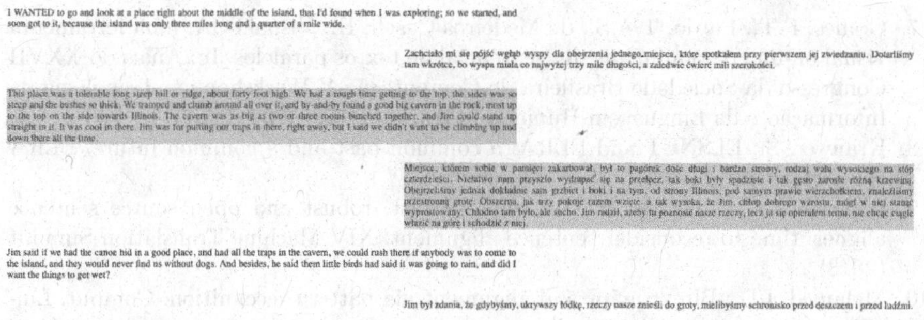

I WANTED to go and look at a place right about the middle of the island, that I'd found when I was exploring; so we started, and soon got to it, because the island was only three miles long and a quarter of a mile wide.

Zachciało mi się pójść wgląb wyspy dla obejrzenia jednego miejsca, które spotkałem przy pierwszem jej zwiedzaniu. Dotarliśmy tam wkrótce, bo wyspa miała co najwyżej trzy mile długości, a zaledwie ćwierć mili szerokości.

This place was a tolerable long steep hill or ridge, about forty foot high. We had a rough time getting to the top, the sides was so steep and the bushes so thick. We tramped and clumb around all over it, and by-and-by found a good big cavern in the rock, most up to the top on the side towards Illinois. The cavern was as big as two or three rooms bunched together, and Jim could stand up straight in it. It was cool in there. Jim was for putting our traps in there, right away, but I said we didn't want to be climbing up and down there all the time.

Miejsce, którem sobie w pamięci zakarbował, był to pagórek dość długi i bardzo stromy, rodzaj wału wysokiego na stóp czterdzieści. Niełatwo nam przyszło wydrapać się na przełęcz, tak boki były spadziste i tak gęsto zarosłe różną krzewiną. Obejrzeliśmy jednak dokładnie sam grzbiet i boki i na tym, od strony Illinois, pod samym prawie wierzchołkiem, znaleźliśmy przestronną grotę. Obszerna, jak trzy pokoje razem wzięte, a tak wysoka, że Jim chłop dobrego wzrostu, mógł w niej stanąć wyprostowany. Chłodno tam było, ale sucho. Jim radził, ażeby tu przenieść nasze rzeczy, lecz ja się opierałem temu, nie chcąc ciągle włazić na górę i schodzić z niej.

Jim said if we had the canoe hid in a good place, and had all the traps in the cavern, we could rush there if anybody was to come to the island, and they would never find us without dogs. And besides, he said them little birds had said it was going to rain, and did I want the things to get wet?

Jim był zdania, że gdybyśmy, ukrywszy łódkę, rzeczy nasze znieśli do groty, mielibyśmy schronisko przed deszczem i przed ludźmi.

Fig. 3. Paragraph alignment of Chap. 8 between the original English (left) and Polish translation (right) of the novel "Adventures of Huckleberry Finn".

5 Conclusions and Ongoing Work

We proposed in this research work a translation dashborad, an NLP-based and data-driven visualization tool, for highlighting intercultural divergence between translated texts and their original source. Based on initial feedback from subject-area experts, we are working on prioritizing and implementing additional requested features. These features include the following: (1) implementing a similarity metric through a combination of automatic assessment, (2) more linguistic coverage: the project is currently working on adding other languages to the corpus, after they have OCR'd and cleaned up a PDF source, and (3) deeper analysis for aligned paragraphs: sentence alignment, word alignment, text similarity and text summarization can support a deeper analysis.

References

1. Braune, F., Fraser, A.: Improved unsupervised sentence alignment for symmetrical and asymmetrical parallel corpora. In: Proceedings of the 23rd International Conference on Computational Linguistics: Posters, pp. 81–89. Association for Computational Linguistics (2010)
2. Druskat, S., Gast, V., Krause, T., Zipser, F.: corpus-tools.org: an interoperable generic software tool set for multi-layer linguistic corpora. In: LREC (2016)
3. Fleury, S., Zimina, M.: Exploring translation corpora with MkAlign. Translation J. **11**(1) (2007)
4. Fraisse, A., Jenn, R., Fishkin, S.F.: Parallel corpora for under-resourced languages using translated fictional texts. In: proceedings of the LREC 2018 Workshop CCURL2018 - Sustaining Knowledge Diversity in the Digital Age. Edited by Claudia Soria, Laurent Besacier, Laurette Pretorius, pp. 39–43. Miyazaki, Japan (2018)
5. Fraisse, A., Tran, Q.T., Jenn, R., Paroubek, P., Fishkin, S.F.: TransLiTex: a parallel corpus of translated literary texts. In: Proceedings of the LREC 2018 Workshop Belt & Road: Language Resources and Evaluation (B&R LRE 2018). Miyazaki, Japan (2018)
6. Gilmanov, T., Scrivner, O., Kübler, S.: Swift aligner, a multifunctional tool for parallel corpora: visualization, word alignment, and (morpho)-syntactic cross-language transfer. In: LREC, pp. 2913–2919 (2014)

7. Gomes, F.T., Pardo, T.A.S., de Medeiros Caseli, H.: VisualTCA: uma ferramenta visual on-line para alinhamento sentencial de textos paralelos. In: Anais do XXVII Congresso da Sociedade Brasileira de Computação-V Workshop em Tecnologia da Informação e da Linguagem Humana (TIL), pp. 1729–1732 (2007)
8. Krauwer, S.: ELSNET and ELRA: a common past and a common future. ELRA Newsletter 3(2) (1998)
9. Lamraoui, F., Langlais, P.: Yet another fast, robust and open source sentence aligner. time to reconsider sentence alignment. XIV Machine Translation Summit (2013)
10. Melamed, I.D.: Bitext maps and alignment via pattern recognition. Comput. Linguist. 25(1), 107–130 (1999)
11. Moore, R.C.: Fast and accurate sentence alignment of bilingual corpora. In: Richardson, S.D. (ed.) AMTA 2002. LNCS (LNAI), vol. 2499, pp. 135–144. Springer, Heidelberg (2002). https://doi.org/10.1007/3-540-45820-4_14
12. Och, F.J., Ney, H.: A systematic comparison of various statistical alignment models. Comput. Linguist. 29(1), 19–51 (2003)
13. Rodney, R.M.: Mark Twain International: A Bibliography and Interpretation of his Wordwide Popularity. Greenwood Press, Westport, CT (1982)
14. Scannell, K.: The crubadan project: corpus building for under-resourced languages. In: Building and Exploring Web Corpora: Proceedings of the 3rd Web as Corpus Workshop, pp. 5–15. Louvain-la-Neuve, Belgium (2007)
15. Smith, N.A., Jahr, M.E.: Cairo: An alignment visualization tool. In: LREC (2000)
16. Varga, D., Halácsy, P., Kornai, A., Nagy, V., Németh, L., Trón, V.: Parallel corpora for medium density languages. Amsterdam Studies In The Theory And History of Linguistic Science Series 4 292, 247 (2007)
17. Xu, Y., Max, A., Yvon, F.: Sentence alignment for literary texts. LiLT (Linguistic Issues in Language Technology) 12 (2015)

Applications and Digital Library Systems

Known by the Company It Keeps: Proximity-Based Indexing for Physical Content in Archival Repositories

Douglas W. Oard[✉]

University of Maryland, College Park, USA
oard@umd.edu

Abstract. Despite the plethora of born-digital content, vast troves of important content remain accessible only on physical media such as paper or microfilm. The traditional approach to indexing undigitized content is using manually created metadata that describes it at some level of aggregation (e.g., folder, box, or collection). Searchers led in this way to some subset of the content often must then manually examine substantial quantities of physical media to find what they are looking for. This paper proposes a complementary approach, in which selective digitization of a small portion of the content is used as a basis for proximity-based indexing as a way of bringing the user closer to the specific content for which they are looking. Experiments with 35 boxes of partially digitized US State Department records indicate that box-level indexes built in this way can provide a useful basis for search.

Keywords: Proximity-based indexing · Archival access · Physical media

1 Introduction

The storyteller Aesop wrote (in Greek) what has been translated as "a man is known by the company he keeps" [1]. In sociology, Aesop's claim is reflected in the concept of homophily, a dictionary definition of which is "the tendency to form strong social connections with people who share one's defining characteristics, as age, gender, ethnicity, socioeconomic status, personal beliefs, etc." [14]. Homophily arises in many contexts, including between people in social network analysis, in organizational dynamics [8], and more metaphorically in, for example, the meaning of terms in natural language processing [3].

Our thesis in this paper is that a form of homophily is to be expected among the content found in archival repositories. Our basis for this is that archivists respect the original order of archival content when performing arrangement and description [18]. In the arrangement task, archivists organize physical materials, typically by placing those materials in folders, placing those folders in boxes, and grouping those boxes into series. Archival materials are generally the records of some organization or individual. Respecting the original order of those records can help to preserve the evidence of the creator's activities that is implicit in that original order. Because archivists consider the evidentiary value of records to be on par with their informational value, this is an important consideration. A second consideration that argues for respecting original order is that doing so makes it possible to open collections for research use with a minimum of work on the archivist's part. Because that original order was useful to the organization or individual that created the records, it is reasonable to assume that users of an archive who put in the effort to learn how a particular collection is ordered will find some value in that ordering [24].

It is this respect for original order in archival arrangement that produces the homophily that we leverage in this paper. Specifically, we hypothesize that if we know something about the content of some records in some archival unit (e.g., folder, box, series, or repository) then we can make some plausible inferences about where certain other records that we have not yet seen might be found. However, it is one thing to reason from first principles that such a claim might be true, and quite another thing to show that such a claim actually is true. In this paper, we show that the claim is true in one specific case, and thus that it could be broadly true, although we leave investigation of the broader question of how widely applicable our claim is for future work.

2 Related Work

Rapid growth in digital content over the last half century has resulted in the initial trickle of digital content reaching archival repositories now becoming a flood. A broad range of tools can be used to find born-digital content, and there has been considerable innovation in that space (e.g., [11,16]). Many such tools could also be used to find content digitized from physical media, such as paper or microfilm, but problems of cost and scale limit the scope of digitization efforts. For example, in the first five months of 2023 the National Archives and Records Administration (NARA) digitized 13 million pages from their holdings of 11.7 billion pages [15]. Even at that impressive rate, 121,000 pages per day, it would take 375 years to digitize the paper holdings of that one repository. Clearly, the problem of finding things on paper will not be going away any time soon.

The first problem faced by someone wishing to find materials on paper is knowing where to look. Citations in the scholarly literature play a particularly prominent role in this process. For example, Tibbo found that 98% of historians followed leads in the published literature [22], and Marsh, et al. found that for anthropologists 73% did so [13]. There are also tools that support search of descriptions created by archivists across multiple repositories, such as Archive-Grid [9]. Once a user knows where to look, their next challenge is to learn how to find what they want there. As Tibbo notes, it is common for scholars to write to or call archivists before visiting a repository [22]. Scholars also make use of finding aids that have been created by archivists to describe (among other things) the nature of the content in a collection, and how that content is arranged and described. Although full-text search of finding aids, which for example Archive-Grid provides, can be useful, in recent years the use of a metadata format called

"Describing Archives: a Content Standard" (DACS) has emerged as an alternative basis for searching the results of the descriptions that archivists create [21].

One limitation of these approaches for finding content on physical media is that they depend entirely on descriptions that are created by archivists. However, the same cost and scale pressures that limit digitization also limit the creation of detailed descriptions [10, 23]. Marsh, for example, notes that of 314 collections in the Smithsonian Institution's National Anthropological Archives, only 25% had an online finding aid as of 2019 [12]. A second limitation is that, as Cox has pointed out, these methods for helping people find archival content were originally designed with scholars in mind, but the general public also makes extensive use of resources found in archives (e.g., for genealogical research), and such users might well need different types of support [5]. For both of these reasons, we see value in creating techniques to guess where specific materials that have not yet been digitized (or otherwise richly described at the level of individual items) might be found. That is the focus of our work in this paper.

3 The "Subject-Numeric Files"

In the United States, the Department of State is responsible for management of foreign relations. Between 1963 and 1973, State maintained its records on paper as "Subject-Numeric Files" [7]. Simplifying somewhat, in this filing system the top-level category is one of 56 three-letter "primary subject" codes (e.g., POL for Political Affairs & Relations), the second-level category indicates a Country (e.g., Brazil), and the third-level category is a numeric code, the meaning of which is specific to each primary subject (e.g., for POL, numeric code 15-1 designates the executive branch of government, and 27-12 designates war crimes). The entire collection includes about 8.6 million pages, held by the United States National Archives and Records Administration (NARA) in College Park, Maryland.

In recent years, Brown University engaged in large-scale digitization of records that shed light on Brazilian politics. As one part of that, Brown arranged for about 14,000 items in NARA's Department of State Subject-Numeric Files to be digitized, all from the POL-Brazil section of those records. They represent parts of the content of a total of 52 boxes. NARA intends to make these records available online, although the links from the NARA catalog to most of these records are not presently working. Fortunately, the Brown University Library makes almost all of the digitized content from 36 of those boxes available,[1] importantly using the same box identifiers. We wrote a crawler to download up to 100 of the records from each of 35 of those boxes (the 36th box had only two digitized files, too few to be useful for our experiments).[2] We also crawled Brown

---

[1] https://library.brown.edu/create/openingthearchives/en/.

[2] The documents that we downloaded were the first (at most) 100 that Brown showed on the results page for each box; results pages were ordered alphabetically by Brown University's title metadata. 100 was more than enough for our experiments, so there was no need to increase the server load by crawling more documents.

University's title metadata for each downloaded document.[3] About 2% of the
PDF files that we downloaded were not actually documents but rather forms
that indicated that a document was not available for scanning; we manually
removed all such cases that could be identified (either by the word "Withdrawal"
in the title metadata, or by viewing PDF files that were small enough—less than
400kB—to suggest that they might be a single page).

This process resulted in 3,205 PDF documents, organized by their original
location at NARA in one of 35 boxes. The smallest number of documents per
box was 22 (box 1925); the largest number was 100 (for eleven of the boxes).
The 35 box numbers are grouped in 8 numeric sequences (1900–1908, 1925–
1934, 1936–1938, 1941–1944, 2129, 2131–2132, 3832–3835, 3837–3838). Boxes
in the NARA's Department of State Subject-Numeric Files have no identifying
metadata beyond the box number, but a box consists of (typically 3 to 6) folders
that hold the actual documents. Brown University metadata includes the label
for the folder in which a document was found, so we crawled that metadata
as well. We can therefore describe a box by the union of its folder labels. For
example, box 1902 contains folders with the following labels:

```
POL 2-3 BRAZ 01/01/1967
POL 5 BRAZ 01/01/1967
POL 6 BRAZ 01/01/1967
```

4   The "BoxFinder" Experiments

The PDF files created by Brown University are searchable, which means that
finding a digitized document can be done with any full-text search system, and
Brown University provides such a service. The situation is quite different, however, for content from those same boxes that has not yet been digitized. When
finding undigitized content is the goal, as is our focus in this paper, all that a
user of NARA's archive would have is folder labels. They would need to request
every box containing any folder labeled with with a subject-numeric code and
date related to their search goal. This is a slow process, since it takes NARA
several hours to deliver a requested box to a user of the archives in the reading
room, and it can easily take hours to examine the records in just one box.

Our ultimate goal is to accelerate this process by recommending to a user
of the archive what box they should look in. We imagine they might use what
we will build one of two ways. In the first, they use it like Google—they type
in a query, and we recommend a box. In the second, they are looking at some
documents, and we recommend a box that we expect contains similar documents.

Whichever type of query we get, we built the box index in the same way. We
pick a few digitized documents from each box, then use the OCR text from those
documents to create an index that can be used to search for a box. The way we
do this is straightforward - we take all the OCR words from some number of

---

[3] Brown University's title metadata is often more concise than NARA's title metadata
for the same document, which for example sometimes also indicates document type.

```
Attached note from the Brazilian Embassy
Background checks
Biographic Information: Vistor Jose Faccione, State Deputy (ARENA) in
    Rio Grande do Sul
Biographic Reporting
Brazil Opts to Counter Poor Image Abroad
Brazilian Laws
Church Newspaper Calls for Democracy
Closure of Brazilian Radio Stations
Daily Media Reaction Report to ITT-Chile Situation
Detention of Fernand Legros
Disability and Death of a President
Ernesto Geisel in Rio
Ester Ferraz
Foreign Minister Gibson Speaks on Brazil's Foreign Policy
GOB Announces Development Goals and Programs for 1970-73
Ineligibilities Again
Itamaraty's Role in Formulation of Brazilian Foreign Policy
Law on Party Loyalty Expected Soon
Monthly Trends Report - December 1971
```

Fig. 1. Some examples of short queries built from title metadata.

pages, starting at the front (e.g., just the first page, or the first two pages) from some number of PDF documents (e.g., 3 documents) that we know actually are in each box. This gives us an index in which there are 35 items that can be found (the 35 boxes), each of which is represented by a single long string of words. If we can use this index to find other documents that are in that same box, then we will have shown that homophily is a useful basis for search, and that a document in this collection can to some extent be "known by the company it keeps."

4.1   Query Formulation

In our experiments, we don't have a real user, so we simulate the two search scenarios. To simulate a "type a query" scenario, we search using Brown University's title metadata for some document as the query (one we have an image of, but that we had not chosen to index).[4] The resulting queries have an average length of 6 terms (min 1, max 26); Fig. 1 shows some examples. If our system can guess which box contains the document from which we got the title, then we expect that it could also do well if a real searcher ever typed a query like that. Of course, searchers might type queries that are better or worse than the document title that we used, but at least this will indicate whether our homophily-based approach can work when it gets a query like the one we gave it.

---

[4] Brown University's title metadata is human-generated; many documents do not actually have titles within the document, and for those that do Brown's title metadata sometimes contains contextual terms missing from the document's actual title.

```
Department o
PAGE 01
47
ACTION SS 7*
INFO CIAE 00,/070 W RIO DE 01693 06I913Z LIMITED OFFICIAL USE
I I 9070
R 06I6TOZ MAR 69
FM AMEMPASSY RIO HE JANFIRO
TO SECSTATE WASHDC 7226
LIMITED OFFICIAL USE RIO DE JANEIRO t693
L I MO IS
FOR VAKY
SUBJECTi DELIVERY OF ROCKEFELLER LETTER
I, IN RFSPONSE TO REQUEST FOR AUDIENCE WITH PRES WE WERE INFORMED
THAT IT NOT CUSTOMARY HERE FOR PRES TO PECEIVF CHARGE D'AFFAIRES
AND PERHAPS I COULD DELIVER IT VIA FONMIN. IT WAS STATED* HOWEVER.
THAT EXCEPTION WOULD BE MADE IN CASE OF U.S. CHARGE IF I So
REQUESTED.
p. IN VIEW FACT I HAD NO OTHER MAJOR SUBSTANTIVE BUSINESS TO DIS-
CUSS AND NOTHING TO ADD TO CONTENTS OF LETTER, I ELFCTED Tn USE
FONMIN CHANNEL FOR DELIVERY* ON THEORY THERE MIGHT SOON BE SIG-
NIFICANT ITEMS i SHOULD TA<E UP DIRECTLY WITH PRES AND IT ADVIS-
ABLE TO SAVr TICKET FOR SUCH AN OCCASION. LETTER WAS DELIVFPED TO
FONMIN THIS MORNING* BELTON
LIMITED OFFICIAL USE
```

Fig. 2. Example of OCR text for the first page of a document.

To simulate the "see a document" query, we use the OCR text from the document that we picked as the basis for the query, and see if the system can guess which box it was from. Figure 2 shows an example of the OCR text from the first page of a document. We call this the query-by-example scenario. Note that this results in a rather long query; on average OCR produced 228 words per page.[5] To limit the complexity of our result tables in this paper, we consistently report results for some number of pages of OCR text that are used both to form the query-by-example and to build the index (e.g., for a box index built from the first page of several documents, our query is built using only the first page of the query-by-example document), although that need not be the case in practice.

4.2   Ranking the Boxes

Whichever type of query we get, we then use bag of words retrieval, ranked with Okapi BM-25 term weights [20] (with $k_1 = 1.2$ and $b = 0.75$), with the Porter stemmer, to create a ranked list of the thirty five boxes, hopefully with the

---

[5] For efficiency reasons, in an actual search system we would also want to do some query term selection (e.g., [17]).

correct box at or near the top.[6] As our measure of success, we count how many times our system (which we call "BoxFinder") guesses the correct box (i.e., the box that actually contains the document the query was made from). To easily compute a percentage, we choose 100 query documents and report how many of that 100 the system got right. We can do this using any number of documents to describe each box, for any number of pages from those documents, and for either way of making a query. For example, as Table 2 shows, if we make the query from the OCR words on the first page of the PDF file, and we use OCR words from the first page of three (other) PDF files to describe each box, then the system is right 27.9% of the time. We call this way of measuring BoxFinder's results Top-1 (since it is the percent of the time that BoxFinder places the correct answer at rank 1). If it were just guessing randomly, with no real idea which box to look in, it would only be right at Top-1 2.9% of the time (i.e., once in every 35 tries).

From this we can conclude BoxFinder is well named - it can find boxes. Of course, 27.9% is a long way from perfect, but it need not be perfect to be useful. Indeed, even when BoxFinder's top result isn't quite right, the right answer is "close" more often than chance would predict. For example, if we look at when BoxFinder's first or second guess is perfect (Top-2), one of those is right 40.4% of the time when we have three first-page training samples per box. Moreover, if we ask how often BoxFinder's Top-1 result is within one box numerically (e.g., ranking box 1903, 1904 or 1905 first when it should have found box 1904), that happens 36.8% of the time with three first-page training samples per box (and we note that this additional benefit from looking "nearby" was obtained despite there being gaps in the box numbering in the test collection we have used).

Of course, guessing randomly is a low baseline. We can instead index terms generated from the labels on the folders in each box. To do this, we must decode subject-numeric codes. The State Department developed a classification guide to help their staff assign codes consistently [6,7]. It is straightforward to replace each code (e.g., POL 12-6) with the corresponding labels (in that case, "POLIT-ICAL PARTIES: Membership. Leaders.").[7] That's a combination of the label for POL 12 ("POLITICAL PARTIES") and the label for POL 12-6 ("Membership. Leaders.") because the State Department classification guide subheadings (in this case, POL 12-6) are meant to be interpreted in the context of the corresponding main heading (in this case, POL 12).

Subject-Numeric codes sometimes also include abbreviations of the names of countries (e.g., PAR for Paraguay, USSR for the Soviet Union, and US for the United States of America), so we also extract and expand those names to a single standard form (e.g., we do not also expand USSR to Union of Soviet Socialist Republics). However, we do not extract or expand "BRAZ" (Brazil), which appears in every folder label in our collection, since its presence everywhere would result in it having no beneficial effect on the ranking of boxes. The folder labels also include dates, from which we extract and include the year (e.g., 1964)

---

[6] We used our own BM-25 implementation, included in code distributed with our data.

[7] The 1963 handbook [6] was updated in 1965 [7]. A few codes had different labels in the two; in such cases, we combined terms for that code from both handbooks.

with the metadata that we index. We elected not to extract and include the month or day from the date because the distribution of dates that we observe makes it clear that these are start dates for a folder, but that a folder can contain documents from several months. We also elected not to index the subject-numeric code itself, since we did not expect the queries used in our experiments to contain such codes (although we note that in a practical application, expert searchers might indeed understand and use subject-numeric codes).

We can also optionally include any scope note text. For example, the scope note for POL 12-6 in the classification guide states "Includes party elections, purges of party, etc. Subdivide by name of leader if volume warrants." Scope notes contain both on-topic terms (e.g., "party elections") and off-topic terms (e.g., "subdivide"), and scope notes can even include negated terms (e.g., the scope note for POL-12 states, in part, "Exclude: Materials on ... legislative matters, for which SEE: POL 15 -2"). Experience from the Text Retrieval Conference (TREC) suggests removing negated terms may have little effect on average, since although retaining negated terms is sometimes harmful, they can also sometimes be helpful (because negated terms often have some relation to the topic) [19].[8] Scope notes can also contain guidance not related specifically to the topic (e.g., "if volume warrants"), but because such guidance is found in many scope notes, those common terms should have little effect on the way boxes are ranked. For these reasons, when we include scope notes, we use the full scope note, with no human editing. Unlike the labels, where we combine the labels for broad topics (e.g., POL 12) and subtopics (POL 12-6), we use only one scope note (in this case, for POL 12-6) because some topic-level scope notes indicate when the topic-level category should be assigned in preference to a subcategory.

5   Evaluation Measure

How well the system ranks boxes depends on which documents describe each box, and which documents we pick as queries. We pick documents to represent each box randomly from within each box, without replacement. To select query documents, we first randomly select the box the query document will be found in. We do this 100 times, with replacement. Then for each of those 100 choices of boxes, we randomly select a query document from that box, being careful not to choose documents that were used to describe that box. This can choose the same query document twice in a set of 100, but such cases are rare. Because of these random choices, BoxFinder evaluation scores will vary depending on the choices that we made, so we run the whole experiment 100 times (randomly choosing the documents to represent each box again, and randomly choosing query documents again), averaging those results to get the percentages we report.

Code and data for the experiments is at https://github.com/oard/BoxFinder.

---

[8] The TREC experiments compared retention to removal of negated query terms, but because ranking relies on term matching we would expect similar results for retention or removal of content terms from the items being indexed.

Table 1. Results using title metadata queries to search OCR from sampled documents. Top-1: % in finding box at rank 1. Top-2: % finding exact box at rank 1 or 2.

Samples	First Page		≤ 2 Pages		≤ 3 Pages		≤ 4 Pages		≤ 100 Pages	
	Top-1	Top-2	Top-1	Top-2	Top-1	Top-2	Top-1	Top-2	Top-1	Top-2
1	10.7	16.9	10.5	17.1	9.5	15.5	9.3	15.5	9.2	15.4
2	13.0	21.1	12.2	19.4	10.8	18.1	11.6	18.6	10.9	18.0
3	14.6	22.1	14.1	21.5	12.9	20.5	13.0	20.2	11.7	19.2
4	15.6	23.6	14.9	23.2	13.8	21.0	13.6	21.4	12.9	20.3
6	16.9	25.4	15.8	24.3	13.7	22.4	13.8	21.9	12.2	20.6
8	16.6	25.0	16.0	24.5	14.8	23.1	14.4	22.6	12.9	21.3
10	18.1	27.1	15.6	24.5	15.0	23.8	15.0	23.5	13.3	22.2

Table 2. Results using query-by-example to search OCR text from sampled documents, using the same page limit for queries and for sampled documents.

Samples	First Page		≤ 2 Pages		≤ 3 Pages		≤ 4 Pages		≤ 100 Pages	
	Top-1	Top-2	Top-1	Top-2	Top-1	Top-2	Top-1	Top-2	Top-1	Top-2
1	16.5	24.5	15.2	22.7	15.2	22.1	14.3	21.5	10.4	16.9
2	23.4	34.4	21.1	29.3	18.4	27.7	18.6	26.9	13.0	19.4
3	27.9	40.4	25.6	34.9	21.8	32,0	22.2	30.5	17.2	25.5
4	31.5	43.7	25.0	36.2	24.1	35,8	24.6	34.8	20.0	28.1
6	34.1	47.4	29.7	42.3	28.6	40.0	27,2	39.2	12.5	32.4
8	35.0	49.0	33.6	46.7	31.3	44.1	29.4	40.5	26.8	38.6
10	39.2	53.5	34.7	47.2	33.0	46.0	32.1	43.9	27.4	38.8

6   Results

We first look at the case in which boxes are represented using sampled OCR text. Following that, we look at how the results would differ if folder labels could also be used as a basis for representing the content of a box.

6.1   Searching Sampled OCR Text

Table 1 summarizes the results for title metadata queries. As we might expect, having a larger number of randomly sampled documents ("samples") to represent a box yields better results. Surprisingly perhaps, it's generally best to use only the first page of each document. One reason for this might be that some documents are very short—32% have only a single page—so we only get more pages from those that are longer.

Table 2 summarizes results for queries built using OCR text from the query document, and Fig. 3 illustrates those results for the Top-2 condition. As can easily be seen, BoxFinder does better with these longer queries. One reason for this

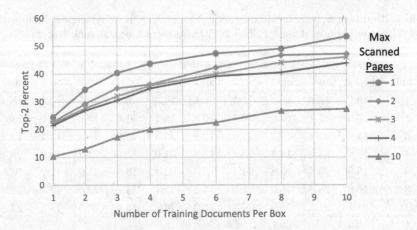

Fig. 3. Learning rate for correct box in Top-2 as scanned documents per box grows, query-by-example condition. Scanning just the first page is best.

is that with short queries (like the ones from title metadata) BoxFinder sometimes finds no matching terms at all, but that doesn't happen very often with longer queries that are based on full-text OCR. Of course, these longer queries have all kinds of strange things in them (from letterhead, message addresses, OCR errors, handwriting that gets misrecognized, etc.), and the document representations suffer from the same problem. Nonetheless, there clearly is a lot of signal here in the midst of all that noise, since BoxFinder is doing better with these longer queries than with the title metadata queries, and it is doing way better than random guessing with either of them.

6.2 Searching with Folder Labels

Table 3 shows that when short (title metadata) queries are used to search documents that are represented only using terms generated from the folder labels, the results are comparable to those reported in Table 1 for using the same queries to search a single page of OCR-generated text. The Top-1 results for searching terms generated from folder labels using short queries was 12.4%, and at Top-2 that same condition had the correct answer in rank 1 or rank 2 17.1% of the time. Only about 70% of the short queries have at least one query term that matches any term resulting from expanding the subject-numeric codes found in the folder

Table 3. Results for searching terms generated from folder labels.

Queries	Repetitions	No Scope Notes		With Scope Notes	
		Top-1	Top-2	Top-1	Top-2
Short: Title metadata	4,200	12.4	17.1	12.4	18.6
Long: First-page OCR	100	5.0	9.5	5.3	9.0

Table 4. Reciprocal rank fusion results, title metadata queries, merging results from searching terms generated from folder labels (no scope notes) and from searching OCR.

Samples	First Page		≤ 2 Pages		≤ 3 Pages		≤ 4 Pages		≤ 100 Pages	
	Top-1	Top-2	Top-1	Top-2	Top-1	Top-2	Top-1	Top-2	Top-1	Top-2
1	14.0	21.5	14.0	21.8	13.3	21.0	13.1	20.5	13.3	20.3
2	15.5	23.4	14.8	22.7	13.9	21.8	14.8	22.6	14.5	23.0
3	15.8	23.5	15.5	23.7	15.1	23.4	15.1	23.0	14.5	23.0
4	16.6	25.2	16.8	24.5	16.2	24.1	16.5	24.0	15.0	23.1
6	17.6	25.7	17.2	25.1	15.8	23.9	16.1	24.1	15.1	23.5
8	17.7	25.9	17.3	25.3	17.7	25.6	16.6	23.8	15.4	23.5
10	19.1	27.5	17.4	25.7	17.1	25.1	16.7	25.1	16.1	24.6

labels (without also indexing the scope notes), but short (title metadata) queries still did far better than the longer OCR-based queries when searching document representations that are based solely on terms generated from folder labels.

Interestingly, the pattern in Tables 1 and 2, where query-by-example was markedly better than using the title metadata as a query, is reversed when ranking based on folder labels. Essentially the broader pattern we see is that a matched condition (using OCR to search OCR, or using metadata to search metadata) is consistently outperforming an unmatched condition. This might be explained by systematic errors in the OCR or by systematic differences in the way language is used in the documents and in Brown University's title metadata. We see a benefit at rank 2 from the inclusion of scope notes when generating terms from folder labels to represent each box, but no benefit at rank 1.[9]

Of course, we need not index terms generated from the folder labels in isolation—we can also use folder labels together with OCR text from sampled documents. We could do this in one of two ways, either concatenating the two representations, or performing two searches (one with each representation) then performing result fusion to create a single ranked list of boxes. We expect that second approach, implemented as reciprocal rank fusion [4], to work better in this case because of mismatched document lengths, so that's the one we tried.[10]

Table 4 shows reciprocal rank fusion results when (short) title metadata is used as the query. As with Tables 1 and 2, these are averages over 100 repetitions. With these short queries, sometimes no terms match at all, resulting in no ranking of the boxes by one of the systems. In such cases, we retain the other ranking unchanged.[11] As can be seen by comparing Tables 3 and 4, this rank fusion results in an improvement over what we achieved using terms generated from folder labels alone. This improvement is both substantial (for example,

---

[9] To measure the benefit of scope notes with short titles more accurately, we average over 4,200 repetitions for our short-query experiments in Table 3.

[10] We set Cormack's discount rate parameter to 60, as Cormack recommends [4].

[11] When neither approach has a term match, we generate an empty list.

compare 15.8 at Top-1 for Reciprocal Rank Fusion with the first page from each of 3 samples in Table 4 to to 12.4 for folder metadata alone in Table 3, a 27% relative improvement; the relative improvement at Top-2 is 38%) and statistically significant (the standard deviation over 42 100-sample averages when searching terms generated from folder labels is 0.33 at both Top-1 and Top-2).

7   Conclusion and Future Work

We close by observing that we have shown that the homophily between digitized and undigitized content that we expected to find in an archival collection can indeed provide a useful signal that can help to improve search for content that has not yet been digitized. There are several ways in which we might push this work further. One thing to try would be to be selective about which parts of a document image to index. For that, we could pay attention not just to the OCR, but to cues from the layout of the words on the page. For example, we might pay particular attention to who sent or received a document, or to the date of the document. We could also use layout analysis to determine what type of document we are looking at (e.g., telegram, letter, memo, or form), and then apply type-specific information extraction, and possibly even type-specific ranking. Speaking of ranking, there's no reason why we need to glom the OCR text from different documents together to make a single representation for each box. Instead, we could make multiple representations, one per document, and then let those representations vote on which box should be chosen. That approach has, for example, been shown to work well for blog search [2].

There is nothing in BoxFinder specific to boxes except the way we tested it; the same ideas could work for folders, series, collections, and entire repositories. Of course, some of the tuning decisions (e.g., how many digitized documents are needed to represent a folder?) will likely differ when applying these ideas at different scales. But tuning would not be hard if we had a collection to tune on. So one key to making BoxFinder into FolderFinder (or SeriesFinder, or ...) is to assemble appropriate collections on which we can train and test. For our experiments in this paper, we assembled a single collection and then used it to see how well our approach of representing a box using OCR from randomly selected documents would do. But when tuning a large number of system details, we'll want training, devtest and evaluation partitions, so we'll need larger collections. Fortunately, the complete NARA Department of State Subject-Numeric files are indeed much larger than the part of that collection that we have used so far, so there is at least one good source for such a collection. But if we want to know how well these ideas work in general, we're going to need several collections, from a variety of sources. So assembling several such collections is a natural next step.

Finally, we have looked only at what can be done using systematic sampling of densely digitized documents, together with quite terse folder-level metadata, using just one test collection. Future work should explore other cases, where the degree of homophily within a box (or other unit) may vary, the available metadata that describes the content is richer (or less rich), and digitization is unevenly distributed across the collection, as is often the case in practice.

Acknowledgements. The author greatly appreciates the comments on this work from Katrina Fenlon, Emi Ishita, Diana Marsh, Toshiyuki Shimizu, Tokinori Suzuki, Yoichi Tomiura, Victoria Van Hyning, and the reviewers.

References

1. Aesop: The Complete Fables. Penguin Classics (1998)
2. Balog, K., Azzopardi, L., de Rijke, M.: Formal models for expert finding in enterprise corpora. In: Proceedings of the 29th Annual International ACM SIGIR Conference on Research and Development in Information Retrieval, pp. 43–50 (2006)
3. Brunila, M., LaViolette, J.: What company do words keep? revisiting the distributional semantics of JR Firth & Zellig Harris. In: Proceedings of the 2022 Conference of the North American Chapter of the Association for Computational Linguistics: Human Language Technologies, pp. 4403–4417 (2022)
4. Cormack, G.V., Clarke, C.L., Buettcher, S.: Reciprocal rank fusion outperforms condorcet and individual rank learning methods. In: Proceedings of the 32nd International ACM SIGIR Conference on Research and Development in Information Retrieval, pp. 758–759 (2009)
5. Cox, R.J., et al.: Machines in the archives: technology and the coming transformation of archival reference. First Monday (2007)
6. Department of State: records classification handbook. https://www.archives.gov/files/research/foreign-policy/state-dept/finding-aids/records-classification-handbook-1963.pdf, visited May 10, 2023 (1963)
7. Department of State: records classification handbook. https://www.archives.gov/files/research/foreign-policy/state-dept/finding-aids/dos-records-classification-handbook-1965-1973.pdf, visited February 8, 2023 (1965)
8. Ertug, G., Brennecke, J., Kovacs, B., Zou, T.: What does homophily do? a review of the consequences of homophily. Acad. Manage. Ann. **16**(1), 38–69 (2022)
9. Falk, P.K.: ArchiveGrid. Tech. Serv. Q. **34**(2), 218–219 (2017)
10. Greene, M., Meissner, D.: More product, less process: revamping traditional archival processing. Am. Archivist **68**(2), 208–263 (2005)
11. Kiusals, D., Leetaru, K.: The declassification engine: the sphere of influence. Website http://diploglobe.declassification-engine.org/, visited May 12, 2023 (2015)
12. Marsh, D.E.: Research-driven approaches to improving archival discovery. IASSIST Q. **43**(2), 1–9 (2019)
13. Marsh, D.E., Andre, S., Wagner, T., Bell, J.A.: Attitudes and uses of archival materials among science-based anthropologists. Arch. Sci., 1–25 (2023)
14. McPherson, M., Smith-Lovin, L., Cook, J.M.: Birds of a feather: homophily in social networks. Ann. Rev. Sociol. **27**(1), 415–444 (2001). https://doi.org/10.1146/annurev.soc.27.1.415
15. National Archives and Records Administration: Record group explorer. Website https://www.archives.gov/findingaid/record-group-explorer, visited February 2, 2023 (2023)
16. O'Connell, K.: The future of email archives: a report from the task force on technical approaches for email archives. Am. Archivist **82**(1), 214–217 (2019)
17. Paik, J.H., Oard, D.W.: A fixed-point method for weighting terms in verbose informational queries. In: Proceedings of the 23rd ACM International Conference on Conference on Information and Knowledge Management, pp. 131–140 (2014)
18. Prom, C., Frusciano, T.S.: Archival arrangement and description. Trends Arch. Pract., Soc. Am. Archivists (2013)

19. Robertson, S.E., Walker, S.: Okapi/Keenbow at TREC-8. In: Proceedings of the Eighth Text Retrieval Conference, pp. 151–162 (1999)
20. Robertson, S.E., Zaragoza, H.: The probabilistic relevance framework: BM25 and beyond. Found. Trends Inf. Retrieval **3**(4), 333–389 (2009). https://doi.org/10.1561/1500000019
21. Society of American Archivists: describing archives: a content standard, version 2022. Website https://saa-ts-dacs.github.io/, visited May 12, 2023 (2022)
22. Tibbo, H.: Primarily history in America: how U.S. historians search for primary materials at the dawn of the digital age. Am. Archivist **66**(1), 9–50 (2003). https://doi.org/10.17723/aarc.66.1.b120370l1g718n74
23. Trace, C.B.: Archival infrastructure and the information backlog. Arch. Sci. **22**(1), 75–93 (2022)
24. Wiedeman, G.: The historical hazards of finding aids. Am. Archivist **82**(2), 381–420 (2019)

Aspect-Driven Structuring of Historical Dutch Newspaper Archives

Hermann Kroll[1]([✉])[iD], Christin Katharina Kreutz[2][iD], Mirjam Cuper[3][iD],
Bill Matthias Thang[1], and Wolf-Tilo Balke[1][iD]

[1] TU Braunschweig, Braunschweig, Germany
{kroll,balke}@ifis.cs.tu-bs.de
[2] TH Köln (University of Applied Sciences), Cologne, Germany
christin.kreutz@th-koeln.de
[3] KB, National Library of the Netherlands, Hague, The Netherlands
mirjam.cuper@kb.nl

Abstract. Digital libraries oftentimes provide access to historical newspaper archives via keyword-based search. Historical figures and their roles are particularly interesting cognitive access points in historical research. Structuring and clustering news articles would allow more sophisticated access for users to explore such information. However, real-world limitations such as the lack of training data, licensing restrictions and non-English text with OCR errors make the composition of such a system difficult and cost-intensive in practice. In this work we tackle these issues with the showcase of the National Library of the Netherlands by introducing a role-based interface that structures news articles on historical persons. In-depth, component-wise evaluations and interviews with domain experts highlighted our prototype's effectiveness and appropriateness for a real-world digital library collection.

Keywords: Historical News Archives · Exploration · Digital Libraries

1 Introduction

Users of digital libraries featuring historical news articles conduct a variety of information interactions such as task planning or searching for and working with information objects [20]. In historical research, historical figures and especially their roles are particularly interesting cognitive access points [19]. Kumpulainen et al. [19] state the need for supporting historians' research by providing domain-specific tools tailored to their needs. One crucial task of researchers is the creation of sub-corpora to answer their research questions [29]. However, finding these sub-corpora, especially when researchers are unfamiliar with the searched historical persons, can be challenging for two reasons. First, the huge size of news article archives might be overwhelming. Second, posing and finding suitable keyword queries to browse such archives is difficult.

Advances in Natural Language Processing (NLP) lead to historic news systems with novel access paths for users to engage with their content [12]. A variety

O. Alonso et al. (Eds.): TPDL 2023, LNCS 14241, pp. 31–46, 2023.
https://doi.org/10.1007/978-3-031-43849-3_4

of such digital library projects has been proposed in the past, e.g., NewsEye [17], ANNO [27], impresso [11], or Cuper's work [5] (see Sect. 2 for a detailed discussion). However, those systems usually rely either on manual curation [5] or at least domain-specific training examples for every implemented step [11]. In contrast, our work bypasses manual curation and the collection of domain-specific training data by utilizing data from Wikipedia (structure information with text examples). This paper introduces a novel system that automatically structures historical news articles on persons and provides an aspect-driven interface to explore a library's content. The central idea is that a person has different roles (e.g., *writer, politician, military person*) and each role has different aspects (e.g., *early life, political career, actions*). Our system should, at best, automatically create sub-corpora for each role and aspect to support research on historical persons. However, traditional methods introduced in the NLP domain typically rely on hand-crafted training data and sometimes artificial benchmarks [30]. We tackled the challenges faced by an actual digital library, namely the National Library of the Netherlands, Koninklijke Bibliotheek (KB) (https://www.kb.nl). Here, no hand-crafted training data and benchmarks were available. Moreover, the library imposed several real-world constraints: (1) The data was available in Dutch, whereas NLP methods are often available in English only. (2) The news articles were based on OCR-scanned newspapers, and hence, came with typical OCR issues (such as incorrect letters or broken paragraphs). (3) The data came with a license prohibiting sending data to APIs like ChatGPT [1].

In addition to those constraints, which are typically not the target in NLP research, we observed an understudied [20] corpus of non-English but Dutch news articles. Our overall goal was thus to build a real-world system that overcomes the typical constraints of a typical digital library. In this work, we therefore strive to support users' data-driven process planning by structuring news articles concerning historical figures by their respective roles. Our prototypical system operates on real data of the KB and bases on automatically generated training data from Wikipedia. We expected our system to help users in the formulation of research questions on the provided data of historical persons.

To tackle our overall research question *How can a digital library design effective access paths to explore their collection?*, we made the following contributions: (1) We discuss and demonstrate how we overcome a digital library's real-world restrictions and constraints (see Sect. 3). (2) We present an effective method for automatically structuring news articles by employing structural background information from Wikipedia with the use case of news articles on historical figures. (3) We evaluate our prototypical system step-by-step and via interviews with five domain experts. Code is available at GitHub[1] and Software Heritage[2].

---

[1] https://github.com/HermannKroll/AspectDrivenNewsStructuring.

[2] https://archive.softwareheritage.org/swh:1:dir:13457c154ed7ad1f571e353c1edf2f87 db61b0ae.

2 Related Work

Related work for our research objective falls into the following categories: (1) related digital library news archive retrieval systems, (2) processing Dutch texts via language models, and (3) text summarization methods.

Digital Library Systems on News Articles. Structuring and exploring news has been a topic of wide research, e.g., summarization [30], the evolution of terms [25], fake news detection [35], clustering [24] and many more. For instance, [24] clusters news articles based on their similarity to pre-computed categories using SVMs. Kumpulainen et al. [19] identified roles of historical persons, relationships between them, and in general, named entities as important cognitive access points to historical documents. Clustering similar news articles has been explored in several concrete applications with real digital library constraints, e.g., NewsEye [17] or ANNO [27]. Another example is the Swiss-Luxembourgish project impresso [11] which utilizes NLP methods like named entity recognition, word embeddings, n-gram search, and information extraction to provide additional information on historical news articles. The KB has developed the Delpher platform: News articles were digitized by OCR tools and Delpher provides a user interface to navigate through their historical newspaper collections. Beyond the traditional keyword-based search, they aimed to organize a part of the KB's newspaper collection differently from the standard search interface [5]. Additionally, the KB manually created subject pages that give more background information on certain topics and related newspapers[3]. Our work's goal was to structure the KB's news articles automatically, at least as much as possible, while meeting the KB's real-world constraints.

Dutch Language Models. Many language models were trained and evaluated on English corpora. Exceptions were models trained in a *multilingual setting* [9,23,37] or ones having been *trained for Dutch*: BERTje [36] is a Dutch BERT [9] model which outperforms the multilingual version [23] of BART [21]. RobBERT [6] is a Dutch RoBERTa model which outperformed BERTje on the sentiment analysis task as well as both BERTje and mBERT on the relative pronoun prediction tasks. A newer version of the model (RobBERT-2022) [7] with a newer Dutch training corpus also outperformed BERTje and RobBERT on the sentiment analysis task. We used the RobBERT-2022 for our text classification.

Text Summarization. The task of text summarization is to produce a concise natural language summary. Nowadays, general-application sequence-to-sequence language models can be fine-tuned to solve the text summarization task, e.g., UniLM [10], T5 [31], BART [21], PEGASUS [40]. Another option is using large language models (LLMs) [41] and prompting in this context. Models like [40] or [21] are restricted to 512 tokens or less, meaning their input must be shorter than 512 tokens. So-called longformer models surpass this restriction by allowing up to 16k tokens as their input, e.g., [2,30,39]. Beyond some remarkable examples like Estonian [16] and Romanian news summarization [28], text summarization models are trained in English [2,21,30,31,40], but they can be fine-tuned for

---

[3] https://www.delpher.nl/thema/geschiedenis/tweede-wereldoorlog.

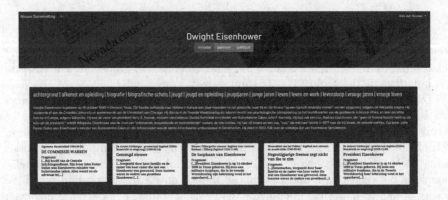

Fig. 1. User interface of our system, URL: https://narrative.pubpharm.de/news.

other languages (here Dutch). The goal of this work was to summarize several articles in a single summary, so the *multi-document summarization* task. PRIMERA [30] is an LED-based [2] state-of-the-art model (ACL2022) for this task. It outperformed single-document models [2,21,40] in different scenarios (news and scientific documents). That is why we used PRIMERA in this work.

3   Conception and Data Acquisition

Our overall goal was to structure news articles to support corresponding research questions on single persons. Each new article consists of a title, the textual content, the release date, and the publishing newspaper. From our viewpoint, each person might have different roles $r \in \mathcal{R}$ (e.g., politician, writer, artist) that come with different aspects r_A (e.g., political career, novels, awards).

Discussion of the Library's Constraints. In brief, we faced the following constraints: (1) The texts stem from OCR-scanned news articles using ABBYY Finereader, (2) texts were written in Dutch (no translation was available), (3) prohibition against sending data to third parties, (4) forced linking to the Delpher system and restriction to show only snippets of the actual data (160 characters at max), and (5) no curated training data for any of our sub-tasks. Those requirements forced us to exclude automated translation services like DeepL and AI assistants like ChatGPT by design. Especially the lack of training data prevented the usage of straightforward approaches like training text classification models. We would have had to collect data for roles and aspects, manually label news articles, and then train classification models. However, creating such data would be cost intensive.

That is why we headed for a different approach: We used the Dutch Wikipedia to gather texts describing different persons, their roles, and the roles' aspects. First, Wikipedia organizes text into different sections describing different *aspects* of entries. Second, Wikipedia enriches an item's text through so-called info boxes that provide structured information, e.g., whether it is a person and has some

Table 1. Statistics for our news article collection: #Art. describes how many articles before filtering and #FArt. after filtering were retrieved for each person.

Person Name (Title/Synonyms)	Role	Life	#Art.	#FArt.
Winston Churchill (Sir Churchill)	politician	1874-1965	47k	8463
Leopold III van Beglië (Leo. III, prins Leo.)	king	1901-1983	26k	1677
Wilhelmina van Oranje-Nassau (prinses Wilhelmina, koningin Wilhelmina)	queen	1880-1962	257k	9416
Jannetje Schaft (Hannie Schaft)	resistance	1920-1945	2056	34
Dwight Eisenhower (majoor-generaal E., Generaal E., president E.)	politician	1890-1969	114k	21k
Anne Frank	war victim	1929-1945	11k	1
Frans Goedhart (Pieter 't Hoen)	resistance	1904-1990	4105	560
Simon Vestdijk	writer	1898-1971	5544	1453
Franklin Roosevelt (president Roosevelt)	politician	1882-1945	165k	16k

roles. For our approach, we used the info boxes to determine a person's role and the Wikipedia texts to learn how certain aspects are described. This approach bypassed the creation of training data, while, however, could cause new problems: It had to be tested if classifiers trained on descriptive Wikipedia texts are transferable and generalizable to Dutch news.

Prototype (User Interface). In constructing the system interface, we strive to carter to McCay-Peet et al.'s [26] five facets supporting serendipity in digital environments: interfaces filled with various information (*trigger-rich*), showcase relationships between information objects (*enables connections*), visual cues (*highlights triggers*), *enables exploration* and provides unanticipated or surprising information (*leads to the unexpected*). Our method's goal was to (1) derive the roles of a person (trigger-rich and exploration) and (2) classify whether a news article's content belongs to one of the role's aspects (connections and unexpected). We used multi-document summarization for each aspect to help users quickly access what is written in the corresponding articles. Users should be able to select different persons and one of the person's known roles. Then users could navigate through different aspects of that role, see a summary for each aspect and a list of articles classified as belonging to that role's aspect (see Fig. 1 for the systems' screenshot and URL). A click on an article forwards users to Delpher.

Historical News Data from the KB. We used a subset of the KB's data for building our system since the KB collected news articles from the 17th century to the recent past. We selected articles for nine famous persons in relation to the second world war with various roles because the KB's Delpher has identified the second world war as a topic users were interested in. We harvested relevant articles by querying for the name and title/pseudonym (see Table 1 for statistics). We only selected items from the newspaper collection with the type 'article'. Then we only kept articles where $\geq 90\%$ of the text was found in a Dutch dictionary, as recommended in [34], to remove noisy and low-quality OCR-scanned data. We also excluded newspapers published by fascist organizations or German authorities with a national socialist agenda. Articles for each person should, on the one hand, carry enough information about the person and, on the other hand, stem from the time when the person was alive. That is why we applied the following additional filters: (1) A news article's release date must be in the corresponding person's life span, (2) the article content must be longer than 100 words, and (3) a person's partial name (e.g., *Frank* for *Anne Frank*) should be mentioned at least three times. Especially the time constraint did filter nearly all articles, except one, of Anne Frank because they were published after her death.

4   System Implementation

Wikipedia Processing. As already mentioned, we used the Wikipedia info boxes to derive a person's role. The information was linked to Wikipedia categories which were organized in a taxonomy, e.g., *British politician* is a specialization of a *politician*. In our context, we understood a person's occupation as a role. We crawled the Dutch *occupation* categories and derived a list of occupations (in sum 30k distinct ones). Then, we iterated through the Dutch Wikipedia XML dumps (March 2023), parsed the info boxes, checked whether a property of the info box was linked to one of those occupations, and if so, we extracted the corresponding page's summary (introduction) and sections plus all occupations. In sum, we derived 259k person pages. While reviewing the pages, we observed many very short pages, e.g., including a brief summary or a single section. However, our goal was to find frequent aspects of well-described roles. So, we removed all pages that (1) had a less than 150 characters summary, or (2) had < 3 sections. Note that we disregarded sections with less than 100 characters and sections that only contained references/literature by using a hand-crafted list. This filtering reduced the number of person pages to 61k. With that, we obtained roles plus thousands of Wikipedia pages for each. Wikipedia sections should, at best, describe one unit of information belonging to a certain aspect of a person.

However, Wikipedia was crafted collaboratively, i.e., through human editing meaning section titles are usually not-canonicalized. For instance, *life, background,* and *curriculum vitae/resume* describe the same, or at least a very similar, aspect of a person. To face this concern, we designed a canonicalization step to cluster semantically similar sections. We applied a pre-trained sentence transformer model (BERT-base-dutch-cased) using the S-BERT Library [32], capable of embedding semantically similar sentences closely in its vector space. To embed a section, we embedded all of its sentences and then computed the mean vector over all sentence vectors. Next, we averaged all section vectors with equal titles (e.g., background sections). Finally, we compared those sections vectors pairwise using the cosine similarity. If two vectors' similarity exceeds a certain pre-defined threshold, we consider those section titles as semantically equivalent. We then computed the transitive closure to determine the set of semantically equivalent section titles, i.e., if a-b and b-c are merged, we also merged a-c. To retain a high precision, we used a similarity threshold of 0.95 in our system.

Aspect Mining and Classification. Next, we mined frequent role aspects by counting how often the aspect (section title or any other section title from that same cluster) was used across all persons of a role (e.g., *writers*). We then computed a relative support, e.g., 0.2 means that 20% of all *writers* have aspect (section tile or any similar title) *background.* We defined a minimum absolute (to ensure enough text examples for aspect training) and a relative support threshold (to ensure frequency within a role). Given a certain person's role, we trained a classifier to predict whether a text belongs to one of the role's aspects. That means we headed for a multi-class classification scenario, e.g., a classifier for role r_1 with aspects a_1, a_2, a_3 must predict one of the aspects, or the negative class (not belonging to the role). First, we retrieved Wikipedia section texts for each aspect. We ensured that each aspect must have at least a minimum number of texts to be considered for training (see aspect mining support threshold). However, some aspects might have more examples than others, which is why we sampled all text examples randomly down to the number of the least frequent aspect, e.g., aspect a_1 and a_2 are sampled down to 100 texts if the least frequent aspect a_3 only has 100 examples. We randomly sampled negative examples (not belonging to the role) from other persons and aspects that do not have the given role r_1. We sampled as many negative examples as we had positive ones, e.g., 100-100-100 positive (three aspects, 100 texts each) and 300 negative examples.

We fine-tuned the Dutch model RobBERT-2022 [7] for the actual text classification. We split our data into train, validation, and test sets (80-10-10). We performed training on train (5 epochs), and searched for hyperparameters (learning rate [1e−3, 1e−4, 1e−5] and decay [0.1, 0.2]) on validation. We picked the best model concerning validation and macro precision because our classification should prefer precision of all classes over recall. We trained a classifier for each role (occupation category of Wikipedia) that had (1) at least three frequent aspects and (2) belongs to the first two category levels in Wikipedia (to select more general roles like *writer* instead of *British writer*). Note that we removed the category suffixes *naar nationaliteit* and *naar beroep.*

News Article Processing. The next step was applying those classifiers to a historical person's actual Dutch news articles. However, a news article might include several different topics, thus, classifying the whole text to one role's aspects could be problematic. So, we computed snippets of the articles that include the person's name: We split the article's content into sentences by using NLTK's [3] sentence split method. We then checked whether a partial name of the person (e.g., *Churchill* or *Winston* for *Winston Churchill*) was included. If so, we considered the sentence relevant and took it and the sentence before and after as additional context information to generate a snippet. The average sentence length computed over Dutch newspaper and Wikipedia articles is 90.3 characters, 3.4% of these sentences have ≤ 19 characters [15]. We only use snippets of three sentences with at least 50 characters to filter out broken or incomplete sentences, corresponding to a minimum average sentence length of ∼16.7 characters each.

For our selected persons, we identified their roles through the info boxes of the corresponding Wikipedia entry. If a role (e.g., *British minister*) was assigned, we also considered its super categories (e.g., *minister* and *person*). We always assigned the role *person* to ensure that our approach also worked in cases when a person did not have an info box (in cases of *Wilhelmina* and *Janeetje Schaft*). Having the roles, we applied the corresponding role classifier to every news article snippet of the person. Note that each snippet could be classified as belonging to several aspects of different roles. This was intended because some aspects of different roles might overlap, e.g., a *politician*'s and *writer*'s *family* or *early life*.

Our last goal was to summarize those snippets into one summary for the users so that they could quickly grasp how the aspect was described in the news articles. However, to the best of our knowledge, multi-document summarization models were unavailable for Dutch. That is why we decided to apply one of the latest English models, namely PRIMERA [30]. We used a fine-tuned news summary PRIMERA model from HuggingFace. However, to apply PRIMERA, we had to translate the Dutch news article snippets into English with OPUS-MT [33], one of the latest open available translation models. The choice of OPUS-MT over using, e.g., the DeepL API, was again made due to our legal constraints. Afterward, PRIMERA's English summaries were translated back to Dutch with OPUS-MT. We translated Dutch texts sentence-wise to English and vice versa. To generate the summaries, we introduced a parameter k to select how many articles snippets should be summarized. In addition to the summaries, we wanted to display fragments of the article snippets in the user interface, to give our users an idea about the article. For the fragment generation, we identified the position where the person's name was mentioned and displayed the surrounding characters and cut if we exceed the 160 characters we were allowed to show.

5   Evaluation

We evaluate our system's components individually (clustering, classification, translation, and summarization) and then report our user study's findings.

Clustering. We exported 221 distinct section titles that occurred in at least 100 Wikipedia articles to ensure enough examples for the clustering and classification. We asked three persons to cluster them manually, i.e., whether two titles semantically belong together. When comparing and discussing their clusters, we observed the following patterns: There was a wide range in clustering regarding the granularity. One annotator clustered everything belonging to one's life as one cluster, whereas a second person created clusters for different periods in life such as *youth* with *early life, youth and training* and *later life* with *death* and *last years*. The annotators had difficulties distinguishing between titles describing a person, e.g., *author*, and titles describing a person's work, e.g., *novel*. But all annotators differentiated between a *politician* and their *political career*. All three annotators agreed to cluster section titles describing different types of *awards*. The annotators disagreed on whether to cluster military and political careers. War-related titles such as *interbellum* and *after the war* also were regarded with uncertainty regarding them being in separate or the same cluster. In general, the annotators found that some section titles were very hard to cluster as the

Table 2. Evaluation results for our Wikipedia text classifiers. We averaged the number of trained aspects and used training samples. Evaluation metrics are macro averaged.

Setting	#Aspects	#Samples	Precision	Recall	F1	Accuracy
Top-5	7.6 ± 3.83	9999 ± 9520	0.95 ± 0.01	0.94 ± 0.03	0.94 ± 0.02	0.95 ± 0.02
Top-10	6.7 ± 3.16	10246 ± 14078	0.94 ± 0.02	0.93 ± 0.02	0.93 ± 0.02	0.94 ± 0.02
Worst-5	6.4 ± 1.74	1285 ± 230	0.80 ± 0.02	0.79 ± 0.03	0.78 ± 0.03	0.82 ± 0.02
Worst-10	5.7 ± 1.95	1545 ± 1340	0.81 ± 0.02	0.81 ± 0.04	0.80 ± 0.03	0.83 ± 0.02
All (43)	6.35 ± 2.88	4254 ± 8215	0.87 ± 0.05	0.88 ± 0.05	0.87 ± 0.05	0.89 ± 0.04

Table 3. Evaluation results of our article snippet classification. For each person, the number of used snippets, different roles, snippets classified as belonging to one aspect, aspects, and classified snippets per aspect are reported.

Name	#Sni.	#Roles	#Classified	#Aspects	Snippets/Aspects		
					Mean±STD	Min	Max
W. Churchill	48k	15	47k	92	508 ± 1587	1	12172
Leopold III	3192	6	1691	42	40 ± 61	1	332
Wilhelmina	40k	1	231	5	46 ± 24	16	76
Jannetje Schaft	76	1	1	1	1 ± 0	1	1
D. Eisenhower	100k	3	36k	20	1780 ± 6631	1	30568
Anne Frank	9	4	1	1	1 ± 0	1	1
Frans Goedhart	2995	2	1132	12	94 ± 283	1	1031
Simon Vestdijk	4989	3	3368	20	168 ± 462	1	2154
F. Roosevelt	80k	7	40k	50	799 ± 3116	1	21926

titles were ambiguous: *Work* could be associated with a person's job, but also with its outcome, e.g., paintings of a painter.

In a subsequent discussion, the three annotators also reviewed the system-generated clusters (41 in total) and commented on them. The annotators were content with most of the clustering but found some clusters which they considered too broad (e.g., *work* together with *bibliography*) or included labels which were seemingly unrelated (e.g., *influence* and *scientist*). They remarked on some titles which were not clustered together: *Work* was not in the same cluster as *works*, *military career* and *political career* belong to different clusters, *life* and *young years* were clustered together but *death* and *early years* were in two different clusters. In brief, the clustering quality was acceptable to continue.

Aspect Classification. We evaluated the aspect classification in three ways: (1) Wikipedia classifier quality measured on test sets, (2) article classification statistics, and (3) rated classified snippets in a manual evaluation. For the aspect mining, we selected an absolute support of 100 examples per aspect to ensure enough examples for the subsequent classification, and a relative support of 0.05 to ensure relevance to the role. With that, we trained classifiers for 43 roles that had at least three different frequent aspects. We applied the classifiers to the Wikipedia test sets to measure the classification quality. The results are reported in Table 2 with additional statistics (avg. training data size, number of aspects). To look at the best and worst performing classifiers (ranked by macro precision to ensure reliable, precise classes), we evaluated five settings: Top-5 classifiers, Top-10 classifiers, Worst-5, Worst-10, and All classifiers. In brief, we concluded two thoughts: The more training data a classifier got, the better its performance was. Top-5 achieved a macro precision of 0.95, while Worst-5 still maintained a precision of 0.8, which we still consider acceptable. The recall was between 0.94 (Top-5) and 0.79 (Worst-10). The number of trained samples was between 10k and 1.2k. However, the deviation was high, e.g., a deviation of 14k for 10k samples. A close look at histograms revealed some outliers, like the role *person* with more than 150k samples. Overall, the classification quality was good.

Table 3 reports statistics on the actual classified news article snippets. For instance, Winston Churchill had up to 15 different roles yielding 47k classified snippets with 92 different role aspects in total. While some role aspects had up to 12k classified snippets, others had only one. Briefly, the number of classified snippets strongly differed between our test persons. Persons like Wilhelmina did not have a role concerning Wikipedia and were hence classified only as a *person*. In our user interface, we show the best-classified snippets plus their summary. That is why we ranked classified snippets by their classification probability and selected the top-5 per person, role, and aspect. From this list with 557 snippets, we randomly sampled 100 entries (role, aspect, snippet) for a manual evaluation.

Three persons rated each entry's correctness and gave explanations if they tagged an entry as incorrect. Counting the majority votes, we obtained 62 correct and 38 incorrect entries with an inter-rater agreement of 0.33 (Krippendorff's α [18]) and 0.32 (Fleiss' κ [13]). Discussing the reasons for the negative ratings revealed that, in many cases, the aspect applied was correctly classified, but the role did not fit. For instance, some aspects like *early life* were way too general to be specific for one role, and hence, deciding whether an *early life* snippet belonged to the role *politician, member of the Parliament*, or *writer* was impossible. Annotators were uncertain about how to rate a statement about a person rather than an action performed by the person. Another encountered issue was distinguishing between pairs of roles which could belong together: *journalist – writer, minister – official, writer – artist*, or *historian – writer*. Such a decision strongly influenced the rating of the aspect classification and oftentimes made raters disagree. Some snippets alone were not enough to rate an entry, e.g., if the award *Karlspreis* is given to *writers*.

Translation. We randomly sampled 100 snippets from all news articles. Two native Dutch speakers read the Dutch snippet and the corresponding translated English version. They rated the syntax of the translation (whether it reads well and is syntactically correct) and the factual correctness (whether the translated facts are still correct). For the syntax, the annotators' ratings for *good-moderate-bad* were 54-28-47 and 38-47-15. The inter-rater agreement was 0.62 (Krippendorff's α) and 0.39 (Fleiss' κ). However, annotators often disagreed in rating a snippet as good or moderate. Counting good and moderate together as

Table 4. Summarization evaluation results. The averaged readability scores, the averaged number of summary sentences, and the averaged reading time are shown per k.

Summary@k	#Sent.	Flesch EN	Flesch NL	Reading Time	Dale-Chall
5	7.7 ± 2.8	70.4 ± 8.8	57.3 ± 9.7	11.9 ± 3.8	9 ± 0.9
10	10.4 ± 4.1	70.1 ± 10.1	57.1 ± 10.2	15.5 ± 4.8	8.8 ± 0.9
20	13.7 ± 5.8	69.8 ± 9.0	56.4 ± 9.0	19.4 ± 5.6	8.8 ± 0.7
30	15.0 ± 5.9	70.2 ± 8.4	56.6 ± 9.4	21.0 ± 6.4	8.7 ± 0.8
40	15.6 ± 6.4	70.5 ± 8.0	57.3 ± 8.8	21.7 ± 6.8	8.7 ± 0.7
50	16.1 ± 6.4	71.3 ± 8.0	57.9 ± 8.3	22.0 ± 6.9	8.7 ± 0.7

one class, we obtained an inter-rater agreement of 0.75 (Krippendorff's α and Fleiss' κ), indicating a fair agreement. In brief, between 82–85% of the translation snippets had a moderate or good syntax. Concerning factual correctness, for *correct-incorrect* the ratings were 82–18 and 85–15. The inter-rater agreement was high, 0.85 (Krippendorff's α and Fleiss' κ). Discussions with both raters revealed that in most cases, when a snippet was marked as factually incorrect, it was due to a minor error. The translation worked well with older Dutch, apart from some mistakes (such as *'Duitschland'*, which was erroneously translated as *'Germanland'*). The translation also handled minor OCR errors or spaces.

Summarization. We evaluated the summarization through (1) automated readability scores and (2) a manual evaluation. We only summarized aspects of roles that had at least five classified snippets per person, otherwise, we did not have enough information to show. In addition, we summarized the most probable 20 article snippets based on classification probability as the multi-document summarization model could only process 4096 tokens as its input and will truncate otherwise. With that, we generated 208 summaries in total. Table 4 reports the following averaged measures: The Flesch readability index [14] quantifies reading ease based on word and sentence length and is language-specific. Scores between 50 and 60 indicate fairly difficult text, while scores between 70 and 80 indicate fairly easy text. The reading time indicates the seconds required to read a text, each character taking 14.69 ms [8]. The new Dale-Chall [4] score gives the reading level of a text as a grade indicating the familiarity of persons from that grade with a list of words. Scores from 8.0 to 8.9 correspond to an 11th/12th-grade student's reading level. We also tested a different number of selected snippets to summarize k, however, except for the number of generated sentences and the required reading time, the scores did not deviate much. We randomly sampled ten summaries plus the 20 snippets used to generate them for three raters. Readability on a *good-average-bad* scale was rated as 0-10-0, 0-10-0 and 1-4-5. The generation quality was hence acceptable. From their discussion of the results we found the following: First, if some snippets supported parts of the summary, they were nearly cited verbatim. Some snippets of different articles were (nearly) identical. Temporal information in the summaries on dates was often bad because the dates were wrong or messed up. Some summaries included hard context breaks between sentences. Moreover, we observed major issues with factual correctness due to hallucinations. Phrases like *"The New York times reports, click here for more"* were generated but not included in the articles. Further, the model also introduced additional, and often wrong, facts about persons, e.g., dates, events, and actions. We assume that such facts and phrases were already learned in PRIMERA's pre-training and fine-tuning for news. However, hallucinated facts in summaries were a major issue. A comparable setting (trained on news, tested on other data) found 51–55% factual consistency [42].

User Interviews. We conducted five independent 30-minute interviews with employees of the KB. The interview partners consented to take part in the study voluntarily and have their voices recorded. They were made aware that they could stop and drop out of the interview at any time without consequences. The process (a mail to the investigator) for later deleting user-specific data was also explained. A week before our semi-structured voice-recorded one-on-one interviews in Dutch took place, participants received an email with a video (https://www.youtube.com/watch?v=0GzIydjts2E) explaining our prototypical system and its URL. Each interview tackled the same guide questions concerning general thoughts, encountered problems, (un)clear elements, helpfulness of the system and components (aspects and summaries), and suggested changes.

Results and Findings. The full questions plus answers are available in our GitHub repository. In general, the interviewees were enthusiastic about the interface. They found it well-arranged and clear. The website immediately provided a lot of information and context about the person in question. Some other remarks were that the interface worked intuitively and that clustering articles per subject was a plus point. The option to be directly referred to the complete articles on Delpher was also mentioned positively. The interviewees believed that a website like this could definitely help certain users (such as researchers), mainly because they immediately get some context about a person instead of only a list of articles. However, they all agreed that some human input was still needed to refine the system's output. The interviewees also provided feedback on the various aspects of the system. They found the roles interesting and a good way to immediately provide information about the person. However, they all had some difficulty in understanding how the roles were chosen as they noticed a lot of overlap between different roles. This led to the question of why these have not been merged (such as the roles *politician* and *politician by party*). Opinions were divided on the aspects. Some found the distinction useful, while others wondered why not all articles belonging to one role were grouped together. They agreed that the multiple labels (clustered section titles of Wikipedia) shown above every aspect should be condensed for clarity for two reasons: The number of labels is unbalanced between aspects, and the sections with many labels caused some confusion, e.g., the aspect with the labels *background*, *biography*, etc. appeared under every role. The interviewees expected it to only belong to the role *person*. Summaries really posed major issues and worried the interviewees. All unanimously agreed that summaries containing incorrect facts are highly problematic for a library. Some also wondered whether the summary added value.

6   Conclusion

In this work, we demonstrated how a digital library can implement an aspect-driven access path to its news collection. We used Wikipedia to bypass the curation of domain-specific and cost-intensive training data. Moreover, our evaluation verified the method's effectiveness on real-world data and the system's value in practice. However, there is still room for improvements, e.g., finding suitable labels for a section cluster, showing and summarizing diverse snippets, and highlighting connections between people. For instance, we could better cater to the requirements of the KB by battling hallucinations in summaries by either fact-checking each sentence against the input summaries and removing unsupported ones or by using an extractive summarization approach [22,38].

References

1. OpenAI's ChatGPT. https://openai.com/blog/chatgpt
2. Beltagy, I., Peters, M.E., Cohan, A.: Longformer: The long-document transformer. CoRR abs/2004.05150 (2020). https://arxiv.org/abs/2004.05150
3. Bird, S.: NLTK: the natural language toolkit. In: ACL 2006, 21st International Conference on Computational Linguistics and 44th Annual Meeting of the Association for Computational Linguistics, 2006. The Association for Computer Linguistics (2006). https://doi.org/10.3115/1225403.1225421
4. Chall, J., Dale, E.: Readability Revisited: The New Dale-Chall Readability Formula. Brookline Books (1995)
5. Cuper, M.: Researching pandemics through time: a Covid-19 inspired data-driven approach to explore historical newspapers. In: Berget, G., Hall, M.M., Brenn, D., Kumpulainen, S. (eds.) TPDL 2021. LNCS, vol. 12866, pp. 227–231. Springer, Cham (2021). https://doi.org/10.1007/978-3-030-86324-1_26
6. Delobelle, P., Winters, T., Berendt, B.: Robbert: a dutch roberta-based language model. In: Findings of the Association for Computational Linguistics: EMNLP 2020. Findings of ACL, vol. EMNLP 2020, pp. 3255–3265 (2020). https://doi.org/10.18653/v1/2020.findings-emnlp.292
7. Delobelle, P., Winters, T., Berendt, B.: Robbert-2022: Updating a dutch language model to account for evolving language use. CoRR abs/2211.08192 (2022). https://doi.org/10.48550/arXiv.2211.08192
8. Demberg, V., Keller, F.: Data from eye-tracking corpora as evidence for theories of syntactic processing complexity. Cognition 109(2), 193–210 (2008). https://doi.org/10.1016/j.cognition.2008.07.008
9. Devlin, J., Chang, M., Lee, K., Toutanova, K.: BERT: pre-training of deep bidirectional transformers for language understanding. In: NAACL-HLT 2019, pp. 4171–4186 (2019). https://doi.org/10.18653/v1/n19-1423

10. Dong, L., et al.: Unified language model pre-training for natural language understanding and generation. In: NeurIPS 2019. pp. 13042–13054 (2019). https://proceedings.neurips.cc/paper/2019/hash/c20bb2d9a50d5ac1f713f8b34d9aac5a-Abstract.html

11. Düring, M., Kalyakin, R., Bunout, E., Guido, D.: Impresso inspect and compare. visual comparison of semantically enriched historical newspaper articles. Inf. **12**(9), 348 (2021). https://doi.org/10.3390/info12090348

12. Ehrmann, M., Bunout, E., Düring, M.: Historical newspaper user interfaces: a review. In: 85th IFLA General Conference and Assembly, Athens, Greece, 24–30 August 2019, pp. 1–24 (2019)

13. Fleiss, J.L.: Measuring nominal scale agreement among many raters. Psychological Bulletin **76**, 378–382 (1971). https://doi.org/10.1037/h0031619

14. Flesch, R.F.: A new readability yardstick. J. Appl. Psychol. **32**(3), 221–33 (1948)

15. Goldhahn, D., Eckart, T., Quasthoff, U.: Building large monolingual dictionaries at the Leipzig corpora collection: From 100 to 200 languages. In: Proceedings of the Eighth International Conference on Language Resources and Evaluation (LREC'12), pp. 759–765. European Language Resources Association (ELRA), May 2012. http://www.lrec-conf.org/proceedings/lrec2012/pdf/327_Paper.pdf

16. Härm, H., Alumäe, T.: Abstractive summarization of broadcast news stories for estonian. Balt. J. Mod. Comput. **10**(3) (2022). https://doi.org/10.22364/bjmc.2022.10.3.23

17. Jean-Caurant, A., Doucet, A.: Accessing and investigating large collections of historical newspapers with the newseye platform. In: JCDL '20: Proceedings of the ACM/IEEE Joint Conference on Digital Libraries in 2020, pp. 531–532. ACM (2020). https://doi.org/10.1145/3383583.3398627

18. Krippendorff, K.: Content analysis (1989)

19. Kumpulainen, S., Keskustalo, H., Zhang, B., Stefanidis, K.: Historical reasoning in authentic research tasks: mapping cognitive and document spaces. J. Assoc. Inf. Sci. Technol. **71**(2), 230–241 (2020). https://doi.org/10.1002/asi.24216

20. Late, E., Kumpulainen, S.: Interacting with digitised historical newspapers: understanding the use of digital surrogates as primary sources. J. Documentation **78**(7), 106–124 (2022). https://doi.org/10.1108/JD-04-2021-0078

21. Lewis, M., Liu, Y., Goyal, N., Ghazvininejad, M., Mohamed, A., Levy, O., Stoyanov, V., Zettlemoyer, L.: BART: denoising sequence-to-sequence pre-training for natural language generation, translation, and comprehension. In: Proceedings of the 58th Annual Meeting of the Association for Computational Linguistics, ACL 2020, pp. 7871–7880 (2020). https://doi.org/10.18653/v1/2020.acl-main.703

22. Liu, Y., Lapata, M.: Text summarization with pretrained encoders. In: Proceedings of the 2019 Conference on Empirical Methods in Natural Language Processing and the 9th International Joint Conference on Natural Language Processing, EMNLP-IJCNLP 2019. pp. 3728–3738. Association for Computational Linguistics (2019). https://doi.org/10.18653/v1/D19-1387

23. Liu, Y., Gu, J., Goyal, N., Li, X., Edunov, S., Ghazvininejad, M., Lewis, M., Zettlemoyer, L.: Multilingual denoising pre-training for neural machine translation. Trans. Assoc. Comput. Linguistics **8**, 726–742 (2020). https://doi.org/10.1162/tacl_a_00343

24. Maria, N., Silva, M.J.: Building a digital library of web news. In: ECDL 2000, vol. 1923, pp. 344–347 (2000). https://doi.org/10.1007/3-540-45268-0_36

25. Marjanen, J., Pivovarova, L., Zosa, E., Kurunmäki, J.: Clustering ideological terms in historical newspaper data with diachronic word embeddings. In: 5th International Workshop on Computational History, HistoInformatics@TPDL 2019. CEUR

Workshop Proceedings, vol. 2461, pp. 21–29. CEUR-WS.org (2019). https://ceur-ws.org/Vol-2461/paper_4.pdf

26. McCay-Peet, L., Toms, E.G., Kelloway, E.K.: Development and assessment of the content validity of a scale to measure how well a digital environment facilitates serendipity. Inf. Res. **19**(3) (2014). http://www.informationr.net/ir/19-3/paper630.html

27. Müller, C.: A N N O - AUSTRIAN NEWSPAPERS ONLINE: Historische österreichische Zeitungen und Zeitschriften online. Eine Digitalisierungsinitiative der Österreichischen Nationalbibliothek (http ://anno.onb.ac.at/). K. G. Saur (2004). https://doi.org/10.1515/9783110944198-023

28. Niculescu, M.A., Ruseti, S., Dascalu, M.: Rosummary: control tokens for Romanian news summarization. Algorithms **15**(12), 472 (2022). https://doi.org/10.3390/a15120472

29. Pfanzelter, E., Oberbichler, S., Marjanen, J., Langlais, P., Hechl, S.: Digital interfaces of historical newspapers: opportunities, restrictions and recommendations. J. Data Min. Digit. Humanit. 2021 (2021). https://doi.org/10.46298/jdmdh.6121

30. Phang, J., Zhao, Y., Liu, P.J.: Investigating efficiently extending transformers for long input summarization. CoRR abs/2208.04347 (2022). https://doi.org/10.48550/arXiv.2208.04347

31. Raffel, C., et al.: Exploring the limits of transfer learning with a unified text-to-text transformer. J. Mach. Learn. Res. **21**, 140:1–140:67 (2020). http://jmlr.org/papers/v21/20-074.html

32. Reimers, N., Gurevych, I.: Sentence-bert: sentence embeddings using siamese bert-networks. In: Proceedings of the 2019 Conference on Empirical Methods in Natural Language Processing. Association for Computational Linguistics, November 2019. https://arxiv.org/abs/1908.10084

33. Tiedemann, J., Thottingal, S.: OPUS-MT - building open translation services for the World. In: Proceedings of the 22nd Annual Conference of the European Association for Machine Translation, EAMT 2020, pp. 479–480. European Association for Machine Translation (2020). https://aclanthology.org/2020.eamt-1.61/

34. van Strien., D., Beelen., K., Ardanuy., M.C., Hosseini., K., McGillivray., B., Colavizza., G.: Assessing the impact of ocr quality on downstream nlp tasks. In: Proceedings of the 12th International Conference on Agents and Artificial Intelligence - Volume 1: ARTIDIGH, pp. 484–496. INSTICC, SciTePress (2020). https://doi.org/10.5220/0009169004840496

35. Vogel, I., Jiang, P.: Fake news detection with the new German dataset "German-FakeNC". In: Doucet, A., Isaac, A., Golub, K., Aalberg, T., Jatowt, A. (eds.) TPDL 2019. LNCS, vol. 11799, pp. 288–295. Springer, Cham (2019). https://doi.org/10.1007/978-3-030-30760-8_25

36. de Vries, W., van Cranenburgh, A., Bisazza, A., Caselli, T., van Noord, G., Nissim, M.: Bertje: a dutch BERT model. CoRR abs/1912.09582 (2019). http://arxiv.org/abs/1912.09582

37. Xue, L., et al.: mt5: a massively multilingual pre-trained text-to-text transformer. In: Proceedings of the 2021 Conference of the North American Chapter of the Association for Computational Linguistics: Human Language Technologies, NAACL-HLT 2021, pp. 483–498 (2021). https://doi.org/10.18653/v1/2021.naacl-main.41

38. Yadav, A., Ranvijay, R., Yadav, R., Maurya, A.K.: State-of-the-art approach to extractive text summarization: a comprehensive review. Multimed. Tools Appl., 1–63, February 2023. https://doi.org/10.1007/s11042-023-14613-9

39. Zaheer, M., et al.: Big bird: transformers for longer sequences. In: Advances in Neural Information Processing Systems 33: Annual Conference on Neural Information Processing Systems 2020 (2020). https://proceedings.neurips.cc/paper/2020/hash/c8512d142a2d849725f31a9a7a361ab9-Abstract.html

40. Zhang, J., Zhao, Y., Saleh, M., Liu, P.J.: PEGASUS: pre-training with extracted gap-sentences for abstractive summarization. In: ICML 2020. 119, pp. 11328–11339, 2020. http://proceedings.mlr.press/v119/zhang20ae.html

41. Zhang, T., Ladhak, F., Durmus, E., Liang, P., McKeown, K.R., Hashimoto, T.B.: Benchmarking large language models for news summarization. CoRR abs/2301.13848 (2023). https://doi.org/10.48550/arXiv.2301.13848

42. Zhang, Z., Elfardy, H., Dreyer, M., Small, K., Ji, H., Bansal, M.: Enhancing multi-document summarization with cross-document graph-based information extraction. In: Proceedings of the 17th Conference of the European Chapter of the Association for Computational Linguistics, pp. 1696–1707. Association for Computational Linguistics, May 2023. https://aclanthology.org/2023.eacl-main.124

PreprintResolver: Improving Citation Quality by Resolving Published Versions of ArXiv Preprints Using Literature Databases

Louise Bloch[1,2,3]([✉]) [iD], Johannes Rückert[1] [iD], and Christoph M. Friedrich[1,2] [iD]

[1] Department of Computer Science, University of Applied Sciences and Arts Dortmund, Emil-Figge-Str. 42, 44227 Dortmund, Germany
{louise.bloch,johannes.rueckert,christoph.friedrich}@fh-dortmund.de
[2] Institute for Medical Informatics, Biometry and Epidemiology (IMIBE), University Hospital Essen, Hufelandstraße 55, 45122 Essen, Germany
[3] Institute for Artificial Intelligence in Medicine (IKIM), University Hospital Essen, Hufelandstraße 55, 45122 Essen, Germany

Abstract. The growing impact of preprint servers enables the rapid sharing of time-sensitive research. Likewise, it is becoming increasingly difficult to distinguish high-quality, peer-reviewed research from preprints. Although preprints are often later published in peer-reviewed journals, this information is often missing from preprint servers. To overcome this problem, the PreprintResolver was developed, which uses four literature databases (DBLP, SemanticScholar, OpenAlex, and CrossRef/CrossCite) to identify preprint-publication pairs for the arXiv preprint server. The target audience focuses on, but is not limited to inexperienced researchers and students, especially from the field of computer science. The tool is based on a fuzzy matching of author surnames, titles, and DOIs. Experiments were performed on a sample of 1,000 arXiv-preprints from the research field of computer science and without any publication information. With 77.94%, computer science is highly affected by missing publication information in arXiv. The results show that the PreprintResolver was able to resolve 603 out of 1,000 (60.3%) arXiv-preprints from the research field of computer science and without any publication information. All four literature databases contributed to the final result. In a manual validation, a random sample of 100 resolved preprints was checked. For all preprints, at least one result is plausible. For nine preprints, more than one result was identified, three of which are partially invalid. In conclusion the PreprintResolver is suitable for individual, manually reviewed requests, but less suitable for bulk requests. The PreprintResolver tool (https://preprintresolver.eu) and source code (https://gitlab.com/ippolis_wp3/preprint-resolver) is available online.

Keywords: Preprint · arXiv · Publication · Research Quality · Digital Library

---

L. Bloch and J. Rückert—These authors contributed equally to the work.

O. Alonso et al. (Eds.): TPDL 2023, LNCS 14241, pp. 47–61, 2023.
https://doi.org/10.1007/978-3-031-43849-3_5

1   Introduction

Preprints are scientific manuscripts that have been uploaded by their authors to public servers (so-called preprint-servers) without being subjected to any peer review process [5]. The original idea of preprints was the publication of research before or during submission to a peer-reviewed journal or conference. More recently, however, most preprint servers also include research that has been submitted after it has been accepted or published in peer-reviewed venues.

ArXiv [18,19] was one of the first internet-based preprint servers developed in 1991 to share preprints in the field of physics. Since then, arXiv has expanded to include the fields of mathematics, computer science, quantitative biology, quantitative finance, statistics, electrical engineering and systems science, and economics. Recently, there have been multiple preprint servers, most of them focusing on specific research areas, e.g., bioRxiv [37] in the field of biology, medRxiv [35] in the field of health sciences, the Social Science Research Network (SSRN) [14] in the field of social sciences and humanities, which later expands to science and engineering, or Humanities Commons [22] in the field of humanities.

In comparison to traditional publication, the release of preprints promises a faster publication of time-sensitive research [1]. In addition, the benefits of preprints include higher attraction [24] and potentially more citations [10,15–17,36], faster feedback from the research community as well as open access publication. While the benefits initially outweigh the disadvantages for the submitter, the disadvantages primarily affect the research community. Due to the lack of peer review, the quality of preprints is not guaranteed which increases the risk of fraudulent preprints and preprints with low research quality. This makes it more difficult to identify quality research, especially for inexperienced researchers. In particular, there is a risk of citing outdated versions of research possibly containing altered or incorrect information [16]. This risk is increased because although preprints are often submitted, accepted, and published in peer-reviewed journals or conference proceedings [1], preprint servers often lack a link to those updated publications [6,12,29].

In this work, the PreprintResolver was developed to resolve published versions of arXiv preprints using four databases. It can help researchers to find the latest published version of preprints. The tool focuses on, but is not limited to, a target group of inexperienced researchers and students in the field of computer science.

2   Related Work

There are a few tools with similar ideas. For example, the SAGE Rejected Article Tracker[1] presented in [21] was developed to track papers rejected by journals, but can also be used to resolve preprints. The Python library requires the input of titles and authors and identifies published versions using CrossRef [34]. Levenshtein distance [27] and a logistic regression model were used to determine

---

[1] SAGE Rejected Article Tracker: https://github.com/sagepublishing/rejected_article_tracker_pkg, Accessed: 2023-07-19.

whether publications were fuzzy matches. The tool is not specialised in resolving preprints which increases the complexity of identifying quality research for inexperienced researchers.

In [12] the tool PreprintMatch[2] is presented that matches preprints uploaded on the BioRxiv and MedRxiv preprint servers to PubMed [7] publications. The tool is based on database dumps. It matches the titles and abstracts using a word vector representation to handle semantic changes. The vectors are ranked by cosine similarity and the top 100 results are compared using the Jaccard similarity [23] of author names and a Support Vector Machine (SVM) [9] trained on a hand-selected dataset. The main differences are the focus on the biomedical domain and the use of database dumps with the risk of outdated information.

A tool named PreprintPublicationLinker[3] uses more recent data by requesting the CrossRef Application Programming Interfaces (API) [6]. It matches preprints from medRxiv with the CrossRef API. The implementation includes a fuzzy comparison of titles, authors, ORCIDs, and publication time. It was tested on a corpus of preprints related to COVID-19 and reached an accuracy of 91.5% (sensitivity: 90.9%, specificity: of 91.9%). The main difference to this work is the focus on the medical domain and the use of a single literature database.

For the arXiv preprint server, which is the focus of this work, the Bibliographic Explorer[4] exists. It provides information about published versions and citations directly as an overlay of the arXiv website. It is based on the databases SemanticScholar [3,25,31], Google Scholar [20], CrossRef/CrossCite, NASA Astrophysics Data System (ADS) [2], and the Inspire HEP API [32]. The tool includes no fuzzy matching of database and preprint information but provides links to the database results directly associated with the `arXiv-id` or DOI. This leads to links to the original arXiv preprints, even though a published version exists, which can be confusing for inexperienced researchers.

Additionally, some case studies use matching algorithms to identify preprint-publication pairs. For example, [29] presents a study investigating how many, and which arXiv preprints were published in the field of computer science. The matching was based on crawled data from CrossRef [34] and Digital Bibliography and Library Project (DBLP) [28]. For papers with unchanged titles, a fuzzy matching of first authors and titles was implemented. A Bidirectional Encoder Representations from Transformers (BERT) [11] model was trained to match preprints and publications with changed titles. The model was trained using a dataset containing arXiv version data as well as data from a CrossRef search.

---

[2] PreprintMatch: https://github.com/PeterEckmann1/preprint-match,   Accessed: 2023-07-19.

[3] PreprintPublicationLinker: https://github.com/gcabanac/preprint-publication-linker, Accessed: 2023-07-19.

[4] arXiv Bibliographic Explorer: https://github.com/mattbierbaum/arXiv-bib-overlay, Accessed: 2023-07-19.

In [26], arXiv preprints are matched to publications in the Web Of Science (WoS) library using a fuzzy matching of titles, journals mentioned in arXiv comments, and first authors. Afterwards, the first characters of the abstracts are compared. During the analysis, 63.7% of the preprints were resolved, but the rate varies by discipline. For example, in computer science, less than 20% were resolved. One reason may be the impact of conferences in this field [30].

For an analysis of citations and altmetrics in preprints, a matching between bioRxiv preprints and CrossRef and Scopus [13] was implemented in [16]. It uses the bioRxiv property of CrossRef, a scan of the bioRxiv websites, and a fuzzy matching including the authors, titles, and abstracts using Scopus as a database. The algorithm resolved 67.6% of the preprints.

In [38] a backward resolving of arXiv preprints is implemented for highly influential computer science conferences. All publications of 63 conferences are identified using the DBLP. An arXiv dump was used to identify corresponding preprints using an exact matching of titles and one author. For 56% of conference articles, a preprint was found.

To the best of our knowledge, there is currently no tool that helps inexperienced researchers identify the most recent publication of an arXiv preprint. The presented tool uses multiple literature databases to resolve preprints from different disciplines and returns the BibTeX citations that can be imported directly into bibliographies. As the tool communicates with the APIs of four literature databases, the data is up to date and no time-intensive downloading of database files is required. The tool[5] and the source code[6] is available online.

3   Literature Databases

This section introduces the databases used to obtain information about arXiv preprints and to find matching peer-reviewed publications. It has to be noted that there is a risk of incorrect or outdated information in all of the databases.

3.1   arXiv

Developed in 1991, arXiv [18,19] was one of the first internet-based preprint servers. The initial aim was to share preprints in the field of physics. Later, arXiv expanded to the fields of mathematics, computer science, quantitative biology, quantitative finance, statistics, electrical engineering and systems science, and economics. Currently, arXiv contains more than 2.2 million preprints and has 2.6 billion total downloads [4]. For linking between preprints and published research,

---

[5] PreprintResolver tool: https://preprintresolver.eu, Available from 2023-08-01.
[6] PreprintResolver source code: https://gitlab.com/ippolis_wp3/preprint-resolver, Accessed: 2023-07-19.

authors are requested to add DOIs and additional information to the preprints after publication[7]. Metadata from arXiv can be requested via a public API[8].

3.2 DBLP

The DBLP computer science bibliography [28] is a bibliographic library of scholarly literature in the computer science domain. In 2023, DBLP contains metadata of more than 6.7 million publications[9]. As conferences and workshops have a high influence in the computer science domain [30], at the time of submission, 48.37% of the publications include conference and workshop papers, whereas 39.38% include journal articles[10]. DBLP provides a public API where users can request publications, venues, and authors[11]. Among other information, requested metadata contains the title, authors, DOI, venue, year, and publication type.

3.3 CrossRef/CrossCite

CrossRef [34] is a DOI registration agency launched in 2000. The original idea was to link research articles from different publishers to improve the citation resolution. CrossRef assigns and links unique identifiers to authors, works, research institutions, and funding. This makes it easier for researchers to find and cite quality research. Recently, CrossRef contains more than 147 million records[12], which were published in more than 120,000 journals and 102,000 conference proceedings. A publicly available REST-API of CrossRef is available online[13] providing metadata and links between research objects.

3.4 SemanticScholar

SemanticScholar [3, 25, 31] is a literature database released in 2015 by the Allen Institute for Artificial Intelligence. It is based on a literature graph that links papers, authors and entities, and aims to help scientists discover and understand scientific literature. Publication metadata includes authors, titles, citation counts, venues, and publication years, among other information. The database

---

[7] arXiv add journal reference: https://info.arXiv.org/help/jref.html, Accessed: 2023-07-19.

[8] arXiv API: https://info.arXiv.org/help/api/user-manual.html, Accessed: 2023-07-19.

[9] DBLP record statistics: https://dblp.org/statistics/recordsindblp.html, Accessed: 2023-07-19.

[10] DBLP publication type statistics: https://dblp.org/statistics/distributionofpublicationtype.html, Accessed: 2023-07-19.

[11] DBLP API: https://dblp.org/faq/How+to+use+the+dblp+search+API.html, Accessed: 2023-07-19.

[12] CrossRef: https://www.crossref.org/06members/53status.html, Accessed: 2023-07-19.

[13] CrossRef API: https://www.crossref.org/documentation/retrieve-metadata/rest-api/, Accessed: 2023-07-19.

contains more than 212 million research items[14]. The publicly available API[15] supports a limited number of queries per time. For this project, a key was requested which increases the number of requests. ArXiv-ids are often directly linked to published versions, and it is possible to request data directly using this id.

3.5 OpenAlex

OpenAlex [33] is a publicly accessible index of information on academic publications, authors, venues, institutions, and concepts which was launched in 2022. The research items in OpenAlex are linked using a graph database which contains more than 209 million academic publications [33] and is growing by about 50,000 per day [33]. Data can be requested via a publicly available REST-API[16]. Among others, the metadata available for publications in OpenAlex contains authors, titles, doi, additional sources (such as arXiv), and citation counts. Currently it is not possible to request arXiv-ids directly in OpenAlex.

4 Methods

This section describes the workflow used to resolve arXiv preprints which is visualized in Fig. 1.

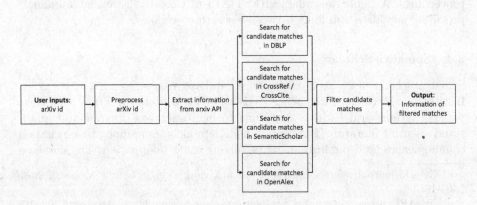

Fig. 1. Workflow used to resolve arXiv preprints based on four literature databases.

---

[14] SemanticScholar: https://www.semanticscholar.org/, Accessed: 2023-07-19.

[15] SemanticScholar API: https://www.semanticscholar.org/product/api, Access: 2023-07-19.

[16] OpenAlex API: https://docs.openalex.org/, Accessed: 2023-07-19.

4.1   User Input

The tool is designed for, but not limited to, a target group of inexperienced researchers. The idea is, to make users aware of the differences between preprints and peer-reviewed research, leading to the requirement for good usability. For this reason, the user has to enter minimal input including only the `arXiv-id` into the interface.

4.2   Preprocess Input

In order to avoid errors, the first step of the pipeline is a preprocessing step. This includes removing leading and closing spaces. Second, as the input may contain the prefixes `"arxiv:"`, `"abs/"`, or `"pdf/"`, the last occurrence of these substrings is identified and all characters before and including these prefixes are removed. Additionally, `".pdf"` is deleted from the end of the input. Thus the resolver can also handle URLs in the form `https://arXiv.org/abs/{arXiv-id}` and `https://arXiv.org/pdf/{arXiv-id}.pdf`. A lower-case version of the extracted `arXiv-id` is used for further processing.

4.3   Extract Information from arXiv API

Using the preprocessed `arXiv-id`, information from the publicly available arXiv-API is requested by `https://export.arXiv.org/api/query?id_list={arXiv-id}`. The response information is used to extract the latest arXiv version, authors, title, DOI, publishing date, categories, and additional information.

4.4   Identify Candidate Matches in Literature Databases

The `arXiv-id`, `title`, and `DOI` extracted from the arXiv API are used to identify candidate matches in the previously introduced literature databases.

DBLP.   The DBLP computer science bibliography is requested for the `title` using the query: `https://dblp.org/search/publ/api?q={title}&format=json&h=5`. This query identifies the top five DBLP candidate matches.

CrossRef/CrossCite.   A two-level query is used to identify candidate matches using the CrossRef and CrossCite APIs[17].

1. If available, the CrossCite API is first requested for the `DOI` using the request: `https://doi.org/{DOI}`.
2. If no valid results are found in the first step, the top 10 CrossRef results are requested using the `title`: `https://api.crossref.org/works?query.bibliographic={title}&sort=score&rows=10`.

---

[17] CrossCite API: https://citation.crosscite.org/docs.html, Accessed: 2023-07-19.

SemanticScholar. Information from SemanticScholar is requested in a three-level query. For all queries, the requested fields are: `title`, `authors`, `journal`, `venue`, `year`, `abstract`, `publicationTypes`, `externalIds`, `isOpenAccess`, `publicationDate`, `fieldsOfStudy`, `s2FieldsOfStudy`, `referenceCount`, `citationCount`, `influentialCitationCount`.

1. The API is queried directly for the given `arXiv-id` using `https://api.semanticscholar.org/graph/v1/paper/ARXIV:{arXiv-id}`.
2. If no valid reference is found in Step 1, and if a DOI is available, the SemanticScholar API is requested for the DOI using `https://api.semanticscholar.org/graph/v1/paper/DOI:{DOI}`.
3. If the previous steps find no valid matches, the API is requested for the `title`: `https://api.semanticscholar.org/graph/v1/paper/search?query={title}`.

OpenAlex. The candidates from OpenAlex are requested in a three-level query.

1. If available, the API is queried for the DOI: `https://api.openalex.org/works/doi={DOI}`.
2. If the previous step shows no results, a search for the `title` is performed using `https://api.openalex.org/works?search={title}`. From this query, the results with a link to the original `arXiv-id` are first filtered.
3. If no matches are identified in the previous steps, the initial candidate matches from Step 2 are filtered.

4.5   Filter Matches

Two approaches have been implemented to filter the candidate matches. The first one is a weak filtering strategy, which is used when the results are identified in the database directly by the `arXiv-id`. The second strategy is a strong filtering which is used for the remaining cases. The weak filtering strategy is a subset of the strong filtering procedure.

Weak Filtering. The idea behind weak filtering is that titles and authors can change during publication, so publications that are directly linked to the preprint in literature databases (SemanticScholar and OpenAlex Step 1) contain more evidence than fuzzy matching. The weak filtering contains the following steps:

1. Exclusion of candidate matches where the preprint is identified as the publication.
2. Exclusion of candidate matches without publication types, or venues.
3. If the DOI is available in both papers, candidate matches with mismatching DOIs are discarded.

Strong Filtering. The matches which are identified without a direct link to the `arXiv-id` are filtered using the following criteria:

1. The weak filtering strategy is applied.
2. For the remaining candidate matches, the titles are compared using fuzzy matching. Titles are accepted if the ratio of the Levenshtein distance [27] and the maximum number of characters in both titles is less than 0.05.
3. The last step is a comparison of the authors. This includes the removal of diacritical marks. Candidates are accepted if the ratio of successfully matched authors and the maximum number of authors of both papers exceeds 0.70.

Table 1. Overview of the arXiv dataset by primary research fields. Publication information is the DOI and journal reference. The dataset was downloaded on 2023-01-19.

Research field extracted from primary arXiv category	# preprints (ratio)	# preprints W/O without information (ratio)	Average preprint versions
Physics	1,234,491 (56.36%)	287,269 (23.27%)	1.53
Mathematics	446,833 (20.40%)	324,414 (72.60%)	1.72
Computer Science	393,434 (17.96%)	306,634 (77.94%)	1.55
Quantitative Biology	24,887 (1.14%)	14,131 (56.78%)	1.49
Quantitative Finance	9,785 (0.45%)	6,935 (70,87%)	1.69
Statistics	41,161 (1.88%)	32,222 (78.28%)	1.75
Electr. Eng. & Systems Service	34,830 (1.59%)	26,712 (76.69%)	1.46
Economics	4,990 (0.23%)	4,229 (84.75%)	1.76
Overall	2,190,411 (100.00%)	1,002,546 (45.77%)	1.58

4.6 Output

The PreprintResolver outputs structured information about the preprint and the candidate publications, as well as citation information. The citation information are provided in the BibTeX format and can thus be added directly to literature databases. Because authors sometimes publish papers with identical titles as journal and conference articles, the PreprintResolver can return multiple results for one database and the user has to choose which publication is most relevant.

5 Experiments and Results

In this section, some experiments are described which were performed to validate the functionality of the tool. The experiments are based on the arXiv Dataset[18] [8] that was published by Cornell University. The dataset was downloaded on 2023-01-19 and includes the metadata of 2, 190, 411 preprints. Table 1

---

[18] arXiv dataset: https://www.kaggle.com/datasets/Cornell-University/arXiv, Accessed: 2023-07-19.

Table 2. PreprintResolver results achieved by resolving a random sample of $1,000$ preprints without any publication information in computer science.

Database	# preprints found	Resolving ratio
DBLP	511	51.1%
CrossRef/CrossCite	468	46.8%
SemanticScholar	487	48.7%
OpenAlex	299	29.9%
Overall	603	60.3%

summarizes the number of preprints, the number of preprints without any information about their publication, and the mean number of versions per preprint and research field. Publication information is the DOI and the journal reference. ArXiv allows authors to select multiple research fields for a preprint. To avoid duplicates in the evaluation process, this work focuses on the primary research field.

The dataset summary shows that the number of preprints differed between research fields. Most preprints are submitted in the initial area of arXiv – physics $(1,234,491; 56.36\%)$. In computer science, the third most preprints $(393,434; 17.96\%)$ were uploaded. The ratios of preprints without any publication information also vary between disciplines. The ratio for the overall data set is 45.77%. Only physics undercuts this ratio (23.27%). The highest ratio of 84.75% was reached in economics. Computer science reached the third highest ratio of 77.94%. The mean number of versions per preprint differs between 1.46 in electrical engineering and systems science and 1.76 in economics. No clear association between the ratio of preprints without publication information and the mean number of versions was investigated.

As this tool focuses on the target group of inexperienced researchers in computer science, the experiments also do. The publication process for scientific journals and conference proceedings can take from a few months to years. To avoid biases, the experiments are based on all preprints with a first submission before January 2022. The computer science data set matching this criterion contains $327,320$ (83.20% of preprints in computer science) preprints. The number of samples without any publication information is $248,671$ (75.97%) in this dataset. For evaluation, a random sample of $1,000$ preprints was drawn from this subset.

The results of the PreprintResolver are summarized in Table 2 and show that 603 (60.3%) preprints were successfully resolved. Most preprints were resolved using DBLP (51.1%) followed by SemanticScholar (48.7%), CrossRef/CrossCite (46.8%), and OpenAlex (29.9%). The Venn diagram in Fig. 2 shows, the contribution of the databases. 186 (18.6%) of the preprints were found in all four databases. For all databases, there were preprints that are individually identified (DBLP: 25; 2.5%, CrossRef/CrossCite: 8; 0.8%, SemanticScholar: 26; 2.6%, OpenAlex: 5; 0.5%). Thus all databases contributed to the final result.

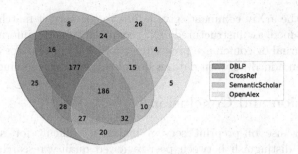

Fig. 2. Venn diagram of the literature database contributions in the PreprintResolver during resolving of a random sample of 1,000 preprints without any publication information in computer science.

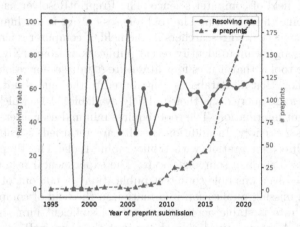

Fig. 3. Plot that shows the number of preprints per year and the resolving rate of the PreprintResolver in the investigated sample of 1,000 preprints in computer science without publication information.

The plot in Fig. 3 shows the number of preprints and the resolving rate over the years. Consistent with the increasing number of preprints the number of preprints in the sample is also increasing. The resolving rate between 1995 and 2009 shows strong fluctuations between 0% and 100%. This can be attributed to the small number of samples (1995: 1; 2009: 8). From 2010, the samples increase and the resolving rate settles between 48.00% (2011) and 64.71% (2021). An increase in the resolving rate can be detected for recent preprints.

For validation, a random sample of 100 of the 603 results resolved by the PreprintResolver were manually checked by comparing the authors, titles, affiliations, and the beginning and end of the abstracts. The results show that the PreprintResolver identified at least one plausible match for all 100 preprints examined. For nine preprints, two different results were identified. Three of these results provide at least one incorrect or untraceable match. For four results it was not possible to determine which was the best match. For two results with two matches, the arXiv comments give a hint to the correct match. Of the 100 preprints examined, an unstructured arXiv comment provides information about the correct journal or conference proceedings for 46 preprints. For one preprint, a DOI has been added between dataset download and the resolving.

6   Discussion and Conclusion

The increasing use of preprint servers makes it difficult for inexperienced researchers to distinguish between peer-reviewed quality research and uncontrolled preprints. Although most preprint servers support the option of linking preprints to published versions, the extent to which this option is used varies between research fields. For example, the experiments in this research identify a deficit in the field of computer science. The PreprintResolver has been developed to overcome this problem. The tool focuses on but is not limited to a target group of inexperienced researchers in the field of computer science. It uses a fuzzy matching algorithm to identify recent publications from arXiv preprints. A strength of the tool is that it uses four literature databases for resolving and the experiments show that all databases contributed to the final result. These literature databases are queried via their publicly available APIs, which guarantees the use of recent information. The tool requires minimal user interactions, making it more user-friendly. In addition, results are returned as BibTeX entries, allowing the direct integration with bibliographic tools. The PreprintResolver has been released as open source software. The experimental results show that the PreprintResolver was able to detect publications of 603 out of 1,000 arXiv preprints with missing publication information in the field of computer science. The resolving rate is stable across years with a sufficient number of samples in the dataset. A manual validation shows that the PreprintResolver identifies at least one plausible result for each of the 100 randomly sampled preprints. For nine samples, the tool identifies more than one result, and for three of these results, one of the results is incorrect or untraceable. This leads to the conclusion, that the PreprintResolver is suitable for individual, manually reviewed requests, but less suitable for bulk requests. Future work includes increasing the number of literature databases, which may increase the resolving ratio. In addition, the matching can be improved, for example, by training machine learning models for filtering of candidate matches. It is expected that such an approach will reduce the number of matches that are erroneously excluded by the strong filtering approach due to title or author changes prior to publication. Another idea is, to expand the supported preprint servers. Research building on this work will investigate the publication rate of arXiv preprints, the recall and precision of the PreprintResolver, and the role of each database on a larger dataset to improve the statistical validity. An extended analysis should also analyse the performance of different thresholds during the strong filtering.

Acknowledgements. This work is part of the BMBF-funded project "Intelligente Unterstützung projekt- und problemorientierter Lehre und Integration in Studienabläufe" (IPPOLIS) (Support code: 16DHBKI050).

The work of Louise Bloch was partially funded by a PhD grant from University of Applied Sciences and Arts Dortmund, Dortmund, Germany.

The authors thank arXiv for use of its open access interoperability.

The authors thank the literature databases CrossRef/CrossCite, DBLP, Semantic-Scholar, and OpenAlex for the use of open access APIs and availability of data.

The authors thank SemanticScholar for providing an API key that allows requesting at a higher rate limit.

References

1. Abdill, R.J., Blekhman, R.: Meta-research: tracking the popularity and outcomes of all bioRxiv preprints. eLife **8**, e45133 (2019). https://doi.org/10.7554/eLife.45133

2. Accomazzi, A.: ADS Services in support of the Discovery, Management and Evaluation of Science Data. Presentation, December 2015. https://doi.org/10.5281/zenodo.34494

3. Ammar, W., et al.: Construction of the literature graph in semantic scholar. In: Proceedings of the 2018 Conference of the North American Chapter of the Association for Computational Linguistics: Human Language Technologies, vol. 3, pp. 84–91. Association for Computational Linguistics, New Orleans - Louisiana (2018). https://doi.org/10.18653/v1/n18-3011, industry Papers

4. arXiv.org: ArXiv annual report 2022. Technical report (2023). https://info.arxiv.org/about/reports/2022_arXiv_annual_report.pdf. Accessed 17 May 2023

5. Berg, J.M., et al.: Preprints for the life sciences. Science **352**(6288), 899–901 (2016). https://doi.org/10.1126/science.aaf9133

6. Cabanac, G., Oikonomidi, T., Boutron, I.: Day-to-day discovery of preprint-publication links. Scientometrics **126**(6), 5285–5304 (2021). https://doi.org/10.1007/s11192-021-03900-7

7. Canese, K., Weis, S.: Pubmed: the bibliographic database. In: The NCBI Handbook 2(1) (2013)

8. Cornell University: ArXiv dataset. Dataset (2023). https://doi.org/10.34740/kaggle/dsv/5621820

9. Cortes, C., Vapnik, V.: Support-vector networks. Mach. Learn. **20**(3), 273–297 (1995). https://doi.org/10.1007/bf00994018

10. Davis, P.M., Fromerth, M.J.: Does the arXiv lead to higher citations and reduced publisher downloads for mathematics articles? Scientometrics **71**(2), 203–215 (2007). https://doi.org/10.1007/s11192-007-1661-8

11. Devlin, J., Chang, M.W., Lee, K., Toutanova, K.: BERT: pre-training of deep bidirectional transformers for language understanding. In: Proceedings of the 2019 Conference of the North American Chapter of the Association for Computational Linguistics: Human Language Technologies, vol. 1, pp. 4171–4186. Association for Computational Linguistics, Minneapolis, Minnesota (2019). https://doi.org/10.18653/v1/n19-1423, long and short papers

12. Eckmann, P., Bandrowski, A.: PreprintMatch: a tool for preprint to publication detection shows global inequities in scientific publication. PLoS ONE **18**(3), e0281659 (2023). https://doi.org/10.1371/journal.pone.0281659

13. Elsevier B.V: Scopus. https://www.scopus.com/home.uri. Accessed 22 May 2023

14. Elsevier B.V: Social Science Research Network (SSRN): Tomorrow's research today. https://www.ssrn.com/index.cfm/en/. Accessed 22 May 2023

15. Feldman, S., Lo, K., Ammar, W.: Citation count analysis for papers with preprints. Preprint (2018). arXiv: 1805.05238v1 [cs.DL]
16. Fraser, N.C., Momeni, F., Mayr, P., Peters, I.: The relationship between bioRxiv preprints, citations and altmetrics. Quant. Sci. Stud. **1**(2), 618 – 638 (2020). https://doi.org/10.1162/qss_a_00043
17. Fu, D.Y., Hughey, J.J.: Meta-research: releasing a preprint is associated with more attention and citations for the peer-reviewed article. eLife **8**, e52646 (2019). https://doi.org/10.7554/eLife.52646
18. Ginsparg, P.: First steps towards electronic research communication. Comput. Phys. **8**(4), 390–396 (1994). https://doi.org/10.1063/1.4823313
19. Ginsparg, P.: ArXiv at 20. Nature **476**(7359), 145–147 (2011). https://doi.org/10.1038/476145a
20. Google Scholar: Google scholar. https://scholar.google.com/. Accessed 22 May 2023
21. Hails, A.J., Day, A.R.: The SAGE rejected article tracker. J. Open Source Softw. **6**(64), 3348 (2021). https://doi.org/10.21105/joss.03348
22. Humanities Commons: Humanities Commons. https://hcommons.org/. Accessed 22 May 2023
23. Jaccard, P.: The distribution of the flora in the alpine zone.1. New Phytologist **11**(2), 37–50 (1912). https://doi.org/10.1111/j.1469-8137.1912.tb05611.x
24. Kelly, D.: SIGIR community survey on preprint services. SIGIR Forum **52**(1), 11–33 (2018). https://doi.org/10.1145/3274784.3274787
25. Kinney, R.M., et al.: The semantic scholar open data platform. Preprint (2023). arXiv: 2301.10140v1 [cs.DL]
26. Larivière, V., Sugimoto, C.R., Macaluso, B., Milojević, S., Cronin, B., Thelwall, M.: ArXiv e-prints and the journal of record: an analysis of roles and relationships. Journal of the Association for Information Science and Technology 65(6), 1157–1169 (2014). https://doi.org/10.1002/asi.23044
27. Levenshtein, V.I.: Binary codes capable of correcting deletions, insertions and reversals. Soviet Phys. Doklady **10**, 707–710 (1966)
28. Ley, M.: The DBLP computer science bibliography: evolution, research issues, perspectives. In: Laender, A.H.F., Oliveira, A.L. (eds.) SPIRE 2002. LNCS, vol. 2476, pp. 1–10. Springer, Heidelberg (2002). https://doi.org/10.1007/3-540-45735-6_1
29. Lin, J., Yu, Y., Zhou, Y., Zhou, Z., Shi, X.: How many preprints have actually been printed and why: a case study of computer science preprints on arXiv. Scientometrics **124**(1), 555–574 (2020). https://doi.org/10.1007/s11192-020-03430-8
30. Lisée, C., Larivière, V., Archambault, E.: Conference proceedings as a source of scientific information: a bibliometric analysis. J. Am. Soc. Inform. Sci. Technol. **59**(11), 1776–1784 (2008). https://doi.org/10.1002/asi.20888
31. Lo, K., Wang, L.L., Neumann, M.E., Kinney, R.M., Weld, D.S.: S2ORC: the semantic scholar open research corpus. In: Proceedings of the 58th Annual Meeting of the Association for Computational Linguistics, pp. 4969–4983 (2020). https://doi.org/10.18653/v1/2020.acl-main.447
32. Moskovic, M.: The INSPIRE REST API. API documentation (2021). https://doi.org/10.5281/zenodo.5788550. https://github.com/inspirehep/rest-api-doc
33. Priem, J., Piwowar, H.A., Orr, R.: OpenAlex: A fully-open index of scholarly works, authors, venues, institutions, and concepts. Preprint (2022), arXiv: 2205.01833v2 [cs.DL]
34. Rachael, L.: CrossRef developments and initiatives: an update on services for the scholarly publishing community from CrossRef. Science Editing **1**(1), 13–18 (2014). https://doi.org/10.6087/kcse.2014.1.13

35. Rawlinson, C., Bloom, T.: New preprint server for medical research. BMJ 365 (2019). https://doi.org/10.1136/bmj.l2301
36. Serghiou, S., Ioannidis, J.P.A.: Altmetric scores, citations, and publication of studies posted as preprints. JAMA **319**(4), 402–404 (2018). https://doi.org/10.1001/jama.2017.21168
37. Sever, R., Roeder, T., Hindle, S., Sussman, L., Black, K.J., Argentine, J., Manos, W., Inglis, J.R.: bioRxiv: the preprint server for biology. Preprint (2019). https://doi.org/10.1101/833400
38. Sutton, C., Gong, L.: Popularity of arXiv.org within computer science. Preprint (2017), arXiv: 1710.05225v1 [cs.DL]

Data Citation and Citation Analysis

How to Cite a Web Ranking and Make it FAIR

Alessandro Lotta[iD] and Gianmaria Silvello[(✉)][iD]

University of Padua, Padua, Italy
{alessandro.lotta,gianmaria.silvello}@unipd.it

Abstract. Citing data is crucial for acknowledging and recognizing the contributions of experts, scientists, and institutions in creating and maintaining high-quality datasets. It ensures proper attribution and supports reproducibility in scientific research. While data citation methods have focused on structured or semi-structured datasets, there is a need to address the citation of web rankings. Web rankings are significant in scientific literature, information articles, and decision-making processes. However, citing web rankings presents challenges due to their dynamic nature. In response, we introduce a new "ranking citation" model and the *Unipd Ranking Citation tool*, designed to generate persistent and machine-readable citations, enhancing reproducibility and accountability in scientific research and general contexts. It is a user-friendly, open-source Chrome extension that employs ontology and RDF graphs for machine understanding and future reconstruction of rankings.

Keywords: Data citation · Ranking citation · Persistent citations

1 Introduction

Data citation has become a central topic in the scholarly domain and has a central role in science communication. Research on data citation has primarily revolved around two key aspects: establishing fundamental principles and developing architectural and computational solutions. Notably, two prominent international initiatives have been dedicated to defining the core principles for data citation. The first initiative, CODATA, published a comprehensive report on data citation principles in 2013 [1]. The second initiative, FORCE 11, presented a consolidated set of principles derived from various working groups in 2014 [12]. These principles underscore that data should be considered a research object worthy of citation, ensuring due recognition for data curators. Furthermore, they outline several key criteria that a citation should uphold, including:

- Enabling identification and access to the referenced data.
- Ensuring the persistence of data identifiers and associated metadata, addressing the issue of fixity.

© The Author(s), under exclusive license to Springer Nature Switzerland AG 2023
O. Alonso et al. (Eds.): TPDL 2023, LNCS 14241, pp. 65–78, 2023.
https://doi.org/10.1007/978-3-031-43849-3_6

- Guaranteeing the completeness of the reference, encompassing all necessary information for data interpretation and comprehension, even beyond the data's lifespan.
- Promoting citation interoperability, allowing humans and machines to interpret and utilize the citations effectively.

Citing data is essential to acknowledge and recognize the contributions made by experts, scientists, and institutions who invest resources and expertise in creating, curating, and maintaining high-quality datasets. By citing data, we ensure that credit is properly attributed to those who deserve it. These datasets are crucial in conducting experiments, testing hypotheses, and advancing scientific knowledge. As their usage becomes more prevalent, it is crucial to acknowledge the efforts and dedication of those involved in producing and maintaining such valuable resources. Furthermore, data citation is vital in facilitating reproducibility in scientific research. We establish a permanent reference to the exact dataset or specific subset utilized in a series of experiments by including data citations. This ensures that others can easily locate and access the same data, enabling them to replicate the research findings and validate the results. Data citations serve as valuable pointers to the precise location of the data for reuse, making data more findable and promoting transparency and accountability in scientific investigations.

The primary emphasis in data citation methods has centered on citing structured or semi-structured datasets [24]. The aim has been to ensure the persistence of citations to specific portions of datasets [20], such as queries to relational [28] or graph databases [23]. Additionally, efforts have been directed toward enabling the retrieval of the exact same data being referenced over time [19]. Another critical aspect is ensuring the accuracy and comprehensiveness of the data citations, guaranteeing that they provide the necessary information to accurately locate and understand the referenced data. The applications of data citation encompass various domains, including the citation of CSV files, scientific centralized or federated databases, result tables generated by web applications, collections of objects obtained through interactive processes, and result sets derived from analytics methods.

Our research primarily focuses on addressing the overlooked aspect of citing web rankings. Web rankings are generated by web applications that utilize search engines to provide relevant data or documents in response to specific user queries. Typically, a user expresses their information needs through a keyword query, and the resulting ranking represents a list of potentially relevant objects for that query. Prominent examples of web rankings include those generated by web search engines like Google and Bing and academic search engines like Google Scholar or Scopus for literature searches. However, search engines are also employed by social networks like Twitter, which generate rankings of relevant tweets based on specific hashtags or keywords. Web rankings play a significant role in scientific literature. For instance, researchers may utilize web rankings to illustrate previous studies' absence by searching on platforms such as Google Scholar or PubMed. They may also present a collection of relevant tweets on a trending societal topic to provide context and motivation for a study. Additionally, web rankings can support decision-making processes by showcasing the results of a patent search on a specialized search engine.

We introduce "citation ranking", a model and an open tool designed to generate FAIR (Findable, Accessible, Interoperable, and Reusable) citations for web rankings. The main challenge we address is the creation of persistent, human- and machine-readable citations for web rankings, which are inherently dynamic and subject to change due to various factors, including user preferences and contextual settings. With "citation ranking", we aim to enable stable referencing to transient web rankings. Currently, it is not feasible to mention a specific ranking, such as papers, web pages, or tweets, and allow third parties, including researchers and the general public, to reproduce and verify the existence of that specific ranking. This poses a significant obstacle to reproducibility and accountability in scientific research and general information articles where web rankings are frequently cited as evidence.

We provide a user-friendly tool that ensures web rankings can be treated as stable and citable objects: the *Unipd Ranking Citation tool*. By doing so, we aim to promote reproducibility and accountability in scientific endeavors and general contexts where web rankings are utilized as evidence. The ultimate goal is to enhance the reliability and transparency of information derived from web rankings, fostering a more robust and trustworthy knowledge ecosystem.

This work provides the first free-to-use and open-source tool to create FAIR and persistent citations of Web rankings. The ranking citation tool is provided as a Chrome plug-in/extension easily usable from a commonly employed browser. We provide a citation model for Web rankings, including human- and machine-readable serializations of the ranking to be cited. To this end, we defined an ontology to create machine-readable Resource Description Framework (RDF) graphs serializing the ranking, enabling inference, machine-understanding, and the reconstruction of the ranking for future purposes. Currently, the *Unipd Ranking Citation tool* works for Google Scholar, Google, Bing, Scopus, and Twitter.

The rest of the paper is organized as follows: Sect. 2 overviews state of the art in data citation, reporting the necessity to cite Web rankings and the absence of viable solutions. Section 3 presents the citation model for Web rankings. Section 4 details the Unipd Ranking Citation tool technical architectures explaining how it has been implemented as an extension of Chrome. Section 5 describes a use case based on Google Scholar. Finally, Sect. 6 draws some final remarks.

2   Background

Within the Research Data Alliance (RDA) initiative, two working groups specifically address the topic of data citation. The first is the Data Citation Working Group (WG),[1] which focuses on establishing methodologies for persistently citing subsets of data derived from queries to structured databases. It aims to

---

[1] https://www.rd-alliance.org/groups/data-citation-wg.html [visited on 22 May 2023].

develop approaches that enable accurate and traceable referencing of specific data portions obtained through querying structured databases.

The second working group is the Complex Citation WG,[2] which concentrates on the citation and distribution of credit for extensive collections of objects. Their focus extends beyond individual data subsets and encompasses the citation practices and mechanisms for acknowledging and attributing credit to large-scale collections of diverse objects. The objective is to devise methods that facilitate proper citation and recognition for researchers and contributors in creating and curating such extensive collections. Both working groups within the RDA initiative play crucial roles in advancing the field of data citation by addressing different aspects of citation methodology. By studying and providing solutions for persistent data subset citation and complex object collection citation, these groups contribute to establishing standardized practices that enhance traceability, reproducibility, and credit attribution in data-intensive research. The activities undertaken by these working groups do not specifically tackle the challenge of citing web rankings. However, it is worth noting that the Data Citation Working Group recognizes the citation of information retrieval rankings, such as those generated by search engines, as a critical issue to address for ensuring the reproducibility of scientific research [21]. To our knowledge, no viable solutions have been proposed to tackle the issue.

[24] provides an extensive overview of state of the art in data citation up to 2018, where the citation of web rankings is never mentioned. Over the past five years, there has been a notable increase in awareness regarding the significance of data citation, leading to the establishment of guidelines for citing datasets by many publishing houses (e.g., Springer Nature [15] and Elsevier).[3] Various domains, including neuroimaging [13], geoscience [2,16], and biology [18,22,26], have explored the incorporation of data citation practices into their research outputs. Numerous studies have delved into the distribution of credit among large groups of scientists who contribute to datasets or data aggregations [7,8,11,17,27]. These works have proposed novel measures, introduced new authorship categories, and explored credit distribution mechanisms [9,10]. Considerable efforts have also been invested in developing infrastructures for depositing datasets, ensuring comprehensive descriptions, and enhancing their discoverability and accessibility [5,6].

Data citation in scholarly graphs has been recognized for its impact and importance. Efforts have been made to extend existing citation graphs to include data, enabling seamless integration of datasets [4]. Furthermore, studies have examined the relationship between datasets and scholarly papers in the scientific discourse, uncovering the connections between them [14]. These endeavors contribute to a more comprehensive understanding of research and facilitate the effective dissemination and utilization of data in scholarly communication [3].

---

[2] https://www.rd-alliance.org/groups/complex-citations-working-group [visited on 22 May 2023].

[3] https://www.elsevier.com/authors/tools-and-resources/research-data [visited on 22 May 2023].

However, despite these initiatives and advancements, none have explicitly targeted rankings' citations. While the importance of data citation has been acknowledged and pursued in various disciplines, the specific challenge of citing web rankings remains unaddressed.

3   Citation Model

In data citation, two fundamental elements comprise a citation: the data object being referenced and the accompanying reference or citation snippet that describes the cited data. The data object must possess persistence, ensuring its continuous accessibility in the exact form as initially cited. Conversely, the reference should possess reusability, allowing machines and humans to interpret and utilize it effectively. Furthermore, the reference should conform to a consistent format observed by other citations referencing the same class of objects, ensuring correctness and completeness. Lastly, an essential characteristic of the reference is its ease of creation, avoiding the need for manual effort during the citation process.

The dynamic and transient nature of web rankings stems from their susceptibility to change based on factors such as the user initiating the query, the contextual circumstances surrounding it, and updates to the underlying index. Therefore, ensuring the longevity of web rankings requires storing them in a format that facilitates long-term preservation while simultaneously enabling machine interpretation and human comprehension.

To ensure human readability, we capture a screenshot(s) of the webpage(s) displaying the ranking to be cited in the PNG (Portable Network Graphics) format. The PNG format is a lossless compressed format widely recognized for its suitability in the long-term preservation of images. It is recommended by institutions such as the Library of Congress for its preservation qualities.[4]

To ensure machine readability, two main steps are taken. Firstly, essential information from the web ranking, including the title, description snippet, URL, position on the page, user, settings, and the main characteristics of the search engines, is extracted. This process involves capturing the key textual components that determine the ranking. This extracted information creates an RDF graph. The RDF graph is a structured representation of the extracted data, enabling machines to interpret and process the information effectively. The key textual elements forming the ranking can be reconstructed from the RDF graph, facilitating machine-based analysis and utilization of the ranking data. Of course, an external service or web application can employ the RDF graph to produce a human-readable replica of the original ranking.

To enhance the machine interpretability of the created RDF graph, we have developed a concise ontology, i.e., the Ranking Citation Ontology (RCO). This ontology serves the purpose of representing the specific domain of interest. Figure 1 reports the graphical representation of the RCO, publicly available at

---

[4] See   https://www.loc.gov/preservation/resources/rfs/stillimg.html   and   https://howtofair.dk/how-to-fair/file-formats/ [last visited on 24 May 2023].

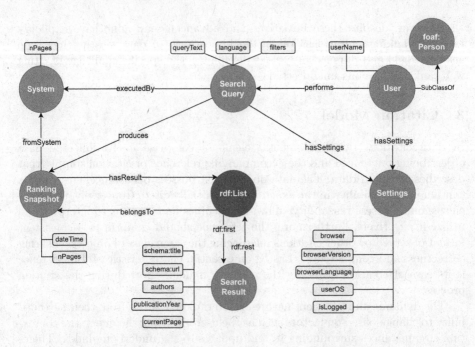

Fig. 1. A graphical representation of the Ranking Citation Ontology

https://rankingcitation.dei.unipd.it/ontology/. We can see that the class User models the user issuing a Search Query to a System. The key properties are the language of the query, the active filters (if any), the text of the query, and the number of result pages the system displayed. The Search Query produces a Ranking Snapshot, which is what we capture (the number of pages captured is a user setting). The Ranking Snapshot is composed of a list (i.e., an RDF List) of Search Results. A Search Result comprises several properties such as the title, the URL, and the current page meaning in which web page the result is displayed. Moreover, we also store the authors and the publication year for search systems like Google Scholar, where a search result corresponds to a scientific paper. Finally, we represent the user and system Settings such as the browser type, version, language, operating system, and if the user was logged in when performing the search.

In the final step, we package the citation artifact using the Research Object (RO) Crate [25]. RO Crate is an openly developed specification offering a lightweight and adaptable packaging format for research objects. It is a structured container encompassing research data, metadata, and contextual information to ensure their integrity, provenance, and discoverability. The format relies on JSON-LD with schema.org annotations, providing a means for data persistence and ensuring long-term accessibility. The RO Crate ontology defines the vocabulary and relationships utilized to describe the contents within an RO Crate. We employ RO Crate to describe the objects stored to preserve a web

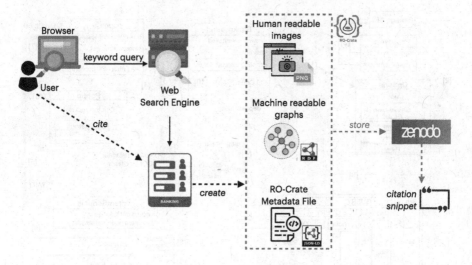

Fig. 2. The ranking citation pipeline.

ranking, associate the screenshot images with the RDF graph, and make the entire citation bundle interpretable. Additionally, the RO Crate contains metadata related to the user, such as their name, ORCID, and affiliation, enabling appropriate attribution of generated citations to the respective user and institution. To facilitate data deposition and guarantee long-term accessibility with robust preservation practices, we combine RO Crate with Zenodo. This integration allows for the seamless deposition of the citation bundle while ensuring enduring accessibility and preservation of the data.

Figure 2 illustrates the key components of the ranking citation model. The process begins with a user issuing a query to a search engine, which generates a ranking. When the user requests a citation for the ranking, three distinct objects are generated and bundled within an RO Crate. These objects include the screenshot images, the RDF graph, and the RO-Crate metadata file. The RO Crate, containing these objects, is then securely stored in Zenodo for long-term preservation, ensuring the persistence and accessibility of the citation. As a result, a consistent citation snippet can be generated, allowing for proper referencing of the ranking.

4   Architecture and Implementation of the Ranking Citation Tool

We developed the proposed model as a Chrome plugin/extension, seamlessly integrating it into a browser for easy use by stakeholders. The "Unipd Ranking Citation Tool" plugin was built using the Chrome Extension CLI development structure. This framework provides a predefined structure with essential folders and source files. The 'src' folder contains the background script, content script,

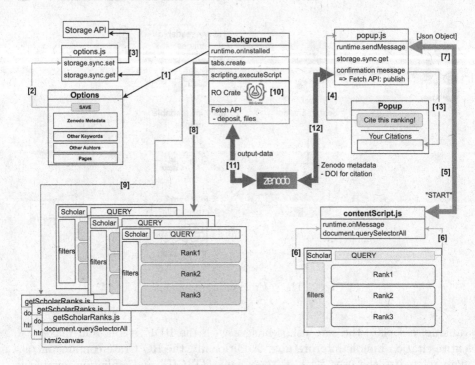

Fig. 3. The *Unipd Ranking Citation Tool* architecture diagram

popup script, and stylesheets for HTML pages. The 'public' folder is composed of the HTML files, including the code for the options page. It also houses subdirectories for storing the required icons and the essential 'manifest.json' file. This file contains crucial information about the extension, such as its name, version, permissions, and declared scripts, enabling proper loading and execution in the browser. The Chrome Extension CLI also configures the Webpack module bundler by providing the necessary configuration files. This integration enables quick and simple development with an automatic reload feature, ensuring that any code changes are immediately reflected in the extension. Furthermore, it simplifies the compilation and packaging process of the extension. The 'build' folder is continuously updated throughout the development process to contain all the finalized files required for using and testing the extension in Chrome. This folder encapsulates the compiled and packaged extension, ready for deployment. The Chrome Extension CLI provides access to Node.js and the Node Package Manager (NPM) for efficient dependency management. This integration enables the easy inclusion and management of external libraries or frameworks.

In Fig. 3 we can see the main components of the *Unipd Ranking Citation Tool* and how they interact. After installing the tool, the background script activates the `onInstalled` listener (step [1] in Fig. 3). This listener triggers the `openOptionsPage` function, which directs the user to the options page specified in the manifest file (step [2]). On this page, the user can configure the settings of

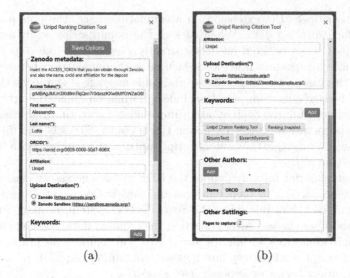

(a)   (b)

Fig. 4. Unipd Ranking Citation Tool: Setting page.

the extension. In Fig. 4, the main settings are displayed, including the Zenodo or Zenodo Sandbox account details, username, and ORCID. The user can choose the Zenodo sandbox for creating temporary or trial citations, or the Zenodo real instance for permanent citations. There are additional sections where users can add keywords for deposit metadata and specify additional authors or collaborators for the project/research. The user must input the respective individuals' names and ORCID for these sections. Finally, a section is dedicated to selecting the desired number of pages to capture during the research process.

After filling in all the required input fields, the user can save the settings by clicking the corresponding button. This action triggers a callback function that utilizes the integrated Chrome Storage API (step [3]) to save the data. The Storage API provides functions for asynchronous data manipulation, such as setting, updating, retrieving, and deleting data, specifically tailored for extensions. Our tool utilizes the "chrome storage sync" area, which synchronizes the data across all Chrome browsers where the user is logged in. If syncing is disabled, it behaves similarly to "storage.local", meaning that the data is cleared when the extension is removed. Using the "chrome storage sync set" function, the saved data is automatically populated in the input fields whenever the options page is reopened, enabling user editing.

Once the settings configuration is complete, users can access the extension's popup, which first checks if the current page URL is supported by the tool (see step [4] in Fig. 3). If not supported, a message is displayed indicating that citations are unavailable on the current page. Below this message, the "Your Citations" section appears, displaying a list of citation cards from previous captures. The "Your Citations" section remains visible regardless of the visited site.

If the user opens the extension on a compatible page, the popup displays a button for capturing data. When clicked, the popup script sends a message to the content script injected into the currently viewed page (see step [5]). The browser's message-passing framework facilitates communication between these scripts. In this case, a one-time JSON-serializable message is sent using the "runtime.sendMessage" function, which includes information about the active page. On the receiving end, the content script implements a "runtime.onMessage" listener to capture any message containing the keyword 'START' (see [5]). Upon receiving such a message, the content script captures the required data from the result page (see [6]).

The content script initially defines the RDF graph's necessary classes, data, and object properties. It then analyzes the page's Document Object Model (DOM) to extract data related to the SearchQuery, System, RankingSnapshot, Settings, and User classes. After collecting the required data, the content script adds the individuals to a JavaScript object that will compose the graph. Finally, the content script sends a response message containing the RDF graph stored as a JSON object back to the popup (see step [7]).

After receiving the content's response, the popup initiates a new simple one-time request to communicate with the background script, sending the received data as the payload. The background script receives the message and opens multiple new pages based on the extension's options settings. The tool utilizes the "chrome.tabs.create" function from the integrated "chrome.tabs" API to create these new pages. It is important to note two aspects of this process: firstly, the filters set during the search process are maintained on the newly opened pages, ensuring consistency. Secondly, a new script is injected into each opened page using the "chrome.scripting.executeScript" function. These injected JavaScript files are responsible for gathering the remaining data necessary for ranking the results. They employ a similar approach to scrape the DOM as described earlier.

The captured ranks consider both the "currentPage" parameter, indicating the page where they are found, and the order assigned by the ranking. Each injected script sends the collected data back to the background script through a one-time request. The background script waits until all the scripts have been completed before proceeding. At this stage, the tool enters the upload phase. In the first phase, an RO Crate is created by defining a JSON object that encapsulates all the entities within the Crate (step [10]). This object includes the context and the graph representing the generated output files, ensuring proper organization within the deposit. Subsequently, the JSON object containing the gathered data and the RO Crate are converted into JavaScript File variables, preparing them for publication.

Next, the deposited metadata is defined, including the title, notes, description, keywords, and authors specified in the options. The files are sent to the server using the JavaScript Fetch API and its asynchronous function "fetch" (step [11]). This step involves three consecutive fetch calls: one for creating the deposit in Zenodo and two for uploading the two files. If the deposit creation is successful, the service responds with the deposit ID, which is necessary for the subsequent uploading process.

Finally, the background script sends a message to the scripts of the opened pages that were used to capture the rankings instructing them to capture a screenshot of each page (step [8]). This passage is executed using the *html2canvas* library[5]. *html2canvas* takes the HTML document's body as input and returns a canvas element representing the entire visible page. The canvas is converted into a blob and subsequently into a file variable, uploaded to the same deposit using a "fetch" call. The scripts injected on each page notify the popup that the screenshots are taken by sending a message.

The final step performed by the extension occurs in the popup script, which prompts the user to confirm the publishing of the deposit to Zenodo or Zenodo Sandbox (step [12]). Upon confirmation, the popup initiates a publish request to the designated upload destination using a fetch call. The response returned by the service is used to construct the citation text on the "Your Citations" section of the popup. If the user doesn't confirm the publication on the upload destination the tool generates a temporary citation, that allows to check if the uploaded files have been generated correctly. These temporary citations are also displayed in the "Your Citations" section inside yellow cards and enable the user to publish the deposit in a second moment by storing the deposit Id.

5   Use Case: Google Scholar

In this use case scenario, we will walk through the process of using the *Unipd Ranking Citation Tool* Chrome extension. To begin, users can update their existing extension or install it from the dedicated web page[6]. This page provides a detailed description of the installation process and usage of the extension. Open a new tab in Google Scholar and enter a query to search for relevant literature. Once the search results are displayed, you can access the extension by clicking on its icon in the browser's top right corner. The extension will present a button indicating the availability of citations on the current page, along with a list of previously published citations as shown in Fig. 5.

By clicking the button, the extension will execute the necessary code in the background script and open a predefined number of new pages (as defined in the options). These pages will gather the data for the rankings on the search results page. The extension will display a confirmation message indicating that the file upload is complete and prompt the user to proceed with publishing on either Zenodo or its Sandbox. After confirming the publishing action, the extension's popup will proceed with the publication process. Once completed, a new card will be displayed, containing the citation for the deposit, Fig. 5. Users can now navigate to Zenodo or its Sandbox and access the upload section to view the deposit. Clicking on the deposit will provide more details about the files contained within, including access to different versions, if available.

---

[5] https://html2canvas.hertzen.com/ [last visited on 30 May 2023.].
[6] https://rankingcitation.dei.unipd.it/.

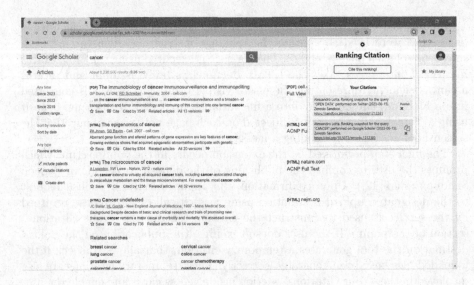

Fig. 5. "Your Citations" as displayed by the Chrome extension tool. The user can copy and paste the automatically created citation snippet pointing to a FAIR and persistent citation.

6   Final Remarks

In summary, our research introduces a novel solution for the citation of web rankings with the development of the *Unipd Ranking Citation tool*. This tool, available as a free and open-source Chrome plugin, addresses the need for FAIR and persistent citations of web rankings. This tool allows users to generate consistent and reliable citation snippets for web rankings, ensuring proper attribution and facilitating reproducibility in scientific research and other contexts.

The *Unipd Ranking Citation tool* represents a significant advancement in the field as it is the first model and tool specifically designed to address the challenges associated with citing web rankings. Currently, the tool is compatible with popular platforms such as Google Scholar, Google, and Twitter. However, our plans involve expanding its functionality to include other widely used rankings in research. It is important to note that the tool relies on parsing the DOM of web pages, and as a result, it is subject to limitations. If the web page's structure being cited changes, the tool's parser may require updates to maintain its functionality. Nonetheless, the *Unipd Ranking Citation tool* provides a viable and practical solution for improving the citation of web rankings, promoting transparency and accountability in scientific research and beyond.

Resources. GitHub Repository:
https://github.com/aleLotta/ranking-citation.git
Unipd Ranking Citation Tool: https://rankingcitation.dei.unipd.it/

References

1. Out of Cite, out of mind: the current state of practice, Polocy, and technology for the citation of data, volume 12. CODATA-ICSTI Task Group on Data Citation Standards and Practices, September 2013
2. Boone, S.C., et al.: Ausgeochem: an open platform for geochemical data preservation, dissemination and synthesis. Geostand. Geoanal. Res. **46**(2), 245–259 (2022)
3. Buneman, P., et al: Why data citation isn't working, and what to do about it. Database J. Biol. Databases Curation, **2020**, baaa022 (2020)
4. Buneman, P., Dosso, D., Lissandrini, M., Silvello, G.: Data citation and the citation graph. Quant. Sci. Stud. **2**(4), 1399–1422 (2021)
5. Burton, A., et al.: The scholix framework for interoperability in data-literature information exchange. D Lib Mag. 23(1/2), 2017
6. Cousijn, H., Feeney, P., Lowenberg, D., Presani, E., Simons, N.: Bringing citations and usage metrics together to make data count. Data Sci. J. **18**(1), 9 (2019)
7. Cullen, M.R., et al.: Population health science as a unifying foundation for translational clinical and public health research. SSM - Popul.Health **18**, 101047 (2022)
8. Devriendt, T., Shabani, M., Borry, P.: Data sharing in biomedical sciences: a systematic review of incentives. Biopreservation Biobanking **19**(3), 219–227 (2021). PMID: 33926229
9. Dosso, D., Davidson, S.B., Silvello, G.: Credit distribution in relational scientific databases. Inf. Syst. **109**, 102060 (2022)
10. Dosso, D., Silvello, G.: Data credit distribution: a new method to estimate databases impact. J. Inf. **14**(4), 101080 (2020)
11. Ewers, R.M., Barlow, J., Banks-Leite, C., Rahbek, C.: Separate authorship categories to recognize data collectors and code developers. Nat. Ecol. Evol. **3**(12), 1610–1610 (2019)
12. FORCE-11. Data citation synthesis group: joint declaration of data citation principles. FORCE11, San Diego, CA, USA (2014)
13. Horien, C., et al.: A hitchhiker's guide to working with large, open-source neuroimaging datasets. Nat. Hum. Behav. **5**(2), 185–193 (2021)
14. Irrera, O., Mannocci, A., Manghi, P., Silvello, G.: A novel curated scholarly graph connecting textual and data publications. J. Data Inf. Q. (2023)
15. Khodiyar, V.: The basics of data citation. https://researchdata.springernature.com/posts/the-basics-of-data-citation, May 2021
16. Li, X., et al.: Boosting geoscience data sharing in china. Nat. Geosci. **14**(8), 541–542 (2021)
17. Mongeon, P., Robinson-Garcia, N., Jeng, W., Costas, R.: incorporating data sharing to the reward system of science: Linking datacite records to authors in the web of science. Aslib J. Inf. Manage. **69**(5), 545–556 (2017)
18. Oza, V.H., et al.: Ten simple rules for using public biological data for your research. PLoS Comput. Biol. **19**(1), e1010749 (2023)
19. Pröll, S., Rauber, A.: A scalable framework for dynamic data citation of arbitrary structured data. In: Proceedings of 3rd International Conference on Data Management Technologies and Applications, pp. 223–230 (2014)
20. Rauber, A., Ari, A., van Uytvanck, D., Pröll, S.: Identification of reproducible subsets for data citation, sharing and re-use. Bull. IEEE Tech. Committee Digit. Libr. Spec. Issue Data Citation **12**(1), 6–15 (2016)
21. Rauber, A., Parsons, M.: Data citation working group Mtg @ P19. https://www.rd-alliance.org/system/files/documents/220623_rda_p19_wgdc_slides.pdf, slide 52, June 2022

22. Sielemann, K., Hafner, A., Pucker, B.: The reuse of public datasets in the life sciences: potential risks and rewards. PeerJ **8**, e9954 (2020)

23. Silvello, G.: A Methodology for Citing Linked Open Data Subsets. D-Lib Mag. **21**(1/2) (2015)

24. Silvello, G.: Theory and practice of data citation. J. Am. Soc. Inf. Sci. Technol. (JASIST) **69**(1), 6–20 (2018)

25. Soiland-Reyes, S., et al.: RO-crate community. In: Groth, P., Goble, C. (eds.) Packaging research artefacts with ro-crate. Data Science **5**(2), 97–138 (2022)

26. Villoutreix, P.: What machine learning can do for developmental biology. Development **148**(1), 01 (2021). dev188474

27. Westoby, M., Falster, D.S., Schrader, J.: Motivating data contributions via a distinct career currency. Proc. R. Soc. B Biol. Sci. **288**(1946), 20202830 (2021)

28. Wu, Y., Alawini, A., Davidson, S.B., Silvello, G.: Data citation: giving credit where credit is due. In: Das, G., Jermaine, C.M., Bernstein, P.A. (eds.) Proceedings of the 2018 International Conference on Management of Data, SIGMOD Conference 2018, pp. 99–114. ACM Press, New York, USA (2018)

Tracing Data Footprints: Formal and Informal Data Citations in the Scientific Literature

Ornella Irrera[1,2](✉) (iD), Andrea Mannocci[2] (iD), Paolo Manghi[2] (iD), and Gianmaria Silvello[1] (iD)

[1] Department of Information Engineering, University of Padova, Padua, Italy
{ornella.irrera,gianmaria.silvello}@unipd.it
[2] National Research Council (CNR-ISTI), Pisa, Italy
{andrea.mannocci,paolo.manghi}@isti.cnr.it

Abstract. Data citation has become a prevalent practice within the scientific community, serving the purpose of facilitating data discovery, reproducibility, and credit attribution. Consequently, data has gained significant importance in the scholarly process. Despite its growing prominence, data citation is still at an early stage, with considerable variations in practices observed across scientific domains. Such diversity hampers the ability to consistently analyze, detect, and quantify data citations.

We focus on the European Marine Science (MES) community to examine how data is cited in this specific context. We identify four types of data citations: formal, informal, complete, and incomplete. By analyzing the usage of these diverse data citation modalities, we investigate their impact on the widespread adoption of data citation practices.

Keywords: Data Citation · Scholarly Graph

1 Introduction

In recent years, there has been a growing recognition of the significance of data within the scholarly communication ecosystem. Data is no longer considered mere byproducts of research but is acknowledged as a valuable resource that can accelerate research, validate experiments, and generate new knowledge. This shift in perception is leading to a transformation in the traditional research ecosystem, in which textual publications were the sole measure of a researcher's work, to a new paradigm where data and publications hold equal importance.

In this evolving landscape, crediting data authors for their released and reused datasets is essential, akin to the recognition given to authors of textual publications [16]. However, citing data presents a significant challenge that must be addressed to ensure that data authors receive the appropriate credit and enable the scientific community to discover and reuse data effectively.

Several international efforts have been made to define how data should be cited in the literature and which information a data citation should contain to properly identify the data and its authors. Nevertheless, until recently, data has

O. Alonso et al. (Eds.): TPDL 2023, LNCS 14241, pp. 79–92, 2023.
https://doi.org/10.1007/978-3-031-43849-3_7

rarely been cited in the literature, and when it was, the citation was inconsistent, leading to the existence of multiple methods of data citation that are often contradictory [21]. For instance, [2] found that more than 370 different citation variants have been used to cite a dataset in the oceanographic community. In addition, [20] showed that *formal* data citations are less common than *informal* citations occurring in the full text of a publication. A universally accepted standard has not been established yet, and some barriers still prevent researchers from sharing their data; the lack of a robust reward system is the most notable [25].

This work delineates the key distinctions between *formal* and *informal* data citations. Our primary goal is to identify the current patterns of data citation and explore the potential ramifications of different citation styles and methods. To address this challenge effectively, we concentrate on a substantial scholarly graph encompassing textual and data citations within the European Marine Science (MES) research community. The MES community was chosen due to its size, active engagement, and well-established data publication and citation practices, as documented in a previous study [14]. Furthermore, in this research, we enhance the existing scholarly graph by incorporating the PDFs of the publications and employing NLP techniques to extract mentions of datasets and software.

Our analysis encompasses the following aspects: (i) identification of prevalent citation practices; (ii) examination of the sections in which data citations are found within the papers; (iii) investigation of the attributes utilized for data identification in citations; (iv) exploration of the publication and data authors to gain insights into data reusability. Our findings demonstrate that only 24.12% of the identified data citations adhere to formal practices, ensuring proper attribution to the data author, unique identification, and persistent access to the dataset. In contrast, most citations are informal, merely mentioning the dataset DOI or title within the publication's full text, without a comprehensive entry in the reference list. Additionally, we have identified the DOI as the most frequently used attribute for referencing datasets and software. Surprisingly, we have observed that citing data is less prevalent than anticipated, as 83% of the data accompanying the publications is not mentioned in the full text. This suggests a significant gap in acknowledging the data used in scholarly research. Furthermore, our analysis reveals that within the MES community, data re-use is not a common practice because creating new datasets specific to the studied use cases is more common than reusing already published and available datasets. As a result of our work, we publicly release a new scholarly graph where publications and cited data are interconnected and whose edges are enriched with information about dataset mentions – e.g., the position of the mention or whether the citation is formal or informal.

The rest of the paper is organized as follows. Section 2 presents related work focusing on analyzing formal and informal data citations; moreover, it provides the key definitions of the terms employed in this work. Section 3 describes the scholarly graph we used for the analysis, how it was built and enriched to analyze data citations. Section 4 reports the main finding of our analyses. Section 5 discusses the main findings of this study, and Sect. 6 draws some final remarks.

2 Background

Related Work. Numerous studies have been conducted to analyze the most common data citation practices, examine the advantages and disadvantages of each practice and its diffusion, and explore how these practices vary across the scientific domains in which they are employed. Despite many efforts to define universally accepted and shared standards for data citation – e.g., [1,7,8,10,26] – there is still no convergence on a common strategy.

The lack of a universally adopted citation standard has resulted in the coexistence of various citation practices both within and across scientific domains [18]. Hence, when studying data citation practices, a very broad definition is often used, which considers not only the citations of a dataset included in a references list but also all its mentions in the text of an article [20,27]. [20] distinguishes between *formal* and *informal* data citations; the former consists of adding an entry about the dataset in the references list of a publication, plus mentioning the entry in the full text. The latter, instead, consists in mentioning the dataset in the full text of a publication without adding a relative entry in the references list. Some works analyze the articles' full text to detect data citation practices. In [28], for example, authors analyzed data citation practices in 600 articles of *PloS One*. [24] proposed a cross-disciplinary study of data citation practices based on the Data Citation Index (DCI). Other studies have analyzed data citation and sharing practices adopted within some scientific domains. In [28], the authors conducted an analysis involving 12 disciplines and studied their data citation, collection, and sharing practices. They found that URL is the most common attribute used to cite datasets in almost all the disciplines; in addition, the 74% of examined publication that used data contains datasets created by the same authors, indicating the tendency to create new datasets instead of re-using the available ones. Similar results have also been found in [11]. Some works investigate data citation practices in disciplines such as earth science [5], bioinformatics [6], social science [17], genetics [19], and astronomy [22]. Almost all the studies detected a high heterogeneity in the citation practices in terms of the dataset attribute cited – e.g., the dataset DOI or its title, the position in the publication's full text of the dataset mention, and the presence of a reference entry related to the dataset in the references list. [20] detected the prevalence of informal citations compared to formal ones. In addition, in [4,17,22,27], the authors detected a high variety of citation behaviors; in particular, [2] detected 377 variant citation formats. Another finding from the cited studies is that the URLs mentioning a dataset does not always guarantee the accessibility to the dataset [27]. Finally, [12,28] found that a common practice is citing data papers instead of the datasets. Although this practice guarantees credit attribution, it does not guarantee access and findability of the dataset.

Definition of Terms. A *scholarly graph* is a heterogeneous, directed, and labeled graph whose nodes represent entities involved in the scholarly domain, while edges define the semantics of the relation between two nodes. *Metadata*, defined as *data about data*, are structured descriptive information about an entity [9]. Metadata sets are associated with the nodes and relations in scholarly graphs and are used to describe the research entities' nodes and the connections between them; the set of metadata associated with a node usually contains information such as the title, abstract, and date of publication of a product. In this work, we considered scholarly graphs representing the following entities: (i) *Publication*: a digital document documenting a research activity; (ii) *Dataset*: a digital research product including measures, or results – datasets are usually archives, figures, tables, CSV files; (iii) *Software*: code generated from a research activity; (iv) *Author*: a person who contributed to the generation of a research product (be it Publication, Dataset or Software).

The scholarly graph created and analyzed in this work contains the following semantics assigned to edges connecting a publication to a dataset (or software): `IsSupplementedBy`, `Cites`, `References`, `HasAuthor`. `IsSupplementedBy` is assigned when a dataset serves as a supplement for a publication, more specifically, the dataset includes additional relevant material that supports the publication [14]; `Cites` is assigned when a publication mentions the datasets in its full text, or when the publication includes the reference to the dataset; `References` when the publication includes the reference of a dataset in the references list; and, `HasAuthor` when an author contributed to a publication or dataset.

According to [3], we consider a *reference* as a short text describing a research entity included in the references list of a publication (i.e., a citation snippet), and a *citation* as the mention of that reference in the full text of a publication. Hence, a dataset can be referenced at most once by a publication, but it can be cited (mentioned) many times. Furthermore, in the following, we introduce the distinction between *formal* and *informal* data citations. *Formal dataset citations* take place when a dataset is mentioned in the publication full text referring to a reference entry in the reference list of the publication [14,20], while *informal dataset citations* take place when the dataset – i.e., its URL, DOI, or title – is mentioned in the publication's full text, but there is not a reference entry of the dataset in the references list of the publication [14,20]. In this work, informal citations comprise also all the datasets included in the references list of a publication but never mentioned in the full text.

We consider formal and informal dataset citation as *incomplete* when it is impossible to determine whether the citation or reference refers to a dataset, a data paper, or none of them. This occurs when there is a lack of URLs or DOIs that allow for the unique identification of the dataset. All the dataset mentions which include the DOI (or URL) are referred to as *complete* citations. In Fig. 1, we illustrate formal and informal data citations in a publication and their representation in the scholarly graph. Datasets A and F are formally cited: they are included in the article's references list and the full text contains a pointer to the reference entry. The formal citation of F is *incomplete* since the reference

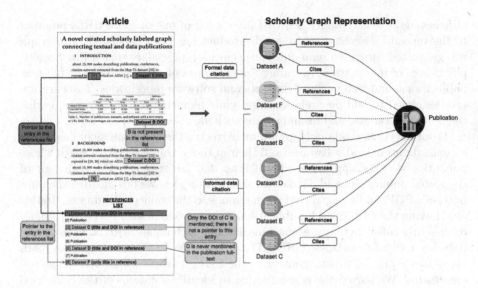

Fig. 1. Representation of formal and informal data citation in literature and in the scholarly graph. Dashed edges represent incomplete data citations. Datasets A and F are formally cited since they are reported in the references list, and there is a pointer to that reference in the full text. Dataset B is mentioned in the full text and not in the references list; Dataset C is mentioned in the references list, and its DOI is mentioned in the full text; Dataset D is mentioned in the references list, but it is never cited; the title of Dataset E is reported in the full text. The citations of E and F are incomplete due to the lack of a DOI or URL able to uniquely identify the datasets.

contains only the title and it is not possible to uniquely identify the dataset. Datasets B, C, D, and E are informally cited: the DOI of B is mentioned in the full text; the DOI of C is mentioned in the full text, it has a reference entry in the references list, but there is no pointer from the mention to the reference list entry; D is mentioned in the references list but not in the full text; the sole title of E is mentioned in the full text: in this case, the citation is incomplete since it is impossible to uniquely identify the dataset.

3   Data and Methods

The scholarly graph considered in this study is described in [14]. It is a curated scholarly graph representing the MES community of OpenAIRE[1]; it comprises 4,047 publications, 5,488 datasets, 22 software, and 21,561 disambiguated authors. It counts 9,692 edges interconnecting publications to datasets and software; edges are labeled with semantics that outline whether a publication is citing, referencing, documenting, or supplementing another research product. Publication, datasets, and software nodes contain the following metadata: title,

---

[1] https://graph.openaire.eu.

abstract, date of acceptance, id, URL(s) – a list of one or more URLs pointing to the repositories where the research product has been deposited. The graph was generated through a semi-automatic curation procedure that utilized multiple sources of information, including the metadata of nodes and edges, full text publications, and web pages of datasets and software repositories. The curation process aimed to add new relationships while removing inaccurate ones, enrich the nodes' metadata, and disambiguate authors.

From the curated scholarly graph, we extracted the subgraph including publications, datasets, and software – and their authors, connected with edges whose semantics were `IsSupplementedBy`, `Cites` and `References`. For each pair of connected publication and dataset (or software) nodes, we downloaded the publication's PDF, and we extracted the mentions to the connected datasets. To this aim, having the PDF of each publication, we processed it with GROBID [15], an open-source software that uses machine learning techniques to extract structured data from scientific articles. GROBID processes the PDF and returns an XML file representing the textual content of the PDF, its sections, as well as the references list. We parsed the generated file to identify mentions of the connected dataset, specifically focusing on mentions of the title, URL, and DOI. If the mention occurred in the references list of the publication, hence the dataset had the related references entry, we assigned the `References` semantics; if the DOI or the titles were mentioned in the full text or the dataset's references entry was cited in the full text, we assigned `Cites`. For each new mention found, we added a new edge. We enriched each edge with the following information: the position of the dataset mentioned in the full text – e.g., the title of the section; additional information about the section – i.e., we assigned *main* if the mention occurred in the full text, *references* if it occurred in the references list, *secondary* if it occurred in footnotes or endnotes, and *captions* if it occurred in figures or tables captions; the attribute mentioned – e.g., whether it was mentioned the DOI or the title; the citation type – e.g., formal, informal, formal incomplete, informal incomplete. As said, we considered a formal citation *incomplete* when the dataset entry in the references list did not include the dataset DOI or it was different from the one provided in the graph. In the resulting graph, if a publication formally cites a dataset, they are connected with a `References` and a `Cites` edges. If the dataset is informally cited in the publication, and the mention occurs in the full text, the dataset will be connected to the publication by a `Cites` edge; the `References` edge is added when the mention occurs in the references list of the publication. In addition, some papers reported a separate list of references dedicated to datasets: also, in this case, we marked these mentions as formal and incomplete since the datasets reference entries were not included in the main list of references. Informal data citations were marked as *incomplete* when only the dataset title was mentioned in the publication's full text. The `IsSupplementedBy` edges have not been modified, as well as the edges connecting research outputs to their authors. The data model of the resulting graph is reported in Fig. 2. Publication, dataset and software nodes share the same set of properties. Edges connect publications to datasets and software, and publications, datasets, and

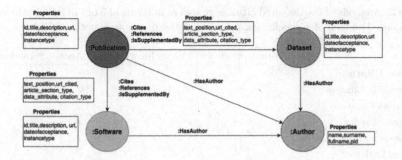

Fig. 2. Graph data model. Inside the rectangles, there are the properties of nodes and relationships. Publications, datasets, and software share the same set of properties. `Cites` and `References` semantics share the same set of properties, the `IsSupplementedBy` semantics, instead, has no properties.

Table 1. Attributes used to mention datasets and software in the references list of an article – `References` labeled edges, and in its full text – `Cites` labeled edges.

	Datasets mentions				Software mentions			
	Title	DOI	Title & DOI	URL	Title	DOI	Title & DOI	URL
References	111	291	480	0	2	7	3	0
Cites	132	761	38	1	0	11	0	0

software to their authors. Edges highlighting authorship relationships have the `HasAuthor` semantics. Edges connecting publications to datasets and software have `Cites`, `References` or `IsSupplementedBy` semantics. The resulting graph [13] is publicly available at https://doi.org/10.5281/zenodo.8006578.

4   Results

This section presents some analysis we performed on the resulting graph. We analyzed all pairs of papers and datasets (or software) connected by at least one edge with the semantics `Cites` or `References` to investigate how they are cited in the literature. The resulting graph counts – 4, 497 datasets, 2, 636 publications, 21 software and 894 `References` labeled edges, 1, 890 `Cites` labeled edges, and 4, 287 `IsSupplementedBy` labeled edges.

To cite a dataset in the literature, attributes such as the title, the DOI, the URL – or a combination of them are commonly used. In Table 1, we report the results of this analysis. The most commonly used attribute to mention a dataset in the references list of a paper – i.e., `References` labeled edge – is the combination of the title and the DOI, used in 480 datasets and 3 software mentions. The DOI without the title has been used in 291 dataset, 7 software mentions, while the title in 111 datasets and 2 software mentions. The URL – intended to link to the data repository and different from the DOI, has never

Table 2. Analysis of the detected citation practices in terms of 5 out of 8 Data Citation Principles. The lack of a checkmark means that the principle is not satisfied.

	Attribution	Evidence	Unique Identification	Access	Importance
Formal Citation					
Reference & Citation	✓	✓	✓	✓	✓
Informal Citation					
Dataset reference	✓		✓	✓	✓
Reference without DOI	✓				✓
Dataset DOI		✓	✓	✓	
Dataset Title		✓			

been used. To mention a dataset in the full text – i.e., the `Cites` labeled edges – the most frequent attribute is the DOI, used 761 times. The title has been used 132 to mention datasets, while the title and the DOI have been used only 38 times. Only 1 dataset URL has been detected. Finally, 11 software DOIs mentions have been detected.

We analyzed how the detected practices comply with 5 of 8 FORCE 11 Data Citation Principles [1]: (i) *Importance*: Data should be considered legitimate, citable products of research; (ii) *Attribution*: data citations should facilitate giving scholarly credit; (iii) *Evidence*: if claim relies upon data, the corresponding data should be cited; (iv) *Unique Identification*: a data citation should include a persistent method for identification; (v) *Access*: Data citations should facilitate access to the data themselves and to such associated metadata, documentation, code, and other materials. The results are depicted in Table 2. Formal citations comply with all the principles. Mentioning a dataset in the references without citing it in the full text complies with the selected principles except for *Evidence* because it does not support any claim in the full text. If the reference lacks the DOI or the provided DOI is wrong, only *Attribution* and *Importance* are satisfied. Mentioning the DOI of a dataset in the full text complies with *Unique Identification* and *Access*, but it is not possible to give credits to contributors; in addition, *Importance* is not satisfied since the dataset is not included in the references section. Finally, mentioning the title of a dataset complies only with *Evidence*; there is not enough information to give credit to contributors and uniquely identify the dataset.

In Table 3, we analyzed the dataset and software citations, distinguishing between *formal* and *informal*, *complete*, and *incomplete* data citations. We found a total of 2,147 dataset citations – this value includes also all the datasets cited more than once in a publication's full text. Only the 24.12% of citations are formal and complete, containing enough information to uniquely identify the cited dataset and attribute it to its authors. The 19.70% is represented by incomplete formal citations: in this case, the lack of DOI prevents accessing and identifying the correct instance of the dataset. Formal dataset citations are the 44% of the entire count of citations. The remaining 56% of the citations are

Table 3. Overview of formal and informal data citations. *Citation only* means that there is not a dataset entry in the references list of the publication. In contrast, *references only* means that there is a reference entry but is never cited. *Complete* citations refer to all the mentions that comprise the DOI of the dataset, *incomplete* citations include only the title of the dataset.

			$p \rightarrow d$ edges (2,147 citations)		$p \rightarrow s$ edges (23 citations)	
			count	%	count	%
Formal	Reference & citation	Complete	518	24.12	5	21.74
		Incomplete	423	19.70	1	4.35
Informal	Citation only	Complete	800	37.26	11	47.82
		Incomplete	132	6.15	0	0
	Reference only	Complete	216	10.06	5	21.74
		Incomplete	58	2.70	1	4.35

informal. The largest portion of informal citations is DOI mentions in the full text without a dataset reference entry – i.e., 37.26%. The datasets' reference entries not mentioned in the full text represent only the 10% of the total. Incomplete informal dataset citations occurred in less than the 10% of cases. Regarding software citations, only one formal and one informal citation are incomplete; the 47.82% is informal – cited in full text without a reference, and the remaining part is equally split between formal and informal citations.

Furthermore, among the pairs of publications and datasets connected with a `References` or `Cites` edge, we found that in 144 publications the connected dataset is both formally and informally cited: the DOI (or the title) of the dataset is mentioned in the full text, and, at the same time, the dataset is present in the reference list of the publication and the related entry is formally cited; this aspect has been noticed in three pairs of publications and software instead.

We investigated the number of formal and informal citations in six date ranges. Our findings indicate that most citations were recorded after 2010, with fewer than 30 citations observed before that year. Additionally, informal complete citations were the prevailing type throughout all the periods starting from 2010. Regarding formal citations, between 2010 and 2014, there is a greater frequency of formal incomplete citations (69) compared to formal complete ones (39). From 2015 to 2019, formal complete and incomplete citations were nearly equal (318 formal complete and 299 incomplete), while after 2020, formal complete citations prevail over incomplete ones – 159 formal complete and 54 incomplete. Informal, incomplete citations are always the least common type.

We studied how many datasets supplementing the publications – connected with a `IsSupplementedBy` labeled edge, are also cited in the full text: 57 pairs of connected publications and datasets are formally cited in full text, 531 are informally cited, and 3,579 are not cited. No software is formally cited, 6 are informally cited, and 12 are not cited.

In the bar plot reported in Fig. 3, we illustrate the positions of a dataset (or software) formal and informal citations in the full text. The largest part

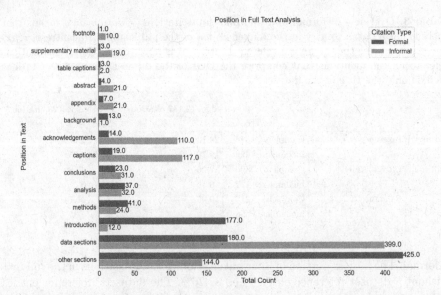

Fig. 3. The bar plot illustrates the positions in the full text of formal and informal citations. In the y-axis there are the possible sections, in the x-axis there is the total count of citations per position.

Table 4. Analysis of authors who contributed to the publication and the connected dataset. We analyzed the pairs of nodes having no authors in common, those having at least one author, and those sharing the entire list of authors.

	No authors	At least one author	All authors
IsSupplementedBy	133	1,612	**2,542**
Cites	300	**475**	398
References	348	**374**	111

of dataset citations is in the introduction, in sections that contain descriptions about the used and generated data – *data sections*, and in one of the sections composing the textual article – *other sections*. Most of the informal citations, instead, are in *data sections*, *other sections*, *acknowledgments*, and *captions*.

We analyzed the authors of the connected research outputs. In Table 4, we show for each semantics how many pairs of nodes do have not any author in common, share at least one author, and share all the authors respectively. The largest part of nodes connected with a IsSupplementedBy labeled edge, share all the authors – 2,542 pairs share all the authors, 1,612 share at least one author (but not all), and 133 pairs have no authors in common. The majority of pairs of nodes connected with Cites and References semantics – 475 and 374 pairs respectively, have at least one author in common; 111 References and 398 Cites labeled pairs have all the authors in common, and 348 References and 300 Cites labeled pairs have disjointed lists of authors.

We analyzed publications, datasets, and software to examine whether there exists a difference among the authors of these three research products. We found 13, 608 distinct publication authors, 9, 804 dataset authors, and 59 software authors. Only 30 authors contributed to publications, datasets, and software; the largest part of authors contributed both to publication and datasets – 8, 759 authors, while 4, 796, 1, 104 and 7 authors contributed only to publications, datasets, and software, respectively. 21 authors contributed to publications and software, while only 1 author to datasets and software.

5   Discussion

About referencing and citing data – **References** and **Cites** labeled relationships – we examined the formal and informal data citations showing that there is not a significant gap between them, accounting for 44% and 56% of the identified citations, respectively. Such a small difference may be related to where the examined datasets are deposited because they mostly belong to Pangaea, Zenodo, Dryad, and Figshare, which promote data citation and provide guidelines that adhere to the 11 data citation principles. However, the lack of a universal way to cite data promotes the coexistence of multiple approaches adopted for data citation. For example, a dataset may be mentioned only in the references list of the publication and be absent from the full text, or vice versa, it may be present only in the full text and not in the references list. It is worth noting that informal citations to datasets are not considered by infrastructures such as OpenCitations [23], which captures formal citations instead and would consequently miss more than half of the detected citations.

Furthermore, there are several different approaches to referring to a dataset – e.g., relying on its DOI, URL, or title. Based on our results, datasets are most commonly cited by including their DOI in the publication, sometimes accompanied by the dataset title. However, there are instances where only the dataset title is provided, resulting in the inability to access the dataset itself. Additionally, it is often observed that when the DOI associated with a dataset is not the one pointing to the dataset repository, the publication is referring not to the dataset itself but to a data paper. This occurs in incomplete formal citations, where an element with the same title as the dataset is cited, but the DOI to the dataset repository is not provided.

The analysis of data citations in different date ranges revealed that citing data is a common practice only in the last decade. In recent years, complete formal citations are becoming more frequent than incomplete ones suggesting a growing consensus on the importance of citing data, a greater interest in following suggested citation practices, and the use of DOIs and persistent URLs.

About supplementary data – i.e., `IsSupplementedBy` labeled edges – we emphasize that despite the close relationship between a publication and its supplementary material, it is rarely cited in the literature. The analysis reveals that out of 4, 287 datasets, 3, 579 (83%) are not cited in the literature. This not only hinders the ability of data authors to diversify their contributions [16] and receive credit but also hinders experiment reproducibility, discovery, and re-use.

Finally, the authors' analysis has allowed us to draw important conclusions regarding the trends of authors in discovering and reusing existing data in the literature. Our results show that when citing data within a publication, there is a tendency to cite datasets produced by the same authors instead of taking advantage of already released datasets. For instance, in pairs of nodes connected by a `Cites` edge, the number of publications and datasets sharing more than one author is more than twice the number of pairs without any common authors. This becomes even more evident when examining supplementary materials: in this case, only 133 pairs do not have any common authors, while more than 2,500 pairs share the entire list of authors. Similar results have been achieved in [11,28]. This finding can be related to the difficulties in re-using datasets and software released by other researchers. Using already released datasets requires a deep understanding of them, which can be acquired by relying on detailed documentation associated with the dataset. However, it is not guaranteed to find good and precise documentation, as its creation is at the discretion of the author. Additionally, most of the time, existing datasets may need to be selected and adapted for the specific use case. These conditions often result in a significant time loss, making it more convenient to create new datasets instead of re-using the already available ones. Furthermore, while there is a high number of authors working on publications, datasets, and software authors often contribute also to publications. This result is related to the lack of a universally adopted approach to citing data and software and a stable and established rewarding mechanism, such as the one for publications, for assigning credits to authors.

6   Conclusions

In this study, we utilized a curated scholarly graph that establishes connections between publications and research data to investigate how datasets and software are cited in the MES scientific literature. To identify dataset (and software) citations, we conducted an analysis of the PDFs of the publications. We focused on several key aspects, including the location of the citation within the full text, the attribute employed to reference datasets, and the categorization of citations as either formal or informal. Our findings confirmed the absence of a standardized approach to data citation. The results indicated a prevalence of informal citations compared to formal citations. The majority of dataset references included both the DOI and the title of the dataset. In cases where dataset mentions occurred within the full text, the dataset DOI emerged as the most frequently used attribute. We discovered that a small fraction of datasets accompanying the literature were cited within full texts, hindering dataset discovery, reuse, and the reproducibility of experiments. Additionally, our analyses revealed that generating new datasets was more prevalent than relying on previously released ones.

References

1. Altman, M., Borgman, C., Crosas, M., Matone, M.: An introduction to the joint principles for data citation. Bull. Assoc. Inf. Sci. Technol. **41**(3), 43–45 (2015)
2. Belter, C.W.: Measuring the value of research data: a citation analysis of oceanographic data sets. PLoS ONE **9**(3), e92590 (2014)
3. Buneman, P., Dosso, D., Lissandrini, M., Silvello, G.: Data citation and the citation graph. Quant. Sci. Stud. **2**(4), 1399–1422 (2021)
4. Callaghan, S.: Preserving the integrity of the scientific record: data citation and linking. Learn. Publish. **27**(5), S15–S24 (2014)
5. Chao, T.C.: Disciplinary reach: investigating the impact of dataset reuse in the earth sciences. Proc. Am. Soc. Inf. Sci. Technol. **48**(1), 1–8 (2011)
6. Costello, M.J., Michener, W.K., Gahegan, M., Zhang, Z.Q., Bourne, P.E.: Biodiversity data should be published, cited, and peer reviewed. Trends Ecol. Evol. **28**(8), 454–461 (2013)
7. Cousijn, H., et al.: A data citation roadmap for scientific publishers. Sci. Data **5**(1), 1–11 (2018)
8. Crosas, M.: The evolution of data citation: from principles to implementation. IASSIST Q. **37**(1–4), 62–62 (2014)
9. Duval, E.: Metadata standards: what, who & why. J. Univers. Comput. Sci. **7**(7), 591–601 (2001)
10. Fenner, M., et al.: A data citation roadmap for scholarly data repositories. Sci. Data **6**(1), 28 (2019)
11. He, L., Nahar, V.: Reuse of scientific data in academic publications: an investigation of Dryad Digital Repository. Aslib J. Inf. Manag. (2016)
12. Huang, Y.H., Rose, P.W., Hsu, C.N.: Citing a data repository: a case study of the protein data bank. PLoS ONE **10**(8), e0136631 (2015)
13. Irrera, O.: MES citations scholarly graph (2023). https://doi.org/10.5281/zenodo.8006578
14. Irrera, O., Mannocci, A., Manghi, P., Silvello, G.: A novel curated scholarly graph connecting textual and data publications. J. Data Inf. Qual. (2023). https://doi.org/10.1145/3597310
15. Lopez, P.: GROBID: combining automatic bibliographic data recognition and term extraction for scholarship publications. In: Agosti, M., Borbinha, J., Kapidakis, S., Papatheodorou, C., Tsakonas, G. (eds.) ECDL 2009. LNCS, vol. 5714, pp. 473–474. Springer, Heidelberg (2009). https://doi.org/10.1007/978-3-642-04346-8_62
16. Mannocci, A., Irrera, O., Manghi, P.: Open science and authorship of supplementary material. Evidence from a research community. arXiv preprint arXiv:2207.02775 (2022)
17. Mooney, H.: Citing data sources in the social sciences: do authors do it? Learn. Publish. **24**(2), 99–108 (2011)
18. Mooney, H., Newton, M.P.: The anatomy of a data citation: discovery, reuse, and credit. J. Librariansh. Scholar. Commun. **1**(1) (2012)
19. Park, H., Wolfram, D.: An examination of research data sharing and re-use: implications for data citation practice. Scientometrics **111**(1), 443–461 (2017). https://doi.org/10.1007/s11192-017-2240-2
20. Park, H., You, S., Wolfram, D.: Informal data citation for data sharing and reuse is more common than formal data citation in biomedical fields. J. Am. Soc. Inf. Sci. **69**(11), 1346–1354 (2018)

21. Parsons, M.A., Duerr, R., Minster, J.B.: Data citation and peer review. EOS Trans. Am. Geophys. Union **91**(34), 297–298 (2010)
22. Pepe, A., Goodman, A., Muench, A., Crosas, M., Erdmann, C.: How do astronomers share data? Reliability and persistence of datasets linked in AAS publications and a qualitative study of data practices among US astronomers. PLoS ONE **9**(8), e104798 (2014)
23. Peroni, S., Shotton, D.: OpenCitations, an infrastructure organization for open scholarship. Quant. Sci. Stud. **1**(1), 428–444 (2020)
24. Robinson-García, N., Jiménez-Contreras, E., Torres-Salinas, D.: Analyzing data citation practices using the data citation index. J. Am. Soc. Inf. Sci. **67**(12), 2964–2975 (2016)
25. Silvello, G.: Theory and practice of data citation. J. Am. Soc. Inf. Sci. **69**(1), 6–20 (2018)
26. Walton, D.W.: Data citation-Moving to new norms. Antarct. Sci. **22**(4), 333–333 (2010)
27. Yoon, J., Chung, E., Lee, J.Y., Kim, J.: How research data is cited in scholarly literature: a case study of HINTS. Learn. Publish. **32**(3), 199–206 (2019)
28. Zhao, M., Yan, E., Li, K.: Data set mentions and citations: a content analysis of full-text publications. J. Am. Soc. Inf. Sci. **69**(1), 32–46 (2018)

Non-citable but not Uncited: A Large-Scale Citation Analysis of Editorials

Tove Faber Frandsen[1](✉) 🆔 and Jeppe Nicolaisen[2] 🆔

[1] University of Southern Denmark, Kolding, Denmark
t.faber@sdu.dk
[2] University of Copenhagen, Copenhagen, Denmark

Abstract. It is widely recognized that the Journal Impact Factor (JIF) can be subject to manipulation, and one such strategy is to publish more editorials. Editorials are considered non-citable and thus excluded from the JIF denominator despite being cited and contributing substantially to the numerator. The strategy is successful if the editorials are cited. Thus, increasing the scientific content of the editorials may result in higher citation counts. This study analyzes the number of editorials published across fields and citations to these to examine if editorials with more scientific content are more cited than editorials with less scientific content. The results show that there is no indication of a general increase over time in editorials with longer reference lists, even though editorials with longer reference lists are found to be cited more.

Keywords: Bibliometrics · Citation analysis · Non-citable documents

1 Introduction

Bibliometric indicators rely on normalization to allow for generalization. Field normalization has, for instance, become a standard procedure among bibliometricians, although many different approaches exist [1]. When working with citation indicators it is vital to consider if citations should be normalized and how [2]. Leydesdorff [3] argues that the journal impact factor was the first attempt to normalize citation distributions by averaging over 2 years. A variety of procedures for normalizing citation distributions have followed since. However, normalization can also become the Achilles' heel of a bibliometric indicator [4]. It may, for instance, open up for gaming the system [5]. This may be illustrated by the journal impact factor (JIF) used by Clarivate Analytics:

$$JIF \ of \ year \ x = \frac{Citations \ in \ x \ to \ items \ in \ J \ (x-1 \ and \ x-2)}{Citable \ items \ in \ J \ (x-1 \ and \ x-2)}$$

This definition of JIF counts citations to items in the numerator that are not necessarily included in the denominator. The numerator of the JIF counts citations to all types of journal publications, whereas the denominator only counts so-called "citable items" [6]. Citable items are defined as articles, notes, and reviews, which means that meeting

O. Alonso et al. (Eds.): TPDL 2023, LNCS 14241, pp. 93–98, 2023.
https://doi.org/10.1007/978-3-031-43849-3_8

abstracts, editorials, letters, news items, corrections, book reviews, biographical items and reprints are considered non-citable items [7]. The asymmetry between the numerator and denominator implies that in principle, JIF could be manipulated by for instance including more editorials [8]. Yet, it should be noted that there is actually little evidence to support that this is actually happening at larger scale [9, 10].

Although the non-citable items are typically seen as second class citizens of the scholarly communication system, they are published in considerable amounts [10, 11]. However, there are great differences across fields and even within fields [6, 12, 13]. The non-citable items have very different characteristics and contain scientific content to a varying degree. Consequently, they are not cited to the same extent. Book reviews and meeting abstracts are cited the least; Discussions, letters and editorials are cited the most [14–16]. Thus, non-citable items do actually not go entirely uncited. On the contrary, they contribute considerably to the impact factor of a journal [17]. Citations to these non-citable items are counted in the numerator of the JIF, but not in the denominator. Therefore, citations to these non-citable items are essentially "free citations" [14, 18]. McVeigh and Mann [6] report that journals in their study accumulated 10% to 20% of their total citations from non-citable items. Similarly, Heneberg [11] reports that non-citable items in 11 journals under study received between 3 to 15% of the total citations to the journals.

Editorials are particularly interesting as they may contribute to the manipulation of JIF in both the numerator and denominator. Increasing use of editorial material will not affect the denominator, but the numerator can be increased through citations to the editorials and by increased use of journal self-citations in the editorials [9]. Obviously, editorials can only be used to manipulate JIF if they are cited. Therefore, more scientific content in the editorials is needed for the manipulation to work. Yet, apart from anecdotal evidence and case stories, little is known about the characteristics of editorials and how they attract citations. The aim of the present study is therefore to analyze the citations to editorials across fields in order to examine if editorials with more scientific content are more cited than editorials with less scientific content.

2   Methods

Data for the study were retrieved from the database Scopus. All editorials published in indexed journals from the year 2000 to 2022 were retrieved and sorted by subject area, number of references, and number of citations. We used the four broad subject areas (Health Sciences; Life Sciences; Physical Sciences; Social Sciences) for the study. The total number of editorials are as follows: Health Sciences (617,860), Life Sciences (173,913), Physical Sciences (206,084) and Social Sciences (215,345).

To study the scientific content aspect, we use the number of references as proxy variable. Specifically, we follow the recommendation of Price [19], and treat editorials with less than 10 references in their literature lists as editorials with less scientific content than those with longer literature lists (10 to 19, 20 to 29, and at least 30 references).

The number of received citations are calculated in two ways: The ratio of uncited/cited editorials; The ratio of editorials cited 0 to 4 times/editorials cited at least 5 times. We are not operating with a fixed citation window. Instead, we operate with the number of citations received on the day of retrieval (March 10, 2023). This means that older editorials consequently have had a much longer period of time to score citations than younger editorials. Therefore, the data only allows for comparisons between subject areas for specific publication years. We calculate the percentage of editorials with varying number of references and cross tabulate these numbers with the different citation ratios. Results are presented as graphs showing percentages year by year.

3   Results

Figure 1 shows the percentage of references in editorials year by year. In all four subject categories, the percentage of editorials with at least 30 references have been radically dropping over time, allowing a slight to moderate increase in the percentage of editorials in the other three categories (0–9 references; 10–19 references; 20–29 references).

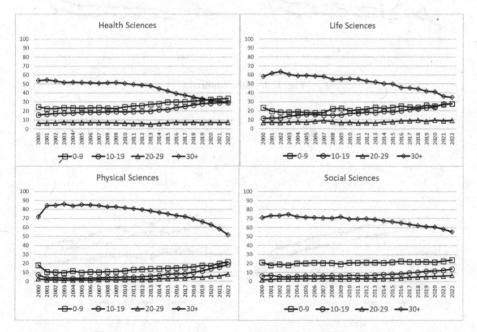

Fig. 1. Number of references in editorials from 2000 to 2022.

Figure 2 shows the percentage of uncited editorials year by year. Focusing on the editorials from the first three reference categories, it is evident that the uncited rate raises dramatically toward the final part of the investigated period. This is of course caused by the gradually shortening of the citation window. However, in all four subject areas, editorials with 0–9 references are generally markedly more uncited than editorials with 10–19 references and 20–29 references. Note also that the editorials with 20–29 references typically are the least uncited category.

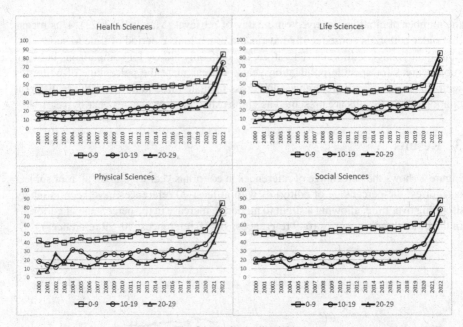

Fig. 2. Uncited editorials

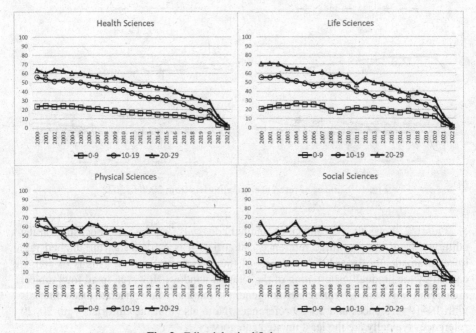

Fig. 3. Editorials cited 5 times or more

Figure 3 shows the percentage of editorials receiving five or more citations. In all three reference categories, the percentages drop radically over time. Of course, this is again caused by the gradual shortening of the citation window. However, there is a clear divide between the three categories. Editorials with 20–29 references score higher percentages than editorials with 10–19 references. Editorials with 0–9 references score by far the lowest percentages in all four subject areas.

4 Discussion and Conclusion

Our results support earlier studies that have found that non-citable documents like editorials are actually cited. Thus, in the four subject categories under study, over 50 percent of the editorials are cited at least once. Consequently, citation measures, including the JIF, are influenced by these alleged "non-citable" documents. Our results also show that the citation impact depends on the number of references in the literature lists. Generally, the more references, the higher impact. To the extent that number of references may be taken as an indicator of scientific content, these results indicate that it is primarily due to their increased scientific content that some categories of editorials are cited much more.

There is, however, a few reservations that need to be made. Our results are based on the document type-categorization of Scopus. If a large amount of the editorials in our study is mis-categorized as such, they might invalidate the results. We can't help noticing the very high number of editorials with 30 or more references in their reference lists. The decline over time may be caused by improved indexing in Scopus. We do not know, and we have not found any evidence of this. However, we have stumbled upon editorials that were wrongly indexed. Continuing along the speculative line, the high number of editorials with many references could potentially be cases of extensive journal self-citation. As noted in the introduction, this practice, if optimally implemented, could boost the JIF of a journal. Again, we have not found any evidence of this in our data.

On a more serious note, the way we define scientific content using a proxy variable based on specific number of references could potentially affect our results. It might be of importance to note that Price was specifically addressing the journal article, and thus not the editorial. It might be the case that other figures should be used for assessing the scholarliness of editorials. Yet, our results clearly indicate that an increase in the number of references go hand in hand with an increase in the number of citations. Thus, in our case, the precise intersection between scholarly/unscholarly does not seem that important. What is important, is the results showing that increased scientific content tend to result in higher citation impact.

Summing up, this study shows that editorials are cited extensively across all fields although to a varying degree. It also shows that citation rates of editorials are tied to the length of the reference list, which means that editorials with longer reference lists are cited more. It therefore seems advantageous for journal editors to include more editorial material with long reference lists. However, there is no indication in this study of a general increase over time in lengthy editorials.

References

1. Haunschild, R., Bornmann, L.: Relevance of document types in the scores' calculation of a specific field-normalized indicator: are the scores strongly dependent on or nearly independent of the document type handling? Scientometrics **127**, 4419–4438 (2022)
2. Ioannidis, J.P.A., Boyack, K., Wouters, P.F.: Citation metrics: a primer on how (not) to normalize. PLoS Biol. **14**, e1002542 (2016)
3. Leydesdorff, L.: Alternatives to the journal impact factor: I3 and the top-10%(or top-25%?) of the most-highly cited papers. Scientometrics **92**, 355–365 (2012)
4. Bensman, S.J.: Distributional differences of the impact factor in the sciences versus the social sciences: an analysis of the probabilistic structure of the 2005 journal citation reports. J. Am. Soc. Inf. Sci. Technol. **59**, 1366–1382 (2008)
5. Larivière, V., et al.: A simple proposal for the publication of journal citation distributions. BioRxiv 062109 (2016)
6. McVeigh, M.E., Mann, S.J.: The journal impact factor denominator: defining citable (counted) items. JAMA **302**, 1107–1109 (2009)
7. http://help.incites.clarivate.com/incitesLiveJCR/9607-TRS/version/17
8. Reedijk, J., Moed, H.F.: Is the impact of journal impact factors decreasing? J. Doc. **64**, 183–192 (2008)
9. Campanario, J.M., González, L.: Journal self-citations that contribute to the impact factor: documents labeled "editorial material" in journals covered by the Science Citation Index. Scientometrics **69**, 365–386 (2006)
10. Frandsen, T.F.: On the ratio of citable versus non-citable items in economics journals. Scientometrics **74**, 439–451 (2008)
11. Heneberg, P.: Parallel worlds of citable documents and others: inflated commissioned opinion articles enhance scientometric indicators. J. Assoc. Inf. Sci. Technol. **65**, 635–643 (2014)
12. Liu, X.L., Gai, S.S., Zhou, J.: Journal impact factor: do the numerator and denominator need correction? PLoS One **11** (2016)
13. Taşkın, Z., Doğan, G., Kulczycki, E., Zuccala, A.A.: Self-citation patterns of journals indexed in the journal citation reports. J. Informetr. **15**, 101221 (2021)
14. Moed, H.F., Van Leeuwen, T.N.: Improving the accuracy of institute for scientific information's journal impact factors. J. Am. Soc. Inf. Sci. **46**, 461–467 (1995)
15. Hu, X., Rousseau, R.: Meeting abstracts: a waste of space? Curr. Sci. **105**, 150–151 (2013)
16. Xue-Li, L., Ya-Hui, W., Shuang-Shuang, G.: Citation characteristics of non-citable documents and contributions to journal impact factor. Curr. Sci. **114**, 1423–1429 (2018)
17. Larivière, V., Sugimoto, C.R.: The journal impact factor: a brief history, critique, and discussion of adverse effects. In: Glänzel, W., Moed, H.F., Schmoch, U., Thelwall, M. (eds.) Springer Handbook of Science and Technology Indicators. Springer Handbooks. Springer, Cham (2019). https://doi.org/10.1007/978-3-030-02511-3_1
18. Bornmann, L., Neuhaus, C., Daniel, H.-D.: The effect of a two-stage publication process on the Journal Impact Factor: a case study on the interactive open access journal Atmospheric Chemistry and Physics. Scientometrics **86**, 93–97 (2011)
19. Price, D.J.: Citation measures of hard science, soft science, technology, and nonscience. Commun. Among Sci. Eng. **1**, 3r22 (1970)

BIP! NDR (NoDoiRefs): A Dataset of Citations from Papers Without DOIs in Computer Science Conferences and Workshops

Paris Koloveas[1,2](✉) ⓘ, Serafeim Chatzopoulos[2] ⓘ, Christos Tryfonopoulos[1] ⓘ, and Thanasis Vergoulis[2] ⓘ

[1] University of the Peloponnese, Tripolis, Greece
{pkoloveas,trifon}@uop.gr
[2] IMSI, Athena RC, Athens, Greece
{schatz,vergoulis}@athenarc.gr

Abstract. In the field of Computer Science, conference and workshop papers serve as important contributions, carrying substantial weight in research assessment processes, compared to other disciplines. However, a considerable number of these papers are not assigned a Digital Object Identifier (DOI), hence their citations are not reported in widely used citation datasets like OpenCitations and Crossref, raising limitations to citation analysis. While the Microsoft Academic Graph (MAG) previously addressed this issue by providing substantial coverage, its discontinuation has created a void in available data. BIP! NDR aims to alleviate this issue and enhance the research assessment processes within the field of Computer Science. To accomplish this, it leverages a workflow that identifies and retrieves Open Science papers lacking DOIs from the DBLP Corpus, and by performing text analysis, it extracts citation information directly from their full text. The current version of the dataset contains more than 510K citations made by approximately 60K open access Computer Science conference or workshop papers that, according to DBLP, do not have a DOI.

Keywords: Citation extraction · Bibliographic metadata · Text mining

1 Introduction

A *(bibliographic) citation* refers to a conceptual (directional) link that connects a research work (usually a publication) which contains a reference to (i.e., "cites") another work (which is being "cited"). During the last decades, citations have become one of the most important types of bibliographic metadata [12]. The main reason for that is that they are often considered as proxies of scientific impact, since a citation can be interpreted as an acknowledgement for the contribution of the cited work into the citing one (although this might not always be the case [1,17]). As a result, they have been instrumental in scientometrics,

O. Alonso et al. (Eds.): TPDL 2023, LNCS 14241, pp. 99–105, 2023.
https://doi.org/10.1007/978-3-031-43849-3_9

becoming the basis for the calculation of various research impact indicators [16]. Such indicators have been used to facilitate scientific knowledge discovery (e.g., they have been used by academic search engines to help researchers prioritise their reading [15]), monitor research production [11], assist research assessment processes, and in many other applications.

Various sources of citation data have become available during the previous decades to address the needs of use-cases like the aforementioned ones. Apart from proprietary and restrictive sources, like Clarivate Analytics' Web of Science, Google Scholar and the Microsoft Academic Graph (MAG) [2], due to the raised popularity of the Open Science movement, a couple of open datasets that provide citations (e.g., OpenCitations[1], the OpenAIRE Graph[2]) have also become available during the last years. Almost all of them report citations as DOI-to-DOI pairs, failing to cover citations that involve publications for which a DOI has not been assigned. This may not be a significant problem for many disciplines, but in Computer Science, a considerable number of conferences and workshops do not assign DOIs to their papers. In addition, in this field, conference and workshop papers are peer reviewed and, historically, serve as important contributions, carrying significant weight in research assessment processes. As a result, if they are not considered during citation analyses, this can overlook an important part of scientific production and even introduce bias. In the past, Microsoft Academic Graph (MAG) was partially covering this gap by also offering citations for papers that do not have a DOI. However, since its discontinuation in December 2021, this data collection is no longer maintained and updated, thus its coverage is continuously declining.

In this work, we introduce BIP! NDR, an open dataset that aims to cover this gap, improving research assessment processes and other relevant applications within the field of Computer Science. The dataset is constructed based on a workflow that identifies and retrieves Open Science publications lacking DOIs from DBLP[3], the most widely known bibliographic database for publications from Computer Science, and then performs text analysis to extract citation information directly from the respective manuscripts. The current version of the dataset contains more than 510K citations made by approximately 60K Computer Science conference or workshop papers that, according to DBLP, do not have a DOI. We plan to frequently update the dataset so that it can become an important resource for citations in Computer Science that are missing from the most important citation datasets. This is a valuable addition to the toolboxes of scientometricians so that they can perform more concrete analysis in the Computer Science domain.

Outline. The rest of the manuscript is organized as follows: in Sect. 2 we elaborate on the technical details related to the production of the BIP! NDR dataset; in Sect. 3 we discuss the structure of the dataset; finally, in Sect. 4 we conclude the work while also discussing future planned extensions.

---

[1] OpenCitations: https://opencitations.net.

[2] OpenAIRE Graph: https://graph.openaire.eu.

[3] DBLP: https://dblp.uni-trier.de/.

2   Dataset Production Workflow

In this section, we discuss the BIP! NDR dataset production workflow and we elaborate on the technical details of its various components. The source code of the production workflow is available as open source on GitHub[4]. A high-level overview of the workflow is depicted in Fig. 1.

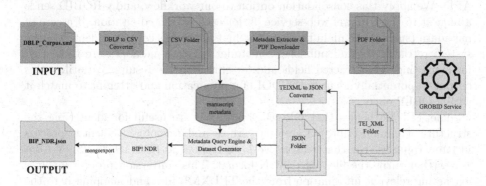

Fig. 1. A high-level overview of the dataset production workflow.

The main input to the workflow is the DBLP Corpus, which we use to collect URLs hosting Open Access manuscripts from the field of Computer Science, focusing on those that do not have a DOI. We collect these manuscripts so that we will be able to extract citations from the respective PDF files. DBLP [5, 6] consolidates scholarly metadata from several open sources which cover the Computer Science field and is largely manually curated and frequently updated. As a result, this collection is ideal for our purposes. Our analysis shows that out of the approximately 320K open access conference publications, approximately 260K do not have a DOI. These publications are the ones that we aim to cover through the evolution of our dataset. The current version of our dataset (v0.1) [4] is based on the November 2022 Monthly Snapshot of DBLP [13]. The DBLP Corpus comes in XML format with all the bibliographic entries together in a single file. Therefore, as a first step, we use `dblp-to-csv`[5] to split the corpus into separate CSV files, grouped by publication type. We further process these CSV files to (a) extract manuscript metadata and store them in a document-oriented database, and (b) follow the included links to download the PDF files of Open Access papers. These operations ensure that the structured manuscript metadata from the DBLP Corpus are easily accessible to our workflow for querying and further processing.

For the next step of our workflow, we needed a tool to extract information from the PDF files while maintaining the headers, structure and sectioning

---

[4] BIP! NDR repository: https://github.com/athenarc/bip-ndr-workflow.
[5] dblp-to-csv: https://github.com/ThomHurks/dblp-to-csv.

of the manuscript. After a thorough evaluation of the literature regarding the tools used for reference extraction from PDFs, we concluded that based both on surveys [9,14], and prominent works that required extensive bibliography parsing [7,10], GROBID [8] is currently the best tool for the task. GROBID converts the PDF files to the TEI XML publication format[6]. Apart from the PDF extraction capabilities, GROBID offers a consolidation option to resolve extracted bibliographical references using services like biblio-glutton[7] or the CrossRef REST API[8]. We apply this consolidation option to our workflow, and GROBID sends a request to the Crossref web service [3] for each extracted citation. If a core of metadata (such as the main title and the first author) is correctly identified, the system retrieves the full publisher's metadata. These metadata are then used for correcting the extracted fields and for enriching the results. We utilize this output to potentially identify the DOI of a publication and attempt to match it with a DBLP entry.

The TEI XML files that GROBID produces are useful for identifying the structure of a manuscript, but are very verbose and are not convenient to process in large volumes. For that reason, we have created a *TEIXML to JSON Converter* that turns the files into JSON format. This conversion process involves extracting relevant information from the TEI XML files and mapping it to the corresponding JSON structure. The resulting JSON files are smaller in size and are compatible with a wide range of tools for processing.

At this point, we have reached the core functionality of our workflow, the process of *querying the DBLP metadata* for the bibliographic references of the papers in our collection. This process queries the manuscript metadata database for each document in the JSON Folder. For each document, we parse the reference list and we first check if a DOI exists in a publication entry. If it exists, we query our database based on the DOI. If a result is returned, we store the `dblp_id`, the `doi`, as well as, the `bibliographic_reference` extracted from the JSON file. Otherwise, we query based on the publication title. On a positive result, we store the previously mentioned fields to the dataset entry. If neither the publication title nor the DOI return a positive result, the publication could not be found in our DBLP metadata, so we store only the `doi` and `bibliographic_reference` from the JSON file. This process ultimately creates the "BIP! NDR" collection which constitutes our dataset.

The final step involved using the *mongoexport* utility to export the "BIP! NDR" collection from MongoDB into the final JSONL file. The exported file served as the culmination of the dataset generation process, providing a structured collection of scholarly data ready for research and analysis.

---

[6] TEI XML format: https://tei-c.org/release/doc/tei-p5-doc/en/html/SG.html.

[7] biblio-glutton: https://github.com/kermitt2/biblio-glutton.

[8] Crossref API: https://www.crossref.org/documentation/retrieve-metadata/rest-api/.

```
{
  "_id":{
    "$oid": "6460a56bda929a01210c1b57"
  },
  "citing_paper": {
    "dblp_id": "conf/ecsa/GasperisPF21"
  },
  "cited_papers": [
    {
      "dblp_id": "journals/sigpro/AlbusacCLVL09",
      "doi": "10.1016/j.sigpro.2009.04.008",
      "bibliographic_reference": "J. Albusac, J. Castro-Schez, L. Lopez-Lopez, D. Vallejo, L. Jimenez-Linares,
        A supervised  learning approach to automate the acquisition of knowledge in surveillance systems,  Signal
        Processing 89 (2009) 2400-2414.  doi:https://doi.org/10. 1016/j.sigpro.2009.04.008, special Section: Visual
        Information Analysis for Security."
    },
    {
      "dblp_id": "journals/cssp/Elhoseny20",
      "doi": "10.1007/s00034-019-01234-7",
      "bibliographic_reference": "M. Elhoseny, Multi-object detection and tracking (modt) machine learning model for real
        -time video surveillance systems, Circuits, Systems, and Signal Processing 39 (2020) 611-630.
        doi:10.1007/s00034-019-01234-7."
    },
    {
      "doi":"10.23919/IRS.2019.8768102",
      "bibliographic_reference":"F. Opitz, K. Dästner, B. v. H. z. Roseneckh-Köhler, E. Schmid, Data analytics and machine
        learning in wide area surveillance systems, in: 2019 20th International Radar Symposium (IRS), 2019, pp. 1-10.
        doi:10.23919/IRS.2019.8768102."
    },
    {
      "dblp_id":"journals/rfc/rfc3411",
      "bibliographic_reference":"D. Harrington, R. Presuhn, B. Wijnen, An architecture for describing simple network
        management protocol (snmp) management frameworks, 2002. doi:10.17487/RFC3411."
    }
  ]
}
```

Fig. 2. Data structure of the BIP! NDR dataset.

3   The BIP! NDR Dataset

In this section we present the structure of the dataset along with some basic statistics of the current version. The dataset is formatted as a JSON Lines (JSONL)[9] file where each line contains a valid JSON object. This file format enables file splitting and data streaming as the dataset grows in size. An indicative record (in JSON format) of the BIP! NDR dataset is depicted in Fig. 2.

Each JSON object has the following three main fields:

1. _id – the unique identifier of each entry
2. citing_paper – an object holding the dblp_id of each citing paper
3. cited_papers – an array that contains the objects that correspond to each reference found in the text of the citing_paper. Each object of the array may contain some or all of the following fields:
   (a) dblp_id – the dblp_id of the cited paper
   (b) doi – the doi of the cited paper
   (c) bibliographic_reference – the raw citation string as it appears in the citing paper

Note that not all the aforementioned fields in (3) are required for a cited_paper to be valid. Specifically, one of the dblp_id or doi identifiers is required for a cited paper to be added in the collection. Finally, the bibliographic_reference exists in all cited_paper objects since it is extracted directly from the PDF files of each citing paper in the dataset.

---

[9] JSON Lines data format: https://jsonlines.org/.

Table 1 summarises some statistics about the BIP! NDR dataset. In particular, 59,663 full texts from Open Access papers were parsed. A total of 1,054,107 references were evaluated, and among them, 511,842 references were successfully matched with corresponding keys from the DBLP database. Additionally, 366,106 DOIs were successfully matched with these DBLP keys. Finally, there were 22,569 DOIs that could not be matched with any DBLP key, indicating that they have not been indexed by DBLP.

Table 1. Statistics of BIP! NDR dataset (current version).

Statistic	#
Total Files Parsed	59,663
Total References Evaluated	1,054,107
DBLP Keys Matched	511,842
DOIs Matched with DBLP Key	366,106
DOIs without DBLP Key	22,569

4   Conclusions

We presented BIP! NDR, a dataset created using text analysis techniques on the DBLP database to extract citation information from the full text of the Open Access papers that do not have an assigned DOI. The dataset offers over 500K citations from Computer Science papers that do not have DOIs, addressing a significant limitation of widely used citation datasets in the field, that fail to cover them. As a result, it enables more comprehensive and accurate research assessment in Computer Science. In the future, we plan to improve the workflow so that it can identify more Open Source publications and to extend the dataset so that it can offer additional metadata for each citation (e.g., a class according to a citation classification algorithm).

Acknowledgements. This work was co-funded by the EU Horizon Europe projects SciLake (GA: 101058573) and GraspOS (GA: 101095129).

References

1. Abu-Jbara, A., Ezra, J., Radev, D.: Purpose and polarity of citation: towards NLP-based bibliometrics. In: Proceedings of the 2013 Conference of the North American chapter of the Association for Computational Linguistics: Human Language Technologies, pp. 596–606 (2013)

2. Färber, M., Ao, L.: The Microsoft academic knowledge graph enhanced: author name disambiguation, publication classification, and embeddings. Quant. Sci. Stud. **3**(1), 51–98 (2022). https://doi.org/10.1162/qss_a_00183

3. Hendricks, G., Tkaczyk, D., Lin, J., Feeney, P.: Crossref: the sustainable source of community-owned scholarly metadata. Quant. Sci. Stud. **1**(1), 414–427 (2020). https://doi.org/10.1162/qss_a_00022

4. Koloveas, P., Chatzopoulos, S., Tryfonopoulos, C., Vergoulis, T.: BIP! NDR (NoDoiRefs): a dataset of citations from papers without DOIs in computer science conferences and workshops. https://doi.org/10.5281/zenodo.7962020

5. Ley, M.: The DBLP computer science bibliography: evolution, research issues, perspectives. In: Laender, A.H.F., Oliveira, A.L. (eds.) SPIRE 2002. LNCS, vol. 2476, pp. 1–10. Springer, Heidelberg (2002). https://doi.org/10.1007/3-540-45735-6_1

6. Ley, M.: DBLP: some lessons learned. Proc. VLDB Endow. **2**(2), 1493–1500 (2009)

7. Lo, K., Wang, L.L., Neumann, M., Kinney, R.M., Weld, D.S.: S2orc: the semantic scholar open research corpus. In: ACL (2020)

8. Lopez, P.: GROBID: combining automatic bibliographic data recognition and term extraction for scholarship publications. In: Agosti, M., Borbinha, J., Kapidakis, S., Papatheodorou, C., Tsakonas, G. (eds.) ECDL 2009. LNCS, vol. 5714, pp. 473–474. Springer, Heidelberg (2009). https://doi.org/10.1007/978-3-642-04346-8_62

9. Meuschke, N., Jagdale, A., Spinde, T., Mitrović, J., Gipp, B.: A benchmark of pdf information extraction tools using a multi-task and multi-domain evaluation framework for academic documents. In: Sserwanga, I., et al. (eds.) Information for a Better World: Normality, Virtuality, Physicality, Inclusivity. LNCS, vol. 13972, pp. 383–405. Springer, Cham (2023). https://doi.org/10.1007/978-3-031-28032-0_31

10. Nicholson, J.M., et al.: scite: A smart citation index that displays the context of citations and classifies their intent using deep learning. Quant. Sci. Stud. 1–17 (2021). https://doi.org/10.1162/qss_a_00146

11. Papastefanatos, G., et al.: Open science observatory: monitoring open science in Europe. In: Bellatreche, L., et al. (eds.) TPDL/ADBIS -2020. CCIS, vol. 1260, pp. 341–346. Springer, Cham (2020). https://doi.org/10.1007/978-3-030-55814-7_29

12. Peroni, S., Shotton, D.M.: Opencitations, an infrastructure organization for open scholarship. Quant. Sci. Stud. **1**(1), 428–444 (2020). https://doi.org/10.1162/qss_a_00023

13. The DBLP Team: DBLP computer science bibliography. Monthly snapshot release of November 2022. https://dblp.org/xml/release/dblp-2022-11-02.xml.gz

14. Tkaczyk, D., Collins, A., Sheridan, P., Beel, J.: Machine learning vs. rules and out-of-the-box vs. retrained: an evaluation of open-source bibliographic reference and citation parsers. In: Proceedings of the 18th ACM/IEEE on Joint Conference on Digital Libraries, pp. 99–108 (2018)

15. Vergoulis, T., et al.: BIP! Scholar: a service to facilitate fair researcher assessment. In: Aizawa, A., Mandl, T., Carevic, Z., Hinze, A., Mayr, P., Schaer, P. (eds.) JCDL '22: The ACM/IEEE Joint Conference on Digital Libraries in 2022, Cologne, Germany, 20–24 June 2022, p. 42. ACM (2022). https://doi.org/10.1145/3529372.3533296

16. Vergoulis, T., et al.: BIP! DB: a dataset of impact measures for scientific publications. In: Leskovec, J., Grobelnik, M., Najork, M., Tang, J., Zia, L. (eds.) Companion of The Web Conference 2021, Virtual Event / Ljubljana, Slovenia, 19–23 April 2021, pp. 456–460. ACM / IW3C2 (2021). https://doi.org/10.1145/3442442.3451369

17. Yousif, A., Niu, Z., Tarus, J.K., Ahmad, A.: A survey on sentiment analysis of scientific citations. Artif. Intell. Rev. **52**(3), 1805–1838 (2019)

Investigating the Relation Between Authors' Academic Age and Their Citations

Rand Alchokr[1]([✉])(iD), Sanket Vikas Joshi[1], Gunter Saake[1](iD), Thomas Leich[2](iD), and Jacob Krüger[3](iD)

[1] Otto-von-Guericke University, Magdeburg, Germany
{rand.alchokr,Sanket.Joshi,saake}@ovgu.de
[2] Harz University and METOP GmbH, Wernigerode, Germany
tleich@hs-harz.de
[3] Eindhoven University of Technology, Eindhoven, The Netherlands
j.kruger@tue.nl

Abstract. The increasing number of authors and consequent publications in computer science can cause some pitfalls, such as understanding the use and fairness of quality indicators for assessing research. In this preliminary work, we aim to examine whether there is a correlation between the citation count and the number of authors contributing to a paper as well as their academic ages. Additionally, we shed light on highly cited papers and compare their authors. For this purpose, we investigate authors' characteristics by conducting data analyses based on a dataset of four prestigious software-engineering-related conferences comprising 5,143 papers and their authors. Our results indicate that the number of authors does not connect to the citation count, but the current academic age of the authors does. We also found that 98% of the highly cited main-track papers had a contribution from at least one senior researcher, whereas none of these papers was written by a junior researcher alone. These first results are a step towards more in-depth research concerning the fair evaluation of computer-science researchers—specifically regarding juniors and their inclusion.

Keywords: Software engineering · Publications · Scientific collaboration · Junior researchers

1 Introduction

In recent years, computer science has undergone rapid evolution, with a notable shift from solitary to collaborative efforts [5,7,10]. Working in teams is generally thought of as a way to benefit from the experiences of researchers from different disciplines, thereby improving knowledge sharing and easing access to resources [6,15,19]. However, the growing trend of scientific collaboration has also raised concerns regarding research assessments. While researchers are increasingly working in teams to publish papers, there is often a lack of transparency regarding their individual contributions, which challenges a fair evaluation. Some journals require disclosure of each researcher's unique contributions,

© The Author(s), under exclusive license to Springer Nature Switzerland AG 2023
O. Alonso et al. (Eds.): TPDL 2023, LNCS 14241, pp. 106–113, 2023.
https://doi.org/10.1007/978-3-031-43849-3_10

but there is currently no standardized framework to precisely measure and assess the contributions of individual authors [22].

Typically, researchers are distinguished based on their expertise, for instance, as junior, mid-level, or senior researchers. However, there is an issue, since quality indicators used for evaluating researchers are the same regardless of their career stage. This has raised questions about the fairness and impact of such indicators on different groups of researchers. Generally, a researcher is assessed based on different measures, the most famous being the *citation count*, which ranks researchers according to their citations, besides other metrics like the *h-index*, *G-index*, or *W-index* [12,14,27] and the rather new *Altmetrics* [23–25]. Analyzing what factors impact such metrics is essential to derive fairer assessments of individual researchers, for instance, for funding agencies and tenure committees [22].

Moving into this direction, *our goal in this paper is to examine whether there are connections between a publication's citation count and the number of authors or their academic ages.* We choose the citation count as a popular assessment method and concentrate on the two variables pertaining to authors' characteristics that may impact citation counts. To the best of our knowledge, researchers' academic age has not been analyzed in depth before. So, we report an analysis on the relationships between these variables and look to find patterns or trends favoring a specific group of researchers if such exist. We defined the following two research questions (RQs) and answer them using a dataset of main-track papers and the corresponding authors' information of four reputable conferences, namely the 1) International Conference on Automated Software Engineering Conference (ASE); 2) Joint European Software Engineering Conference and Symposium on the Foundations of Software Engineering (ESEC/FSE); 3) International Conference on Software Engineering (ICSE); and 4) Joint Conference on Digital Libraries (JCDL), that we extracted from dblp:[1]

RQ₁. Does the number of authors contributing to a paper affect its citation count?

RQ₂. Is there a correlation between authors' academic age and the citation count?

Our work is an initial step for a more comprehensive analysis to identify and develop fair metrics and quality indicators to evaluate researchers.

2   Background

There have been various proposals for how to assess research. For instance, Hirsch [14] suggested the h-index, which attempts to calculate a researcher's output and influence over time using the number of papers receiving citations. However, this metric has limitations, since it assigns equal importance to all papers and ignores their age [26]. To address this limitation to some extent,

---

[1] https://dblp.uni-trier.de/.

Table 1. Overview of our dataset.

conference	period	# unique papers	# unique authors
ASE	1991–2020	1,070	2,465
ESEC/FSE	1987–2020	1,193	2,530
ICSE	1976–2020	2,300	4,357
JCDL	2001–2020	580	1,390
total		5,143	8,730

variants of the h-index have been proposed, like the contemporary or trendy h-index—which consider a paper's publication year or age [26]. The citation count is the most widely used metric to assess researchers, and has often been relevant in career decisions [18,20]. However, in a collaborative scientific environment in which researchers combine their knowledge and contribute to multi-author papers, crediting the authors fairly becomes a challenging task that needs to be tackled [5,15,21]. Multiple studies emphasize the role of collaboration specifically with highly cited scholars, as it benefits early career researchers to gain experience and improve their careers [7,9]. This opinion is also shared among early career researchers themselves [6,20]. Nonetheless, different opinions exist when it comes to citations and collaborative papers. A study shows that an increase in the number of co-authors has a definite impact on productivity in terms of the number of papers published [16], but this does not always mean more citations [2,17]. However, a contradicting result indicates that co-authored publications receive more citations because collaboration improves the transfer and synthesis of knowledge [1]. Noteworthy, we found that the assessment metrics reported in such studies are the same for all researchers, albeit their expertise or academic age. Academic age is an important characteristic that we have investigated more deeply in recent research [3–6]. Yet, the impact of ignoring such characteristics when utilizing metrics or the correlations between these characteristics and the citation count is unknown.

3   Methodology

We performed a retrospective study in which we examined a dataset extracted from dblp based on our RQs. Note that we studied papers published at conferences, because computer science focuses more on conferences than journals [11]. Namely, we examined the research tracks of three major software-engineering conferences (ASE, 1991; ESEC/FSE, 1987; ICSE, 1976) and one software-related conference (JCDL, 2001). We gathered all papers since the first edition (years in previous hyphens) of each conference until 2020 by crawling paper and author data from dblp using Python scripts. Note that each author has a website on dblp that acts as an identifier to distinguish authors with the same name. For validation, we compared the data manually against the official data from the ACM.[2]

---

[2] https://dl.acm.org/.

If we could not clearly identify research-track papers due to missing data, especially for older conferences, we used a proxy by excluding papers with fewer than seven pages. In Table 1, we summarize the number of unique authors and papers for all four conferences. Since dblp does not provide citation counts, we fetched this data from Scopus—a permissive citation database by Elsevier.[3] Note that the total number of unique authors (8,730) is not the sum of the last column, since we counted each author only once across all conferences. For a more robust analysis, we used a subset of our dataset comprising highly-cited papers only (≥ 25 citations) and papers with a publishing year until 2010. Furthermore, we divided the resulting dataset (808 papers) into the following subsets: (i) PRE-2000 (114); (ii) POST-2000 (694); and (iii) PRE- and POST-2000 combined (808). We used regression analysis and in-depth data exploration via Python and KNIME [8] to analyze our data.

Academic age is the number of years an author has actively published until a particular paper, and must be calculated individually for each researcher based on a paper's publication year and the author's first paper's publication year (not restricted to the four conferences). For the *current academic age*, we replace the paper publication year with the author's last paper publication year:

$$Age_{academic} = Year_{paper} - Year_{firstPaper} + 1 \qquad (1)$$

To distinguish researchers based on their academic age, we classified them as: *Juniors* (academic age ≤ 3) have up to three years of academic experience and only recently started working in research [18]. For *mid-level* researchers ($3 < $ academic age ≤ 15), we used the upper limit of 15, since we identified it as the "Golden Age" of software-engineering researchers [4]. Lastly, we labeled researchers with an academic age above 15 years as *seniors* (academic age > 15).

4 RQ_1: Number of Authors and Citations

First, we investigated whether more authors contributing to a paper impacts the citation count of that paper. This direction is inspired by research on public health indicating that the number of citations decreases as the number of authors increases [2]. Using qualitative data analysis, we checked for connections between the *number of authors* and the *citation count* across all three datasets. For all three, we found that most papers have been written by a team of two, three, or four authors. The paper with the highest number of citations (more than 1,000) was authored by three researchers. Moreover, we observe that the number of citations does not increase with the number of authors. So, we conclude that having more authors seems to have no bearing on citations, despite more authors likely increasing the visibility and dissemination of the paper—since it is exposed to more networks and personal contacts While we require further research in this direction, it seems that other factors like the topic of the paper and its quality or the author's reputation and academic age may be more important [18, 20].

---

[3] https://www.scopus.com.

Table 2. Coefficients and Statistics.

data	variable	coefficient	std. error	p-values	R^2	adjusted R^2
PRE-2000	Current author age	0.398	0.845	0.637	0.005	−0.004
	Academic age	−0.456	1.557	0.769	0.005	−0.004
POST-2000	Current author age	1.507	0.445	0.001	0.005	0.004
	Academic age	−2.028	0.592	0.001	0.005	0.004
PRE-POST	Current author age	0.863	0.357	0.016	0.002	0.001
	Academic age	−1.235	0.502	0.014	0.002	0.001

5 RQ_2: Academic Age and Citations

Regarding the age of a paper's authors, we investigated the **null hypothesis:** "The authors' ages (current author age, academic age) do not impact the citation count." For this purpose, we first used statistical inference (regression modeling) to determine what kind of relationship exists between the dependent *citation count* and the independent variables *current author age* as well as *academic age* [13]. The null hypothesis generally rejects the theory that independent variables do not impact the result, while the alternate hypothesis is precisely the opposite. In Table 2, we can see the values for the coefficients for the *current author age* and *academic age*. For the **PRE-2000** dataset, we see positive coefficients for the *current author age*, which means that a positive effect on the citation count exists. The *academic age* has a negative coefficient, which means that the citation count decreases as the academic age increases. However, the academic age has a higher error rate than the current author's age. Seeing the significance values, we cannot make a strong inference from these findings, since the values suggest that the dataset is too small to draw any conclusions. R-squared or R^2 is a metric that measures the proportion of the dependent variable's variance that the independent variables account for collectively. According to its value, only 0.5% of citation-count fluctuations can be attributed to our dependent variables. Adjusted-R^2 is a more accurate version of R^2. The R^2 value increases as we add the independent variables, but the adjusted-R^2 value increases only when the independent variable strongly influences the dependent variable. A negative value signifies that the impact of the independent variables is very low on the dependent variable for this dataset, at the least.

In the two other datasets, we had more data. Interestingly, we found that the explanatory variables *current author age* and *academic age* influenced the citation count. The former positively, and the latter negatively. The p-values are less than the significance level of 0.05. Thus, we could partly reject the null hypothesis, for one variable, which eventually means our alternative hypothesis partly holds in this scenario. So, the age features seem to impact the citation count. The R^2, and adjusted-R^2 values are positive, because the explanatory variable impact the response variable.

To further explore the data, we compared the three categories of researchers as illustrated in Fig. 1. According to (a), the seniors' percentage surpasses other researchers with a gradual increase for juniors. In (b), we can see that seniors comprise the highest percentage of first authors in multi-authored papers. After investigating our datasets deeply, we found that juniors are on average third authors, whereas mid-levels and seniors are on average second authors. Via (c), we mainly checked how many papers researchers have written without collaboration across different groups (e.g., seniors with juniors) We can see that for **PRE-2000** no paper was authored exclusively by one or more junior researchers, whereas senior researchers wrote 57 papers alone, compared to one paper written by mid-level researchers only. Moving to **POST-2000**, again none of the junior researchers wrote a publication alone. Mid-level researchers published 11 single-author papers, while seniors wrote 250 papers. Consequently, in the **PRE and POST-2000** dataset, there are also no papers written solely by juniors. These insights suggest that for a paper to be cited frequently, it must have a contribution from a senior researcher.

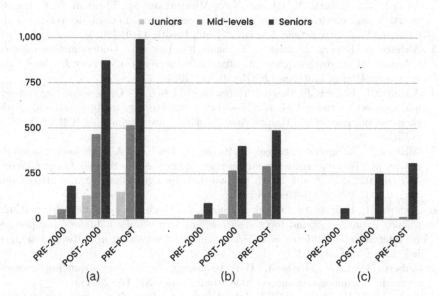

Fig. 1. In-depth data exploration. (a): Researchers contributing to papers with ≥ 25 citations; (b): Papers with $\geq$ citations & first author from a specific group; (c): Papers with citations ≥ 25 & single-authored by a specific group.

6   Conclusion

In this paper, we have reported an initial analysis of the relationship between citation count and two features (number of researchers contributing and their academic age) using data of 808 highly-cited papers from the software-engineering community. Overall, the results indicate that the number of authors contributing does not relate to a paper being cited highly, but that the current age of authors is an influential factor. We also found that 98% of these highly-cited papers had a contribution from at least one senior researcher with around 60% as first authors and no paper written solely by a junior researchers. Therefore, our results indicate that comparing two groups of researchers based on citation-related indicators is unfair because it is highly influenced by the *age* factor. Consequently, we believe that researchers should be compared based on their actual contribution and there is a need for a consistent framework with which the contribution of every researcher can be determined. The results also emphasize the role of collaboration in helping early-career researchers.

References

1. Adams, J.: Collaborations: the rise of research networks. Nature **490** (2012)
2. Ahmed, A., Mastura, A., Ghafar, N.A., Muhammad, M., Ebrahim, N.A.: Impact of article page count and number of authors on citations in disability related fields: a systematic review article. Iranian J. Publ. Health **45**(9) (2016)
3. Alchokr, R., Krüger, J., Shakeel, Y., Saake, G., Leich, T.: Understanding the contributions of junior researchers at software-engineering conferences. In: Joint Conference on Digital Libraries (JCDL). IEEE (2021)
4. Alchokr, R., Krüger, J., Shakeel, Y., Saake, G., Leich, T.: On academic age aspects and discovering the golden age in software engineering. In: International Workshop on Cooperative and Human Aspects of Software Engineering (CHASE). ACM (2022)
5. Alchokr, R., Krüger, J., Shakeel, Y., Saake, G., Leich, T.: A closer look into collaborative publishing at software-engineering conferences. In: Silvello, G., et al. (eds.) - TPDL 2022. LNCS, vol. 13541, pp. 395–402. Springer, Cham (2022). https://doi.org/10.1007/978-3-031-16802-4_38
6. Alchokr, R., Krüger, J., Shakeel, Y., Saake, G., Leich, T.: Peer-reviewing and submission dynamics around top software-engineering venues: a Juniors' perspective. In: International Conference on Evaluation and Assessment in Software Engineering (EASE). ACM (2022)
7. Aubert Bonn, N., Pinxten, W.: Advancing science or advancing careers? researchers' opinions on success indicators. PLoS ONE **16** (2021)
8. Berthold, M.R., et al.: KNIME: the Konstanz information miner. In: Preisach, C., Burkhardt, H., Schmidt-Thieme, L., Decker, R. (eds.) Data Analysis, Machine Learning and Applications. Studies in Classification, Data Analysis, and Knowledge Organization, Springer, Heidelberg (2008). https://doi.org/10.1007/978-3-540-78246-9_38
9. van den Besselaar, P., Sandström, U.: Measuring researcher independence using bibliometric data: a proposal for a new performance indicator. PLoS ONE **14** (2019)
10. Bukvova, H.: Studying research collaboration: a literature review. All Sprouts Content (2010)
11. Chen, J., Konstan, J.A.: Conference paper selectivity and impact. Commun. ACM **53**(6) (2010)

12. Egghe, L.: An improvement of the h-index: the g-index. ISSI Newsl. **2**(1) (2006)
13. Freedman, D.A.: Statistical Models: Theory and Practice. Cambridge University Press (2009)
14. Hirsch, J.E.: An index to quantify an individual's scientific research output. Proc. Natl. Acad. Sci. **102**(46) (2005)
15. Katz, J.S., Martin, B.R.: What is research collaboration? Res. Policy **26**(1) (1997)
16. Lee, S., Bozeman, B.: The impact of research collaboration on scientific productivity. Soc. Stud. Sci. **35**(5) (2005)
17. Levitt, J., Thelwall, M.: Long term productivity and collaboration in information science. Scientometrics **108** (2016)
18. Li, W., Aste, T., Caccioli, F., Livan, G.: Early coauthorship with top scientists predicts success in academic careers. Nat. Commun. **10**(1) (2019)
19. Melin, G.: Pragmatism and self-organization: research collaboration on the individual level. Res. Policy **29**(1) (2000)
20. Nicholas, D., et al.: Early career researchers' quest for reputation in the digital age. J. Scholar. Publish. **49** (2018)
21. Qi, M., Zeng, A., Li, M., Fan, Y., Di, Z.: Standing on the shoulders of giants: the effect of outstanding scientists on young collaborators' careers. Scientometrics **111** (2017)
22. Sauermann, H., Haeussler, C.: Authorship and contribution disclosures. Sci. Adv. **3**(11) (2017)
23. Shakeel, Y., Alchokr, R., Krüger, J., Leich, T., Saake, G.: Are altmetrics useful for assessing scientific impact? A survey. In: International Conference on Management of Digital EcoSystems (MEDES). ACM (2022)
24. Shakeel, Y., Alchokr, R., Krüger, J., Saake, G., Leich, T.: Altmetrics and citation counts: an empirical analysis of the computer science domain. In: Joint Conference on Digital Libraries (JCDL). IEEE (2022)
25. Shakeel, Y., Alchokr, R., Krüger, J., Saake, G., Leich, T.: Are altmetrics proxies or complements to citations for assessing impact in computer science? In: Joint Conference on Digital Libraries (JCDL). IEEE (2022)
26. Sidiropoulos, A., Katsaros, D., Manolopoulos, Y.: Generalized hirsch h-index for disclosing latent facts in citation networks. Scientometrics **72** (2007)
27. Wu, Q.: The w-index: a significant improvement of the h-index. arXiv preprint arXiv:0805.4650 (2008)

Discovering Science

On Retraction Cascade? Citation Intention Analysis as a Quality Control Mechanism in Digital Libraries

Muhammad Usman(✉) ⓘ and Wolf-Tilo Balke ⓘ

Institute for Information Systems, TU Braunschweig, Braunschweig, Germany
{usman,balke}@ifis.cs.tu-bs.de

Abstract. The amount of information in digital libraries (DLs) has been experiencing rapid growth. With the intense competition for research breakthroughs, researchers often intentionally or unintentionally fail to adhere to scientific standards, leading to the retraction of scientific articles. When a paper gets retracted, all its citing articles have to be verified to ensure the overall correctness of the information in digital libraries. Since this subjective verification is extremely time and resource-consuming, we propose a triage process that focuses on papers that imply a dependence on retracted articles, thus requiring further reevaluation. This paper seeks to establish a systematic approach for identifying and scrutinizing scholarly works that draw upon retracted work by direct citations, thus emphasizing the importance of further evaluation within the scholarly discourse. Firstly, we categorized and identified the intention in the citation context using verbs with predicative complements and cue phrases. Secondly, we classified the citation intentions of the retracted articles into dependent (if the citing paper is based on or incorporates part of the cited retracted work) and non-dependent (if the citing article discusses, criticizes, or negates the cited work). Finally, we compared the existing state-of-the-art literature and found that our proposed triage process can aid in ensuring the integrity of scientific literature, thereby enhancing its quality.

Keywords: Retraction Analysis · Citation Intention · Digital Libraries

1 Introduction

Building new research results upon existing work is a central pillar of scientific progress. The existing quality control peer-review process serves as a solid and (to some degree) accepted foundation for developing new ideas. Moreover, it serves as a benchmark to assess some new ideas' plausibility and possible benefits, then allows discussing, reproducing, expanding, or challenging previous results, but also to contrast new ideas against the current state of the art. Supporting this discourse according to the FAIR principles[1] is a central responsibility for modern digital libraries. Here digital libraries,

---

[1] While the FAIR principles were originally designed for scientific data management and stewardship, their adaptation to scientific publications is quite straightforward, see FAIR Principles - GO FAIR (go-fair.org).

on the one hand, act as classical knowledge providers to make scientific results findable and accessible. On the other hand, they also have to actively ensure that publications can quickly and safely be used and are bound to offer conflicting, inconsistent, and sometimes even contradictory content due to comprehensively representing scientific discourse. Yet over time, they will provide a rich and commonly accepted body of new insights building on and citing the original research.

Due to a growing number of instances, processes for quality control in digital libraries also need to reflect on how to deal with publications that suffer from scientific misconduct, e.g., plagiarism, fabrication, or falsification [1]. The retractions of publications are not caused by differing opinions, experimental results, or theories but by either an intention to deceive or at least gross negligence of scientific standards. The governance of the retraction process is currently limited to alerting the scientific community when some previously published article has been found to include either explicit misconduct, such as deliberately misleading claims or fabricated data, or other serious errors that render a study's results and conclusions unreliable or irreproducible. Indeed, the number of retracted articles is continuously increasing across fields. According to *Retraction Watch* (RW), the number of retracted studies increased by 800% between 2010 and 2020 compared to before 2010. As of April 2023, the *RW* database[2] lists over 43,000 retractions, including the reasons for these retractions.

However, what should a governance structure for handling retractions within a concise digital library need to consider? A retraction does not only affect the retracted paper but may also affect all papers citing the original research in the worst case, leading to a cascade of retractions. This paper focuses on the triage process to screen out the studies that need reconsideration because their scientific argument depends on the referenced retracted article. We conducted our experiments on over 1000 citing papers of retracted articles. Our experimental findings assist in determining the papers that are partially or entirely dependent on a cited retracted work, i.e., which need to be reevaluated to ensure whether the retraction of a cited paper does not change the findings of citing work.

2   Related Work

Retraction is a prolonged process requiring extensive discussion and investigation to raise serious concerns [2]. The objective of a retraction is to discredit the alleged article and alert the scientific community about its validity. In related work, we focus on citation intention analysis and citation behavior of retracted articles.

2.1   Citation Intention Analysis

A citation context is a concise summary of the concept described in the respective cited reference, consisting of one or multiple contiguous sentences. It provides evidence from scientific literature to support, explain, or build a hypothesis [3]. However, citations of the scientific article are of unequal importance depending on the intention of the citation [4]. The citation analysis offers insight into citations' qualitative and quantitative behavior.

---

[2] Retraction Watch Database (retractiondatabase.org).

More than 150 types of citation intention classes exist in the literature [8], and several studies have investigated citation intentions, e.g., [6, 7].

Jiang et al. performed citation intention analysis and made an intriguing observation. They found that the models with the best overall performance were not the best in per-class performance [9]. This suggests that citation intention classification remains a challenging task that requires further exploration and development of more specialized classification for individual categories. Te et al. (2022) investigated the specialized categories of citation intention (critical and non-critical), which is crucial for identifying potential errors and encouraging self-correction of scientific findings [10]. More recent works categorize the intention of citations as important, non-important [11, 12], and influential, non-influential [13]. Numerous ontologies are available to classify the intent of the citation, including FaBiO or CiTO [14]. The CiTO classifies citation intention into 41 empirical categories. However, if we had perfect ontology annotation of citation context, would that solve to cascade citations of retracted articles?

2.2 Citation Behavior of Retracted Articles

The period from publication to retraction takes up to three years on average. During this period and even after the retraction, the citations of retracted articles continued to increase [18]. Of course, it is permissible to cite a retracted article, provided the reader is made aware of the retraction. Yet, several authors have raised concerns about the frequent use of retracted articles without referencing the retraction notice [19].

Research on the citation behavior of retracted articles focused on quantitative aspects, such as citation growth and alt-metrics [20]. In 2021, Heibi and Peroni performed a citation analysis of Wakefield's retracted work [21], claiming an (in reality non-existent) association between vaccinations and autism [22]. They found that Wakefield's citations continued to increase after retraction, but most citations are for general discussions. Heibi and Peroni recently performed quantitative and qualitative analyses on the citations of retracted articles in humanities [23]. They observed no decline in the total number of citations following the retraction. However, a few citations' contexts expressed a negative sentiment. In addition, Heibi and Peroni observed that the health sciences have a higher level of awareness about citing a retracted publication than the humanities and social sciences.

In 2020, Fu and Schneider introduced a system to determine if an article's conclusion is based on cited work [24, 25]. Their approach showcased promising results; however, the system requires substantial contributions from human experts, making the process arduous. For instance, in their case study on citing non-reproducible code, the researchers formulated specific questions to assess the impact on the citing article. Despite its novelty, the subjective mining of arguments and the need for substantial input from experts deterred the implementation of the system. In contrast, this paper proposes a novel and automated approach to categorizing articles by identifying the dependency between citing and cited retracted articles.

3 Methodology

Identifying and flagging papers that reference and, to some degree, depending on claims from retracted articles remain a persistent challenge for state-of-the-art digital libraries. To address this, we primarily focused on the following research question: *To what extent can we reliably distinguish between the citations of the retracted articles that depend on it and those that do not?* Our process involves collecting, annotating citations, and developing a classification model to predict which articles require reevaluation (see Fig. 1).

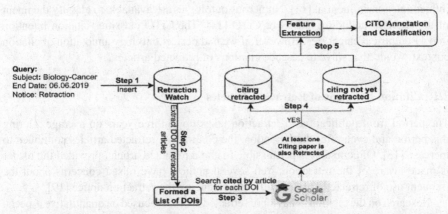

Fig. 1. We started with a collection of citations of retracted articles, identified the instances where both citing and cited articles are retracted, and then extracted their features. Secondly, we classified the citations based on the behavior of the citations into dependent and non-dependent.

3.1 Dataset Selection

To collect papers that cite the retracted articles, we first used *Retraction Watch*[3], a free, comprehensive online database, to form a list of retracted articles. We considered the retracted articles from the Biology-Cancer domain as a preliminary study. We then collected citing papers of retracted articles using *Google Scholar*. The existing datasets on citations of retracted articles suffer from limitations, such as incomplete coverage of all citations, potential biases resulting from analyzing different subsets of citing articles, and reliance on individual high-profile retraction case studies [24–27]. Given these limitations, considering various retraction cases, considering all their citations is of utmost importance to maintain a fair investigation.

Our selection process was rigorous and explicit. Our search endeavors yielded intriguing observations, revealing a recurring phenomenon wherein articles citing retracted publications undergo subsequent retractions. These compelling instances lend

---

[3] Retraction Watch Database (retractiondatabase.org).

substantial credence to our underlying hypothesis, highlighting the necessity for reassessment when referencing articles associated with retraction. Therefore, after careful consideration, we sought out retracted articles, ensuring that each article contained at least one instance where the citing article was also retracted. Given this condition, we found 28 articles and considered all of their subsequent, over 1000 citing articles, as a preliminary investigation. We extracted the title, authors, informed citation (If an author cited the retraction notice also or at least included the word "Retract", "Retraction" "Retracted" in reference or citation text), self-citations, citation context (one sentence before and after citation sentence), frequency of citation, citation section, journal, publication year, and Digital Object Identifier (DOI) for all articles.

3.2 Taxonomy Building

The citation intentions' definition often overlaps and has diffuse meaning. Furthermore, the annotator's mental models create a proliferation of competing perspectives that may conflict [16]. There are several ontologies, but we opted for the CiTO developed by SPAR because it describes a citation's nature *factually* and *rhetorically*. No other OWL ontology provides as extensive a set of citation properties as CiTO [15]. However, not all properties are equally adaptable. Some categories lead to overlapping meanings, and projects often use fragments of the CiTO distinctive properties, e.g., Journal of Cheminformatics [17]. To reduce the risk of getting the contradictory annotation, we categorize CiTO properties into five groups that cover all possible distinct intentions of referencing a scientific article; *"inconsistent"*, *"discuss"*, *"consistent"*, *"use material"*, and *"build-upon"* based on their given CiTO definition (see Table 1). For instance, we found that the CiTO functions of *"discusses"* and *"describes"* both relate to explaining the cited work, while *"confirms"* and *"cites as evidence"* are associated with showing similarities with the cited work. Therefore, by using rhetorical definitions, we grouped *"discusses"* or *"describes"* into *"discuss"* and *"confirms"* or *"cites as evidence"* into *"consistent"*. We then divide the defined five groups into *"dependent"* and *"non-dependent"* based on the impact each

Table 1. Categorization of CiTO-Properties

Inconsistent	Discuss	Consistent	Use Material	Build-upon
deride ridicule refutes critiques disagree disputes corrects retracts	parodies, qualifies, credit, discusses, describes, reviews, Information, quotation, Related, metadata, authority, Assertion, replies, background,recommended documents, data source, compiles, excerpt from, links to, plagiarizes, solution, agrees with	obtain support cites as evidence, speculates on, confirms	uses { conclusions, data, method}	updates, extend

category can have on the citing article (see Table 2). On the one hand, articles that incorporate a part of a retracted work demonstrate dependence, and those that show consistencies with an unreliable source of information also require a close look. On the other hand, articles discussing, negating, contrasting, or criticizing the retracted work in citation context show the non-dependence, which is acceptable and does not harm scientific literature. The generalized decision rules for determining the dependency in the citation context are shown in Table 3.

Table 2. Definition and Example of Dependent and Non-Dependent Categorize

Intent Category and Definition			Example
Non-Dependent	Inconsistent Discuss	The citation provides context for the problem, concept, method, topic, and field relevance or credits, discusses, recommends, critiques, refutes, or disagrees with the work	It was found that supplementation with curcumin, a dominant component of Indian spice, could upregulate miRNA-200 and downregulate miRNA-21 [58]
Dependent	Consistent Use Material Build upon	The citation shows consistencies and similarities in results/ conclusion with the cited work or uses its method, data, or conclusion to build on it	The MTT assay was performed as described previously [19] These findings are in agreement with our observation that FoxM1 upregulates MMP-2 and MMP-9 in U2OS osteosarcoma cells and support the notion that MMP-2 and MMP-9 play a role in FoxM1-dependent tumor invasion [50]

Table 3. The generalized rules for determining the dependency of citation context

Analyze	Action
Does the citation context incorporate a part of retracted work?	Yes: Citation context is dependent No: Proceed to the next question
Does the citation context show consistency with the finding of retracted work?	Yes: Citation context is dependent No: proceed to the next question
Does the citation context discuss the retracted work?	Yes: Citation context is non-dependent No: Further assessment may be required

3.3 Citation Intention Annotation

To identify the dependency in the citation context, we utilized Stanford linguist Levin's instructions for *verbs with predicative complements* [29]. Due to their grammatical complementarity, these verbs are more naturally classified than nouns or prepositional phrases [30]. We extracted the verbs from the citation context with the help of the Stanford NLP toolkit, which implies dependency. However, the extracted verbs can also be part of the citation context with a non-dependency citation intent, where they are incorporated for some other purpose instead of referring to dependency on retracted work. Two university graduates with expertise in semantics, document analysis, and text classification conducted the annotation process. They observed verbs with predictive complements and identified cue phrases that may indicate the presence of dependency in the citation context. We also formed a list of example cue phrases from our dataset, indicating the dependency on cited work (see Table 4).

Table 4. The table shows the Verbs with Predicative Complements and Cue phrases that can imply dependency in the citation context.

Verbs	Cue Phrases
Incorporate, consider, consist, derive, depend, adopt, employ, produce, extend, confirm, prove, apply, induce, use, compare, add, suggest, base, support, relate, verify, ensure, promote, facilitate, indicate, accept, establish, reveal, obtain, agree, influence, similar, favor, yield, illustrate, encourage, compliment, convince, validate, evidence, evolve, inspire, emphasize, utilize	In line with [R], Consistent with [R], supported by a recent report [R], In agreement with [R], experiments performed as [R], Similar to [R] Procedures described in [R] Substantiated by recent evidence [R], Aligned with the findings in [R],

To further mitigate the likelihood of mistakes in the annotation process, we collaborated with an English language expert to address potential linguistic ambiguities. This collaborative effort enabled us to establish a 0.87 inter-agreement score. We discovered that most citations to retracted articles focused on discussing the referenced article, compared to only 11% employing the content of referenced article materialistically. We now perform statistical analysis and build a robust classifier to effectively discern the citations with dependency on the cited retracted article.

3.4 Citation Patterns of Retracted Articles

The retraction of scientific articles is a critical problem, as it can harm scientific progress and damage the reputation of the scientific community. Therefore, it is essential to understand how often retracted articles are cited, how researchers cite, and whether or not authors know about the retraction. Through an analysis of the various correlations outlined below that we observed in our study, it is possible to gain insights into how the scientific community responds to the issue of retracted articles. This can aid in identifying areas where additional efforts are required to enhance awareness and prevent the dissemination of misinformation.

Pre- and Post-Retraction Citations: Modern digital libraries such as Google Scholar and PubMed emphasize retracted studies to inform readers about the credibility concerns present in literature. Despite this, the citations of retracted articles continued to rise. However, we observed that, after some time, the citations dropped sharply; only 17% came in the five years following the retraction, compared to 83% in the previous five years.

Informed Citation of Retracted Articles: It is acceptable to cite retracted work, provided the author is aware of the retraction. It is recommended to reference both the original publication and the retraction notice, as they offer digital object identifiers (DOIs). Despite the considerable efforts made by DLs to bring attention to the retraction, only 1% of the references after the retraction contained the term "retracted" within the reference. This finding implies that the author's lack of awareness regarding the retraction could be attributed to either negligence or insufficient dissemination of the retraction notice. This required the scientific community's attention to take further steps to prevent the propagation of misinformation.

Pre- and Post-Retraction Dependent Citations: Researchers cite an article in good faith in the pre-retraction period, as they are not aware of the retraction at that time. However, in post-retraction time, the lack of awareness and ignorance of authors about the retraction caused no significant difference in the number of dependent instances after the retraction. We found that 15% and 13% of citations in pre- and post-retraction times are dependent, respectively. Having dependent citations in pre-retraction time can be considered an honest mistake, but only cases of gross negligence can result in such an outcome during the period following retraction.

Dependent Self-Citations: It is common practice for scientists to do self-citations to expand their research. However, it could have severe consequences if the referenced literature is subsequently retracted. It was observed that a notable proportion of dependent citations consist of self-citations, and all of the self-citations dependent on the original work are present in the pre-retraction phase and are in good faith, in contrast to only one in the post-retraction phase. It raised concerns about the self-citations of retracted articles and required intention from the scientific community to evaluate such cases critically.

Frequency of Citation: The "frequency of citation," or the number of times a specific article is referred to within the body of a citing article, is considered a strength of the correlation between the citing and cited articles. We observed that 40% of the time, papers containing potentially dependent citations referred to a retracted article more than once.

4   Experimental Settings and Result

We utilized a dataset of citations manually extracted from scientific articles for experiments. The citation text contains markups to references in the bibliography, such as [12], (12), (Author et al.), which is not helpful for the classifiers that we aim to design to identify dependencies in text. To remove citation references from the text, we employ a regular expression (\([^\)]*,[^\)]*\)). A few citation references also required manual omission, as there are different styles for referring to articles in the text, for example, a superscript type of reference. We used the NLTK library for preprocessing data for machine learning classifiers. The NLTK library contains "no", "nor", and "not" words as stop words, which are useful in the citation context, so we have excluded such words from the list that can carry the semantic meanings. In addition, to deal with words with multiple terms, we used bigram vectorization for classification with conventional machine learning algorithms. We conducted experiments using 10-fold cross-validation, with an 80–20 split for training and testing. We conducted experiments using 10-fold cross-validation. Our dataset contains imbalanced classes, so we focused on weighted precision, recall, and F1 scores as our evaluation metrics. Weighted precision, recall, and F1-score are vital evaluation metrics for imbalanced datasets. Weighted precision measures the accuracy of positive predictions, and Weighted recall gauges the model's ability to capture actual positive instances. Weighted F1-score combines precision and recall, providing a balanced overall performance assessment. Our experiments involved the use of several machine learning classifiers, including naive Bayes, logistic regression, and support vector machine, as well as deep learning models such as Long Short-Term Memory (LSTM) [31] and Bidirectional Encoder Representations from Transformers (BERT) [32]. By using multiple models and considering various performance metrics, we were able to gain a comprehensive understanding of the effectiveness of our approach.

In the experimental setting for LSTM, we utilized the Keras tokenizer. The tokenized sequences are prerequisites for data input into the model. We designed the neural network architecture with an embedding layer, an LSTM layer with dropout regularization, and a dense layer with a sigmoid activation function. We chose the LSTM layer due to its proven suitability for processing sequential data such as text. The dropout regularization was implemented to prevent overfitting, while the dense layer used a sigmoid activation function to assign a probability score to each class. In the experimental setting for BERT, we used a pre-trained BERT-base-uncased model. The model is fine-tuned for the "dependent" and "non-dependent" categories. We used the Adam optimizer [33] with binary cross-entropy as the loss function to optimize the model's performance for LSTM and BERT. We trained the models for ten epochs to promote comprehensive learning from the data and achieve improved classification performance; by hit and trial, we found that more epochs add no value.

Our experiments revealed that deep learning models, particularly the LSTM and BERT, outperformed conventional classifiers in categorizing dependent and non-dependent instances. The LSTM achieved the highest weighted precision of 0.94, followed by BERT with 0.90 (See Table 5). The LSTM has achieved better results than a BERT model, and for a small dataset, it gets trained faster than tuning the pre-trained counterparts [34], causing a better performance than BERT. The machine learning models SVM, logistic regression, and naive Bayes also yield promising results in classifying dependent and non-dependent instances and achieved weighted precision of 0.89, 0.87, and 0.81, respectively. Given that the data is not comprehensive for training, there is room for improvement. Ambiguities in language introduce the potential for false-positive and false-negative classifications. For instance, the citation context, *"The study by Johnson*

Table 5. Classification of "Dependent" and "Non-Dependent" Citation Intention

Classifier	Weighted-Precision	Weighted-Recall	Weighted-F1-score
SVM	0.89	0.85	0.87
LR	0.87	0.81	0.84
Naïve Bayes	0.81	0.80	0.80
LSTM	0.94	0.93	0.94
BERT	0.90	0.91	0.90

et al. provided valuable insights into the topic, which were further discussed in this paper." can be interpreted as both dependent and non-dependent. This ambiguity highlights the challenge of accurately determining the dependency status of citation contexts. Enhancing the training dataset with more diverse examples and incorporating additional contextual information is vital to disambiguate such cases and improve classification performance. The supplementary material utilized in this study is available for access[4].

The implications of our findings are significant in terms of identifying articles that cite and depend on retracted articles. Our classifiers provide the ability to flag such articles, ensuring the integrity of digital libraries. This capability allows us to effectively pinpoint articles that require further scrutiny, thereby preventing the potential dissemination of unreliable information. By considering our approach, researchers and library curators can play a crucial role in maintaining the quality and trustworthiness of the literature. This, in turn, fosters an environment conducive to reliable and accurate scientific advancements.

5 Qualitative Comparison with a Manual Approach

In 2022, Addepalli et al. [25] tested a keystone framework [24] to find the dependency of citing articles on Wakefield's retracted article [21]. It was published in 1998, and after years of discussion, Wakefield's work was partially retracted in 2004 and fully retracted in 2010 [5]. According to *Retraction Watch*[5], the reasons for its retraction are *data* fabrication and *result* manipulation. We have applied our approach to the same set of citing articles for comparison as used by Addepalli et al.

In Addepalli et al.'s work [25], two annotators performed the annotation based on the flow chart. One annotator marked two instances as *dependent*, nine as *up to professional*, and the second marked two as *dependent* and seven as *up to professional*. Both marked the remaining citing papers as *independent* of Wakefield's work. However, they agreed in only one instance of *up to professional* before the discussion. This significant pre-discussion divergence, caused by the conflicting understanding of the annotation rules or a flow chart's disputed meaning, leads to different results. We identified five articles that dependently cited Wakefield's retracted article. In two of those

---

[4] https://github.com/Conferences2023/TPDL.
[5] Retraction Watch Database (retractiondatabase.org).

instances, we found an agreement with Addepalli et al. The article with dependency either cites Wakefield's work to show consistency with their result or incorporates the methodology or data. Overall, we found an agreement of above 90%, where most citing articles independently cited Wakefield's work. Table 6 compares contradicting predictions about dependency or non-dependency with the reason for our different judgments. Our approach has several benefits over the existing approach. Firstly, our approach is not limited to case studies, where an explicit argument must be defined to uncover dependency, making it highly adaptable and applicable. Secondly, we recognize citations' vital role in representing rhetorical relations and information flow in linking scientific articles within digital libraries and show how information in the articles is interconnected. Furthermore, the extension of our approach holds the potential to contribute to quality control in digital libraries significantly. By incorporating our methodology into modern digital library systems, we can introduce a layer of scrutiny to identify and stop the spread of misinformation.

Additionally, we conducted a metaphorical comparison with *Scite*[6]. It categorized the citations into *supporting*, *monitoring*, and *contrasting*. The *supporting* category represents citations with identical results. The *monitoring* encompasses citations with discussions, and the *contrasting* category includes citations that present differing opinions. During our analysis, we observed that two instances we marked as dependent were also categorized as supporting in Scite. Furthermore, one of the dependent instances from Addepalli et al.'s study is categorized as independent by our approach and monitoring by Scite. However, it is essential to note that Scite does not currently encompass all the citations available. For instance, Wakefield's article is cited in over 4000 articles listed in *Google Scholar*, whereas Scite only displays less than 2500 citations.

Table 6. Comparative Analysis of Diverging Judgments and Contributing Reason

PMID	Existing work [3]	Our Approach	Reason
12142948	up to professional	dependent	incorporate data
15622451	independent	dependent	based on
19917212	independent	dependent	consistent findings
16003130	independent	dependent	incorporate data
12773694	dependent	independent	Discussion
15526989	dependent	independent	Discussion
15031638	dependent	independent	Discussion

6 Discussion and Conclusion

Scientific articles are not stand-alone entities but are interconnected by citations. Researchers cite existing articles to make an argument for their new findings. When an article gets retracted, citing articles whose conclusion depends on it must also be

---

[6] Scite: see how research has been cited.

reconsidered. Despite increasing citations of retracted articles, modern digital libraries do not flag such cases. In this paper, we effectively analyzed and classified over 1,000 citations of retracted articles based on the intention in the citation context into dependent and non-dependent. We can infer that the reliability of findings is questioned when an article indicates the dependency on a fallacious source of information. In an ideal world, we can eliminate this problem if all citations are explicitly annotated with the intention of its citation so that when a cited paper gets retraction, its subsequent citing paper that depends on its fallacious claims also gets retraction.

Moreover, we uncovered some instances where citing and cited papers were retracted, despite the citing paper having no dependency on the retracted work. Such retraction cases are identified based on subjective evaluation from journal editors or third-party investigators. Retraction is a critical task, and the existing state of art process takes up to three years on average to retract scientific articles. This opens the discussion of how close we are to having a system capable of retracting a paper and underscores the need for a more robust retracting system. We identified four cases of citations of retracted articles based on citation intention (see Fig. 2).

	Dependent	Non- Dependent
Retracted	Case 1: 2.9%	Case 2: 6.0%
Non-Retracted Yet	Case 3: 7.7%	Case 4: 83.5%

Fig. 2. The correlation between the citation intention and the retraction

Case I: When a cited article gets retraction due to errors or misconduct, which raises questions about the accuracy and reliability of the citing paper. In such cases, it is essential to consider the impact of these errors on the citing paper. Depending on the extent to which the citing paper depends on the retracted work, it may be necessary to retract the citing paper as well, to prevent the spread of misinformation. Case 4: Retraction is a procedure carried out by publishers and editors to indicate that an article is invalid due to misconduct or errors that undermine the credibility of the findings. There is no harm in citing retracted work if the researcher is aware of its retraction status and employs it solely for background information or to discuss the scientific problem at hand. It is imperative to acknowledge that retracted literature can impede scientific progress and compromise the integrity of subsequent research. However, it remains plausible that the aforementioned article gets retracted due to potential misrepresentation of its methodology, data, or results based on an arbitrary investigation, as discussed in [28] (Case 2). We identified instances to triage the process to screen out the studies that implied dependency on cited retracted articles that are not retracted yet (Case 3). Therefore, we must thoroughly investigate such instances before concluding about the subsequent retraction.

7 Limitation and Future Work

Although our study provides valuable insights for citations of retracted articles, we identified a potential shortcoming in our current approach. Our current approach relied on explicit indicators in the citation context that implied dependency on the cited work. It can be problematic when the paper implicitly implies dependence, which could result in papers depending on retracted work without any indication in the citation context being overlooked. In future work, we will explore more sophisticated methods for identifying implicit indicators and consider the full text to categorize articles that require reevaluation. Moreover, recognizing the need for a more comprehensive understanding of retractions in science, we plan to expand our scope and aim to formulate a comprehensive dataset and train language models to use it across fields to identify articles with dependencies on unreliable sources of information.

Acknowledgments. Supported by the Deutsche Forschungsgemeinschaft (DFG, German Research Foundation): PubPharm – the Specialized Information Service for Pharmacy (Gepris 267140244).

References

1. Resnik, D.B.: From baltimore to bell labs: reflections on two decades of debate about scientific misconduct. Account Res. **10**, 123–135 (2003). https://doi.org/10.1080/08989620300508
2. Bar-Ilan, J., Halevi, G.: Temporal characteristics of retracted articles. Scientometrics **116**(3), 1771–1783 (2018). https://doi.org/10.1007/s11192-018-2802-y
3. Hernández-Alvarez, M., Gomez, J.M.: Survey about citation context analysis: tasks, techniques, and resources. Nat. Lang. Eng. **22**(3), 327–349 (2016). https://doi.org/10.1017/S1351324915000388
4. Aljohani, N.R., Fayoumi, A., Hassan, S.U.: An in-text citation classification predictive model for a scholarly search system. Scientometrics **126**(7), 5509–5529 (2021). https://doi.org/10.1007/s11192-021-03986-z
5. The Editors of The Lancet Retraction—Ileal-Lymphoid-Nodular Hyperplasia, Non-Specific Colitis, and Pervasive Developmental Disorder in Children. Lancet **375**, 445 (2010). https://doi.org/10.1016/S0140-6736(10)60175-4
6. Cohan, A., Ammar, W., van Zuylen, M., Cady, F.: Structural scaffolds for citation intent classification in scientific publications. In: Proceedings of NAACL-HLT, pp. 3586–3596 (2019). https://doi.org/10.18653/v1/N19-1361
7. Bakhti, K., Niu, Z., Yousif, A., Nyamawe, A.S.: Citation function classification based on ontologies and convolutional neural networks. In: Learning Technology for Education Challenges: 7th International Workshop, LTEC 2018, Žilina, Slovakia, August 6–10, 2018, Proceedings 7, pp. 105–115. Springer International Publishing (2018). https://doi.org/10.1007/978-3-319-95522-3_10
8. Ihsan, I., Qadir, M.A.: CCRO: citation's context & reasons ontology. IEEE Access **7**, 30423–30436 (2019). https://doi.org/10.1109/ACCESS.2019.2903450
9. Jiang, X., Cai, C., Fan, W., Liu, T., Chen, J.: Contextualised modelling for effective citation function classification. In: Proceedings of the 2022 6th International Conference on Natural Language Processing and Information Retrieval, pp. 93-103 (2022). https://doi.org/10.1145/3582768.3582769
10. Te, S., Barhoumi, A., Lentschat, M., Bordignon, F., Labbé, C., Portet, F.: Citation context classification: critical vs. non-critical. In: Proceedings of the Third Workshop on Scholarly Document Processing, pp. 49–53 (2022)
11. Valenzuela, M., Ha, V., Etzioni, O.: Identifying meaningful citations. In: AAAI Workshop: Scholarly Big Data, vol. 15, p. 13 (2015)

12. Wang, M., Zhang, J., Jiao, S., Zhang, X., Zhu, N., Chen, G.: Important citation identification by exploiting the syntactic and contextual information of citations. Scientometrics **125**, 2109–2129 (2020). https://doi.org/10.1007/s11192-020-03677-1

13. Zhu, X., Turney, P., Lemire, D., Vellino, A.: Measuring academic influence: not all citations are equal. J. Assoc. Inf. Sci. Technol. **66**, 408–427 (2015). https://doi.org/10.1002/asi.23179

14. Peroni, S., Shotton, D.: FaBiO and CiTO: ontologies for describing bibliographic resources and citations. J. Web Semant. **17**, 33–43 (2012). https://doi.org/10.1016/j.websem.2012.08.001

15. Mayernik, M.S., Phillips, J., Nienhouse, E.: Linking publications and data: challenges, trends, and opportunities. D-Lib Mag. **22**(5/6), 11 (2016). https://doi.org/10.1045/may2016-mayernik

16. Ciancarini, P., Iorio, A.D., Nuzzolese, A.G., Peroni, S., Vitali, F.: Evaluating citation functions in CiTO: cognitive issues. In: European Semantic Web Conference, pp. 580–594. Springer, Cham (2014). https://doi.org/10.1007/978-3-319-07443-6_39

17. Willighagen, E.: Two years of explicit CiTO annotations. J. Cheminformatics **15**(1), 14 (2023). https://doi.org/10.1186/s13321-023-00683-2

18. Hsiao, T.-K., Schneider, J.: Continued use of retracted papers: temporal trends in citations and (lack of) awareness of retractions shown in citation contexts in biomedicine. Quant. Sci. Stud. **2**, 1144–1169 (2021). https://doi.org/10.1162/qss_a_00155

19. Bar-Ilan, J., Halevi, G.: Post retraction citations in context: a case study—Scientometrics **113**(1), 547–565 (2017). https://doi.org/10.1007/s11192-017-2242-0

20. Feng, L., Yuan, J., Yang, L.: An observation framework for retracted publications in multiple dimensions. Scientometrics **125**, 1445–1457 (2020). https://doi.org/10.1007/s11192-020-03702-3

21. Wakefield, A., et al.: RETRACTED: ileal-lymphoid-nodular hyperplasia, non-specific colitis, and pervasive developmental disorder in children. Lancet **351**, 637–641 (1998). https://doi.org/10.1016/S0140-6736(97)11096-0

22. Heibi, I., Peroni, S.: A qualitative and quantitative analysis of open citations to retracted articles: the Wakefield 1998 et al.'s case. Scientometrics **126**(10), 8433–8470 (2021). https://doi.org/10.1007/s11192-021-04097-5

23. Heibi, I., Peroni, S.: A quantitative and qualitative open citation analysis of retracted articles in the humanities Quant. Sci. Stud. 1–46 (2022).https://doi.org/10.1162/qss_a_00222

24. Fu, Y., Schneider, J.: Towards knowledge maintenance in scientific digital libraries with the keystone framework. In: Proceedings of the ACM/IEEE Joint Conference on Digital Libraries in 2020. ACM: New York, NY, USA, August 2020; pp. 217–226 (2020). https://doi.org/10.1145/3383583.3398514

25. Addepalli, A., Subin, K.A., Schneider, J.: Testing the keystone framework by analyzing positive citations to Wakefield's 1998 paper. In: International Conference on Information, pp. 79–88. Springer, Cham (2022). https://doi.org/10.1007/978-3-030-96957-8_9

26. Schneider, J., Ye, D., Hill, A.M., Whitehorn, A.S.: Continued post-retraction citation of a fraudulent clinical trial report, 11 years after it was retracted for falsifying data. Scientometrics **125**, 2877–2913 (2020). https://doi.org/10.1007/s11192-020-03631-1

27. Hsiao, T.K., Schneider, J.: Continued use of retracted papers: temporal trends in citations and (lack of) awareness of retractions shown in citation contexts in biomedicine. Quant. Sci. Stud. **2**(4), 1144–1169 (2021). https://doi.org/10.1162/qss_a_00155

28. Williams, P., Wager, E.: Exploring why and how journal editors retract articles: findings from a qualitative study. Sci. Eng. Ethics **19**(1), 1–11 (2013). https://doi.org/10.1007/s11948-011-9292-0

29. Levin, B.: English verb classes and alternations: a preliminary investigation. University of Chicago Press (1993)

30. Kipper, K., Korhonen, A., Ryant, N., Palmer, M.: A large-scale classification of English verbs. Lang. Resour. Eval. **42**, 21–40 (2008). https://doi.org/10.1007/s10579-007-9048-2
31. Sherstinsky, A.: Fundamentals of recurrent neural network (RNN) and long short-term memory (LSTM) network. Physica D **404**, 132306 (2020). https://doi.org/10.1016/j.physd.2019.132306
32. Devlin, J., Chang, M.W., Lee, K., Toutanova, K.: Bert: pre-training of deep bidirectional transformers for language understanding. arXiv preprint arXiv:1810.04805 (2018). https://doi.org/10.48550/arXiv.1810.04805
33. Zhang, Z.: Improved Adam optimizer for deep neural networks. In: 2018 IEEE/ACM 26th International Symposium on Quality of Service (IWQoS), pp. 1–2. IEEE (2018). https://doi.org/10.1109/IWQoS.2018.8624183
34. Ezen-Can, A.: A comparison of LSTM and BERT for small corpus. arXiv preprint arXiv:2009.05451 (2020). https://doi.org/10.48550/arXiv.2009.05451

Using Semi-automatic Annotation Platform to Create Corpus for Argumentative Zoning

Alaa El-Ebshihy[1,2,3]([✉]) [iD], Annisa Maulida Ningtyas[1,4] [iD], Florina Piroi[1,2] [iD],
Andreas Rauber[1] [iD], Ade Romadhony[5] [iD], Said Al Faraby[5] [iD],
and Mira Kania Sabariah[5] [iD]

[1] Technische Universität Wien, Vienna, Austria
{alaa.el-ebshihy,annisa.ningtyas,florina.piroi}@tuwien.ac.at,
rauber@ifs.tuwien.ac.at
[2] Research Studios Austria, Data Science Studio, Vienna, Austria
[3] Alexandria University, Alexandria, Egypt
[4] Universitas Gadjah Mada, Yogyakarta, Indonesia
[5] Telkom University, Bandung, Indonesia
{aderomadhony,saidalfaraby,mirakania}@telkomuniversity.ac.id

Abstract. Argumentative Zoning (AZ) is a tool to extract salient information from scientific texts for further Natural Language Processing (NLP) tasks, e.g. scientific articles summarisation. AZ defines the main rhetorical structure in scientific articles. The lack of large AZ annotated benchmark datasets along with the manual annotation complexity of scientific texts form a bottle neck in utilizing AZ for scientific NLP tasks. Aiming to solve this problem, in previous work, we presented an AZ-annotation platform that defines and uses four categories, or zones (*Claim, Method, Result, Conclusion*) that are used to label sentences in scientific articles. The platform helps to create benchmark datasets to be used with the AZ tool. In this work we look at the usability of the said platform to create/expand datasets for AZ. We present a annotation experiment, composed of two annotation rounds, selected scientific articles from the ACL anthology corpus are annotated using the platform. We compare the user annotations with a ground truth annotation and compute the inter annotation agreement. The annotations obtained in this way are used as training data for various BERT-based models to predict the zone of a given sentence from a scientific article. We compare the trained models with a model trained on a baseline AZ corpus.

Keywords: Argumentative Zoning · Annotation · Benchmark creation

1 Introduction

For any research topic, there exist various available scientific articles from conferences, journal publications etc. Usually, the abstracts of the articles do not provide enough insights about the salient information in the article. Due to this, it is usually difficult for a researcher, especially young researchers and students, to decide whether to proceed reading the full paper text or not and whether it is relevant to their own work.

Extracting salient information in scientific literature is a known challenge, and NLP techniques are becoming increasingly crucial in trying to address it. The information to be extracted is part of the main components of any research article, which are:

the research questions, hypothesis, methodology, results and conclusions. One of the approaches that are used to identify these components is *Argumentative Zoning (AZ)* [18]. AZ refers to the examination of the argumentative status of sentences in scientific articles and their assignment to specific argumentative zones. Its main goal is to collect sentences that belong to predefined categories (i.e. zones), such as "claim" or "method". AZ is useful as a tool for downstream NLP tasks; e.g. scientific article summarisation [5,7,9,12,16] and research articles theme classification [6].

Automatic AZ identification has been approached in previous work as a supervised learning problem to train a model with annotated scientific articles [1,3,14,16–18]. The bottle neck in training these algorithms is that the training data is obtained by manual annotation of scientific articles, a work that is complex and often not feasible [20] due to the technical document structure, the length of the articles, the necessity of domain expertise. Teufel et al. [18] introduced an annotation schema of seven AZ labels , which was later updated [17]. Accusto et al. [1] proposed a fine grained annotation schema with eleven categories for AZ.

Although there are ongoing efforts to create annotated corpus as training data for AZ models, the main challenge is expanding and creating an AZ corpus on complete papers, not only abstracts, and for domains other than the Computational Linguistics (CL)[1]. With this goal in sight, we proposed in previous work, a platform for the systematic annotation and, consequently, the creation of new benchmarks to be used for training AZ identification algorithms [8]. The platform uses a simplified a schema of four labels that identify the claims, methods, conclusion and results. Sentences from a scientific article are selected and labeled by a previously trained algorithm and users are asked to verify and correct the labels. In this work, we examine the feasibility of our platform in creating an annotated AZ corpus and the use of the annotated data in automatic AZ identification. More concretely:

1. we present an annotation experiment to annotate selected scientific articles by conducting two annotation rounds (online and onsite) with bachelor and master students using the AZ annotation platform.
2. we build a new AZ corpus using collected annotations from the annotation rounds in addition to using it to expand an existing AZ corpus in a previous work [1].
3. we use the constructed AZ corpora to train Bert-based models for AZ identification and compare their performance against a baseline model.

2   Related Work

Argumentative zoning (AZ) is defined as "the analysis of the argumentative status of sentences in scientific articles". The theory of AZ was formalized by Simone Teufel in her PhD thesis in 1999 [18]. There, Teufel introduced a manual annotation scheme for scientific articles, focusing on argumentative zones and rules with predefined zones (i.e. labels) to annotate 48 computational linguistic (CL) papers by categorizing each sentence into one of 7 zones: *BKG, OTH, OWN, AIM, TXT, CTR* and *BAS*. In her work, Teufel provided an approach that combined traditional hand-engineered features, meta-discourse features, and classification techniques to automatically classify sentences in

---

[1] Previous work mainly focused on CL domain.

scientific articles into argumentative zones [18]. It included the release of 80 CL hand-annotated articles, where each sentence was labeled with one of the above mentioned zones. Though the corpus is a strong gold standard, it is relatively small in size.

Later, a more fine grained schema of 17 zones was introduced, extending to the Chemistry domain [16,17]. This work was a step towards showing the applicability of the AZ theory to different domains. However, the small corpus issue is still present, with the annotation of only 30 papers from the Chemistry domain and 9 papers from the Computational Linguistics domain. Recently, deep learning methods have been used in automatic AZ identification [14], with the obvious conclusion that the AZ identification is sensitive to the type of embedding used. In addition to the CL and chemistry domains, the AZ theory was applied to other domains; e.g. biomedical, physics and biochemistry domains [10,11,13].

Argument mining is similar to AZ. Accuosto et al. [1–3] define argument mining as the automated process of identifying arguments, their components, and relationship within text. In subsequent studies, they proposed an annotation schema for identifying argumentative units and relations specifically in scientific abstract [1–3] and introduced an annotation schema that aimed to add argumentative components and relations to a small subset of 60 abstracts obtained from the SciDTB corpus [19]. Their objective was to identify the boundaries of each argumentative unit [2,3], experimenting with sentences as argumentative units [1]. As a result of this work, the authors published a manually annotated corpus of 225 CL abstracts and 285 biomedical abstracts and used it to fine-tune a BERT based model for argument mining.

Bless et al. [4] introduced an annotation tool for LaTeX documents that differs from previous approaches in identifying argumentative zones. Their tool employs scientific knowledge graphs to annotate machine-actionable metadata (i.e. zones), specifically allowing researchers to annotate their publication while writing the manuscript.

To address the challenge of creating labeled corpora for AZ identification, we presented an AZ annotation platform [8] . Inspired by previous work [1,18], we define a simplified AZ annotation schema. This schema is used to assign labels to selected sentences in scientific articles, which users can then correct or agree with, thus facilitating the annotation process.

3   Manual Annotation for AZ Corpus Creation

Aiming to create AZ corpus, we conducted an annotation task to collect sentences from selected scientific articles labelled with one of four predefined argumentative categories (i.e. zones): *Claim*, *Method*, *Result*, and *Conclusion*. We want to assure the good performance of the annotators by comparing their annotation against a ground truth and to assess the same level of understanding of annotators of the task. We did two annotation rounds with students from Telkom University[2] who were asked to annotate selected scientific articles using an AZ annotation platform [8]. The user interface of the platform in the second annotation round[3] differs slightly from the one used in the first round[4] (see

---

[2] https://telkomuniversity.ac.id/.

[3] https://riset.fanzru.dev/login.

[4] https://ir-group.ec.tuwien.ac.at/artu_az_annotation/.

Fig. 1), where the modifications include usability improvements collected in a feedback form after the first annotation round.

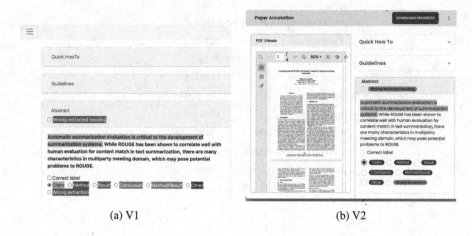

(a) V1   (b) V2

Fig. 1. The UI of the annotation platform: V1 is used in the first annotation round, and V2 in the second round.

In the following, we give more details about the AZ annotation platform, the participants per each annotation round, the selection of the scientific articles to annotate, and describe each annotation round.

3.1 AZ Annotation Platform

In this section, we give a brief overview of the annotation platform [8]. Our platform takes PDF scientific articles as input from the user, and selects/highlights sentences from each section of the article based on their similarity with the abstract sentences. We define four AZ categories that cover the main components of scientific articles: *Claim*, *Method*, *Result* and *Conclusion*. Each selected sentence is labeled with one of these categories where we use a pre-trained BERT model based on the approach proposed by Accuosto et al. [1] to predict the argumentative category of the sentences. We map each of the original argumentative category labels to one of our defined four AZ categories (Table 1). At the end of the process, the platform uses the annotations to create summaries for the annotated article. Evaluating the generated summaries, however, is not the focus of this paper.

3.2 Participants

The study was conducted with bachelor and master students in their last year, who volunteered after call for participation in the annotation study. 22 and 11 students responded to the calls for the first and the second annotation rounds respectively. To understand their comprehension skills and English language proficiency, we asked the

Table 1. Mapping the Accuosto et al. [1] annotation schema to ours.

AZ categories in [1]	Our AZ categories
proposal	Claim
proposal_implementation	Method
observation	Result
result	Result
result_means	Method
conclusion	Conclusion
means	Method
motivation_problem	Claim
motivation_hypothesis	Claim
motivation_background	Claim
information_additional	Claim

students to fill a questionnaire in which they indicated their EPrT score[5] Fig. 2 shows the distribution of the EPrT scores among participants in round 1 (Fig. 2a) and round 2 (Fig. 2b). Most of the participants have score greater than 450 which shows that they can understand common phrases in academic text.

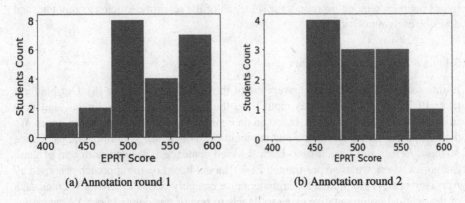

(a) Annotation round 1   (b) Annotation round 2

Fig. 2. Distribution of EPrT scores among participants.

3.3 Selecting and Assigning Articles

We selected 48 and 8 scientific articles to annotate for the first and the second annotation rounds, respectively. Most of the articles were selected from the ACL anthology[6] as the annotators' background is in the Text Mining and Natural Language Processing

---

[5] English Proficiency Test. https://lac.telkomuniversity.ac.id/en/course/eprt-preparation/.

[6] https://aclanthology.org/.

domain. Figure 3 shows the distribution of the selected articles according to the topic of the article per each round. In each round, one of the selected papers was assigned to all of the students in the annotation round and was, thus, used to assess the quality of the student annotations against a ground truth annotation[7]. This allowed us to remove low quality annotations from the final set of annotations. The rest of the papers were assigned to three students, each, in both rounds so we can have later better judgement for the evaluation of the Inter-Annotator-Agreement (IAA) rates.

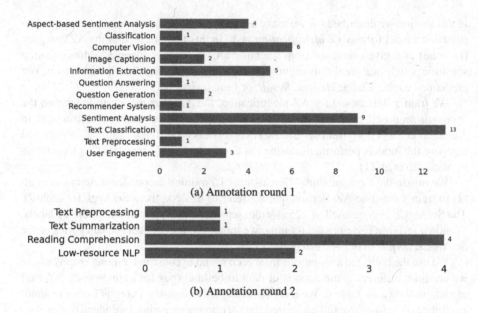

Fig. 3. Main topic distribution of the selected articles.

3.4 Annotation Rounds

As previously mentioned, two annotation rounds were held using two different versions of the platform's user interface while maintaining the same core model (i.e. backend):

Annotation Round 1: In this round we used the version of the platform which was published in our previous work [8]. Annotation instructions were given to the students via an online session and the guidelines[8] were provided as further material to them. The students were given a two weeks time frame to complete the annotations offline and deliver their annotated data.

---

[7] The first author of this paper is the ground truth annotator.

[8] Annotation guidelines available at: https://owncloud.tuwien.ac.at/index.php/s/lqyUgQmAb Zg2cf3.

Annotation Round 2: based on the feedback collected from the previous round, in the second round we used a slightly modified interface. This round was held as an onsite one day workshop with the students. The annotation workshop motivation and instructions were presented to the students. In addition, assistance was given to the students during the annotation workshop by answering their questions.

4   Making Use of Annotations

In this section we describe how we make use of the collected annotations to train a classification model for the ***AZ identification*** task. In this task we predict the AZ category (i.e zone) of a given sentence from scientific article. That is, given a sentence from a scientific article we predict its argumentative category by labeling it with one of our predefined zones: *Claim, Method, Result,* or *Conclusion.*

We train a Bert model for AZ identification, the ***AZ-Bert*** model, following on the approach proposed by Accuosto et al. [1]. Using the same parameter settings as in Accuosto et al. [1], we train several AZ-Bert models on different training corpora and compare the models performance using the Computational Linguistic (CL) test corpus in Accuosto et al. [1].

We utilize the Computational Linguistic (CL) training corpus from Accuosto et al. [1] to train a baseline AZ-Bert model, we refer to this corpus as **SciArgCL** (Table 2). The SciArgCL is composed of 225 abstract sentences labeled with one of the 11 labels, as shown in Table 1. Before the training, we transform the original AZ categories of the SciArgCL corpus to our AZ categories (Table 1).

We use the collected annotations from each round to construct training corpus where we consider different combinations of data to build corpus for training each AZ-Bert model, as shown in Table 2. We use two strategies to construct corpus from the annotated data: (1) using the full annotated data without processing (we identify this data from the first and the second rounds with the ids **R1** and **R2** respectively), and (2) defining criteria to filter out the corpus from low quality annotations (identified by **FR1** and **FR2** for the first and the second round respectively). The details of constructing and filtering the training corpus are mentioned in Sect. 5.

Table 2. Description of corpora used to train AZ-Bert models in different experiments.

Description	Training data name	Sentences number
Baseline data set	SciArgCL	1048
Expansion with whole set of annotation	SciArgCL + R1	4268
	SciArgCL + R2	1556
	SciArgCL + R1 + R2	4776
Expansion while removing low quality annotations	SciArgCL + FR1	2997
	SciArgCL + FR2	1369
	SciArgCL + FR1 + FR2	3318
Collected annotation as a standalone corpus	FR1	1949
	FR2	321
	FR1 + FR2	2270

We have two types of the experiments: (1) *Expansion* experiments where we expanded the SciArgCL dataset with combinations of R1, R2, FR1 and FR2 (Table 2) to train AZ-Bert models and measure the impact of the expansion on the model performance, and (2) *Standalone* experiments where we use FR1 and FR2 to construct a standalone training corpus, from collected annotations, for AZ-Bert to measure whether we can construct a training corpus for AZ identification using our annotation platform. We consider only the FR1 and FR2 for the *Standalone* experiments because the AZ-Bert model performed better on the expanded data using FR1 and FR2.

5   Results

In this section, we present the results for (1) the annotation task (Sect. 3) by assessing the quality of the annotation using ground truth annotation and measure the same level of understanding for the annotators of the task by means of Inter Annotator Agreement (IAA), and (2) the AZ-Bert experiments (Sect. 4) by comparing the performance of trained AZ-Bert against a baseline model.

5.1   Annotation

Annotation performance: recall, in Sect. 3.3, that we assigned one paper to be annotated by all students during each annotation round[9]. The first author of this paper annotated both articles where we consider her annotation as ground truth annotation. We compute the metrics: *Precision*, *Recall*, and *F-measure* of the students' annotation against the ground truth to measure the students annotation performance. We compute each metric per each zone. In Table 3, we report the average performance among all students annotation per each zone and the weighted average (W. Average) performance. In terms of performance results, we notice the following:

1. Generally, sentences which belong to the *Claim* zone are easy to be identified this is because these sentences usually contain clear phrases that make them easy to be labeled (e.g. *"In this work, we propose"*, *"We present"*, etc.).
2. In the first round, the performance of identifying sentences belonging to the *Method* zone is very low. This is because the sentences that were extracted and originally labelled as *Method* sentences by the platform were sentences which described previous work and not the original work of the annotated paper. For example the sentence: *"In the SemEval 2017 Task 4 (Rosenthal et al., 2017), a thorough 5x coverage annotation scheme is used (each tweet is annotated by at least five people)."* describes methodology in a previous work which is cited by the article being annotated, however it was labelled by the platform as a *Method* sentence. According to our definition of the *Method* zone, that it should contain sentences that define methodology for the annotated paper not a previous work. For the case of a sentence belong to a

---

[9] In the first round: [Sentiment Analysis: It's Complicated!] (Kenyon-Dean et al., NAACL 2018) In the second round: [Estimation of Conditional Probabilities With Decision Trees and an Application to Fine-Grained POS Tagging] (Schmid & Laws, COLING 2008).

previous work, we define an extra category called *Other*, this category identifies sentences describing previous work and we ignore the sentences with *Other* category from the collected annotated corpus. However, assessing the annotation results, it became obvious that the use of the *Other* category was not clear to the students in the first round which we clarified for them in the second round.

3. The annotation performance in the second annotation round is higher than that of the first. This is expected since the second round took place on-site, under direct guidance. For clearer analysis of the second annotation round performance, we divided the annotators of this round into two groups: (1) *Old* annotators - participated in both rounds, and (2) *New* annotators - participated in the second round only and we calculated the weighted average performance of each group (rows OW. Average and NW. Average in Table 4). As expected the performance of *Old* annotators is higher than that of the *New* ones since they have prior knowledge of the task.

Table 3. The average of the students annotation performance (in terms of *Precision, Recall* and *F-measure*) during each annotation round per each zone and the weighted average performance of all zones.

Label	Round 1			Round 2		
	Precision	Recall	F-measure	Precision	Recall	F-measure
Claim	**0.85 ± 0.13**	**0.87 ± 0.16**	**0.85 ± 0.12**	**0.95 ± 0.05**	**0.85 ± 0.17**	**0.89 ± 0.11**
Method	0.13 ± 0.28	0.27 ± 0.46	0.15 ± 0.30	0.86 ± 0.12	0.63 ± 0.11	0.72 ± 0.10
Result	0.00 ± 0.00	0.00 ± 0.00	0.00 ± 0.00	0.61 ± 0.19	0.72 ± 0.25	0.61 ± 0.15
Conclusion	0.49 ± 0.50	0.53 ± 0.51	0.5 ± 0.5	0.00 ± 0.00	0.00 ± 0.00	0.00 ± 0.00
W. Average	0.68 ± 0.20	0.61 ± 0.17	0.61 ± 0.17	**0.82 ± 0.06**	**0.70 ± 0.10**	**0.74 ± 0.08**
OW. Average				0.83 ± 0.05	0.71 ± 0.03	0.75 ± 0.03
NW. Average				0.80 ± 0.06	0.69 ± 0.13	0.72 ± 0.10

Inter Anotator Agreement (IAA): Each paper was annotated by three annotators in addition to the paper that was annotated by all of the students during each annotation round. We use these annotations to compute the pair wise inter-annotator's agreement using Kappa κ Cohen score to assess the same level of understanding of different annotators for the task definition. We report in Table 4 the average with the standard deviation, minimum and maximum of the pairwise agreements. Noticing the results in the first row, the agreements are *moderate* for both annotation rounds. We were expecting based on the annotation performance results (Table 3), that the agreement in the second annotation round should be higher than that of the first. For further analysis of the results, we filtered the annotations by removing low quality annotations considering the average F-measure (Table 3) as a threshold for the annotation quality and removed all instances of annotations for annotators with performance less than the threshold. Then, we recomputed the agreement using the filtered corpus (last three rows in Table 4). We notice that the interpretation of the agreement raised to *substantial* for both rounds. After filtering the annotators, we notice that the minimum agreement (the last row in

Table 4) of the second round is relatively high compared to the first round which shows that the annotators tends to have the same understanding of the task in the second annotation round more than the first round.

Table 4. The pairwise agreement between annotators using Cohen's κ coefficient.

Description	Cohen's κ	Round 1	Round 2
Considering whole set of annotation	Avg. pairwise	0.519±0.279	0.450 ± 0.143
	Maximum	1.000	0.754
	Minimum	0.013	0.058
Removing low quality annotations	Avg. pairwise	0.768±0.258	0.605 ± 0.095
	Maximum	1.000	0.754
	Minimum	0.090	0.419

5.2 AZ Identification

We looked at the usefulness of the collected annotated corpus in addressing the AZ identification task (recall Sect. 4). To construct the training corpus from collected annotated sentences, we label the sentences by considering the majority voting of papers assigned by multiple annotators, where we broke ties randomly, and the ground truth annotations for the single papers in both rounds. We trained several AZ-Bert models using different combination of training corpora, as shown in Sect. 4 and Table 2. For the expansion and creation of standalone corpus, we experiment per annotation round and merging corpora from both rounds. To filter out the low quality annotations, we consider the average F-measure (Table 3) as a threshold for the annotation performance where we removed all instances of annotations for annotators with performance less than the threshold to build the final filtered corpus.

Table 5 shows the performance of the AZ-Bert models trained using different corpora on the CL test set used by Accuosto et al. [1] in terms of *Precision*, *Recall* and *F-measure*. To assure that the results are not random, we repeat each experiment four times and we report for the average performance and the standard deviation. In the following, we discuss the results of each of the *Expansion* and *Standalone* experiments.

Expansion Experiments: We notice that the models trained by expanding SciArgCL with R2 and FR2 (**bolded** values in Table 5) achieves higher performance than the baseline and the best performance is achieved after filtering for low quality annotations (i.e. the row **SciArgCL + FR2**). We measure the significance *F-measure* improvement of the model trained using SciArgCL + FR2 over the one using SciArgCL using a t-test, we got $p\_value = 0.049$ which we interpret as statistical significant change. On the other hand, expanding SciArgCL with data collected from the first annotation round (i.e. R1 and FR1) does not help in improving the AZ-Bert performance, where the baseline is statistically significantly higher in performance. This result matches with the annotation performance results (see Table 3) where the annotation performance of the second

Table 5. Performance of repeated experiments (mean±std) of the AZ-BERT models trained on different corpus on the CL test set from [1].

Experiment Type	Training data	Results		
		Precision	Recall	F-measure
Baseline	SciArgCL	0.686±0.016	0.684±0.008	0.683±0.013
Expansion	SciArgCL + R1	0.622±0.043	0.609±0.040	0.614±0.041
	SciArgCL + R2	**0.692±0.028**	0.677±0.037	0.682±0.030
	SciArgCL + R1 + R2	0.613±0.042	0.602±0.038	0.607±0.040
	SciArgCL + FR1	0.632±0.021	0.628±0.013	0.629±0.017
	SciArgCL + FR2	**0.715±0.028**	**0.720±0.037**	**0.716±0.030**
	SciArgCL + FR1 + FR2	0.645±0.042	0.630±0.038	0.636±0.040
Standalone	FR1	0.628±0.008	0.564±0.015	0.589±0.010
	FR2	0.581±0.056	0.570±0.021	0.568±0.024
	FR1 + FR2	0.639±0.005	0.585±0.007	0.610±0.006

annotation round is better than that of the first. When the annotation instructions were carefully clarified for the students, the annotators performance increased and it helps in an overall improvement of the AZ identification task. This verifies also the usefulness of collecting annotated corpus using our AZ annotation platform, when the annotation quality is high, to extent corpus for AZ identification.

Standalone Experiments: with these experiments, we aim to study the usefulness of the annotation platform to construct a standalone AZ corpus using collected annotations. We chose to train AZ-Bert models with the filtered corpus (i.e. FR1 and FR2) only and ignore the whole set based on the *Expansion* experiments results. As shown in Table 5, the performance of the AZ-Bert model built using the standalone corpus is significantly less than the baseline which is verified by a t-test which gives a $p\_value < 0.05$ when we measure the significance of the high value of the baseline F-measure with respect to the models trained using the standalone corpus. The performance of the AZ-Bert model of trained with FR1+FR2 achieves higher performance than that from each round alone (i.e. FR1 alone and FR2 alone) with significant F-measure improvement ($p\_value = 0.005$). This result shows that increasing collected corpus with more annotated data helps in the AZ-Bert model improvement. It is expected that results from the collected annotation would not improve over the baseline, but we assume that this result accepted given that: (1) the annotations are done in a semi-automatic way which reduces the effort and the time for the annotation process, (2) they are done by students compared to expert annotators who build the SciArgCL corpus [1], (3) the number of collected annotated articles are fewer compared to the base line (56 articles vs. 225 articles), and (4) the tool helps to collect annotation on paper level with less effort, by suggesting automatic annotations, if it is compared to do annotation on abstract level [1].

6   Conclusion and Future Work

With the aim to solve the problem of creating benchmark data for Argumentative Zoning (AZ) identification, we proposed in a previous work an AZ annotation platform that helps user to annotate given PDF scientific articles with a simplified AZ schema of four zones: *Claim, Method, Result,* and *Conclusion.* In this paper, we present our work on the design and execution of an annotation experiment to collect sentences from scientific articles labeled with AZ categories, using the platform. The experiment consisted of two annotation rounds, online and onsite, with bachelor and master students from Telkom University. The aim of the annotation experiment was to collect AZ annotated corpus where we evaluated the students annotation performance using ground truth annotation and using the agreement between annotators to analyse the students understanding of the task. We utilize the collected annotations to train AZ-Bert models using different training corpora and compare the performance of the trained models with an AZ-Bert model trained on a baseline corpus (SciArgCL). We experiment with two settings: expanding the SciArgCL corpus with collected annotations and using the annotations as a stand alone training corpora. Though only one model achieved better performance over the baseline, we consider that the performance is accepted given that the platform helped to reduce the cost of the annotation process and creating AZ corpus in terms of time and effort and without need of domain experts.

As future work, we plan to use the platform to create benchmark data set which helps for scientific articles summarisation. By its original design, the platform generates two types of article summaries at the end of the annotation process; one is based on improving a previous work [7] and the other using the users annotations. We collected feedback for the generated summaries using pre and post-questionnaires during the annotation rounds described in this paper. We are planning to use the collected feedback to refine the summarisation pipeline as a step to build informative summaries [15] for scientific articles using the argumentative zones. In addition, we plan to analyse the potential of the tool to create AZ corpora for domains other than the Computational Linguistics domain.

Acknowledgement. This work was a part from the *Artificial Researcher in Science: Efficient Publication Mining* project (ID:2241716) and supported by the ASEAN European Academic University Network (ASEA-UNINET), Project Number: ASEA 2021 22/TU/Proj. 1

References

1. Accuosto, P., Neves, M., Saggion, H.: Argumentation mining in scientific literature: from computational linguistics to biomedicine. In: Frommholz I, Mayr P, Cabanac G, Verberne S, editors. BIR 2021: 11th International Workshop on Bibliometric-enhanced Information Retrieval, 1 April 2021, Lucca, Italy. Aachen: CEUR; 2021, pp. 20–36. CEUR Workshop Proceedings (2021)
2. Accuosto, P., Saggion, H.: Transferring knowledge from discourse to arguments: a case study with scientific abstracts. In: Stein, B., Wachsmuth, H., (eds.) Proceedings of the 6th Workshop on Argument Mining, 1 August 2019, Florence, Italy. Stroudsburg: Association for Computational Linguistics, pp. 41–51. ACL (Association for Computational Linguistics) (2019)

3. Accuosto, P., Saggion, H.: Mining arguments in scientific abstracts with discourse-level embeddings. Data Knowl. Eng. **129**, 101840 (2020). https://doi.org/10.1016/j.datak.2020. 101840, https://www.sciencedirect.com/science/article/pii/S0169023X20300446

4. Bless, C., Baimuratov, I., Karras, O.: Scikgtex - a latex package to semantically annotate contributions in scientific publications (2023)

5. Contractor, D., Guo, Y., Korhonen, A.: Using argumentative zones for extractive summarization of scientific articles. In: Proceedings of COLING 2012, pp. 663–678. The COLING 2012 Organizing Committee, Mumbai, India, December 2012. https://aclanthology.org/C12-1041

6. E. Mendoza, Ó., et al.: Benchmark for research theme classification of scholarly documents. In: Proceedings of the Third Workshop on Scholarly Document Processing, pp. 253–262. Association for Computational Linguistics, Gyeongju, Republic of Korea, October 2022. https://aclanthology.org/2022.sdp-1.31

7. El-Ebshihy, A., Ningtyas, A.M., Andersson, L., Piroi, F., Rauber, A.: ARTU/TU Wien and artificial researcher@ LongSumm 20. In: Proceedings of the First Workshop on Scholarly Document Processing, pp. 310–317. Association for Computational Linguistics, November 2020. https://doi.org/10.18653/v1/2020.sdp-1.36, https://www.aclweb.org/anthology/2020. sdp-1.36

8. El-Ebshihy, A., Ningtyas, A.M., Andersson, L., Piroi, F., Rauber, A.: A platform for argumentative zoning annotation and scientific summarization. In: Proceedings of the 31st ACM International Conference on Information & Knowledge Management, CIKM 2022, pp. 4843–4847. Association for Computing Machinery, New York, NY, USA (2022). https:// doi.org/10.1145/3511808.3557193

9. Goldsack, T., Zhang, Z., Lin, C., Scarton, C.: Domain-driven and discourse-guided scientific summarisation. In: Kamps, J., Goeuriot, L., Crestani, F., Maistro, M., Joho, H., Davis, B., Gurrin, C., Kruschwitz, U., Caputo, A. (eds.) Advances in Information Retrieval, pp. 361–376. Springer Nature Switzerland, Cham (2023). https://doi.org/10.1007/978-3-031-28244-7_23

10. Guo, Y., Korhonen, A., Liakata, M., Silins, I., Sun, L., Stenius, U.: Identifying the information structure of scientific abstracts: an investigation of three different schemes. In: Proceedings of the 2010 Workshop on Biomedical Natural Language Processing, pp. 99–107. Association for Computational Linguistics, Uppsala, Sweden, July 2010. https://aclanthology.org/W10-1913

11. Guo, Y., Silins, I., Stenius, U., Korhonen, A.: Active learning-based information structure analysis of full scientific articles and two applications for biomedical literature review. Bioinformatics **29**(11), 1440–1447 (2013). https://doi.org/10.1093/bioinformatics/btt163

12. Liakata, M., Dobnik, S., Saha, S., Batchelor, C., Rebholz-Schuhmann, D.: A discourse-driven content model for summarising scientific articles evaluated in a complex question answering task. In: Proceedings of the 2013 Conference on Empirical Methods in Natural Language Processing, pp. 747–757. Association for Computational Linguistics, Seattle, Washington, USA, October 2013. https://aclanthology.org/D13-1070

13. Liakata, M., Teufel, S., Siddharthan, A., Batchelor, C.: Corpora for the conceptualisation and zoning of scientific papers. In: Proceedings of the Seventh International Conference on Language Resources and Evaluation (LREC 2010). European Language Resources Association (ELRA), Valletta, Malta, May 2010. http://www.lrec-conf.org/proceedings/lrec2010/pdf/644_Paper.pdf

14. Liu, H.: Automatic Argumentative-Zoning Using Word2vec. CoRR abs/1703.10152 (2017). http://arxiv.org/abs/1703.10152

15. Saggion, H., Lapalme, G.: Generating indicative-informative summaries with SumUM. Comput. Linguist. **28**(4), 497–526 (2002). https://doi.org/10.1162/089120102762671963, https://www.aclweb.org/anthology/J02-4005

16. Teufel, S., Moens, M.: Summarizing scientific articles: experiments with relevance and rhetorical status. Comput. Linguist. **28**(4), 409–445 (2002)
17. Teufel, S., Siddharthan, A., Batchelor, C.: Towards domain-independent argumentative zoning: evidence from chemistry and computational linguistics. In: Proceedings of the 2009 Conference on Empirical Methods in natural language processing, pp. 1493–1502 (2009)
18. Teufel, S., et al.: Argumentative zoning: Information extraction from scientific text. Ph.D. thesis, Citeseer (1999)
19. Yang, A., Li, S.: SciDTB: discourse dependency TreeBank for scientific abstracts. In: Proceedings of the 56th Annual Meeting of the Association for Computational Linguistics (Volume 2: Short Papers). pp. 444–449. Association for Computational Linguistics, Melbourne, Australia, July 2018. https://doi.org/10.18653/v1/P18-2071, https://aclanthology.org/P18-2071
20. Yasunaga, M., et al.: ScisummNet: a large annotated corpus and content-impact models for scientific paper summarization with citation networks. In: Proceedings of AAAI 2019 (2019)

CORE-GPT: Combining Open Access Research and Large Language Models for Credible, Trustworthy Question Answering

David Pride[✉], Matteo Cancellieri, and Petr Knoth

The Knowledge Media Institute, The Open University, Milton Keynes, UK
{david.pride,matteo.cancellieri,petr.knoth}@open.ac.uk

Abstract. In this paper, we present CORE-GPT, a novel question-answering platform that combines GPT-based language models and more than 32 million full-text open access scientific articles from CORE (https://core.ac.uk). We first demonstrate that GPT3.5 and GPT4 cannot be relied upon to provide references or citations for generated text. We then introduce CORE-GPT which delivers evidence-based answers to questions, along with citations and links to the cited papers, greatly increasing the trustworthiness of the answers and reducing the risk of hallucinations. CORE-GPT's performance was evaluated on a dataset of 100 questions covering the top 20 scientific domains in CORE, resulting in 100 answers and links to 500 relevant articles. The quality of the provided answers and relevance of the links were assessed by two annotators. Our results demonstrate that CORE-GPT can produce comprehensive and trustworthy answers across the majority of scientific domains, complete with links to genuine, relevant scientific articles.

1 Introduction

LLMs demonstrate a remarkable ability to process and interpret natural language, understanding various nuances and intricacies of human language. They excel at text generation, crafting coherent and contextually relevant responses or content, ranging from casual conversations to technical articles. However, these are predictive models and cannot be relied upon to provided reliable sources or citations for any generated text.

In order to better understand the problem, we used the GPT3.5 and GPT4 models to answer 50 questions from across ten different domains, and to provide the five top sources/citations for each of the answers. Each row in Fig. 1 shows the results for a single answer. A green dot represents a genuine, factual citation with a paper that exists or a link that goes directly to the paper itself. A red dot represents a completely fictional paper that simply does not exist. The yellow dots were used where there was what we termed *conflation*, meaning the provided citation or source was not real, but used either a mix of real titles or real author names or then linked to a completely different paper entirely. This shows that 22% of references for GPT3.5 and less than 20% for GPT4 were factual.

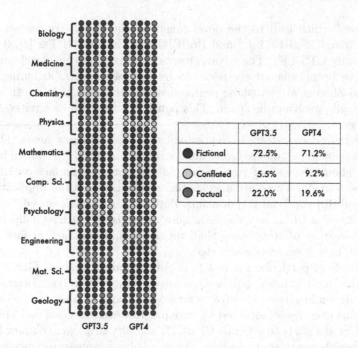

	GPT3.5	GPT4
● Fictional	72.5%	71.2%
○ Conflated	5.5%	9.2%
● Factual	22.0%	19.6%

Fig. 1. Citations to answers given by LLMs. Each row represents 5 sources/citations for a single answer. Overall, 72.5% of citations provided by GPT3.5 were fictional. This figure was 71.2% for GPT4

Whilst it can be argued that GPT3.5 and GPT4 were not designed to reference evidence [1], it can be widely observed that people have attempted to use them for these purposes and that it would be valuable if they could be used in this way. In this paper, we address this issue by introducing CORE-GPT. Our main contributions are:

– We provided empirical evidence demonstrating that GPT3.5 and GPT4 cannot be relied upon to generate sources of references.
– We provide a solution that combines the power of GPT models and a global open research corpus to deliver a credible and trustworthy question-answering solution, accompanied with references to research literature.
– Our question-answering solution is capable of providing answers including references to recently published research without the need for retraining the GPT models.

2   Related Work

The term Large Language Model has been in existence for many decades, however the LLMs we focus on here are extensions of the *transformer* model architecture introduced in 2017 by Vaswani et al. in their seminal paper *'All you need is attention'* which lead to the development of the BERT transfomer models and its siblings (SciBERT [2] and RoBERTa [3]) and to GPT-2 [4], 3 [5] and most recently GPT4 [6]. The advancements and overall recent developments in LLMs have been exhaustively reviewed by several scholars, including Fan et al. [7] and Zhao et al. [8], whose comprehensive surveys offer in-depth analyses of this rapidly evolving discipline. This paper will therefore not reiterate these developments.

LLMs have demonstrated remarkable capabilities in many areas. There are however significant challenges associated with the use of LLMs. There has been concerns about the risk of plagiarism and the potential impact on education and assessment [9]. There are also specific concerns about the implications for the medical [10] and legal [11] domains. Beyond these domain-specific concerns, the robustness of LLMs has also been questioned. Issues such as hallucinations, or the generation of statements that appear credible but are in fact entirely fabricated, have been widely reported.

In a study of particular interest to scientists and researchers, Gao et al. [12] showed that models based on the Generative Pre-training Transformer (GPT) architecture could generate abstracts for scientific articles that were often indistinguishable from those authored by humans. However, Alkaissi and McFarlane [13] conducted a study to evaluate ChatGPT's ability to answer complex biomedical and healthcare-related questions. Their results demonstrated mixed quality in the generated responses, with answers consisting of a blend of factual information and fabricated content. Crucially, when ChatGPT was asked to provide citations and PubMed IDs to support its answers, all the provided references were fictional, and the given PubMed IDs were simply sequences of random numbers with no relation to existing papers. This research, corroborated by additional studies [14], underscores a profound problem with LLMs generating authentic-sounding but entirely fictional content.

These challenges and the results shown in Table 1 highlight a significant hurdle that needs to be overcome in order to be able to leverage the abilities of LLMs for question answering whilst limiting the potential for false or misleading answers. The focus of our work in this paper is on addressing this credibility gap, by proposing a novel approach that combines Open Access scientific literature with LLMs to enhance the reliability and trustworthiness of these systems.

3 Our Solution - CORE-GPT

3.1 CORE-GPT Workflow

CORE-GPT has been developed specifically to address the problems discussed in the previous sections. We use a three-stage approach to returning answers to user questions with links to relevant full-text papers in CORE.

In Stage 1, the original question is passed to the GPT4 API with several instructions.

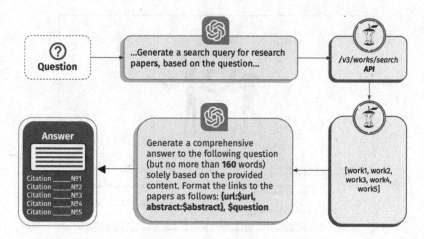

Fig. 2. CORE-GPT workflow.

- Identify the key terms within the question
- Enrich with close synonyms
- Formulate this into a search query.

A sample question and search formatted response can be seen below:

Original user question
What strategies can be implemented to improve literacy rates in rural primary schools in developing countries?
Formatted query
strategies improve literacy rates rural primary schools developing countries OR low-income OR underdeveloped OR third-world

In Stage 2, the formatted search query is then passed to the CORE API which returns the five most relevant papers where the full-text content is available. Stage 3 is the key to the novel solution provided by CORE-GPT. We pass the titles and abstracts returned in Stage 2 back to the GPT4 API with further instructions:

Generate a comprehensive answer to the following question (but no more than 160 words) solely based on the content provided. Format the links to the papers as follows: furl:\$url, abstract:\$abstract, \$question

Our evaluation shows that this critical third stage is largely effective at constraining the model to base its reply only on the supplied input. The answer and provided links are then shown to the user. The full workflow can be seen in Fig. 2

3.2   The CORE-GPT User Interface

Initially, CORE-GPT will be made available on the CORE website as a new web-based question/answer platform (Fig. 3). Further development will allow for the service to be made available via the CORE API. This is discussed in the Future Work section (Sect. 8.) A sample result is shown in Fig. 4.

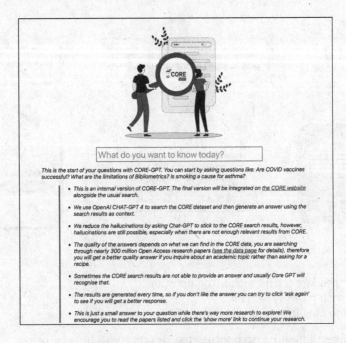

Fig. 3. CORE-GPT user interface.

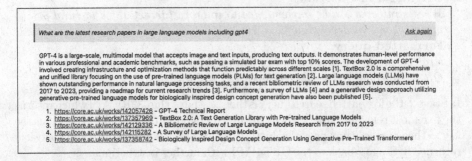

Fig. 4. CORE-GPT Sample results including very recently published papers (less than one month since publication.)

3.3 Benefits of CORE-GPT

The key benefit of CORE-GPT is in ensuring that the content of the generated answers is drawn from published scientific literature, which is then subsequently referenced. This greatly reduces the potential for hallucinations. There are further benefits derived from the constraints placed on the model. In our evaluation, there were instances where, despite the massive-scale corpus that CORE-GPT draws its answers from, there was not enough relevant content to formulate a comprehensive answer. Below is an example question from the questions dataset used for the evaluation were this was the case;

"What are the potential long-term health impacts of regular use of over-the-counter pain medications on the liver and kidney function in young adults?"

In cases like these, the GPT4 model is capable of recognising the lack of relevant responses. If a complete answer cannot be given, the user will be informed with the following type of message;

"Regular use of over-the-counter (OTC) pain medications can potentially impact liver and kidney function in young adults. *However, the provided results do not offer specific information* on the long-term health impacts of such medications on these organs. *To obtain a comprehensive answer, further research on this topic would be necessary.*"

In our evaluation we found that whilst this type of answer was understandably low scoring in terms of comprehensiveness and utility, it scored highly for trustworthiness. The key factor here is that the model is forced to be honest when it does not know something. This greatly reduces the potential for hallucinations and increases the overall viability and usability of CORE-GPT in academic question/answering.

Another key benefit is intrinsically linked to the way CORE operates as an Open Access infrastructure. Anyone who has used the latest GPT models will almost certainly be familiar with the response *'I'm sorry for the inconvenience. As an AI model with a knowledge cutoff in September 2021, I don't have real-time information'.* CORE however is constantly aggregating content from the global network of Open Access repositories and as soon as a document is indexed in CORE, it is available to CORE-GPT to be used in answers and cited. The search shown in Fig. 4 was undertaken during the second week of May 2023. The results contain papers published as recently as April 2023. As CORE-GPT is designed to work in this way, this removes the knowledge cut-off date experienced when using just the GPT models themselves.

4   Evaluation Methodology

4.1   Data Sources

CORE-GPT is designed to provide citations to the research papers used to formulate the answers. All cited research papers are drawn from the CORE corpus of Open Access research literature. CORE is currently the one of the largest aggregators of OA scholarly knowledge, aggregating content from the global network of almost 11,000 institutional, pre-print and publisher repositories and, as of May 2023, hosts over 32 million full-text research papers [15].

Table 1. Size of the CORE collection as of January 2023.

Metadata records	291,151,257
Records with full text	32,812,252
Records with abstract	94,521,867
Records with full-text link	139,000,000[†]
Data providers	10,744
Number of CORE data provider countries	150
Estimated number of languages of collected content	118

[†]Estimate based on analysis

4.2 Question Generation

Our first task was to generate a dataset of questions that could be used to test the performance of CORE-GPT and also to compare this performance against large language models such as GPT3.5 and GPT4. Additionally, we wanted to ascertain whether the models themselves and also CORE-GPT were more successful in some domains and less successful in others. We therefore generated a dataset of questions based on the split of domains in the CORE dataset. The domains with the largest amount of full text content in CORE were selected. We added education as the final domain to give 20 domains.

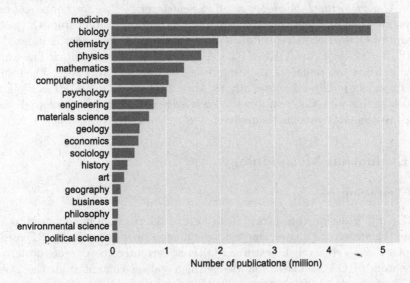

Fig. 5. Subject distribution of a sample of 20,758,666 CORE publications.

To aid in the rapid development of the questions dataset, we elected to use a large language model. GPT-4 was chosen for its recency and known abilities for this task. Using the list of domains previously discussed, the OpenAI GPT-4 API was used to generate the questions using the following prompt;

messages=["role": "system", "content": "*write a graduate level research question in the following domain, only reply with the body of the question itself:*", "role": "user", "content": *domain,*]

Five questions were generated from each domain for a total of 100 questions. Overall, the question generation methodology was effective and allowed for rapid generation of the questions dataset. There are however some potential limitations that this method may introduce which are discussed in the Discussion section (Sect. 6.) The datasets of all questions and answers with accompanying citations can be found in the Github repository for this study[1].

4.3 Evaluation Metrics

Effectively evaluating CORE-GPT requires a two-step approach as both the given answer and the provided citations must be validated. We elected to use three metrics for each of the answers as follows:

- **Comprehensive:** How comprehensively is the question answered?
- **Trust:** How trustworthy is the answer?
- **Utility:** How useful is the answer?

For the citations, we use **relevance** as the metric, that is how relevant is the given reference to the original question. To enable evaluation of the results, a browser-based evaluation platform was developed which sequentially displayed each of the 100 questions and answers and the title, abstracts and links to the five papers for each answer. For each question, the three answer metrics shown above and the relevance score for each of the citations could be assigned a value from zero to ten.

Table 2. Inter-annotator agreement for each classification

Class	Agreement (k)
Comprehensiveness	0.792
Trust	0.760
Utility	0.748
Cite 1	0.808
Cite 2	0.727
Cite 3	0.665
Cite 4	0.717
Cite 5	0.651

Two annotators were retained and were given written instructions and training using the evaluation platform with sample data. Inter-annotator agreement for

---

[1] https://github.com/oacore/core-gpt-evaluation.

each metric was measured using Cohen's Kappa with quadratic weights. This measure was chosen for the task as it accounts for both small and large differences of opinion more accurately than unweighted Kappa. The results for the inter-annotator agreement can be seen in Table 2.

5   Results

5.1   Quality of Answers

Using the evaluation platform, the annotators were asked to rank each answer according to the three metrics introduced previously, *comprehensiveness*, *trust* and *utility*. Each of these metrics could be scored from 0 (not at all) to 10 (completely) for each answer. Figure 6 shows the mean comprehensiveness, trust and utility scores for the answers from each of the 20 domains. CORE-GPT performs exceptionally well across most domains, but is less successful in a few areas. In 75% of the domains, the mean comprehensive, trust and utility score was 8 points or greater, and 9 points or greater in over half of the domains, indicating that CORE-GPT provides highly relevant, factual and, most importantly, referenced answers. A full breakdown of all scores is shown in Tables 3 and 4. It is worth noting that in the domains where the answers were deemed by the annotators to be less comprehensive and less useful, the trust scores remained fairly high (>6 across all domains) indicating that overall the given answers were considered trustworthy.

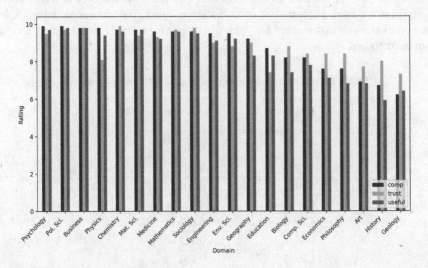

Fig. 6. Mean comprehensiveness, trust and utility scores for each domain ordered by mean comprehensiveness.)

We investigated whether there was a relationship between the domain scores for comprehensiveness, trustworthiness and utility and the number of research papers in CORE for each respective domain (Fig. 5). However, we found only a weak correlation (Pearson's R0.23, n = 20), indicating that having less research content in some domains does not fully explain the lower performance in these areas. CORE is a comprehensive source of multidisciplinary research content [16] and it might be that the domains in which there is genuinely less content are not necessarily insufficiently represented in CORE.

We further examined whether the length of the abstracts given to the model to generate the answers had an impact on the quality scores for the answers. There is a wide variance in mean abstract length across the domains, from economics (171 words) to engineering (329 words), we were therefore interested to see if this influenced the scores for comprehensiveness and utility. However, we observed no correlation between these scores and the mean abstract lengths in each domain.(Pearson's $r = -0.02, n = 20$)

5.2 Citation Relevance

In contrast to the results for GPT3.5 and GPT4 shown in Fig. 1, all citations provided by CORE-GPT are, by design, links to genuine research papers. Therefore the evaluation was based on testing not the existence of these papers, but their relevance to the user's original question. The annotators were asked to rank each citation from 0 (not relevant at all) to 10 (completely relevant). Figure 7 shows the mean relevance score for each of the five citations across all domains.

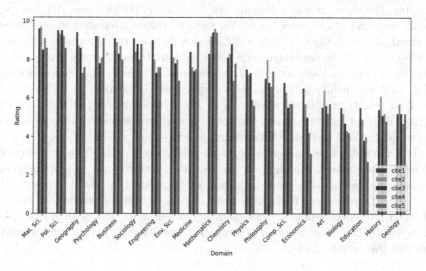

Fig. 7. Mean citation relevance scores for each domain. (Ordered by relevance score for first citation.)

Based on the previously discussed Fig. 6 we observed that CORE-GPT provides comprehensive, trustworthy and useful answers for the majority of the

Table 3. Mean answer quality scores for all domains.

Domain	Comp	Trust	Utility	Mean
Pol. Sci.	9.9	9.7	9.8	9.80
Business	9.8	9.8	9.8	9.80
Chemistry	9.7	9.9	9.6	9.73
Psychology	9.9	9.5	9.7	9.70
Mathematics	9.6	9.7	9.6	9.63
Sociology	9.6	9.8	9.5	9.63
Mat. Sci.	9.7	9.4	9.7	9.60
Medicine	9.6	9.3	9.2	9.37
Engineering	9.5	9	9.1	9.20
Env. Sci.	9.5	8.8	9.2	9.17
Physics	9.8	8.1	9.4	9.10
Geography	9.2	9.0	8.3	8.83
Education	8.7	7.4	8.3	8.13
Comp. Sci.	8.2	8.4	7.8	8.13
Biology	8.2	8.8	7.4	8.13
Economics	7.6	8.4	7.1	7.70
Philosophy	7.6	8.4	6.8	7.60
Art	6.9	7.7	6.8	7.13
History	6.7	8	5.9	6.87
Geology	6.2	7.3	6.4	6.63

Table 4. Mean citation relevance scores for all domains.

Domain	cite1	cite2	cite3	cite4	cite5	Mean
Pol. Sci.	9.5	9.3	9.5	9.2	8.6	9.22
Mathematics	8.3	9.2	9.4	9.6	9.4	9.18
Mat. Sci.	9.6	9.7	8.5	9.1	8.6	9.10
Psychology	9.2	9.2	7.8	8.1	9.1	8.68
Sociology	9.1	8.4	8.8	8	8.8	8.62
Business	9.1	8.9	8.3	8.7	8	8.60
Geography	9.4	8.7	8.6	7.3	7.6	8.32
Chemistry	8.1	8.3	8.8	6.9	7.8	7.98
Medicine	8.4	7.6	7.4	7.5	8.9	7.95
Env. Sci.	8.8	8.1	7.8	8	6.9	7.92
Engineering	9	8	7.3	7.6	7.6	7.90
Philosophy	7	8	6.8	6.6	7.4	7.16
Physics	7.5	7.2	7.3	5.9	5.6	6.70
Comp. Sci.	6.8	6.3	5.5	5.7	5.7	6.00
Art	5.5	6.4	5.6	5.2	5.7	5.68
History	5.4	6.1	5.1	5.2	4.8	5.32
Geology	5.2	5.7	5.2	4.7	5.2	5.20
Economics	6.5	5.7	5	4.2	3.1	4.90
Biology	5.5	5.2	4.7	4.3	4.2	4.78
Education	5.5	4.9	3.8	4.0	2.7	4.17
Mean	7.68	7.54	7.06	6.79	6.78	

domains. However, in some domains, such Geology, History and Art, comprehensiveness and utility were lower. We were therefore interested to find out to what extent the ability of CORE-GPT to provide good-quality answers is linked to the quality of the retrieved references. We found that there is a very strong correlation between the relevance of the retrieved references and comprehensiveness, trust and utility across domains respectively (Pearson $r = 0.77$ (comp.); $r = 0.83$ (trust); $r = 0.80$ (utility), $n = 20$). This suggests that the ability to retrieve relevant references with respect to a user's question has a major impact on the quality of CORE-GPT's answers.

The annotators were asked to score the relevance of each of the five retrieved references separately, enabling us to test the performance of our reference retrieval functionality. A well optimised ranking function should retrieve the most relevant references first. As a result, we expected to observe that the top retrieved references would be assigned higher relevance scores than the latter references by the annotators on average. The results reported in Table 4 indeed confirms this trend.

6   Discussion

Whilst the overall performance of CORE-GPT is very good, there are still some limitations to consider. CORE-GPT draws its answers and references from the body of Open Access literature. Whilst OA now covers a growing proportion of published scientific articles, there is still a significant quantity that is locked behind publishers' paywalls which CORE-GPT cannot currently access. However this problem, and the issues with current publishing paradigms in general, extend far beyond the scope of this study.

It should be noted that whilst CORE-GPT was tested across a wide range of domains, only five questions per domain were used for the evaluation. This was to limit the burden on the annotators who validated 100 answers and checked all 500 links to references. Further evaluation could therefore be undertaken with a larger cohort of annotators.

In the questions dataset, a small number of questions are somewhat basic and not really at the level that would be expected of a research question. Further, it can be seen that there is overlap in the phrasing of some questions, leading to similar questions in some domains. Whilst this reduced the variety of questions by a small margin, we remain confident in the overall results presented here.

Across all domains there is very strong correlation between the comprehensiveness, trust and utility scores for the answers and the relevance of the citations (Pearson $r = 0.77$ (comp.); $r = 0.83$ (trust); $r = 0.80$ (utility), $n = 20$) This indicates that it is access to high quality, relevant literature that is central to delivering high quality answers.

7   Conclusion

In this paper we introduce CORE-GPT a framework that combines LLMs and massive-scale Open Access scientific corpora to deliver a trustworthy, evidence-based question-answering platform. CORE-GPT is an overtly simple, yet elegant solution to the problems that arise when LLMs are asked to provide factual, evidence-based answers. Our evaluation results demonstrate that the answers provided by CORE-GPT are, on the whole, comprehensive, useful and most importantly trustworthy. Further, all references generated by the platform are, by design, genuine research papers held within CORE.

8   Future Work

The results from the evaluation show that CORE-GPT performs well across the majority of scientific domains. This provides a strong foundation to now develop a range of applications using the central CORE-GPT architecture. The initial version of CORE-GPT uses the titles and abstracts of the five most relevant papers as source for the given answers. Due to the limitations in the number of tokens that can be passed to the GPT4 model it is not currently possible to pass the entire full-text content of all papers. This is something that will undoubtedly change in the future and may lead to even stronger results.

Our initial plan includes making the current version of CORE-GPT available as an addition to the CORE API V3.0. Further, CORE provides a range of management tools for repositories and we see strong potential in developing both an embedded repository version of the service and also a recommender system for repositories based on the CORE-GPT architecture.

Data and Code Availability. All data and software code used for the evaluation of CORE-GPT are available to promote transparency and reproducibility of the findings. The dataset of questions and answers and the source code used for the analysis and visualisations in this study are accessible on the CORE-GPT GitHub repository (https://github.com/oacore/core-gpt-evaluation). Any questions or requests for further information can be addressed to the corresponding author.

References

1. LSE: LSE (ed.): New AI tools that can write student essays require educators to rethink teaching and assessment. The London School of Economics and Political Science; 2022. Accessed 18 May 2023. https://blogs.lse.ac.uk/impactofsocialsciences/2022/05/17/new-ai-tools-that-can-write-student-essays-require-educators-to-rethink-teaching-and-assessment/

2. Beltagy, I., Lo, K., Cohan, A.: SciBERT: a pretrained language model for scientific text. arXiv preprint arXiv:1903.10676 (2019)

3. Liu, Y., Ott, M., Goyal, N., Du, J., Joshi, M., Chen, D., et al.: RoBERTa: a robustly optimized bert pretraining approach. arXiv preprint arXiv:1907.11692 (2019)

4. Radford, A., Wu, J., Child, R., Luan, D., Amodei, D., Sutskever, I., et al.: Language models are unsupervised multitask learners. OpenAI blog. **1**(8), 9 (2019)

5. Brown, T., Mann, B., Ryder, N., Subbiah, M., Kaplan, J.D., Dhariwal, P., et al.: Language models are few-shot learners. Adv. Neural. Inf. Process. Syst. **33**, 1877–1901 (2020)

6. OpenAI. OpenAI (ed.): GPT-4 Techincal Report. OpenAI; 2023. Accessed 24 Apr 2023. https://cdn.openai.com/papers/gpt-4.pdf

7. Fan, L., Li, L., Ma, Z., Lee, S., Yu, H., Hemphill, L.: A bibliometric review of large language models research from 2017 to 2023. arXiv preprint arXiv:2304.02020 (2023)

8. Zhao, W.X., Zhou, K., Li, J., Tang, T., Wang, X., Hou, Y., et al.: A survey of large language models. arXiv preprint arXiv:2303.18223 (2023)

9. Kasneci, E., Seßler, K., Küchemann, S., Bannert, M., Dementieva, D., Fischer, F., et al.: ChatGPT for good? On opportunities and challenges of large language models for education. Learn. Individ. Differ. **103**, 102274 (2023)

10. Shen, Y., Moy, L. (ed.): ChatGPT and other large language models are double-edged swords. Radiological Society of North America (2023)

11. Armstrong, K.: BBC (ed.). ChatGPT: US lawyer admits using AI for case research. BBC (2023). Accessed 30 May 2023. https://www.bbc.co.uk/news/world-us-canada-65735769

12. Gao, C.A., Howard, F.M., Markov, N.S., Dyer, E.C., Ramesh, S., Luo, Y., et al.: Comparing scientific abstracts generated by ChatGPT to original abstracts using an artificial intelligence output detector, plagiarism detector, and blinded human reviewers. bioRxiv. 2022:2022–12

13. Alkaissi, H., McFarlane, S.I.: Artificial hallucinations in ChatGPT: implications in scientific writing. Cureus **15**(2), 35179 (2023)

14. McMichael, J., SMU (ed.): Artificial intelligence and the research paper: a librarian's perspective. SMU; 2023. Accessed 30 May 2023. https://blog.smu.edu/smulibraries/2023/01/20/artificial-intelligence-and-the-research-paper-a-librarians-perspective/
15. Knoth, P., et al.: CORE: A Global Aggregation Service for Open Access Papers. Publication due June, Nature Scientific Data (2023)
16. Gusenbauer, M.: Search where you will find most: comparing the disciplinary coverage of 56 bibliographic databases. Scientometrics **127**(5), 2683–2745 (2022)

A Robust Approach for Hybrid Personalized Recommender Systems

Le Nguyen Hoai Nam[1,2]($\boxtimes$) (iD)

[1] Faculty of Information Technology, University of Science, Ho Chi Minh City, Vietnam
lnhnam@fit.hcmus.edu.vn
[2] Vietnam National University, Ho Chi Minh City, Vietnam

Abstract. The personalization of services for users is one of the most crucial objectives of digital platforms. This objective is accomplished by integrating automated recommendation components into information systems. The increasing computational power and storage capacity available today have opened up opportunities to deploy a combination of diverse approaches to enhance the accuracy of the recommendation process. Compared to previous research, the distinguishing feature of this study is the introduction of an approach that combines not only computational aspects but also data types. In terms of computation, our approach integrates both item-based and user-based recommendations. Regarding data type, we utilize all three common data types, i.e., user ratings, user reviews, and user interactions, to learn user preferences for recommendations. This comprehensive combination has demonstrated its effectiveness through experiments.

Keywords: Collaborative filtering · recommender systems · personalization

1 Introduction

Recommender systems play a vital role in enterprise information systems. These systems enable users to easily access items that match their interests, facilitating precise and time-saving decision-making [1, 2]. With such benefits, recommendation components have become essential to implementing information systems. Evidence of this can be seen in the significant number of users on digital platforms who make purchases based on recommender systems [3].

To successfully provide recommendations, recommender systems always strive for effective approaches to predict user preferences. Collaborative filtering is one of the most popular approaches for this task, comprising two primary classes: latent factor models and neighbor models. Latent factor models concentrate on representing users and items through latent factors, which enable precise prediction of user preferences for items [4, 5]. However, interpreting the underlying meanings of these latent factors can be challenging. In contrast, neighbor models offer greater interpretability [6–8]. Nowadays, the interpretability of a recommendation model is considered as significant as its accuracy [8, 9].

Neighbor models predict the preference of a user u for an item i by leveraging the preferences for i observed from users who share similar preferences with u, known as neighbor users. In addition to such neighbor-user models, this principle can also be implemented into neighbor-item models. Neighbor-item models entail aggregating the ratings of u for items that are similar to i, referred to as neighbor items. To improve the accuracy of recommendations, many studies have focused on combining the preference predictions from both neighbor-user and neighbor-item models [10, 11]. This paper aims to contribute to the advancement of combined neighbor models, as follows:

- Traditionally, neighbor models rely on observed preferences to identify neighbor users and neighbor items. However, beyond observed preferences, recommender systems can also gather interactions and textual reviews from users [12, 13]. The distinctive feature of this paper is the integration not only of the two computational aspects (neighbor-item model and neighbor-user model) but also of all three popular user profile types (user preferences, user reviews, and user interactions).
- However, the integrations mentioned above may lead to an increase in computational expenses. Hence, our objective is to put forth efficient solutions to address the implementation challenges associated with our proposed approach.

2 Related Works

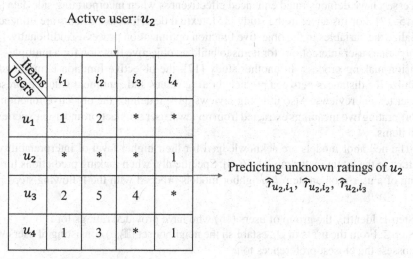

Fig. 1. An description of a recommender system

2.1 Recommendation Problem Statement

Recommendation models are trained based on item preferences observed by users. These preferences typically consist of numeric ratings assigned by users to items ($r_{u,i} \neq *$ where $u = 1 \ldots m$, $i = 1 \ldots n$, m is the number of users, and n is the number of items). The trained models help predict unknown ratings ($r_{u,i} = *$ where $u = 1 \ldots m$ and $i = 1 \ldots n$). In Fig. 1, it is necessary to predict u_2's rating for i_1, i_2, and i_3. The items that receive the highest predicted ratings will be recommended to u_2.

2.2 Recommendation Models

Collaborative filtering is one of the most popular approaches for rating predictions, comprising two primary classes: latent factor models and neighbor models. In the latent factor models, a set of latent factors is learned by optimizing an objective function. Consequently, the rating that a user assigns to an item ($\hat{r}_{u,i}$) can be predicted by multiplying their respective vectors defined by the latent factors ($\vec{z}_u$ $u = 1 \ldots m$ and $\vec{h}_i$ $i = 1 \ldots n$) [12–14], as follows:

$$\hat{r}_{u,i} = \vec{z}_u \cdot \vec{h}_i \tag{1}$$

The objective functions for learning latent factors are typically constructed based on the principle of optimizing the difference between the observed rating values and the predicted rating values. These objective functions, along with their optimization processes, have demonstrated enhanced effectiveness when incorporating side data [12, 13, 15–17]. For instance, in the study [15], textual descriptions of items are utilized to initialize the variables in the objective function optimization process. Additionally, [12] incorporates user interactions for items to build an objective function for a multiple-step decision-making process. In another study [17], the objective function is modified to optimize the distances between predicted rating values and sentiment values expressed in user textual reviews. Also utilizing reviews, [13] redefines the objective function by incorporating two meanings extracted from reviews: user satisfaction and user experience with items.

The neighbor models are acknowledged for their higher level of interpretability in contrast to the latent factor models [6–8]. Specifically, when making predictions for the rating of a user u on an item i, neighbor models proceed with the following steps [18, 19]:

- Step 1: Identify the group of users ($\mathbb{U}_i$) who have provided ratings for i.
- Step 2: From the users in $\mathbb{U}_i$, establish the neighbor set ($\mathbb{T}_{u,i}$) consisting of users who possess the closest preferences to u.
- Step 3: Compute the average of the observed ratings assigned by the users $v \in \mathbb{T}_{u,i}$ to i ($r_{v,i}$), resulting in an estimation of u's rating for i ($\hat{r}_{u,i}$), as follows:

$$\hat{r}_{u,i} = \mu_u + \frac{\sum_{v \in \mathbb{T}_{u,i}} sim_{u,v} \cdot (r_{v,i} - \mu_v)}{\sum_{v \in \mathbb{T}_{u,i}} |sim_{u,v}|} \tag{2}$$

where μ_u and μ_v denote the averages of the observed ratings of user u and user v, respectively. Step 2 requires the similarity of preferences between user u and each user

v in the set $\mathbb{U}_i$, denoted by $sim_{u,v}$. Some typical methods for calculating similarity are as follows. For Jaccard [20], the more items two users rate in common, the higher their similarity. Going into the details of each rating value, PCC [21] is the cosine of two vectors containing the shared ratings of the two users. MSD [22] uses the absolute difference in shared ratings. [23] calculates the similarity of two users by combining their consistent extreme behaviors and individual extreme behaviors.

In addition to considering observed ratings, observed reviews are also incorporated in the computation of user preference similarity. For example, the authors in [24] calculate the similarity between two users by averaging the distances between their review vectors, which are obtained through a topic modeling technique. In [25], the similarity using reviews is combined with the similarity using ratings. This integration of both rating-based and review-based similarities enhances the accuracy of the similarity calculation.

The aforementioned predictive approaches can also be implemented using a neighbor-item model, where the focus is on neighbor items instead of neighbor users. Accordingly, a user's preference for an item is calculated by aggregating the ratings expressed by the user after experiencing the neighbor items. Several studies have explored rating predictions by combining both the neighbor-user and neighbor-item models. Specifically, [10] employed Singular Value Decomposition on the combined matrix of user numeric ratings and item textual descriptions to derive user/item vectors in the Bert space. Cosine similarity was then calculated for each pair of user/item vectors in the Bert space. These similarity measures were subsequently employed to identify the neighbor users and neighbor items within the combined model. Compared to [10], the difference of [11] lies in the implementation of Singular Value Decomposition on each user/item cluster. Subsequently, the transformed vector of each item/user is utilized to calculate the cosine similarity with other users/items within the same cluster only. Both approaches, [10] and [11], apply the unweighted averaging technique to combine the rating predictions from both neighbor-user and neighbor-item models.

3 Motivation

In addition to ratings, a user's characteristics can also be revealed through his/her inter-actions in the system, such as clicking, purchasing, or viewing items. Compared to rating data, this data can be collected easily and rapidly through software integrated into the system. After interacting with and rating an item, users often write a review to express their emotions and experiences related to the item. In this paper, we aim to combine not just **T**wo computational **A**spects (neighbor-user model and neighbor-item model) but also **T**hree popular user **P**rofile types (user preferences, user reviews, and user interactions) to enhance neighbor-based recommendation processes. With that idea, we name the proposed approach in this paper **TATP**.

In our recent research, we have introduced two latent factor models: SC1 [12], which combines user interactions and ratings, and UI2R [13], which combines user reviews and ratings. These models have demonstrated remarkable effectiveness in predicting ratings. The integration of rating, interaction, and review data has facilitated the learning of latent factor vectors for more accurate representations of users and items. Building upon this finding, our goal is to leverage these vectors to improve the quality of neighbor users and neighbor items in the TATP. The detailed process is illustrated in Sects. 4.1 and 4.2.

These combinations increase the computational cost of TATP, which significantly impacts the scalability of the system. To address this issue and make TATP more comprehensive, we have proposed an alternative version of TATP that aims to reduce computational expenses. However, it is important to note that reducing computational costs will inevitably lead to a trade-off with the accuracy of rating predictions. In Sect. 4.3, we will provide a specific implementation of TATP.

4 Our Proposed Approach, TATP

4.1 Hybrid Model

Firstly, we employ our previous recommendation models, SC1 [12] and UI2R [13], to derive user and item vectors. SC1 [12] is a latent factor model that integrates user interaction data and rating data. In particular, SC1 captures the steps of a decision-making process in the following manner:

- A user interacts with an item based on compatibility $(\hat{t}_{u,i})$ between the initial user vector $(\overrightarrow{d}_u\, u = 1\dots m)$ and the initial item vector $(\overrightarrow{b}_i\, i = 1\dots n)$, as follows:

$$\hat{t}_{u,i} = \overrightarrow{d}_u \cdot \overrightarrow{b}_i \tag{3}$$

- Following the interaction on the item, the user engages with it, and ultimately provides a rating $(\hat{r}_{u,i})$ by aligning the final user vector $(\overrightarrow{z}_u\, u = 1\dots m)$ with the final item vector $(\overrightarrow{h}_i\, i = 1..n)$, as follows:

$$\hat{r}_{u,i} = \overrightarrow{z}_u \cdot \overrightarrow{h}_i \tag{4}$$

Using the collected interactions and ratings ($t_{u,i} \neq *$ and $r_{u,i} \neq *$ with $u = 1\dots m$ and i = 1...n), we can estimate both the initial and final user/item vectors. These two optimizations are solved with the constraint that the initial user/item vectors act as the starting values for the corresponding final user/item vectors in the Stochastic Gradient Descent process, as follows:

$$\min_{\substack{\overrightarrow{d}_u, \overrightarrow{b}_i \\ u = 1\dots m \\ i = 1\dots n}} \frac{1}{2} \cdot \sum_{\{(u,i)|u=1\dots m \wedge i=1\dots n \wedge t_{u,i}\neq *\}} \left(t_{u,i} - \hat{t}_{u,i}\right)^2$$

$$\Leftrightarrow \min_{\substack{\overrightarrow{d}_u, \overrightarrow{b}_i \\ u = 1\dots m \\ i = 1\dots n}} \frac{1}{2} \cdot \sum_{\{(u,i)|u=1\dots m \wedge i=1\dots n \wedge t_{u,i}\neq *\}} \left(t_{u,i} - \overrightarrow{d}_u \cdot \overrightarrow{b}_i\right)^2$$

$$\min_{\substack{\overrightarrow{z}_u, \overrightarrow{h}_i \\ u = 1\dots m \\ i = 1\dots n}} \frac{1}{2} \cdot \sum_{\{(u,i)|u=1\dots m \wedge i=1\dots n \wedge r_{u,i}\neq *\}} \left(r_{u,i} - \hat{r}_{u,i}\right)^2$$

$$\Leftrightarrow \min_{\substack{\vec{z}_u, \vec{h}_i \\ u=1\ldots m \\ i=1\ldots n}} \frac{1}{2} \cdot \sum_{\{(u,i)|u=1\ldots m \wedge i=1\ldots n \wedge r_{u,i} \neq *\}} \left(r_{u,i} - \vec{z}_u \cdot \vec{h}_i \right)^2$$

$$Subject\ to: \vec{z}_u^{(0)} = \vec{a}_u\ u = 1\ldots m \wedge \vec{h}_i^{(0)} = \vec{b}_i\ i = 1\ldots n \tag{5}$$

In contrast to SC1, UI2R [13] is designed to combine textual reviews and numerical ratings in a latent factor model. Each review is encoded into a vector using the Bert model ($\vec{v}_{u,i} \neq *$). The distinctive feature of this model lies in its consideration of the Bert review vectors as the representation of contextual factors. These factors have a direct influence on the user's rating for the item ($\hat{r}_{u,i}$). This influence is incorporated into the objective function to learn the user vectors ($\vec{k}_u\ u = 1\ldots m$) and item vectors ($\vec{y}_i\ i = 1\ldots n$) in the following manner:

$$\hat{r}_{u,i} \approx \vec{k}_u \cdot \vec{y}_i$$

$$\min_{\substack{\vec{k}_u, \vec{y}_i \\ u=1\ldots m \\ i=1\ldots n}} \frac{1}{2} \cdot \sum_{\{(u,i)|u=1\ldots m \wedge i=1\ldots n \wedge r_{u,i} \neq *\}} \left(r_{u,i} - \hat{r}_{u,i} - \vec{k}_u \cdot \vec{v}_{u,i} - \vec{y}_i \cdot \vec{v}_{u,i} \right)^2$$

$$\Leftrightarrow \min_{\substack{\vec{k}_u, \vec{y}_i \\ u=1\ldots m \\ i=1\ldots n}} \frac{1}{2} \cdot \sum_{\{(u,i)|u=1\ldots m \wedge i=1\ldots n \wedge r_{u,i} \neq *\}} \left(r_{u,i} - \hat{r}_{u,i} - \vec{k}_u \cdot \vec{v}_{u,i} - \vec{y}_i \cdot \vec{v}_{u,i} \right)^2$$

$$\tag{6}$$

In the combined latent factor spaces, users and items are represented as specified vectors. Therefore, it is straightforward to implement the cosine similarity to calculate the similarity of two users (u and v)/two items (i and j):

$$sim_{u,v}^{(Rating\&Interaction)} = cosine(\vec{z}_u, \vec{z}_v) = \frac{\vec{z}_u \cdot \vec{z}_v}{\|\vec{z}_u\| \cdot \|\vec{z}_v\|}$$

$$sim_{u,v}^{(Rating\&Review)} = cosine(\vec{k}_u, \vec{k}_v) = \frac{\vec{k}_u \cdot \vec{k}_v}{\|\vec{k}_u\| \cdot \|\vec{k}_v\|}$$

$$sim_{i,j}^{(Rating\&Interaction)} = cosine(\vec{h}_i, \vec{h}_j) = \frac{\vec{h}_i \cdot \vec{h}_j}{\|\vec{h}_i\| \cdot \|\vec{h}_j\|}$$

$$sim_{i,j}^{(Rating\&Review)} = cosine(\vec{y}_i, \vec{y}_j) = \frac{\vec{y}_i \cdot \vec{y}_j}{\|\vec{y}_i\| \cdot \|\vec{y}_j\|} \tag{7}$$

Let the neighbor sets $\mathbb{T}_{u,i}^{(Rating\&Interaction)}$ and $\mathbb{T}_{u,i}^{(Rating\&Review)}$ respectively denote the set of users who have provided ratings for an item i and have the highest similarities ($sim_{u,v}^{(Rating\&Interaction)}$ and $sim_{u,v}^{(Rating\&Review)}$) with a user u. Now, the process of predicting the rating of u for i in the neighbor-user model ($\hat{r}_{u,i}^{(U\_Rating\&Interaction)}$ and $\hat{r}_{u,i}^{(U\_Rating\&Review)}$) would be as follows:

$$\hat{r}_{u,i}^{(U\_Rating\&Interaction)} = \mu_u + \frac{\sum_{v \in \mathbb{T}_{u,i}^{(Rating\&Interaction)}} sim_{u,v}^{(Rating\&Interaction)} \cdot (r_{v,i} - \mu_v)}{\sum_{v \in \mathbb{T}_{u,i}^{(Rating\&Interaction)}} \left| sim_{u,v}^{(Rating\&Interaction)} \right|}$$

$$\hat{r}_{u,i}^{(U\_Rating\&Review)} = \mu_u + \frac{\sum_{v \in \mathbb{T}_{u,i}^{(Rating\&Review)}} sim_{u,v}^{(Rating\&Review)} \cdot (r_{v,i} - \mu_v)}{\sum_{\mathbb{T}_{u,i}^{(Rating\&Review)}} \left| sim_{u,v}^{(Rating\&Review)} \right|} \qquad (8)$$

Similarly, the prediction process in the neighbor-item model ($\hat{r}_{u,i}^{(I\_Rating\&Interaction)}$ and $\hat{r}_{u,i}^{(I\_Rating\&Review)}$) is implemented as follows:

$$\hat{r}_{u,i}^{(I\_Rating\&Interaction)} = \mu_u + \frac{\sum_{j \in \mathbb{W}_{i,u}^{(Rating\&Interaction)}} sim_{i,j}^{(Rating\&Interaction)} \cdot (r_{u,j} - \mu_u)}{\sum_{j \in \mathbb{W}_{i,u}^{(Rating\&Interaction)}} \left| sim_{i,j}^{(Rating\&Interaction)} \right|}$$

$$\hat{r}_{u,i}^{(I\_Rating\&Review)} = \mu_u + \frac{\sum_{j \in \mathbb{W}_{i,u}^{(Rating\&Review)}} sim_{i,j}^{(Rating\&Review)} \cdot (r_{u,j} - \mu_u)}{\sum_{j \in \mathbb{W}_{i,u}^{(Rating\&Review)}} \left| sim_{i,j}^{(Rating\&Review)} \right|} \qquad (9)$$

where $\mathbb{W}_{i,u}^{(Rating\&Interaction)}$ and $\mathbb{W}_{i,u}^{(Rating\&Review)}$ represent the sets of items that have been rated by user u and have the highest similarities ($sim_{i,j}^{(Rating\&Interaction)}$ and $sim_{i,j}^{(Rating\&Review)}$) with i.

As mentioned in Sect. 3, we aim for a comprehensive hybrid approach to rating predictions. The comprehensiveness lies in not only combining both user-based and item-based implementations but also incorporating interaction, review, and rating data. Therefore, we utilize the weighted average to achieve the final rating ($\hat{r}_{u,i}$), as follows:

$$\hat{r}_{u,i} = \alpha \cdot \hat{r}_{u,i}^{(U\_Rating\&Interaction)} + \beta \cdot \hat{r}_{u,i}^{(U\_Rating\&Review)} + \gamma \cdot \hat{r}_{u,i}^{(I\_Rating\&Interaction)} + \sigma \cdot \hat{r}_{u,i}^{(I\_Rating\&Review)}$$
$$(10)$$

4.2 Weight Estimation

Many previous hybrid models often assign equal weights to their individual models ($\alpha = \beta = \gamma = \sigma$ in Eq. (10)). However, in reality, the individual models can have varying levels of accuracy in different application domains. Therefore, setting equal weights may not be the optimal choice. In this paper, the weights (α, β, γ, and σ) are determined through an estimation process using a subset of observed data called the validation set

$\mathbb{H}$. Specifically, we use Eq. (8, 9) to make predictions for each rating in the validation set, and then aggregate them using Eq. (10). Optimizing the difference between the observed ratings in the validation set ($r_{u,i} \in \mathbb{H}$) and their predictions ($\hat{r}_{u,i}$) helps determine α, β, γ, and σ. Our advantage lies in the parallel optimization towards both the observed rating and the inferred ratings from observed reviews (the rating $r\prime_{u,i}$ inferred from the review of user u for item i, as proposed in [17]). This parallel optimization is particularly effective in situations where there is an inconsistency between the reviews and the ratings provided by the users. The detailed objective function for weight estimation is as follows:

$$\min_{\alpha,\beta,\gamma,\sigma} \frac{1}{2} \cdot \sum_{r_{u,i} \in \mathbb{H}} \left(\left(r_{u,i} - \hat{r}_{u,i} \right)^2 + \left(r\prime_{u,i} - \hat{r}_{u,i} \right)^2 \right) + \frac{\lambda}{2} \left(\alpha^2 + \beta^2 + \gamma^2 + \sigma^2 \right)$$

$$\Leftrightarrow \min_{\alpha,\beta,\gamma,\sigma} \frac{1}{2} \cdot \sum_{r_{u,i} \in \mathbb{H}} \left(\begin{matrix} \left(\begin{matrix} r_{u,i} - \alpha.\hat{r}_{u,i}^{(U\_Rating\&Interaction)} - \beta.\hat{r}_{u,i}^{(U\_Rating\&Review)} \\ -\gamma.\hat{r}_{u,i}^{(I\_Rating\&Interaction)} - \sigma.\hat{r}_{u,i}^{(I\_Rating\&Review)} \end{matrix} \right)^2 \\ + \left(\begin{matrix} r\prime_{u,i} - \alpha.\hat{r}_{u,i}^{(U\_Rating\&Interaction)} - \beta.\hat{r}_{u,i}^{(U\_Rating\&Review)} \\ -\gamma.\hat{r}_{u,i}^{(I\_Rating\&Interaction)} - \sigma.\hat{r}_{u,i}^{(I\_Rating\&Review)} \end{matrix} \right)^2 \end{matrix} \right) + \frac{\lambda}{2} \left(\alpha^2 + \beta^2 + \gamma^2 + \sigma^2 \right)$$

$$(11)$$

The last part in Eq. (11) is a Tikhonov regularization to prevent overfitting with the weight λ. Equation (11) can be solved as a bridge regression.

4.3 Efficient Implementation

In general, the implementation of a neighbor model consists of two stages: offline and online.

- During the offline stage, the model computes the similarity between each pair of users/items using a selected similarity metric.
- The online stage is performed based on the sets of neighbor users/items, which are easily determined by the similarity scores calculated in the offline stage. Using these neighbor sets, the model predicts the ratings of the active user for items that he/she has not yet discovered.

However, in scenarios where the number of users/items is large, calculating pairwise similarities for all user/item pairs in the offline stage becomes computationally infeasible. One approach to address this issue is to cluster users/items, allowing for similarity calculations only within each cluster [18, 19]. However, clustering users/items in the sparse space of preferences often leads to suboptimal clustering results. This can result in a significant decline in the performance of subsequent neighbor-based recommendations. It is important to highlight that in the offline stage, we have successfully obtained user vectors, i.e., $\overrightarrow{z}_u$ and $\overrightarrow{k}_u$ $u = 1 \ldots m$, and item vectors, i.e., $\overrightarrow{h}_i$ and $\overrightarrow{y}_i$ $i = 1 \ldots n$, in a combined space of ratings, reviews, and interactions. We apply concatenation to these vectors to create a unique vector for each item and user, i.e., $\overrightarrow{x}_u$=concatenation($\overrightarrow{z}_u, \overrightarrow{k}_u$) $u = 1 \ldots m$ and $\overrightarrow{d}_i =$ concatenation($\overrightarrow{h}_i, \overrightarrow{y}_i$) $i = 1 \ldots n$. This technique is commonly used in previous research to integrate different representations of an object. Instead of clustering sparse preference vectors, we cluster the concatenated vectors, as follows:

$$\text{Clustering } \vec{x}_u \ u = 1...m; \quad \text{clustering } \vec{d}_i \ i = 1...n$$

$$sim_{u,v} \text{ if } u \text{ and } v \text{ belong to the same cluster.} \tag{12}$$

$$sim_{i,j} \text{ if } i \text{ and } j \text{ belong to the same cluster}$$

5 Experiment

5.1 Experiment Setup

In the experiments, our method will be compared with the following approaches:

- [23]: Neighbor-User model relying solely on Ratings (NuRa)
- [24]: Neighbor-User model relying solely on Reviews (NuRe)
- [25]: Neighbor-User model combining Ratings and Reviews (NuRaRe)
- [11]: Neighbor-User and Neighbor-Item model relying solely on Ratings (NuNiRa)
- [10]: Neighbor-User and Neighbor-Item model combining Ratings and Reviews (NuNiRaRe) where the item description is formed by aggregating reviews.
- Our proposed approach: Neighbor-User and Neighbor-Item model combining Ratings, Reviews, and Interactions (TATP).

The parameters for the latent factor models SC1 and UI2R to learn user/item vectors in TATP are set as follows:

- Learning rate is 0,003
- Regularization weight is 0,02
- The number of latent factors is 60

5.2 Dataset

To conduct the experiments, we selected three popular Amazon datasets containing both ratings and reviews. Their details are presented in Table 1. The experimental datasets are randomly divided into 65% for training and 25% for testing.

Table 1. The datasets.

	# users	# items	# ratings and reviews
Video games	24,303	10,672	231,780
Clothing-Accessories	39,387	23,033	278,677
Gourmet food	14,681	8,713	151,254

Inspired by [12, 26, 27], we simulate user interaction data as follows. If a user provides a rating for an item, it can be inferred that the user has interacted with the item. This simulation does have a limitation, as it overlooks instances where users interact with items but do not provide ratings. However, given the vast number of items available, omitting these cases introduces negligible bias to the overall results.

5.3 Measure

RMSE is utilized to assess the accuracy of recommendation models, as follows:

$$RMSE = \sqrt{\frac{\sum_{(u,i)\in\mathbb{T}}\left(\hat{r}_{u,i} - r_{u,i}\right)^2}{|\mathbb{T}|}} \tag{13}$$

where $\mathbb{T}$ is the test set.

5.4 Experimental Results

Figure 2 illustrates the RMSE results of the experimental approaches. It is evident that the hybrid approaches, i.e., NuRaRe, NuNiRa, NuNiRaRe, and TATP, yield better results compared to the individual approaches, i.e., NuRe and NuRa. Among the hybrid approaches, our approach TATP outperforms the others. The reason for this is

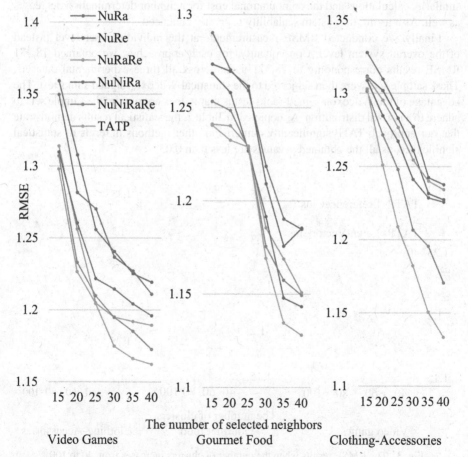

The number of selected neighbors

Video Games   Gourmet Food   Clothing-Accessories

Fig. 2. The RMSE results when the number of selected neighbors increases from 15 to 40.

that TATP utilizes more information and performs more comprehensive calculations compared to the other approaches. Furthermore, leveraging both the observed ratings and observed reviews to implement a bridge regression for learning the weights of the individual models also proves to be highly effective. Due to the inherent sparsity of the recommendation problem, combining more data and computations naturally leads to significantly improved accuracy in the recommendation process. Although there is a trade-off in terms of increased computational costs, the continual advancements in computational power and storage capacity have made this trade-off more feasible and acceptable.

Fixing the number of neighbors optimally for each approach on each experimental dataset, we perform user/item clustering to enhance scalability as presented in Sect. 4.3. Figure 3 shows that the clustering in our combined space (TATP + LatentVectorClus) proves to be more effective compared to that in the preference space [18, 19] (TATP + PreferenceClus). This effect becomes more pronounced as the number of clusters increases. Note that as the number of clusters increases, the number of users/items within each cluster gradually decreases. This means that the number of pairs requiring similarity calculations and the computational cost for neighbor determination decreases as well. As a result, the system scalability is greatly enhanced.

Finally, we conducted RMSE measurements at the individual user level instead of the overall system level. Consequently, for each approaches, we obtained 78,371 RMSE results corresponding to 78,371 users across all three experimental datasets. These sample sets were then subjected to the statistical Wilcoxon signed-ranks test. The advantage of the Wilcoxon signed-ranks test is that it does not require the sample sets to adhere to a normal distribution. As depicted in Table 2, the statistical results demonstrate that our approach TATP significantly outperform other methods in terms of statistical significance, as all the obtained p-values are less than 0.05.

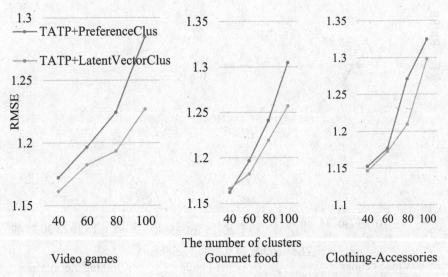

Fig. 3. The RMSE results when the number of clusters increases from 40 to 100.

Table 2. The results of the statistical Wilcoxon signed-ranks test.

TATP >> NuNiRaRe p-value = 0.0152	TATP >> NuNiRa p-value = 0.0067	TATP >> NuRaRe p-value = 0.0081	TATP >> NuRe p-value = 0.0029

6 Conclusion and Future Work

In terms of computation, this paper combines both user and item aspects to effectively utilize both neighbor users and neighbor items in predicting ratings. Regarding data, this paper integrates three common types of user profiles, including user ratings, user reviews, and user interactions, into the training process. The parameters of our hybrid model are estimated using a bridge regression. The experimental results on various datasets demonstrate that our approach performs better than both individual approaches and other hybrid approaches.

The main drawback of our proposed approach is its substantial computational overhead. This arises from the implementation of diverse individual approaches on various user profile types. Although we have proposed a version to reduce computational expenses, the reduction is not significant. Therefore, in the future, we aim to redesign the proposed approach with parallel processing. This will facilitate successful deployment on a distributed Hadoop.

Acknowledgments. This research is funded by the University of Science, VNU-HCM under grant number CNTT 2022-01.

References

1. Duan, R., Jiang, C., Jain, H.K.: Combining review-based collaborative filtering and matrix factorization: a solution to rating's sparsity problem. Decis. Support Syst. **156**, 113748 (2022)
2. Ahmadian, M., Ahmadi, M., Ahmadian, S.: A reliable deep representation learning to improve trust-aware recommendation systems. Expert Syst. Appl. **197**, 116697 (2022)
3. Ahmadian, S., Ahmadian, M., Jalili, M.: A deep learning based trust-and tag-aware recommender system. Neurocomputing **488**, 557–571 (2022)
4. Nam, L.N.H.: Towards comprehensive profile aggregation methods for group recommendation based on the latent factor model. Expert Syst. Appl. **185** (2021)
5. Nam, L.N.H.: Profile aggregation-based group recommender systems: moving from item preference profiles to deep profiles. IEEE Access **10**, 6218–6245 (2022)
6. Noshad, Z., Bouyer, A., Noshad, M.: Mutual information-based recommender system using autoencoder. Appl. Soft Comput. **109**, 107547 (2021)
7. Sun, X., Zhang, L.: Multi-order nearest neighbor prediction for recommendation systems. Digital Signal Process. **127**, 103540 (2022)
8. Nam, L.N.H.: Towards comprehensive approaches for the rating prediction phase in memory-based collaborative filtering recommender systems. Inf. Sci. **589** (2022)
9. Vultureanu-Albişi, A., Bădică, C.: A survey on effects of adding explanations to recommender systems (2022)

10. Hoang, B.N.M., Vy, H.T.H., Hong, T.G., Hang, V.T.M., Nhung, H.L.T.K., Nam, L.N.H.: Using Bert Embedding to improve memory-based collaborative filtering recommender systems. In: 2021 RIVF International Conference on Computing and Communication Technologies (RIVF), pp. 1–6. IEEE (2021)

11. Nilashi, M., Ibrahim, O., Bagherifard, K.: A recommender system based on collaborative filtering using ontology and dimensionality reduction techniques. Expert Syst. Appl. **92**, 507–520 (2018)

12. Nam, L.N.H.: Latent factor recommendation models for integrating explicit and implicit preferences in a multi-step decision-making process. Expert Syst. Appl. **174** (2021)

13. Nam, L.N.H.: Incorporating textual reviews in the learning of latent factors for recommender systems. Electron. Commerce Rese. Appl. **52** (2022)

14. Noulapeu Ngaffo, A., Choukair, Z.: A deep neural network-based collaborative filtering using a matrix factorization with a twofold regularization. Neural Comput. Appl. **34**(9), 6991–7003 (2022)

15. Khan, Z., Iltaf, N., Afzal, H., Abbas, H.: Enriching non-negative matrix factorization with contextual embeddings for recommender systems. Neurocomputing **380**, 246–258 (2020)

16. Yengikand, A.K., Meghdadi, M., Ahmadian, S.: DHSIRS: a novel deep hybrid side information-based recommender system. Multimedia Tools Appl. 1–27 (2023)

17. Shen, R.P., Zhang, H.R., Yu, H., Min, F.: Sentiment based matrix factorization with reliability for recommendation. Expert Syst. Appl. **135**, 249–258 (2019)

18. Nikolakopoulos, A.N., Ning, X., Desrosiers, C., Karypis, G.: Trust your neighbors: a comprehensive survey of neighborhood-based methods for recommender systems. Recommender Systems Handbook, pp. 39–89 (2021)

19. Aggarwal, C.C.: Neighborhood-based collaborative filtering. Recommender Systems: The Textbook, pp. 29–70 (2016)

20. Koutrika, G., Bercovitz, B., Garcia-Molina, H.F.: Expressing and combining flexible recommendations. In: Proceedings of the 35th SIGMOD International Conference on Management of Data (SIGMOD 2009), Providence, RI, USA, vol. 29 (2009)

21. Herlocker, J.L., Konstan, J.A., Borchers, A., Riedl, J.: An algorithmic framework for performing collaborative filtering. In: ACM SIGIR Forum, vol. 51, no. 2, pp. 227–234. New York, NY, USA: ACM (2017)

22. Su, X., Khoshgoftaar, T.M.: A survey of collaborative filtering techniques. Adv. Artif. Intell. **2009** (2009)

23. Feng, C., Liang, J., Song, P., Wang, Z.: A fusion collaborative filtering method for sparse data in recommender systems. Inf. Sci. **521**, 365–379 (2020)

24. Musto, C., de Gemmis, M., Semeraro, G., Lops, P.: A multi-criteria recommender system exploiting aspect-based sentiment analysis of users' reviews. In Proceedings of the Eleventh ACM Conference on Recommender Systems, pp. 321–325 (2017)

25. Ghasemi, N., Momtazi, S.: Neural text similarity of user reviews for improving collaborative filtering recommender systems. Electron. Commer. Res. Appl. **45**, 101019 (2021)

26. Aggarwal, C.C.: An introduction to recommender systems. In: Recommender Systems, pp. 1–28. Springer, Cham (2016)

27. Pan, R., Scholz, M.: Mind the gaps: weighting the unknown in large-scale one-class collaborative filtering. In: Proceedings of the 15th ACM SIGKDD International Conference on Knowledge Discovery and Data Mining, pp. 667–676 (2009)

Readability Measures as Predictors of Understandability and Engagement in Searching to Learn

Yasin Ghafourian[1,2]([✉]) [iD], Allan Hanbury[2] [iD], and Petr Knoth[3] [iD]

[1] Research Studios Austria FG, Vienna 1090, Austria
yasin.ghafourian@researchstudio.at
[2] Technische Universität Wien, Vienna 1040, Austria
[3] Knowledge Media Institute, Open University, Milton Keynes, UK

Abstract. Search engines have become essential tools for learning, providing access to vast amounts of educational resources. However, selecting the most suitable resources from numerous options can be challenging for learners. While search engines primarily rank resources based on topical relevance, factors like understandability and engagement are crucial for effective learning as well. Understandability, a key aspect of text, is often associated with readability. This study evaluates eight commonly used readability measures to determine their effectiveness in predicting understandability, engagement, topical relevance, and user-assigned ranks. The empirical evaluation employs a survey-based methodology, collecting explicit relevance feedback from participants regarding their preferences for learning from web pages. The relevance data was then analyzed concerning the readability measures. The findings highlight that readability measures are not only reliable predictors of understandability but also of engagement. Specifically, the FKGL and GFI measures demonstrate the highest and most consistent correlation with perceived understandability and engagement. This research provides valuable insights for selecting effective readability measures to tailor search results to the users' learning needs.

Keywords: Empirical Evaluation · Relevance · Understandability · Engagement · Readability Measures · User Study

1 Introduction

Search engines provide access to large quantities of learning resources contributing to the trend of using web search as a means for learning [3,8]. However, it can be challenging for learners to choose which resources are most suitable from many of the available options [10,13]. Search engines typically rank resources by their topical relevance, but other characteristics, such as understandability and engagement of the learning resources, are also important to learners.

Several readability measures have been established in the literature. They have been used to assess the complexity of written text and estimate its reading difficulty. In 1969, G. Harry McLaughlin, the creator of one of the widely used readability measures, defined readability as: "the degree to which a given class of people find certain reading matter compelling and comprehensible [17]." As a result, readability is inherently linked to engagement and understandability.

Although there are several categories of approaches in the literature to measure the readability of text, More research is needed to assess their performance in different use cases. Vajjala's survey [23] summarizes two decades of literature on Automatic Readability Assessment (ARA) and concludes that a clear understanding of effective modeling techniques is still lacking in ARA.

Readability measures consider surface-level language features in web pages, such as sentence structure and word choice. Therefore, lengthy sentences, multi-syllabic words, and uncommon vocabulary typically yield readability scores indicating a more complex text. Readability is one of the aspects of the text that contributes to its understandability [5,26]. Thus, readability has been used in the literature as a proxy for understandability [18,30,31]. Table 1 provides a summary of eight of the most frequently used readability measures.

Table 1. Summary of the most common readability measures. S, W, Syl, and Ch show the number of sentences, words, syllables, and characters in the text respectively. W_Polly shows the number of words with 3 or more syllables, and W_long is the number of words with 6 or more characters. DC_DW is the number of difficult words after excluding Dale-Chall's list of 3,000 common words.

Readability Measure	Abbreviation	Formula	Description
Flesch-Kincaid Grade Level Index [12]	FKGL	$11.8 \times (\frac{Syl}{W}) + 0.39 \times (\frac{W}{S}) - 15.59$	Outputs a score as a U.S. grade level needed to understand the text. It can also mean the years of education needed to read the text.
Gunning's Fog Index [9]	GFI (or FOG)	$0.4 \times (\frac{W}{S} + (100 \times \frac{W\_Polly}{W}))$	The Gunning Fog Index formula promotes shorter, plain English sentences for better readability scores, while scores above 12 become difficult for most readers.
Flesh Reading Ease [7]	FRE	$206.835 - 1.015 \times \frac{W}{S} - 84.6 \times \frac{Syl}{W}$	Outputs a number between 0 and 100. The easier the text, the higher the score that it receives.
Coleman-Liau Index [4]	CLI	$0.0588 \times (\frac{Ch}{W} \times 100) + 0.296 \times (\frac{S}{W} \times 100) - 15.8$	Originally developed to help the U.S. Office of Education, CLI approximates a U.S. grade level to understand the text.
Dale-Chall Readability index [6]	DCI	$0.1579 \times (\frac{DC\_DW}{W} \times 100) + 0.0496 \times (\frac{W}{S})$	Outputs a score that corresponds to the U.S. grade system and is based on the use of familiar English words.
Automated Readability Index [22]	ARI	$0.5 \times (\frac{W}{S}) + 4.71 \times (\frac{Ch}{W}) - 21.43$	Outputs a number that approximates the grade needed to understand the text according to U.S. school grade system (from kindergarten to college)
The Lasbarhetsindex [2]	LIX	$\frac{W}{S} + (\frac{W\_long}{W} \times 100)$	Originally developed by a Swedish scholar, LIX is based on a word factor and a sentence factor. It favors the texts with shorter words (less than 6 characters) and sentences.
SMOG Grading [17]	SMOG	$3.1291 + 1.0430 \times \sqrt{\frac{W\_Polly}{S} \times 30}$	This formula estimates the educational years required to comprehend a text with values corresponding from the 4th grade to the college level in the U.S. grading system

Our Study in this paper is the first that empirically evaluates the predictive capacity of these eight readability measures under the same experimental conditions in a searching to learn context. We aim to assess the degree to which they can be used as predictors of the understandability, engagement, and topical relevance of web pages as perceived by users as well as the rank that the users would assign to these web pages for learning. Our results contribute to a better understanding of the differences in performance and consistency of readability measures, thus helping to select the most effective readability measures in tailoring search results towards the needs of learners.

Our methodology is based on a survey design and proceeds by first collecting explicit relevance feedback focused on participants' preferences for learning about a topic from a set of Web pages. We then analysed how the relevance data provided is associated with the readability measures listed above in Table 1. More specifically, we aim to answer the following two questions:

Research Question 1. To what extent are existing readability measures associated with the perceived understandability, engagement, topical relevance, and user-assigned ranks?

Research Question 2. To what extent are existing readability measures consistent in estimating the perceived understandability, engagement, topical relevance, and user-assigned ranks?

The key contributions of this work are: 1) We show that readability measures are not only good predictors of understandability (as they have been used as a proxy for understandability), but also of engagement of web pages 2) We show that FKGL and GFI are the readability measures with the highest and the most consistent correlation with perceived understandability and engagement.

2   Methodology

Our methodology employs a survey design to gather explicit relevance feedback from online participants' preferences for learning about a specific topic. We selected four topics and created a knowledge test consisting of 10 questions for each topic in survey format, using available online quizzes. This test, administered only once at the start of the survey, aimed to assess participants' existing knowledge of the topics and provide us with insights on the topic knowledge distribution among them. Next, we sampled 10 web pages for each topic using Google as search engine and SerpAPI[1] as a tool to retrieve the results returned by Google. For each topic, we submitted a query that covered the most important concepts in its knowledge test 10 times from different locations and in 10-minute intervals. We then merged the 10 retrieved search engine result pages (SERPs) in a paginated manner and sampled a link from each page of the merged SERP.

For each topic, more than 50 participants were hired from Prolific[2] resulting in a total of 207. Participants were instructed to re-rank the given web pages in descending order based on their opinion of how suitable they found the web pages

---

[1] https://serpapi.com.
[2] https://www.prolific.co/.

for learning about the topic. Simultaneously, they were asked to provide three labels for each web page on a 5/7 point Likert scale: 1) the topical relevance, 2) the understandability, and 3) the level of engagement offered by the web page meaning its motivational value for learning about the topic.

Having conducted the survey, we proceeded to calculate the readability value for each web page in our collection using eight different readability measures from Table 1. To extract readability features, we pre-processed the documents using trafilatura[3]. It is worth noting that Palotti et al. [19] have done an investigation on the impact of web page pre-processing on readability measure values.

3   Results

Table 2 provides an overview of the participants who took part in each of the four topics, including their demographic distribution, average declared knowledge of the topic, and average obtained knowledge score after taking the knowledge test.

Table 2. An overview of participants' demographics and characteristics. The Average Declared Knowledge is reported using a 5-point Likert scale and the attained Average Knowledge Test Scores are mapped to the same scale to allow comparison.

Topic Name	Number of Participants	Time Spent on the Survey (Minutes)		Gender Distribution			Age Distribution						Average Declared Knowledge (1-5)	Average Knowledge Test Score	Difference between Declared Knowledge Score and Test Score
		Mean	Standard Deviation	Female	Male	Other	18-24	25-34	35-44	45-54	55+			
World War 2	56	21.25	10.37	44%	56%	0%	5%	51%	22%	15%	7%	3.4	3.48 (62%)	0.08
Financial Literacy	51	22.10	10.12	45%	55%	0%	12%	27%	37%	20%	4%	3.1	3.20 (55%)	0.10
Covid-19	50	18.8	7.41	58%	40%	2%	12%	52%	18%	14%	4%	3.82	2.84 (46%)	0.98
Theory of General Relativity	50	26.62	14.12	44%	54%	2%	4%	38%	28%	24%	6%	2.26	2.32 (33%)	0.06

In order to investigate the association between the readability of web pages and the perceived relevance of those web pages, we utilized the Pearson correlation. Pearson correlation explores the strength and direction of the relationship between user-assigned values and readability measures for research question 1. To study the consistency of the readability measures for research question 2, the standard deviation of correlations across topics is used as a measure of variation.

Most readability measures, with the exception of Flesch Reading Ease (FRE), are inherently designed so that a higher readability score indicates lower text understandability and, more difficult text. In FRE, a higher score signifies higher text understandability and lower difficulty. We have taken this inherent behaviour of readability functions into account during the conversion of the user-assigned labels of relevance from the Likert scale to values to allow for a straightforward comparison. As a result, in the converted Likert values, a lower

---

[3] https://trafilatura.readthedocs.io.

Table 3. Pearson correlations between user-provided labels and readability measures across topics. FRE • is the measure obtained from negating FRE. The values associated with $FKGL^\rho$ and GFI^σ are marked in bold as $FKGL^\rho$ is the readability measure with the highest average correlation with all labels across topics, and GFI^σ is the most consistent readability measure across topics in all dimensions of relevance, as it has the lowest mean standard deviation.

Label Name	Readability Measure	Mean of Correlations	SD of Correlations	Label Name	Readability Measure	Mean of Correlations	SD of Correlations
Understandability	$FKGL^\rho$	**0.645**	**0.077**	Engagement	$FKGL^\rho$	**0.566**	**0.121**
	GFI^σ	**0.642**	**0.074**		GFI^σ	**0.566**	**0.094**
	FRE •	0.640	0.070		SMOG	0.560	0.122
	SMOG	0.639	0.042		FRE •	0.559	0.157
	ARI	0.593	0.079		ARI	0.526	0.132
	LIX	0.573	0.074		LIX	0.507	0.151
	DCI	0.434	0.455		DCI	0.424	0.388
	CLI	0.399	0.231		CLI	0.360	0.385
Rank	$FKGL^\rho$	**0.526**	**0.217**	Topical Relevance	DCI	0.277	0.452
	GFI^σ	**0.511**	**0.184**		FRE •	0.275	0.350
	FRE •	0.504	0.280		$FKGL^\rho$	**0.270**	**0.261**
	ARI	0.501	0.246		ARI	0.265	0.325
	SMOG	0.489	0.231		GFI^σ	**0.239**	**0.197**
	LIX	0.454	0.261		SMOG	0.223	0.244
	DCI	0.413	0.494		CLI	0.194	0.586
	CLI	0.329	0.503		LIX	0.193	0.286

value indicates a higher preference. For example, "Very Easy" in the understandability label was assigned the value of 1, while "Very Difficult" received the value of 7.

Table 3 shows the results of computing the Pearson correlation between each of the user-assigned values as one variable and each readability measure as the other variable. The correlations were calculated for each pair of label and measure, and then the mean and standard deviation of these correlations were calculated across all topics. The results from Table 3 confirm that the readability measures, apart from DCI and CLI, show high consistency across topics for understandability and to a large degree also for engagement. For the topical relevance and rank, the standard deviations are substantially higher indicating that these readability measures are not necessarily good predictors for them.

Among the readability measures, $FKGL$ stands out with the highest mean correlation across all user-assigned labels, while GFI demonstrates the highest consistency across all topics for all labels. The alignment of these two measures with the two labels that have shown the highest correlation with them (understandability and engagement) for all 4 topics is illustrated in Fig. 1. A closer look at Fig. 1 reveals that both the $FKGL$ and GFI measures exhibit a moderate to strong estimation of user-assigned understandability and engagement across all topics. Moreover, the figure highlights an interesting observation: the correlation values for each topic using both the $FKGL$ and GFI measures are nearly identical. These findings suggest that there is a consistent and robust

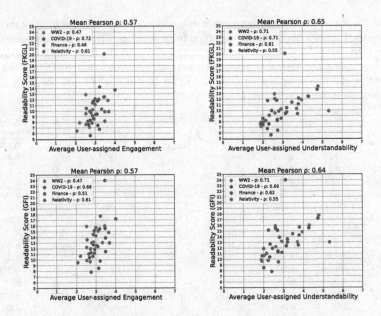

Fig. 1. Alignment of FKGL and GFI with values from user-provided labels, understandability, and engagement. Each dot is a web page.

relationship between these two measures and user-assigned understandability, and user-assigned engagement, regardless of the topic under consideration.

4   Discussion and Related Work

Readability measures have been used in combination with other frameworks to assess the understandability of text across different domains. Some works can be mentioned from the health informatics domain [1, 25, 27, 29]. It has also been previously shown that using readability measures to model text comprehensibility and personalize the search results to the user's understandability level can lead to significant improvements in content ranking [20, 30]. Readability measures have been also investigated in user studies as estimators and predictors of user-provided data concerning understandability, comprehensibility, etc. [11, 24, 28]. For instance, Leroy et al. [14] measured the association between values calculated by readability formulas and values assigned by users to a pair of difficult and easy sentences to measure the effectiveness of a text simplification tool.

Our work in this paper is the first study that looks into evaluating the predictive power of readability measures in a searching to learn context. We have asked our survey participants to provide scores for understandability, engagement, and topical relevance of web pages as they are re-ranking the pages for learning. This work falls in the same category as prior studies which empirically evaluate the performance of readability measures by conducting a user study and measuring the relationship between the user-provided data and the readability measures.

It comes as no surprise for us to see that user-assigned values for understandability exhibit the highest correlation with readability measures. However, it is intriguing to note that these measures serve also as predictors for engagement and, to a considerable extent, for topical relevance although with a weaker correlation with rank, indicating a less pronounced association. A slight surprise is that these measures demonstrate a weaker correlation with topical relevance compared to rank, despite topical relevance being commonly regarded as the primary component influencing the rank. This suggests that understandability and engagement might be equally, if not more, closely linked to rank. This observation is in line with the literature on information retrieval, stating that the overall relevance is not merely a function of topical relevance, but it is a multi-aspect concept including aspects like understandability, novelty, reliability, and other aspects. [5,16,21]. Similarly, the results of a user study by Li et. al [15] exploring a multidimensional user relevance model, concluded that "Topicality" does not show a significant contribution to users' relevance judgment.

5 Conclusion

In this paper, we studied the performance of eight of the most frequently used readability measures in predicting understandability, topical relevance, and engagement of online web pages as perceived by users in a learning context. We measured this performance in terms of correlation and consistency. We showed how each of these measures is correlated which each of the user-provided labels and how consistent is each measure across topics. We found out that not only are these measures moderate-strong predictors of understandability, but also they are good predictors of engagement as well. We also found out that in particular, two reading measures of FKGL and GFI have shown the highest correlation and consistency on average with all the user-provided labels. In our future work, we aim to assess the accuracy of readability measures in personalizing search results based on users' understanding of a topic, as estimated by those measures. We will explore this using our assessment of users' knowledge on the topic that are obtained through online quizzes before directing them to relevant web pages.

Acknowledgements. This work was supported by the EU Horizon 2020 ITN/ETN on Domain Specific Systems for Information Extraction and Retrieval - DoSSIER (H2020-EU.1.3.1., ID: 860721).

References

1. Adkins, A.D., Singh, N.N.: Reading level and readability of patient education materials in mental health. J. Child Family Stud. **10**, 1–8 (2001)
2. Björnsson, C.H.: Readability of newspapers in 11 languages. Reading Res. Q. **18**, 480–497 (1983)
3. Câmara, A., Roy, N., Maxwell, D., Hauff, C.: Searching to learn with instructional scaffolding. In: Proceedings of the 2021 Conference on Human Information Interaction and Retrieval, pp. 209–218 (2021)

4. Coleman, M., Liau, T.L.: A computer readability formula designed for machine scoring. J. Appl. Psychol. **60**(2), 283 (1975)
5. Cosijn, E., Ingwersen, P.: Dimensions of relevance. Inf. Process. Manage. **36**(4), 533–550 (2000)
6. Dale, E., Chall, J.S.: A formula for predicting readability: instructions. Educ. Res. Bull. **27**, 37–54 (1948)
7. Flesch, R.F., et al.: Art of readable writing (1949)
8. Gadiraju, U., Yu, R., Dietze, S., Holtz, P.: Analyzing knowledge gain of users in informational search sessions on the web. In: Proceedings of the 2018 Conference on Human Information Interaction & Retrieval, pp. 2–11 (2018)
9. Gunning, R.: The Technique of Clear Writing. McGraw-Hill. New York (1952)
10. Head, A.J., Eisenberg, M.B.: What today's college students say about conducting research in the digital age. Project Inf. Literacy Prog. Rep. **4**(7) (2009)
11. Kauchak, D., Leroy, G., Hogue, A.: Measuring text difficulty using parse-tree frequency. J. Assoc. Inf. Sci. Technol. **68**(9), 2088–2100 (2017)
12. Kincaid, J.P., Fishburne, R.P., Jr., Rogers, R.L., Chissom, B.S.: Derivation of new readability formulas (automated readability index, fog count and flesch reading ease formula) for navy enlisted personnel. Technical Report, Naval Technical Training Command Millington TN Research Branch (1975)
13. Lee, S.S., Tay, S.M., Balakrishnan, A., Yeo, S.P., Samarasekera, D.D.: Mobile learning in clinical settings: unveiling the paradox. Korean J. Med. Educ. **33**(4), 349 (2021)
14. Leroy, G., Kauchak, D., Mouradi, O.: A user-study measuring the effects of lexical simplification and coherence enhancement on perceived and actual text difficulty. Int. J. Med. Inf. **82**(8), 717–730 (2013)
15. Li, J., Zhang, P., Song, D., Wu, Y.: Understanding an enriched multidimensional user relevance model by analyzing query logs. J. Assoc. Inf. Sci. Technol. **68**(12), 2743–2754 (2017)
16. Mao, J., et al.: When does relevance mean usefulness and user satisfaction in web search? In: Proceedings of the 39th International ACM SIGIR conference on Research and Development in Information Retrieval, pp. 463–472 (2016)
17. Mc Laughlin, G.H.: Smog grading-a new readability formula. J. Read. **12**(8), 639–646 (1969)
18. Palotti, J., Goeuriot, L., Zuccon, G., Hanbury, A.: Ranking health web pages with relevance and understandability. In: Proceedings of the 39th international ACM SIGIR Conference on Research and Development in Information Retrieval, pp. 965–968 (2016)
19. Palotti, J.R.D.M., Zuccon, G., Hanbury, A.: The influence of pre-processing on the estimation of readability of web documents. In: Proceedings of the 24th ACM International on Conference on Information and Knowledge Management, pp. 1763–1766 (2015)
20. Palotti, J.R., et al.: CLEF eHealth evaluation lab 2015, task 2: Retrieving information about medical symptoms. In: CLEF (Working Notes), pp. 1–22 (2015)
21. Pasi, G.: Contextual search: issues and challenges. In: Holzinger, A., Simonic, K.-M. (eds.) USAB 2011. LNCS, vol. 7058, pp. 23–30. Springer, Heidelberg (2011). https://doi.org/10.1007/978-3-642-25364-5_3
22. Smith, E.A., Senter, R.: Automated readability index, vol. 66. Aerospace Medical Research Laboratories, Aerospace Medical Division, Air . . . (1967)

23. Vajjala, S.: Trends, limitations and open challenges in automatic readability assessment research. In: Proceedings of the Thirteenth Language Resources and Evaluation Conference. pp. 5366–5377. European Language Resources Association, Marseille, France, June 2022. https://aclanthology.org/2022.lrec-1.574

24. Verma, M., Yilmaz, E., Craswell, N.: On obtaining effort based judgements for information retrieval. In: Proceedings of the Ninth ACM International Conference on Web Search and Data Mining, pp. 277–286 (2016)

25. Wu, D.T., et al.: Applying multiple methods to assess the readability of a large corpus of medical documents. Stud. Health Technol. Inf. **192**, 647 (2013)

26. Xu, Y., Chen, Z.: Relevance judgment: what do information users consider beyond topicality? J. Am. Soc. Inf. Sci. Technol. **57**(7), 961–973 (2006)

27. Yan, X., Song, D., Li, X.: Concept-based document readability in domain specific information retrieval. In: Proceedings of the 15th ACM International Conference on Information and Knowledge Management, pp. 540–549 (2006)

28. Yaneva, V., Evans, R.: Six good predictors of autistic text comprehension. In: Proceedings of the International Conference Recent Advances in Natural Language Processing, pp. 697–706 (2015)

29. Yılmaz, F.H., Tutar, M.S., Arslan, D., Çeri, A.: Readability, understandability, and quality of retinopathy of prematurity information on the web. Birth Def. Res. **113**(12), 901–910 (2021)

30. Zuccon, G.: Understandability biased evaluation for information retrieval. In: Ferro, N., Crestani, F., Moens, M.-F., Mothe, J., Silvestri, F., Di Nunzio, G.M., Hauff, C., Silvello, G. (eds.) ECIR 2016. LNCS, vol. 9626, pp. 280–292. Springer, Cham (2016). https://doi.org/10.1007/978-3-319-30671-1_21

31. Zuccon, G., Koopman, B.: Integrating understandability in the evaluation of consumer health search engines. In: MedIR@ SIGIR, pp. 32–35 (2014)

Classification of Visualization Types and Perspectives in Patents

Junaid Ahmed Ghauri[1]([✉]) [iD], Eric Müller-Budack[1,2] [iD], and Ralph Ewerth[1,2] [iD]

[1] TIB – Leibniz Information Centre for Science and Technology, Hannover, Germany
{junaid.ghauri,eric.mueller,ralph.ewerth}@tib.eu
[2] L3S Research Center, Leibniz University, Hannover, Germany

Abstract. Due to the swift growth of patent applications each year, information and multimedia retrieval approaches that facilitate patent exploration and retrieval are of utmost importance. Different types of visualizations (e.g., graphs, technical drawings) and perspectives (e.g., side view, perspective) are used to visualize details of innovations in patents. The classification of these images enables a more efficient search in digital libraries and allows for further analysis. So far, datasets for image type classification miss some important visualization types for patents. Furthermore, related work does not make use of recent deep learning approaches including transformers. In this paper, we adopt state-of-the-art deep learning methods for the classification of visualization types and perspectives in patent images. We extend the *CLEF-IP* dataset for image type classification in patents to ten classes and provide manual ground truth annotations. In addition, we derive a set of hierarchical classes from a dataset that provides weakly-labeled data for image perspectives. Experimental results have demonstrated the feasibility of the proposed approaches. Source code, models, and datasets are publicly available (https://github.com/TIBHannover/PatentImageClassification).

Keywords: patent image classification · deep learning · digital libraries

1 Introduction

Patents are legal documents that represent intellectual properties to exclude others from making, using, or selling inventions. The number of patent applications submitted to patent organizations like *WIPO* (World Intellectual Property Organization), *EPO* (European Patent Office), and *USPTO* (United States Patent and Trademark Office) is rapidly rising. For example, the *WIPO* received more than three million patent applications in 2021 [35]. Details of the inventions proposed in patents are typically presented using text and images [14]. Different visualization types are used to efficiently convey information, e.g., block diagrams, graphs, and technical drawings [9]. In some cases, technical drawings are illustrated in more than one perspective (e.g., top or front view) to depict details [34]. Novel information and multimedia retrieval methods are

O. Alonso et al. (Eds.): TPDL 2023, LNCS 14241, pp. 182–191, 2023.
https://doi.org/10.1007/978-3-031-43849-3_16

necessary to facilitate search, organization, and exploration of patents in digital libraries [19, 29], e.g., to allow human assessors to find relevant patents (prior art) and possible plagiarism [11, 14], as well as to assess the novelty of the inventions presented.

According to a recent survey paper on patent analysis [14], there has been a lot of progress for tasks like patent retrieval [24, 25, 32, 38] and patent image classification [9, 15, 34] due to the advancements in deep learning. We mainly focus on image classification since visualizations contain important information of patents [5, 11, 14]. However, patents can depict various visualization types that require specific information extraction techniques, e.g. for tables [4, 21, 22, 28] or structured diagrams [8, 12, 16, 33]. So far, there have been some approaches for image type classification in scientific documents [10, 20] but the application domain and images differ in terms of style, structure, etc. compared to patent images. For patents specifically, Jiang et al. [9] suggested a deep learning model for image type classification and applied it to the *CLEF-IP 2011 dataset* [24]. However, existing datasets [9, 15, 24] on image type classification contain different classes that miss some important types used in patents. The image perspective is another important aspect since it helps to analyze technical aspects of the same drawing from different viewing angles. To the best of our knowledge, there is only one approach for the classification of image perspectives [34] which only considers textual information from captions to determine the perspective of the associated image. Overall, works for visualization type and perspective classification have not leveraged recent deep learning approaches [26, 27, 31, 37], particularly vision-language models such as CLIP (Contrastive Language-Image Pretraining) [26], that have achieved tremendous progress in various image classification tasks.

In this paper, we address the aforementioned limitations. Our contributions can be summarized as follows: (1) We present approaches that adopt state-of-the-art methods from computer vision [6, 26, 27, 31, 37] for patent image type and perspective classification. (2) We extend the CLEF-IP dataset [9, 24] with the class of *block circuit* as this can depict important technological innovations along with manual annotations to provide all ground-truth labels. (3) We extracted perspective class labels from dataset by Wei et al. [34] that uses textual descriptions for perspective detection. We also identified a class hierarchy with three levels of complexities and 2, 4, and 7 perspective classes, respectively. (4) We conduct an in-depth analysis of the proposed approaches on the datasets created for visualization type and perspective classification. Overall, we achieved promising results and provide strong baselines based on state-of-the-art approaches.

The rest of the paper is organized as follows. Section 2 describes the proposed approach and architecture for image type and perspective classification in patents. The experimental setup, dataset, and results are reported in Sect. 3. Section 4 concludes the paper and outlines potential future research directions.

2   Image Type and Perspective Classification in Patents

This section proposes approaches for visualization type and perspective classification in patents. For both individual tasks, the goal is to find models $\psi(I) \to y$

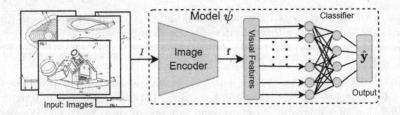

Fig. 1. Pipeline for patent image classification including visual feature extraction and classification using a multilayer perceptron (MLP) for the respective classes.

that predict the correct class y for a given image I. In general, we follow the pipeline in Fig. 1. Unlike related work, we first use novel deep learning models including convolutional neural networks (CNNs, Sect. 2.1) and the vision-language transformer *CLIP* [26] (Section 2.2) to extract features **f** from patent images. Second, we use a multilayer perceptron (MLP) to predict the probabilities $\hat{\mathbf{y}} = \langle \hat{y}_1, \hat{y}_2, \ldots, \hat{y}_c \rangle$ for the c classes of the given task.

2.1 Patent Classification Using CNN Models

We selected four CNNs (notation in bold), i.e., ***ResNet*-*50*** [6], ***RegNet Y-16GF*** [27], ***EfficientNetV2*-*M*** [31], and ***ResNeXt*-*101(64×4d)*** [37], which have been proven to produce promising results in image classification tasks, as backbones to extract features **f**. We use the official implementations and set the number of neurons in the last fully-connected layer to the number of classes c for the given task. During training, we finetune the weights of the *entire network* using the cross-entropy loss between the one-hot encoded ground-truth vector $\mathbf{y} = \langle y_1, y_2, \ldots, y_c \rangle$ and the predicted probabilities $\hat{y}$. Finetuning the entire network including the image encoder typically provides better results than solely training a classifier since features specific to patent images can be learned [7,18].

2.2 Patent Classification Using CLIP

To compare the CNN-based approach to recent vision-language models, we apply *CLIP* [26] that has achieved promising results in many downstream applications. We use the vision transformer (ViT-B/32) [3] of *CLIP* to extract the visual features **f** from the input images. Since finetuning of transformers requires much more data [17,18], we decided to freeze the weights of the image encoder during training. Instead, we use a multilayer perceptron (MLP) comprising three fully-connected layers with 256, 128, and 64 neurons to learn a feature representation for patent images. Finally, we apply another fully-connected layer to predict the probabilities $\hat{y}$ for c classes. As for the CNN models (Sect. 2.1), we use the cross-entropy loss between the ground truth and predictions to optimize the MLP. In the remainder of this paper, this model is denoted as ***CLIP+MLP***.

Table 1. Statistics for the extended CLEF-IP 2011 (left) and USPTO-PIP dataset with different granularities (right) for two (C_2), four (C_4), and seven classes (C_7).

Image Type	Train	Val	Test
Block Circuit	450	50	100
Chemical	5362	595	112
Drawing	5009	556	274
Flowchart	279	31	102
Genesequence	5385	598	24
Graph	1497	166	193
Maths	5355	595	126
Program	5016	557	26
Symbol	1421	157	17
Table	4952	550	66

Perspective Type	Train	Val	Test	C_2	C_4	C_7
• Perspective View	6140	150	150	✓	✓	✓
• Non-Perspective	18470	900	900	✓	✗	✗
• Left-Right	4767	300	300	✗	✓	✗
• Left	2407	150	150	✗	✗	✓
• Right	2360	150	150	✗	✗	✓
• Bottom-Top	6060	300	300	✗	✓	✗
• Bottom	2800	150	150	✗	✗	✓
• Top	3260	150	150	✗	✗	✓
• Front-Rear	7643	300	300	✗	✓	✗
• Front	5184	150	150	✗	✗	✓
• Rear	2459	150	150	✗	✗	✓

3   Experimental Setup and Results

In this section, we present the experimental setup (Sect. 3.1) and results for visualization type (Sect. 3.2) and perspective classification (Sect. 3.3).

3.1   Experimental Setup

In the following, we provide details on the datasets for visualization type and perspective classification, evaluation metrics, and implementation.

Extended CLEF-IP 2011 Dataset: We use the 2011 benchmark dataset of CLEF-IP [24] for visualization type classification. However, it does not cover *block and circuit diagrams*, which are an important type of visualization frequently used in patents. We added this category as a tenth class and collected images by querying EPO's publication server (https://data.epo.org/publication-server/). Finally, an annotator with background in computer science has manually labeled 600 images depicting *block and circuit diagrams* out of five thousand candidate images. The dataset statistics are provided in Table 1 (left).

USPTO-PIP Dataset: For the perspective classification task, we use the dataset presented by Wei et al. [34] based on patents collected from the USPTO. In this dataset, meta information including image perspectives has been automatically extracted from captions. We processed the data to extract the most common (more than 1000 samples) perspective labels (e.g., *left view, perspective*) and identified a class taxonomy (Table 1, right) covering 2, 4, and 7 classes. We use this information to compile the *USPTO-PIP* dataset for patent image perspective (PIP) classification from images.

Evaluation Metric: According to related work on image classification [2,3,36,39], we use top-1 accuracy as a metric for evaluation. To account for the different number of test samples for image types, we compute the macro-average.

Table 2. Performance of different models on the extended CLEF-IP dataset for image type classification (left) as well as the USPTO-PIP dataset for perspective classification on different granularities (right) with two (C_2), four (C_4), and seven classes (C_7).

Model	Accuracy %
ResNet [6]	81.60
EfficientNetV2 [31]	83.61
ResNeXt [37]	**85.01**
RegNet [27]	80.20
CLIP [26] + MLP	82.44

Model	Accuracy %		
	C_2	C_4	C_7
ResNet [6]	88.80	58.20	36.91
EfficientNetV2 [31]	90.92	66.90	41.01
ResNeXt [37]	**92.71**	**68.30**	**42.88**
RegNet [27]	87.70	62.50	34.80
CLIP [26] + MLP	87.15	59.75	33.40

Fig. 2. Confusion matrices [%] for patent image type (a) and perspective classification for seven classes (C_7, b) using the *ResNeXt* model [37].

Implementation Details: Models are trained for 200 epochs with batch size 32 using the respective training data for a given task (Table 1) and Adaptive Moment Estimation (Adam) [13] with a learning rate of 10^{-3}. We choose the best model according to the loss of the validation data for evaluation.

3.2   Results for Visualization Type Classification

We compared the models presented in Sect. 2 on the test data of the *Extended CLEF-IP 2011 Dataset*. According to Table 2 (left), finetuned CNNs like *ResNeXt* [37] and *EfficientNetV2* [31] are superior to *CLIP* [26]+*MLP* which only finetunes an MLP for classification. However, *CLIP* [26]+*MLP* can be finetuned much faster and with little resources while outperforming two CNN models (*ResNet* [6], *RegNet* [27]). Overall, the *ResNeXt* model achieves the highest accuracy (85%). The confusion matrix in Fig. 2(a) provides an overview of its performance for the individual image types. Wrong classification results can mainly be explained by the visual similarities of examples between two classes. For example, as shown in Fig. 3(a) and (b), *drawings* are mostly confused with

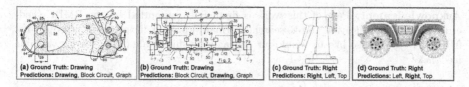

Fig. 3. Examples for correct (green) and wrong (red) top-1 predictions. (Color figure online)

block and *circuit diagrams* that share similar visual elements. However, the correct prediction in these cases is within the top-2 predictions.

3.3 Results for Perspective Classification

Results for patent image perspective classification are reported in Table 2 (right). As we mentioned earlier, we consider three granularity levels with like two (C_2), four (C_4), and seven classes (C_7). Overall, the same conclusion can be drawn for perspective type classification (Section 3.2). Again, the best results are achieved by *ResNeXt* [37] for all three granularity levels. The confusion matrix in Fig. 2(b) shows that most mistakes are made for classes that belong to the same parent class (e.g., *left* vs. *right* side views) and thus are expected to be more similar, as also illustrated in Fig. 3(c) and (d). Comparing both tasks, image perspective classification on the finest granularity is much more challenging than image type classification due to the high similarity of classes.

4 Conclusion

In this paper, we presented approaches based on recent deep learning models including CNNs and vision-language transformers for the classification of visualization types and perspectives in patents. For this purpose, we first processed and extended available datasets from the related work for training and evaluation. In our experiments, we achieved promising results in particular using CNN-based models that outperform transformers with fixed weights in the image encoder for both tasks. We specifically observed problems distinguishing classes with similar visual attributes. Particularly, the classification of similar image perspectives (e.g., *left* and *right* side view) is very challenging. For future work, we aim to explore more efficient finetuning techniques for vision-language models such as prompt learning [1,40,41] or parameter-efficient finetuning [7,23,30] of the entire network. Moreover, it is worth investigating hierarchy-aware models or multi-head classifiers to leverage the taxonomy of image perspectives.

Acknowledgment. Part of this work is financially supported by the BMBF (Federal Ministry of Education and Research, Germany) project "ExpResViP" (project no: 01IO2004A). We also like to thank our colleague Sushil Awale (TIB) for his valuable feedback.

References

1. Chen, G., Yao, W., Song, X., Li, X., Rao, Y., Zhang, K.: PLOT: prompt learning with optimal transport for vision-language models. In: International Conference on Learning Representations, ICLR 2023, Kigali, Rwanda, 1–5 May 2023. OpenReview.net (2023). https://openreview.net/pdf?id=zqwryBoXYnh

2. Chen, X., et al.: PaLI: a jointly-scaled multilingual language-image model. In: International Conference on Learning Representations, ICLR 2023, Kigali, Rwanda, 1–5 May 2023. OpenReview.net (2023). https://openreview.net/pdf?id=mWVoBz4W0u

3. Dosovitskiy, A., et al.: An image is worth 16x16 words: transformers for image recognition at scale. In: International Conference on Learning Representations, ICLR 2021, Virtual Event, Austria, 3–7 May 2021. OpenReview.net (2021). https://openreview.net/forum?id=YicbFdNTTy

4. Gralinski, F., et al.: Kleister: a novel task for Information Extraction involving Long Documents with Complex Layout. arXiv preprint abs/2003.02356 (2020). https://arxiv.org/abs/2003.02356

5. Hanbury, A., et al.: Patent image retrieval: a survey. In: Workshop on Patent Information Retrieval, PaIR 2011, Glasgow, Scotland, UK, 24 October 2011. ACM (2011). https://doi.org/10.1145/2064975.2064979

6. He, K., Zhang, X., Ren, S., Sun, J.: Deep residual learning for image recognition. In: IEEE Conference on Computer Vision and Pattern Recognition, CVPR 2016, Las Vegas, NV, USA, 27–30 June 2016. IEEE Computer Society (2016). https://doi.org/10.1109/CVPR.2016.90

7. Houlsby, N., et al.: Parameter-efficient transfer learning for NLP. In: International Conference on Machine Learning, ICML 2019, 9–15 June 2019, Long Beach, California, USA. PMLR (2019)

8. Hu, X., Zhang, L., Liu, J., Fan, J., You, Y., Wu, Y.: GPTR: Gestalt-Perception Transformer for Diagram Object Detection. arXiv preprint abs/2212.14232 (2022). https://doi.org/10.48550/arXiv.2212.14232

9. Jiang, S., Luo, J., Pava, G.R., Hu, J., Magee, C.L.: A convolutional neural network-based patent image retrieval method for design ideation. In: International Design Engineering Technical Conferences & Computers and Information in Engineering Conference, IDETC-CIE 2020, Online, Virtual, 17–19 August 2020. The American Society of Mechanical Engineers (ASME) (2020). https://doi.org/10.1115/DETC2020-22048

10. Jobin, K.V., Mondal, A., Jawahar, C.V.: DocFigure: a dataset for scientific document figure classification. In: IAPR International Workshop on Graphics Recognition co-located with International Conference on Document Analysis and Recognition, GREC@ICDAR 2019, Sydney, Australia, 22–25 September 2019. IEEE (2019). https://doi.org/10.1109/ICDARW.2019.00018

11. Joho, H., Azzopardi, L., Vanderbauwhede, W.: A survey of patent users: an analysis of tasks, behavior, search functionality and system requirements. In: Information Interaction in Context Symposium, IIiX 2010, New Brunswick, NJ, USA, 18–21 August 2010. ACM (2010). https://doi.org/10.1145/1840784.1840789

12. Kembhavi, A., Salvato, M., Kolve, E., Seo, M., Hajishirzi, H., Farhadi, A.: A diagram is worth a dozen images. In: Leibe, B., Matas, J., Sebe, N., Welling, M. (eds.) ECCV 2016. LNCS, vol. 9908, pp. 235–251. Springer, Cham (2016). https://doi.org/10.1007/978-3-319-46493-0_15
13. Kingma, D.P., Ba, J.: Adam: a method for stochastic optimization. In: International Conference on Learning Representations, ICLR 2015, San Diego, CA, USA, 7–9 May 2015 (2015)
14. Krestel, R., Chikkamath, R., Hewel, C., Risch, J.: A survey on deep learning for patent analysis. World Pat. Inf. **65**, 102035 (2021). https://doi.org/10.1016/j.wpi.2021.102035
15. Kucer, M., Oyen, D., Castorena, J., Wu, J.: DeepPatent: large scale patent drawing recognition and retrieval. In: IEEE/CVF Winter Conference on Applications of Computer Vision, WACV 2022, Waikoloa, HI, USA, 3–8 January 2022. IEEE (2022). https://doi.org/10.1109/WACV51458.2022.00063
16. Lee, K., et al.: Pix2Struct: Screenshot Parsing as Pretraining for Visual Language understanding. arXiv preprint abs/2210.03347 (2022). https://doi.org/10.48550/arXiv.2210.03347
17. Li, X.L., Liang, P.: Prefix-tuning: optimizing continuous prompts for generation. In: Annual Meeting of the Association for Computational Linguistics and the International Joint Conference on Natural Language Processing, ACL/IJCNLP 2021, Virtual Event, 1–6 August 2021. Association for Computational Linguistics (2021)
18. Lian, D., Zhou, D., Feng, J., Wang, X.: Scaling & shifting your features: a new baseline for efficient model tuning. In: Conference on Neural Information Processing Systems, NeurIPS 2022, New Orleans, Louisiana, 28 Nov 2022 – 9 Dec 2022 (2022)
19. Miric, M., Jia, N., Huang, K.G.: Using supervised machine learning for large-scale classification in management research: the case for identifying artificial intelligence patents. Strateg. Manag. J. **44**(2), 491–519 (2022)
20. Morris, D., Müller-Budack, E., Ewerth, R.: SlideImages: a dataset for educational image classification. In: Jose, J.M., et al. (eds.) ECIR 2020. LNCS, vol. 12036, pp. 289–296. Springer, Cham (2020). https://doi.org/10.1007/978-3-030-45442-5_36
21. Nazir, D., Hashmi, K.A., Pagani, A., Liwicki, M., Stricker, D., Afzal, M.Z.: HybridTabNet: towards better table detection in scanned document images. Appl. Sci. **11**(18), 8396 (2021). https://doi.org/10.3390/app11188396
22. Paliwal, S.S., Vishwanath, D., Rahul, R., Sharma, M., Vig, L.: TableNet: deep learning model for end-to-end table detection and tabular data extraction from scanned document images. In: International Conference on Document Analysis and Recognition, ICDAR 2019, Sydney, Australia, 20–25 September 2019. IEEE (2019). https://doi.org/10.1109/ICDAR.2019.00029
23. Pan, J., Lin, Z., Zhu, X., Shao, J., Li, H.: ST-adapter: parameter-efficient image-to-video transfer learning. In: Conference on Neural Information Processing Systems, NeurIPS 2022, New Orleans, Louisiana, 28 Nov 2022 - 9 Dec 2022 (2022)
24. Piroi, F., Lupu, M., Hanbury, A., Zenz, V.: CLEF-IP 2011: Retrieval in the Intellectual Property Domain. In: CLEF 2011 Labs and Workshop, Notebook Papers, 19–22 September 2011, Amsterdam, The Netherlands. CEUR Workshop Proceedings. vol. 1177. CEUR-WS.org (2011). https://ceur-ws.org/Vol-1177/CLEF2011wn-CLEF-IP-PiroiEt2011.pdf

25. Pustu-Iren, K., Bruns, G., Ewerth, R.: A multimodal approach for semantic patent image retrieval. In: Workshop on Patent Text Mining and Semantic Technologies co-located with International Conference on Research and Development in Information Retrieval, PatentSemTech@SIGIR 2021, July 11–15, 2021. ACM (2021)
26. Radford, A., et al.: Learning transferable visual models from natural language supervision. In: International Conference on Machine Learning, ICML 2021, Virtual Event, 18–24 July 2021. PMLR (2021). http://proceedings.mlr.press/v139/radford21a.html
27. Radosavovic, I., Kosaraju, R.P., Girshick, R.B., He, K., Dollár, P.: Designing network design spaces. In: IEEE/CVF Conference on Computer Vision and Pattern Recognition, CVPR 2020, Seattle, WA, USA, 13–19 June 2020. Computer Vision Foundation/IEEE (2020). https://doi.org/10.1109/CVPR42600.2020.01044
28. Schreiber, S., Agne, S., Wolf, I., Dengel, A., Ahmed, S.: DeepDeSRT: deep learning for detection and structure recognition of tables in document images. In: IAPR International Conference on Document Analysis and Recognition, ICDAR 2017 (2017). https://doi.org/10.1109/ICDAR.2017.192
29. Song, K., Ran, C., Yang, L.: A digital analysis system of patents integrating natural language processing and machine learning. Technol. Anal. Strateg. Manag. **34**, 1–17 (2022)
30. Sung, Y.L., Cho, J., Bansal, M.: VL-adapter: parameter-efficient transfer learning for vision-and-language tasks. In: Conference on Computer Vision and Pattern Recognition, CVPR 2022, 19 Jun 2022 - 24 Jun 2022. IEEE/CVF (2022)
31. Tan, M., Le, Q.V.: EfficientNetV2: smaller models and faster training. In: Proceedings of the International Conference on Machine Learning, ICML 2021, 18–24 July 2021, Virtual Event. PMLR (2021)
32. Vrochidis, S., Moumtzidou, A., Kompatsiaris, I.: Concept-based patent image retrieval. World Pat. Inf. **34**(4), 292–303 (2012). https://doi.org/10.1016/j.wpi.2012.07.002
33. Wang, S., Zhang, L., Luo, X., Yang, Y., Hu, X., Liu, J.: RL-CSDia: Representation Learning of Computer Science Diagrams. arXiv preprint abs/2103.05900 (2021), https://arxiv.org/abs/2103.05900
34. Wei, X., Wu, J., Ajayi, K., Oyen, D.: Visual descriptor extraction from patent figure captions: a case study of data efficiency between BiLSTM and transformer. In: Joint Conference on Digital Libraries, JCDL 2022, Cologne, Germany, 20–24 June 2022. ACM/IEEE (2022), https://doi.org/10.1145/3529372.3533299
35. WIPO Statistics Database: IP Facts and Figures (2023). https://www.wipo.int/en/ipfactsandfigures/patents. Accessed 24 July 2023
36. Wortsman, M., et al.: Model soups: averaging weights of multiple fine-tuned models improves accuracy without increasing inference time. In: International Conference on Machine Learning, ICML 2022, 17–23 July 2022, Baltimore, Maryland, USA. PMLR (2022). https://proceedings.mlr.press/v162/wortsman22a.html
37. Xie, S., Girshick, R.B., Dollár, P., Tu, Z., He, K.: Aggregated residual transformations for deep neural networks. In: Conference on Computer Vision and Pattern Recognition, CVPR 2017, Honolulu, HI, USA, 21–26 July 2017. IEEE Computer Society (2017). https://doi.org/10.1109/CVPR.2017.634

38. Yang, L., Gong, M., Asari, V.K.: Diagram image retrieval and analysis: challenges and opportunities. In: Conference on Computer Vision and Pattern Recognition, CVPR Workshops 2020, Seattle, WA, USA, 14–19 June 2020. IEEE/CVF (2020). https://doi.org/10.1109/CVPRW50498.2020.00098

39. Yu, J., Wang, Z., Vasudevan, V., Yeung, L., Seyedhosseini, M., Wu, Y.: CoCa: contrastive captioners are image-text foundation models. Trans. Mach. Learn. Res. **2022**, 2835–8856 (2022). https://openreview.net/forum?id=Ee277P3AYC

40. Zhou, K., Yang, J., Loy, C.C., Liu, Z.: Conditional prompt learning for vision-language models. In: Conference on Computer Vision and Pattern Recognition, CVPR 2022, New Orleans, LA, USA, 18–24 June 2022. IEEE/CVF (2022). https://doi.org/10.1109/CVPR52688.2022.01631

41. Zhou, K., Yang, J., Loy, C.C., Liu, Z.: Learning to prompt for vision-language models. Int. J. Comput. Vis. (IJCV) **130**(9), 2337–2348 (2022)

Monitoring and Publishing Science

It's Not Just GitHub: Identifying Data and Software Sources Included in Publications

Emily Escamilla[1] , Lamia Salsabil[1] , Martin Klein[2]([⊠]) , Jian Wu[1] ,
Michele C. Weigle[1] , and Michael L. Nelson[1]

[1] Old Dominion University, Norfolk, VA, USA
{evogt001,lsals002}@odu.edu, {jwu,mweigle,mln}@cs.odu.edu
[2] Los Alamos National Laboratory, Los Alamos, NM, USA
mklein@lanl.gov

Abstract. Paper publications are no longer the only form of research product. Due to recent initiatives by publication venues and funding institutions, open access datasets and software products are increasingly considered research products and URIs to these products are growing more prevalent in scholarly publications. However, as with all URIs, resources found on the live Web are not permanent. Archivists and institutions including Software Heritage, Internet Archive, and Zenodo are working to preserve data and software products as valuable parts of reproducibility, a cornerstone of scientific research. While some hosting platforms are well-known and can be identified with regular expressions, there are a vast number of smaller, more niche hosting platforms utilized by researchers to host their data and software. If it is not feasible to manually identify all hosting platforms used by researchers, how can we identify URIs to open-access data and software (OADS) to aid in their preservation? We used a hybrid classifier to classify URIs as OADS URIs and non-OADS URIs. We found that URIs to Git hosting platforms (GHPs) including GitHub, GitLab, SourceForge, and Bitbucket accounted for 33% of OADS URIs. Non-GHP OADS URIs are distributed across almost 50,000 unique hostnames. We determined that using a hybrid classifier allows for the identification of OADS URIs in less common hosting platforms which can benefit discoverability for preserving datasets and software products as research products for reproducibility.

Keywords: Web Archiving · GitHub · arXiv · Digital Preservation · Memento · Open Source Software

1 Introduction

The definition of a research product has broadened to include datasets and software products, away from the idea that a paper publication is the only form of research product. In many cases in scientific research, access to the original data

Supported by the Alfred P. Sloan Foundation.

and software is the lynch pin of reproducibilty, the ability for other researchers to reproduce or replicate the results of a study. Reproducibility allows for verification of published results as well as further advancement built on the previous methodology. Additionally, publication venues and funding institutions encourage, and in some cases mandate, the sharing of related research objects such as datasets and software. The data and software products produced by researchers, like all Web resources, are subject to content drift [6] and link rot [7]. As such, the notion of access to and reproducibility of research objects is in jeopardy. Therefore, Web archiving efforts are needed to discover, capture, and preserve these research products. However, archivists and archival institutions must be able to find the data and software products created by the researcher in order to preserve them. Some researchers attempt to make their code available for the long-term by self-archiving: depositing their own materials into a repository or archive. However, of academics who write source code, only 47.2% self-archive that code [8]. Additionally, there is no single platform for researchers to deposit or host their research products. Figure 1 shows the Web page where Jefferson Lab, a U.S. Department of Energy Office of Science National Laboratory, hosts the documentation for their CEBAF Online Data Acquisition (CODA) framework. A URI to this Web page was included in over 40 articles in the arXiv[1] corpus, a dataset of 1.58 million STEM pre-print articles used in this study. Both the number of times the URI was included in scholarly publications and the importance of the research institution as a US national laboratory reflect that the size of the platform is incongruent with the importance of its contents. Like the Jefferson Lab, various disciplines and institutions have their own niche hosting platforms, but these may be missed by larger Web preservation efforts like Web archives or Software Heritage due to the relatively small scale of the hosting platforms.

Software Heritage[2], a non-profit repository, is solely focused on the preservation of software on the Web with the goal "to collect, preserve, and share all software that is publicly available in source code form". They use a combination of crawling and user-submitted requests to discover software products to preserve. Smaller, more niche platforms may be less likely to be discovered resulting in their holdings being less likely to be preserved by Software Heritage without researchers depositing their code. Unlike Software Heritage, Web archives are not solely focused on the preservation of software. Web archives, like Internet Archive, work to archive the Web at large and allow users to experience what a given URI would have looked like at a given point in time. Web archives capture live Web pages, known as URI-Rs, and create a archived copies of the Web page, known as URI-Ms or mementos, with an associated Memento-datetime, the date and time that the URI-R was archived. In their attempt to discover and archive the Web, Web archives may capture Web-based data and software hosting platforms, but this form of incidental archiving is not sufficient for ensuring the preservation of data and software for reproducibility.

---

[1] https://arxiv.org.

[2] https://softwareheritage.org/.

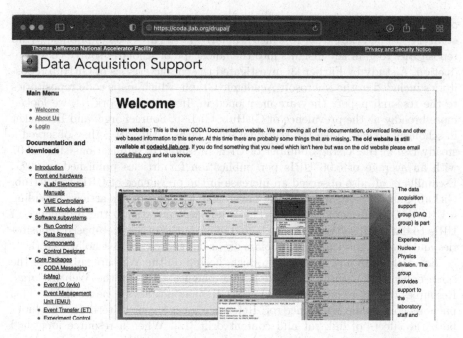

Fig. 1. Landing page for https://coda.jlab.org/drupal/

There are a number of popular code and data repositories including Zenodo[3], GitHub[4], Figshare[5], and Dryad[6]. References to these repositories may be easy to identify by their well-known URIs. We assume that there are other URIs that also point to software and data repositories, so our study is focused on discovering URIs to open-access data and software (OADS) products in order to identify some of the other platforms that scholars are referencing as OADS URIs. We used a classifier system to identify URIs to open access data and software products in scholarly publications. We found that GitHub, GitLab, SourceForge, and Bitbucket account for 33% of all OADS URIs. We also found that the remaining OADS URIs are distributed across almost 50,000 different Web pages. URIs to the European Council for Nucleur Research (CERN) were the most common with 4,953 URIs, but URIs to CERN still only accounted for 1.92% of all non-GHP OADS URIs.

2   Related Work

Previous studies have investigated the links between software repositories and scholarly publications. However, most studies have focused their investigations

---

[3] https://zenodo.org.
[4] https://github.com.
[5] https://figshare.com.
[6] https://datadryad.org.

on links to scholarly publications from software repositories. Wattanakriengkrai et al. [14] studied the extent to which scholarly papers are cited in public GitHub repositories to gain key insights into the landscape of scholarly source code production. A study by Färber [3] investigated the characteristics of GitHub repositories included in the Microsoft Academic Graph, which maps code repositories to the research papers they are mentioned in. In previous work [1], we looked more broadly at the prevalence of GitHub, GitLab, SourceForge, and Bitbucket in scholarly articles. Like the study by Klein et al. [7] in 2014, they observed a steady rise in the average number of URIs in scholarly publications since 2007 with an average of 5.06 URIs per publication for articles published in 2021. Escamilla et al. also observed an increase in the prevalence of URIs to GitHub, GitLab, SourceForge, and Bitbucket over time with one in five articles including a URI to GitHub alone in 2021. This study will investigate the prevalence of URIs to data and software products and identify the other Web-based repositories and hosting services that scholars are using and citing in scholarly work.

Scholarly data and software products hosted on the Web are subject to the same ephemeral nature of the Web that plagues URIs to the Web at large. Resources that were once available at a URI may not always be available. This phenomenon is called reference rot. Reference rot is a general term that includes both the effects of link rot and content drift [13]. When a resource identified by a URI is missing, the URI has experienced link rot. When the information identified by a URI changes over time and no longer represents what the author originally intended, the URI has experienced content drift. In a 2014 study, Klein et al. [7] studied the prevalence of reference rot in a dataset of 3.5 million scholarly articles published from 1997 to 2012 from three corpora: arXiv, Elsevier, and PubMed Central. They discovered that one in five articles is impacted by reference rot. For articles that contain at least one URI to the Web at large, seven out of ten articles are impacted by reference rot. Jones et al. [6] took the study a step farther and investigated the prevalence of content drift within the dataset used by Klein et al. They found that 75% of all URIs referenced in the scholarly articles have been impacted by content drift and no longer reflect what the author originally intended.

3   Methodology

For our study, we analyzed the arXiv corpus. arXiv is a pre-print service for STEM disciplines and its corpus contains over 2 million submissions [4]. In April 2007, the arXiv identifier scheme changed to accommodate a larger number of submissions and to address other categorization issues.[7] We decided that beginning our corpus in April 2007 would give us a nearly 15-year time period to study and be sufficient for our analysis. arXiv allows authors to submit multiple versions of their article. In the case of multiple versions, we considered the latest version of each submission to be most representative of what the author intended,

---

[7] https://arxiv.org/help/arxiv_identifier.

so we used only the latest version for our analysis which resulted in a corpus of 1.58 million pre-prints.

To determine whether a URI links to an open access dataset or software resource, we used a hybrid classifier proposed in our previous work [11] for each article in the corpus. The classifier transforms each article into a text file using the PDFMiner[8] Python library. By employing a regular expression, it scans the text to identify and extract sentences that contain URIs. Given the extracted sentences, the hybrid classifier combines two approaches: a heuristic classifier and a learning-based classifier. The heuristic classifier removes URIs that fall into two categories: those belonging to 54 major publishers such as Springer, Wiley, and Sagepub, and those that end with ".pdf". This is because publisher URIs are typically not associated with datasets or software repositories, and .pdf files are typically not datasets or software. The learning-based classifier is trained on a dataset of labeled sentences that contain URIs. The labeled samples are classified as either open access datasets/software (OADS), or not (non-OADS) as shown in Table 1. The learning-based classifier uses this information to learn how to classify new URIs. In our previous study, we found that the hybrid classifier is more accurate than either the heuristic classifier or the learning-based classifier alone. This is because the heuristic classifier eliminates many irrelevant URIs, and the learning-based classifier is able to classify the remaining URIs accurately.

Table 1. Sentences containing OADS and non-OADS URLs.

Sentences containing the URI	Category
The dataset is available at http://ibm.biz/multishapeinsertion	OADS
Code and materials for reproducing the experiment as well as all data and analysis scripts are open and available at https://github.com/hawkrobe/pragmatics_of_perspective_taking	OADS
This article is available from: http://www.nature.com/articles/srep01037	Non-OADS
All these scenes can be seen in our video at https://youtu.be/RcWHXL2vJPc	Non-OADS

After all of the URIs have been classified, we filtered out URIs that were out of scope for this study. In following the methods used by Klein et al. [7] to identify URIs to the "Web at large", we filtered out URIs with a scheme other than HTTP or HTTPS, localhost, and private/protected IP ranges. Because we wanted to focus on data and software repositories, we filtered out URIs that would likely point to publications such as URIs to arXiv, Elsevier RefHub,[9] CrossRef Crossmark [5], and some HTTP DOIs. DOIs resolve to artifacts, most commonly

---

[8] https://pypi.org/project/pdfminer/.
[9] https://refhub.elsevier.com.

papers. Because we were working to identify URIs to data and software, we chose to include DOIs to Zenodo, Dryad, figshare, and Open Science Framework (OSF), as they are known to resolve to data and software artifacts, while removing all other DOIs. Links to Elsevier RefHub and CrossRef Crossmark function similarly to DOIs and are often added by the publisher. We decided to exclude DOI and DOI-like references following Klein et al.'s assumption that, for the most part, such artifacts are in-scope for existing archiving and preservation efforts such as LOCKSS [9], CLOCKSS [10], and Portico [2].

We used the regular expressions introduced in our previous study [1] to identify URIs to GitHub, GitLab, SourceForge and Bitbucket from the extracted URIs. Collectively, we will refer to URIs to one of these four Git hosting platforms (GHPs) as GHP URIs. OADS URIs that are not URIs to one of these four GHPs will be referred to as non-GHP OADS URIs.

4   Results

With the extracted and classified URIs, we looked at the overall distribution of URIs and the distributions of URIs classified as OADS and non-OADS. In Fig. 2, we looked at the average number of OADS, non-OADS, and total URIs per publication. The average number of URIs, OADS URIs, and non-OADS URIs per publication rose steadily from 2007 to 2021. In 2007, there were an average of 0.416 URIs per publication with 0.111 OADS URIs per publication and 0.306 non-OADS URIs per publication. Those averages nearly tripled across all three categories by 2021. In 2021, there were an average of 1.273 URIs per publication with 0.433 OADS URIs per publication and 0.841 non-OADS URIs per publication. This shows that authors have been increasingly including URIs, both OADS and non-OADS URIs, in their publications. With a growing number of included URIs comes a growing need to archive the resources that these authors are including in their research with the understanding that authors included the URIs because they were important to their study or were a result of their research.

With an understanding of the general trends of URI usage, we next looked at the distribution of OADS and non-OADS URIs. We also separated the GHP URIs from the other OADS URIs to gain an understanding of the prevalence of GHP URIs over time. We chose GitHub, GitLab, Bitbucket, and SourceForge as popular GHPs to represent GHP URIs. As shown in Fig. 3, we found that both the prevalence and the distribution of the URIs changed across the time period. The percentage of non-OADS URIs has slightly declined meaning that authors are including a higher proportion of OADS URIs to non-OADS URIs in recent years. The percentage of GHP URIs has significantly increased from less than 1% in 2007 to around 15% of all URIs in 2021. Despite the overall increase in the prevalence of OADS URIs seen in Fig. 2, there has been a decrease in the percentage of non-GHP OADS URIs as shown in Fig. 3. This means that the growth in the prevalence of OADS URIs has largely been due to an increase in the inclusion of GHP URIs within publications.

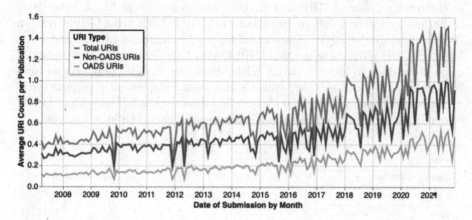

Fig. 2. Average number of URIs per arXiv pre-print by publication date. The blue line represents the number of URIs our machine learning model classified as non-OADS as an average per publication (y-axis) per publication month (x-axis). The orange line represent the number of URIs our machine learning model classified as OADS as an average per publication. The red line represents the total number of URIs we extracted from the publications as an average per publication. (Color figure online)

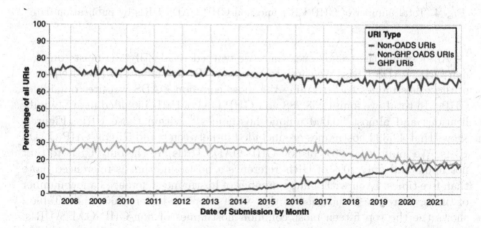

Fig. 3. Percentage of GHP URIs, non-GHP OADS URIs, and non-OADS URIs by publication date. The blue line represents the percent of URIs our machine learning model classified as non-OADS (y-axis) per publication month (x-axis). The orange line represents the percent of URIs our machine learning model classified as OADS, excluding GHP URIs. The green line represents the percent of URIs that were GHP URIs. (Color figure online)

The increase of the prevalence of GHP URIs is also reflected when we look at the total number of GHP and OADS URIs over time in Fig. 4. From 2007 to 2015, there were a 500 to 1000 more non-GHP URIs than GHP URIs. In 2015, the number of GHP URIs started to steadily increase. In 2020 and 2021, for every GHP URI, there is a non-GHP OADS URI. This shows that utility of using a classifier to identify OADS URIs, especially in older publications from 2007 to 2015. We also see that, while GitHub is an independently popular GHP, we must look beyond GitHub to identify and discover the full breadth of OADS resources being referenced and produced by researchers even in recent year.

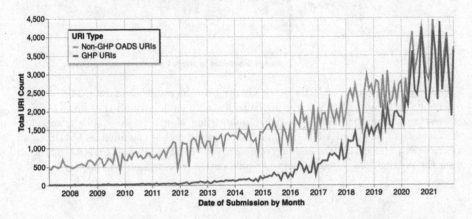

Fig. 4. Total number of GHP URIs and non-GHP OADS URIs by publication date

After seeing the trends over time, we wanted to identify the most common non-GHP OADS URIs. We chose to compare URI hostnames and the frequency of those hostnames to determine the most common OADS websites outside of GHPs. In total, we found 258,288 non-GHP OADS URIs included in arXiv publications and almost 50,000 unique hostnames[10] within those URIs. Figure 5 shows that 49,392 hostnames are included in between 0 and 50 non-GHP OADS URIs. We found that 63% of non-GHP OADS URIs are the only URIs to that hostname and only 10% of URIs reference a hostname that is referenced more than five times. Even with a large number of hostnames referenced a few number of times, there are 19 hostnames that were referenced over 1000 times. Table 2 shows the the top fifteen most common hostnames of non-GHP OADS URIs. However, it is worth noting that the most popular hostname, cds.cern.ch, only accounts for 1.92% of all non-GHP OADS URIs. Therefore, there are a large number of platforms used by scholars to host data and software which increases the difficulty of archiving data and software products for reproducibility. The diversity of the platforms used and referenced by scholars makes it difficult to

---

[10] The full dataset is available at https://github.com/elescamilla/Extract-URLs/blob/main/classifier_results/count_oads_non_ghp_hostnames.csv.

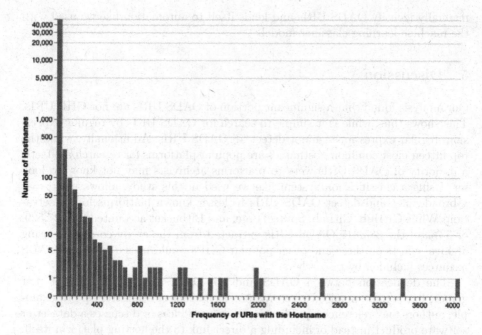

Fig. 5. A histogram showing the frequency of the hostname in non-GHP OADS URIs (x-axis) and the number of hostnames that shared that frequency (y-axis)

Table 2. The top 15 most common hostnames for non-GHP OADS URIs and their frequencies

Hostname	Frequency
cds.cern.ch	4,953
www.sciencedirect.com	3,119
archive.ics.uci.edu	2,632
adsabs.harvard.edu	2,031
www.ncbi.nlm.nih.gov	1,998
www.cosmos.esa.int	1,996
physics.nist.gov	1,651
fermi.gsfc.nasa.gov	1,627
heasarc.gsfc.nasa.gov	1,500
cran.r-project.org	1,446
doi.org	1,337
www.w3.org	1,289
www.nature.org	1,275
archive.stsci.edu	1,243
en.wikipedia.org	1,228

manually identify OADS URIs and lends itself to automation like we used with the machine learning classifier model.

5 Discussion

Our analysis found that a significant portion of OADS URIs are not GHP URIs. This shows that, while is it simple to search for OADS URIs by regular expression, regular expressions cannot detect all OADS URIs. Additionally, while the top fifteen most common hostnames are popular platforms for research artifacts, a majority of OADS URIs were to platforms archivists may not know to look for. Using a classification system like we used in this study, allows us to cast a broader net and detect OADS URIs to lesser known platforms for preservation. While GitHub, GitLab, SourceForge, and Bitbucket accounted for 127,529, or 33%, of the 385,817 OADS URIs extracted from the arXiv corpus, focusing archival efforts on these and other popular GHPs would miss 67% of the OADS resources included by researchers.

The delineation between OADS and non-OADS may seem clear at first glance, but is more nuanced when we look at current citation trends. For example, authors may reference a publication that introduces or discusses a dataset or software product instead of including a direct link to the hosting platform itself. This tendency may be due to the value of publication citations within academia or due to established practices within a discipline or institution, but it results in the possibility of indirect links to OADS via paper publications. For example, ScienceDirect is a digital library of journal articles and book chapters which are non-OADS, but indirect links to OADS could result in ScienceDirect URIs being classified as OADS. Figure 6 shows the reference for a ScienceDirect publication cited in an arXiv article [12]. The ScienceDirect publication was classified as an OADS URI by our machine learning classifier model despite it being a paper publication. Figure 7 shows the reference being cited in the context of the author listing out available packages for solving DMFT equations. While the citation itself is to a paper publication, the author is using the citation to indicate a soft-

[14] S. Choi, P. Semon, B. Kang, A. Kutepov, G. Kotliar, Comdmft: A massively parallel computer package for the electronic structure of correlated-electron systems, Computer Physics Communications 244 (2019) 277 – 294 (2019). doi:https://doi.org/10.1016/j.cpc.2019.07.003. URL   http://www.sciencedirect.com/science/article/pii/S0010465519302140

Fig. 6. The reference for a ScienceDirect publication cited in an arXiv publication and classified as an OADS URI despite being a paper publication.

ware package discussed in the publication. This is one example of the delineation between OADS and non-OADS being more nuanced than it may first appear.

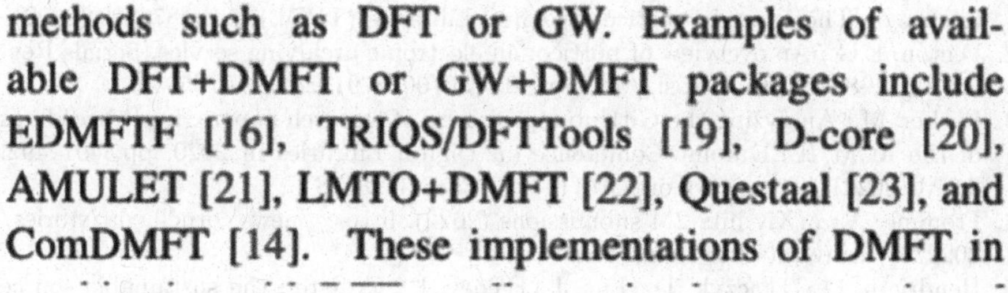

methods such as DFT or GW. Examples of available DFT+DMFT or GW+DMFT packages include EDMFTF [16], TRIQS/DFTTools [19], D-core [20], AMULET [21], LMTO+DMFT [22], Questaal [23], and ComDMFT [14]. These implementations of DMFT in

Fig. 7. The citation of the ScienceDirect publication. The author is listing out available software packages and includes a citation to the ScienceDirect publication and URI.

Our machine learning classifier model, despite good performance found in previous studies [11], fine tuning, and a large training set, was not perfect, as can be expected when extracting and classifying millions of URIs from 1.58 million scholarly articles. It incorrectly classified some GHP URIs as Non-OADS. In some cases, these GHP URIs were located in the footnote or in other locations that lacked the necessary context sentence around the target URI for proper classification. Despite the limitations and inaccuracies, we are remain confident that utilizing machine learning models to classify OADS and non-OADS URIs will allow researchers and archivists to more easily identify less popular or niche platforms for preservation.

6 Conclusion

Researchers are increasingly including URIs to the Web at large and also to open access data and software (OADS). However, the multitude of hosting platforms, including institutional or discipline-specific platforms, available to researchers makes it more difficult for archivists to identity these platforms and archive their contents to facilitate long-term reproducibility. We used a machine learning classification system to identify OADS URIs outside of the popular GHP URIs that can be found with regular expressions. We found that GHP URIs only account for 33% of all OADS URIs and that non-GHP OADS URIs are dispersed across nearly 50,000 unique hostnames.

References

1. Escamilla, E., Klein, M., Cooper, T., Rampin, V., Weigle, M.C., Nelson, M.L.: The rise of GitHub in scholarly publications. In: Proceedings of the International Conference on Theory and Practice of Digital Libraries (TPDL), pp. 187–200 (2022)
2. Fenton, E.G.: An overview of portico: an electronic archiving service. Serials Rev. **32**(2), 81–86 (2006). https://doi.org/10.1080/00987913.2006.10765036
3. Färber, M.: Analyzing the GitHub repositories of research papers. In: Proceedings of the ACM/IEEE Joint Conference on Digital Libraries in 2020, pp. 491–492. ACM (2020). https://doi.org/10.1145/3383583.3398578
4. Fromme, A.: arXiv hits 2M submissions (2022). https://news.cornell.edu/stories/2022/01/arxiv-hits-2m-submissions
5. Hendricks, G., Tkaczyk, D., Lin, J., Feeney, P.: Crossref: the sustainable source of community-owned scholarly metadata. Quant. Sci. Stud. **1**(1), 414–427 (2020). https://doi.org/10.1162/qss_a_00022
6. Jones, S.M., Van de Sompel, H., Shankar, H., Klein, M., Tobin, R., Grover, C.: Scholarly context adrift: three out of four URI references lead to changed content. PLOS ONE **11**, 1–32 (2016). https://doi.org/10.1371/journal.pone.0167475
7. Klein, M., et al.: Scholarly context not found: one in five articles suffers from reference rot. PLOS ONE **9**, 1–39 (2014). https://doi.org/10.1371/journal.pone.0115253
8. Milliken, G., Nguyen, S., Steeves, V.: A behavioral approach to understanding the git experience. In: Proceedings of the HICSS-54, p. 7239 (2021). https://doi.org/10.24251/HICSS.2021.872
9. Reich, V., Rosenthal, D.S.H.: LOCKSS: a permanent web publishing and access system. D-Lib Mag. **7**(6), 1082–9873 (2001). https://doi.org/10.1045/june2001-reich
10. Reich, V.: CLOCKSS-It takes a community. Serials Librarian **54**(1–2), 135–139 (2008). https://doi.org/10.1080/03615260801973968
11. Salsabil, L., et al.: A study of computational reproducibility using URLs linking to open access datasets and software. In: Companion Proceedings of the Web Conference 2022, pp. 784–788 (2022)
12. Singh, V., Herath, U., Wah, B., Liao, X., Romero, A.H., Park, H.: DMFTwDFT: an open-source code combining dynamical mean field theory with various density functional theory packages. Comput. Phys. Commun. **261**, 107778 (2021). https://doi.org/10.1016/j.cpc.2020.107778
13. Van de Sompel, H., Klein, M., Shankar, H.: Towards robust hyperlinks for web-based scholarly communication. In: Watt, S.M., Davenport, J.H., Sexton, A.P., Sojka, P., Urban, J. (eds.) CICM 2014. LNCS (LNAI), vol. 8543, pp. 12–25. Springer, Cham (2014). https://doi.org/10.1007/978-3-319-08434-3_2
14. Wattanakriengkrai, S., et al.: GitHub repositories with links to academic papers: public access, traceability, and evolution. J. Syst. Softw. **183**, 111117 (2022). https://doi.org/10.1016/j.jss.2021.111117

A Graph Neural Network Approach for Evaluating Correctness of Groups of Duplicates

Michele De Bonis[1]($\boxtimes$)(iD), Filippo Minutella[3], Fabrizio Falchi[1](iD),
and Paolo Manghi[1,2](iD)

[1] Istituto di Scienza e Tecnologie dell'Informazione "A. Faedo" - ISTI (CNR),
Pisa, Italy
{michele.debonis,paolo.manghi,fabrizio.falchi}@isti.cnr.it
[2] OpenAIRE AMKE, Pisa, Italy
paolo.manghi@openaire.eu
[3] TIM S.p.A., Pisa, Italy
filippo.minutella@telecomitalia.it

Abstract. Unlabeled entity deduplication is a relevant task already studied in the recent literature. Most methods can be traced back to the following workflow: entity blocking phase, in-block pairwise comparisons between entities to draw similarity relations, closure of the resulting meshes to create groups of duplicate entities, and merging group entities to remove disambiguation. Such methods are effective but still not good enough whenever a very low false positive rate is required. In this paper, we present an approach for evaluating the correctness of "groups of duplicates", which can be used to measure the group's accuracy hence its likelihood of false-positiveness. Our novel approach is based on a Graph Neural Network that exploits and combines the concept of Graph Attention and Long Short Term Memory (LSTM). The accuracy of the proposed approach is verified in the context of Author Name Disambiguation applied to a curated dataset obtained as a subset of the OpenAIRE Graph that includes PubMed publications with at least one ORCID identifier.

Keywords: entity deduplication · correctness · graph neural networks · author name disambiguation

1 Introduction

Entity deduplication (or disambiguation) refers to the process of identifying duplicates within a given collection of entity metadata descriptions. The primary objective of this process is to group the equivalent entities into distinct groups of duplicates, thereby increasing the data quality and saving storage space. The deduplication process is particularly relevant for providers who curate collections that must be indexed and made available for user search.

Before the advent of machine learning, the most popular approaches were based on a three-stage workflow:

O. Alonso et al. (Eds.): TPDL 2023, LNCS 14241, pp. 207–219, 2023.
https://doi.org/10.1007/978-3-031-43849-3_18

Blocking preliminary blocking stage to group "potentially equivalent" entities to limit the number of comparisons;

Similarity match pairwise comparisons stage inside each block to check for equivalence and to draw similarity relationships between equivalent entities;

Deduplication identification of groups of duplicates (equivalent entities) by closing the meshes in the graph resulting from the previous phase.

This type of approach persists nowadays when the entities bear a well-described set of metadata attributes and the collection curator demands strong control and explainability over the results [1–3]. On the other hand, evaluating the quality (e.g. via metrics) of the groups of duplicates when these are label-less becomes as challenging as inefficient. Measuring quality is essential, to refine or improve the results, or to provide a level of confidence to the consumers of the deduplicated collection. Given the nature of the problem, where the main objective is to have a low number of wrong groups of duplicates, it is important to have an evaluation measure able to give a score to a group independently from the others. In this way, the data quality can be increased by excluding from the final graph all the groups with a low score by cutting their similarity relations.

In this paper, we address this problem by exploiting a Graph Neural Network (GNN) approach, relying on a twofold intuition: (*i*) the similarity match stage described above generates a graph where nodes represent the entities and relationships indicate the equivalence between two nodes; and (*ii*) the deduplication stage generates a set of distinct graphs, whose nodes have no relationships with nodes of other graphs. In the last few years, many different architectures involving deep learning and graphs have been proposed, with GNN methods becoming very popular in the research community. Typically, such methods encode the information in every node of the graph through a feature-extraction algorithm and subsequently generate node embeddings by encoding information about the node's topology via message passing with other nodes in the neighborhood. GNN methods have been proven effective in node and graph classification, where node embeddings are merged to represent the whole graph. Most popular examples of GNNs are the Graph Convolutional Network (GCN) [4], the Graph Attention Network (GAT) [5], Graph Isomorphism Network (GIN) [6] and Graphormer [7], which brings the concept of NLP transformers on Graphs.

In light of these observations, we propose a custom model capable of processing groups of duplicates to evaluate their correctness regarding a percentage indicator. The model is then applied in a real-case scenario of scholarly communication to duplicate author names. More specifically, it is trained in a supervised way using a custom dataset of ORCID-provided authors coming from PubMed[1] article metadata records collected by the OpenAIRE Graph[2] [8–10]. To define the model, a preliminary analysis of known Graph Neural Networks has been carried out and a 3-layered GAT was identified as the most promising. The model has been customized in two ways. Firstly, by adding edge weights that reflect the similarity match between two nodes and a node betweenness centrality [11]

---

[1] https://pubmed.ncbi.nlm.nih.gov.

[2] https://graph.openaire.eu.

measure that reflects the pivotal role of a node in a graph in terms of shortest paths. Secondly, by adding a further LSTM layer [12], before the classifier for the prediction. A sigmoid function is subsequently applied to the classifier output to transform the result into a percentage measure of correctness. Once the model has been trained over labeled data, it can be used to classify groups with no available labels (i.e. the majority of those resulting from a real-case scenario) as the nature of groups of duplicates depends on the algorithm used for the deduplication and therefore remains the same. Our experiments have shown the approach to be effective with both big and small groups with an accuracy of circa 90%.

The paper is organized as follows: Sect. 2 describes the current status of the research on the topic; Sect. 3 describes the methodology used to conduct the research; Sect. 4 provides a description of the developed architecture together with the experimental results; Sect. 5 discusses the obtained results; Sect. 6 concludes the paper providing some hints for the future directions of this research.

2   State of the Art

The literature does not address the problem of assessing the quality of groups of duplicate entities. However, since the groups created after a deduplication process correspond to clusters of equivalent data (entities), *clustering evaluation metrics* may be considered a valuable solution. Two classes of metrics exist: "extrinsic measures" when the ground truth label is required, and "intrinsic measures" when the ground truth label is not required. Known metrics in these fields are the *Rand Index*, the *Mutual Information*, the *V-measure*, and the *Fowlkes-Mallow score* when speaking about intrinsic measure, while the *Silhouette Coefficient*, the *Calinski-Harabasz Index*, and the *Davies-Bouldin Index* when speaking about extrinsic measure. In order to use such metrics for the evaluation it is important to think of the group of duplicates as a set of points in an n-dimensional space, and in some cases to define a measure of distance between such points. The evaluation of deduplication by means of the metrics described above does not allow the evaluation of each group independently from the others, as the final score provided by the formulas of each metric is either inefficient to be computed or descriptive of the whole deduplication.

The evaluation of a deduplication result can be sometimes performed by heavily relying on persistent identifiers of entities [13] (e.g. the DOI) but it is not guaranteed that the measure is trusty, as the persistent identifier for the evaluation is not often available for every entity in the collection of a real-case scenario.

The graph classification problem has been studied in literature and surveys on this topic summarise several methods [14,15]. The methods described in the surveys classify molecules and proteins in a supervised fashion by giving acceptable accuracy ranges. Nonetheless, such methods are not directly applicable to groups of duplicates because of the different and particular nature of such groups, having a dense or sparse distribution of relations that is not directly indicative of the correctness of the group.

As claimed by the authors, the best approach for classifying a graph is Graphormer [7], which brings the transformer concept into Graph Neural Networks. Nonetheless, the nature of transformers makes such architectures' training and inference process extremely slow or feasible only when a high computation power is available, which is not the case in most scenarios.

3   Methodology

The research of this paper has been conducted by following three steps: (*i*) the preparation of the dataset to be used as training, validation, and testing set; (*ii*) the preliminary experiments on base Graph Neural Network architecture to highlight the advantages and the disadvantages of each model; and (*iii*) the implementation, training, and validation of the final model architecture to be used for the classification of groups of duplicates.

The dataset preparation has been performed by mimicking a real-case scenario when a standard framework for deduplication has been applied. In this research we used FDup [16], a framework for efficient data deduplication using decision tree-based matching. The FDup framework delivers a full deduplication workflow in a single easy-to-use software based on Apache Spark Hadoop, where developers can customize the blocking and the similarity matching via an intuitive configuration file. In particular, the similarity matching function is engineered as a decision tree that drives the comparisons of the fields of two records as branches of predicates and allows early-exit strategies to save computation time.

The code is available on GitHub[3] and it is written in Python by using the Deep Graph Library[4] (DGL), a Pytorch-based library which implements fast and memory-efficient message passing primitives for training Graph Neural Networks. All the models have been trained using an *NVIDIA GeForce RTX 3060 Laptop GPU*.

4   Results

4.1   Dataset Preparation

Since this is aimed to be classified as a supervised way of training a Graph Neural Network for graph classification, the main objective of the research is to have a proper dataset to test the goodness of the findings. We decided to use Author Names Disambiguation as an example, and we extracted only Authors with an ORCID identifier provided by PubMed records in the OpenAIRE Graph. The identifier will be used as a label to determine the correctness of a group.

The first step of the dataset preparation consists of extracting the authors from PubMed records. Every author extracted from a publication comprises personal fields and fields inherited by the respective publication. Such fields are:

---

[3] https://github.com/micónis/dedup-groups-evaluator.

[4] https://www.dgl.ai.

- full name (i.e. *"Surname, Name"* or *"Surname, N."*)
- the co-authors list (i.e. the list of authors belonging to the same publication as a list of strings)
- the abstract of the publication

Since the deduplication algorithm needs meaningful information for the comparison, the abstract of the publications has been processed with the Latent Dirichlet Allocation (LDA) [17]. To this aim, the abstracts of the publications have been tokenized (i.e. transformed into vectors of words excluding the stop-words), and vectorized (by means of a Bag of Word model) using the Dewey Decimal Classification [18] as a dictionary. Various models of LDA have been trained over the vectorized abstracts by varying the number of topics. The perplexity score over the testing set has been fined-tuned to reach the optimal number of topics for the collection, which resulted in 15, as depicted in Fig. 1.

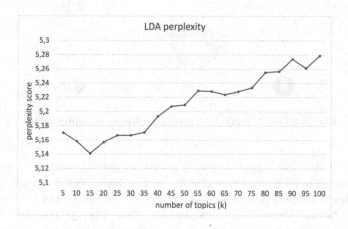

Fig. 1. LDA perplexity score varying the number of topics

Once the optimal LDA model in terms of perplexity is obtained, every abstract has been processed to produce a 15-sized topic vector assigned to the publication's author names to describe authors in terms of the topics they touched upon. The collection of enriched author names is deduplicated at this stage by applying FDup. The framework has been configured as follows:

- preliminary Last Name First Initial (LNFI) blocking stage to identify potentially equivalent authors as authors sharing the surname and the first letter of the first name; in particular, authors having the same surname and the same initial letter of the name are considered potentially equivalent and therefore processed by the similarity matching function (i.e. *"Sandra Smith"* and *"Steven Smith"* will end up in the same block as they share the same blocking key - *"smiths"*);

– pairwise similarity matching based on comparing the co-authors lists and LDA topic vectors. The similarity on the co-authors' lists is measured by counting the number of common names among the lists (i.e. number of similar names), while the cosine similarity measures the similarity on the topic vectors. Note that the threshold of the co-authors similarity has been set empirically to 2, while the threshold of the topic vectors similarity has been set to 0.5 after a False Positive - False Negative analysis varying the threshold on all the possible comparisons. The FDup decision tree used for this purpose is depicted in Fig. 2.

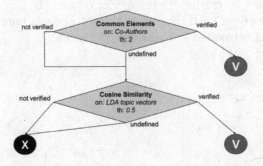

Fig. 2. FDup decision tree used for authors' disambiguation

The result of the deduplication creates groups of authors sharing at least 2 co-authors and/or having a cosine similarity of their topic vectors greater than 0.5. Such groups have been processed and prepared to be the proper training set for the Graph Neural Network. To this aim, they have been labeled and manually classified into positive groups (i.e. all the authors in the group have the same ORCID), or negative groups (i.e. the group has authors with different ORCIDs). Subsequently, 2-sized groups have been removed (i.e. they are pairs), and the dataset has been balanced to have the same number of positive and negative samples. Statistics on the groups are reported in Table 1. The dataset used for this research is available on Zenodo.org [19]. Note that the total number of positive and negative groups has been balanced, but the dataset reflects the common situation in real-case scenarios where the number of wrong groups increases with the size of the groups.

4.2 Preliminary Experiments

In order to provide meaningful features to the Neural Networks, the abstract associated with each author has been further processed via a pre-trained BERT Sentence Embedding model called *bert-base-multilingual-cased*. BERT [20] is a method of language representation able to extract high-quality language features from text data, guaranteeing that similar texts produce similar embeddings.

Table 1. Training dataset statistics

	positive	negative
global	25,450	25,450
groups of 3	12,291	6,699
groups of 4 to 10	11,882	12,107
groups of more than 10	1,277	6,644
total	50,900	

Once the BERT embedding for each graph node has been created, the dataset has been divided into training, validation, and testing set with a ratio of 60%, 20%, and 20%. The idea is to exploit the message passing to update node embeddings with topology information coming from the neighborhood and consequently apply a readout (e.g. aggregation of node embeddings) to have the final graph embedding classified (as usual in graph classification tasks). We decided to test 3 base architectures using the most popular GNN layers. Such architectures are described below:

- GCN3: a 3-layered Graph Convolutional Network;
- GAT3: a 3-layered Graph Attention Network;
- Graphormer: a 6-layered graph transformer with Spacial Encoding and Degree Encoding, as described in the original paper [7].

In every case, the network is finalized by a Linear transformation layer inputted to a sigmoid function to obtain the value as a percentage to be used as a score for evaluating a group. Each architecture has been trained and tested to stop the training process once the overfitting condition was verified (i.e. the loss on the testing set increasing for more than 20 epochs). We chose the best model for each architecture by taking the one from the epoch with the lower loss. Subsequently, models have been evaluated by measuring their performances on the validation set.

Results depicted in Table 2 showed the GAT3 model to be the most promising approach for this kind of activity, confirming the outcomes of the literature claiming that putting attention on neighborhoods' features brings better results.

Table 2. Preliminary experiments on base Graph Neural Networks

model	Acc	TPR	TNR	FPR	FNR	Precision	F1-Score
Graphormer	75.91	85.02	66.56	33.43	14.97	72.29	78.14
GCN3	78.76	81.63	75.81	24.18	18.36	77.59	79.59
GAT3	81.73	87.16	76.17	23.82	12.83	78.96	82.86

4.3 Final Model Architecture

Once the best base model has been pointed out, the final architecture to be used for the purpose of this research has been developed. The intuition behind the approach is in the intrinsic characteristics that make a group of duplicates wrong.

The first source of errors is in the clustering key that defines initial blocks to limit the number of comparisons. In other words, each node in the graph must include in its encoding also some sort of encoding for the field used for the blocking. Since the strategy adopted for the purpose of this experiment is to apply the LNFI on the authors' names, the encoding of each node should include also an encoding for author names. The type of encoding used for this purpose is a Bag of Letters-like method, a simplifying representation that imitates the most common Bag of Words representation used in natural language processing and information retrieval. Each author name is coded in a 55-sized feature vector in which each element indicates the frequency of a specific letter in the name (the size of 55 indicates the number of characters in the alphabet used as a dictionary). Such kind of encoding is sufficient to achieve good results since it guarantees a good representation of typos, which may be present in author names but are still coded in similar vectors (in case of typing errors leading to letters swapped in positions, the encoding is exactly the same). An example of how an author name is encoded is shown in Fig. 3. To better describe the differences among the names in the group, each edge has been weighted with the Jaro-Winkler distance between the two names. This way each edge is normalized with the degree of similarity of the names of its nodes.

Fig. 3. Simplified example of the author name encoding

The second source of error lies in one (or more) nodes leading to the creation of bigger groups. Such nodes have been identified as "bridges" because they are usually poorly described nodes (with a missing first name, and missing co-authors) matching with nodes belonging to different groups for their intrinsic characteristics, creating bigger groups putting together different entities. Examples of bridges are depicted in Fig. 4, where authors with missing first names matched with authors with two different names resulting in the creation of a big wrong group of duplicates after the closure of the meshes.

In order to emphasize such nodes, we developed a centrality encoder that gives a higher weight to nodes which can be potentially a bridge. For this purpose, we used the betweenness centrality measure, which detects the influence a node has over the flow of information in a graph. It is often used to find nodes that serve as a bridge from one part of a graph to another because it measures how

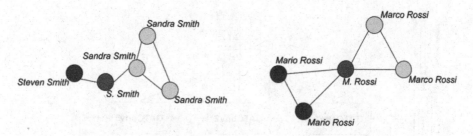

Fig. 4. Example of bridges in a disambiguation graph

many times, in proportion, the path needs to pass from a specific node to reach another.

To complete the model, we added an LSTM to process the output of the GAT convolutional layers. This intuition comes from the fact that groups in the dataset are not of the same length and a smaller group may be flattened by passing through a high number of convolutional layers. On the contrary, bigger groups must pass through more layers for better representation. In this economy, the concatenation of the outcome of every GAT convolutional layer is inputted to the LSTM which will be able to learn to which extent to consider the results of the first layers of the network (meaningful for small groups) combining them with results of the last layer of the network (meaningful for big groups). Following the previous description, our final architecture is depicted in Fig. 5.

Table 3 reports the results obtained for the testing set using the newly created model, dividing them on the nature of the block to better describe how the model behaves. It is shown as the model has an accuracy of about 90% on each class of groups.

Table 3. Experiments on the final architecture

model	Acc	TPR	TNR	FPR	FNR	Precision	F1-Score
GAT3NamesEdgesCentrality	89.87	93.03	86.62	13.37	6.96	87.71	90.29
(in groups of 3)	88.56	95.05	76.75	23.24	4.94	88.14	91.46
(in groups of 4 to 10)	88.77	91.48	85.98	14.01	8.59	87.08	89.22
(in groups of more than 10)	96.25	88.64	97.81	2.18	11.35	89.29	88.97

5   Discussion

Usually, a deduplication process ends up with a series of groups with different sizes: smaller groups are the most probable while bigger groups are less. Conversely, the number of wrong groups among bigger groups is higher because

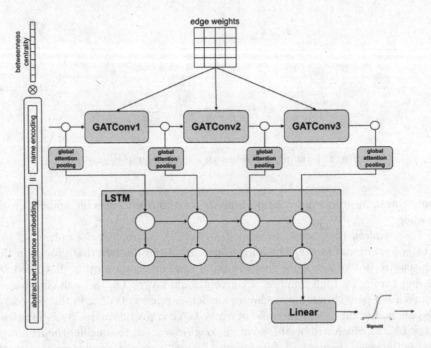

Fig. 5. Final architecture for the classification of a group of duplicates

finding bridges on a more extensive set of nodes is easier. The dataset we created for this research perfectly reflects the environment described above, as table numbers suggest a coherent distribution among wrong and correct groups. Note that the accuracy of the process is not directly comparable to any other architecture of the literature as emerged that the use case was not studied in other research.

The results in terms of accuracy and other metrics depicted in tables for each model architecture tested in this research showed that the main lack of base approach was the misalignment of the accuracies on groups of different sizes. Smaller groups tend to bring down the whole accuracy because the information of the first layers is lost as the other layers of the network process the input. Adding the LSTM at the end of the network allows for overcoming this limitation as it considers meaningful information coming from previous processing steps when needed. In fact, the results of the final model with the LSTM show a balanced accuracy between smaller groups, leading to a higher average accuracy among all the groups in the dataset.

It is important to notice that the accuracy of groups with more than 10 entities is very promising, as such groups are the most difficult to be individuated. The percentages of True Positives, True Negatives, False Positives, and False Negatives fit with the use case, as in this kind of activities is important not to have False Negatives which tend to bring the quality of the data to a lower level.

A fixed threshold has been set on the network output for training. Such threshold identifies a correct group when the output score is greater than 0.5, while identifies a wrong group when the output score is lower than 0.5. A threshold analysis on the scores of the False Negatives and False Positives allows the fine-tuning of such threshold to reduce the number of errors. Increasing the threshold on the final score increases the model's overall accuracy. The outcome of the Graph Neural Network can be consequently used to correct wrong groups (i.e. those with a low score) and to promote correct groups (i.e. those with a high score).

In the end, it is important to mention that the approach is meant to work also for other types of entities since the correctness of a group depends on attributes of the same nature (e.g. titles when the deduplication is performed over publications, legal names when the deduplication is performed over organizations, etc.). The concept of the bridge remains the same in every scenario and does not depend on the type of entity to be deduplicated.

6 Conclusions and Future Works

In this paper, we presented a Graph Neural Network based on the Graph Attention mechanism and the Long Short Term Memory to classify groups of duplicates created by a standard deduplication algorithm. The architecture is provided with a custom encoding for the betweenness centrality of each node and a Bag Of Letters model for the name of the author encoding. The experiments performed on the custom dataset created for this purpose showed acceptable measures of accuracy considering the typical use case of the deduplication activity.

Accuracy can be further increased by including in the encodings entity attributes used by the deduplication algorithm in charge of performing the pairwise comparisons, as experiments suggested that the source of errors lies in poorly described fields.

The approach described in this paper uses the Author Name Disambiguation as an example use case but it is possible to turn it into a general purpose approach. The "bridge" problem depends not on the entity type being deduplicated but on the 3-stage entity linking paradigm formed by entity blocking, pairwise matching, and closing meshes. To turn the approach into a general purpose, it is sufficient to act on the feature type used to feed the Graph Neural Network in a way that they describe the entity attribute responsible for the equivalence of a pair of entities. The initial ground truth to train the Graph Neural Network with can be created by performing the deduplication on entities with identifiers (e.g. ORCID) to be used for the labeling of groups. Once the network has been trained over the ground truth, it can be used to evaluate the correctness of groups even when they do not contain entities with an identifier.

Acknowledgements. This work was partially funded by the EC H2020 projects OpenAIRE-Nexus (Grant agreement 101017452) and FAIRCORE4EOSC (Grant agreement 101057264).

References

1. Manghi, P., Atzori, C., De Bonis, M., Bardi, A.: Entity deduplication in big data graphs for scholarly communication. Data Technol. Appl. **54**(4), 409–435 (2020)
2. He, Q., Li, Z., Zhang, X.: Data deduplication techniques. In: 2010 International Conference on Future Information Technology and Management Engineering, vol. 1, pp. 430–433. IEEE (2010)
3. Kolb, L., Thor, A., Rahm, E.: Dedoop: efficient deduplication with hadoop. Proc. VLDB Endow. **5**(12), 1878–1881 (2012). https://doi.org/10.14778/2367502.2367527
4. Zhang, S., Tong, H., Xu, J., Maciejewski, R.: Graph convolutional networks: a comprehensive review. Comput. Soc. Netw. **6**(1), 1–23 (2019). https://doi.org/10.1186/s40649-019-0069-y
5. Veličković, P., Cucurull, G., Casanova, A., Romero, A., Lio, P., Bengio, Y.: Graph attention networks. arXiv preprint arXiv:1710.10903 (2017)
6. Xu, K., Hu, W., Leskovec, J., Jegelka, S.: How powerful are graph neural networks? arXiv preprint arXiv:1810.00826 (2018)
7. Ying, C., et al.: Do transformers really perform badly for graph representation? Adv. Neural Inf. Process. Syst. **34**, 28877–28888 (2021)
8. Manghi, P., Houssos, N., Mikulicic, M., Jörg, B.: The data model of the OpenAIRE scientific communication e-infrastructure. In: Dodero, J.M., Palomo-Duarte, M., Karampiperis, P. (eds.) MTSR 2012. CCIS, vol. 343, pp. 168–180. Springer, Heidelberg (2012). https://doi.org/10.1007/978-3-642-35233-1_18
9. Manghi, P., et al.: The openaire research graph data model. Zenodo (2019) .
10. Manghi, P., et al.: Openaire research graph dump (2022)
11. Ausiello, G., Firmani, D., Laura, L.: The (betweenness) centrality of critical nodes and network cores, pp. 90–95, July 2013
12. Hochreiter, S., Schmidhuber, J.: Long short-term memory. Neural Comput. **9**, 1735–1780 (1997)
13. Vichos, K., et al.: A preliminary assessment of the article deduplication algorithm used for the openaire research graph (2022)
14. Errica, F., Podda, M., Bacciu, D., Micheli, A.: A fair comparison of graph neural networks for graph classification. CoRR abs/1912.09893 (2019). http://arxiv.org/abs/1912.09893
15. Tsuda, K., Saigo, H.: Graph classification, pp. 337–363. Springer, US, Boston, MA (2010). https://doi.org/10.1007/978-1-4419-6045-0_11
16. De Bonis, M., Manghi, P., Atzori, C.: FDup: a framework for general-purpose and efficient entity deduplication of record collections. PeerJ. Comput. Sci. **8**, e1058 (2022)
17. Blei, D.M., Ng, A.Y., Jordan, M.I.: Latent dirichlet allocation. J. Mach. Learn. Res. **3**, 993–1022 (2003)
18. Scott, M.L., SCOTT, M.L.: Dewey Decimal Classification. Libraries Unlimited (1998)
19. De Bonis, M.: Deduplication groups evaluator data benchmark. https://doi.org/10.5281/zenodo.7997279, June 2023
20. Devlin, J., Chang, M., Lee, K., Toutanova, K.: BERT: pre-training of deep bidirectional transformers for language understanding. CoRR abs/1810.04805 (2018). http://arxiv.org/abs/1810.04805

Synthesizing Web Archive Collections into Big Data: Lessons from Mining Data from Web Archives

Shawn M. Jones[1]([⊠]) [iD], Himarsha R. Jayanetti[2] [iD], Martin Klein[1] [iD],
Michele C. Weigle[2] [iD], and Michael L. Nelson[2] [iD]

[1] Los Alamos National Laboratory, Los Alamos, USA
{smjones,mklein}@lanl.gov
[2] Old Dominion University, Norfolk, USA
hjaya002@odu.edu, {mweigle,mln}@cs.odu.edu

Abstract. Web archives are sources of big data. When presenting human visitors with archived web pages, or mementos, web archives often apply user interface augmentations to assist them. Unfortunately, these augmentations present challenges for natural language processing, computer vision, and machine learning methods. Thus, big data researchers must apply special techniques to web archives when acquiring mementos. This paper details these techniques so that future projects can more easily create datasets and conduct research. We review 22 web archives and discuss the methods needed to re-synthesize a memento to something close to its original capture without augmentations. We close by discussing options for improving the state of memento sharing for big data efforts.

Keywords: Web archive collections · WARCs · data science · big data

1 Introduction

With potentially billions of documents available [33], web archives are a growing big data resource. Researchers have extracted data from them for numerous studies [1,5,8,9,14,26,29,36,41,43,50]. Most of this data gathering has been done manually or with custom tools developed during the research effort. Developing such tools requires knowledge gathered through trial-and-error, experience, and discussions with the web archiving community. As part of the Dark and Stormy Archives Project [23,24,27] (DSA), we develop tools for automatically discovering, acquiring, and summarizing individual archived pages as well as themed collections. We acquired this knowledge through our research and development process. Here we share our findings so that others can more easily execute big data efforts on public web archives.

Web archives capture a web page's current, or **live**, version as a **memento**. Web archives often store mementos in **WebARChive (WARC)** [20] files. Typically, web archiving platforms do not publicly share these WARCs with outsiders. Many existing tools [15,40,44] require that users have access to the original

O. Alonso et al. (Eds.): TPDL 2023, LNCS 14241, pp. 220–229, 2023.
https://doi.org/10.1007/978-3-031-43849-3_19

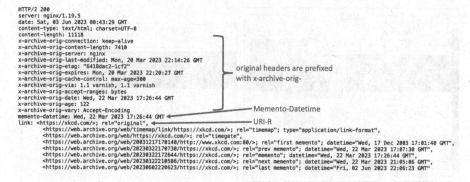

Fig. 1. HTTP headers from a memento at the Internet Archive's Wayback Machine showing the information available via the Memento Protocol and `x-archive-orig-` headers. Annotations are in red. Headers have been abridged and formatted.

WARC files to perform any analysis. Machine clients outnumber human visitors to web archives [4, 21], indicating a need for this knowledge to be centralized into a single work. Here we address the following research question:

How does an actor (machine or human) **re-synthesize** *a memento from the web archive's user interface so that it most closely matches what the web archive originally captured? From the moment of capture, we need (1) the original HTTP headers, (2) the original content, (3) the original URL, and (4) the date and time of capture.*

We provide this work for those who use web archives as a data source. We close by suggesting some improvements that the web archiving community can make so that such research and development is easier for other projects in the future.

2   Background

Using an **original resource** URL, or **URI-R**, web archives apply crawling software, such as Heritrix [18, 42], Brozzler [19] or Webrecorder [39], to capture live web resources as mementos. Each memento is an observation from the time of capture, its **Memento-Datetime**. A memento is identified at the web archive using a **URI-M**.

In our re-synthesis, we use the Memento Protocol [25, 46] supported by more than 20 public web archives. Memento provides a special `Memento-Datetime` HTTP header as well as special relations for the `Link` header, as shown in Fig. 1. These help machine actors discover the URI-R and Memento-Datetime. Additionally, Memento provides a special resource, the **TimeMap**, which provides a listing of all URI-Ms and associated Memento-Datetimes for a URI-R.

When a visitor's browser issues a request for a URI-M, the web archive's **playback engine** (e.g., OpenWayback [17], pywb [38]) uses the URI-R and Memento-Datetime to find the associated WARC record. Web archive playback engines then augment the content in that record before returning it to the

(a) augmented   (b) augmentations removed

Fig. 2. A comparison of an augmented Trove memento from the collection *Tourism* with its augmentations removed. Note the absence of the calendar, banner, and other navigational elements on the right.

browser. These **augmentations** create a better user experience for human visitors, but complicate our ability to automate certain types of analysis. Machine actors require the **raw memento** free of these augmentations.

One popular augmentation is to add branding and navigational elements to each memento. We show an example for a Trove memento[1] in Fig. 2. These augmentations identify the archive and provide humans with links to other resources at the archive [2,3]. Tools that apply standard NLP techniques, such as term frequency [22], can present skewed results because these noisy terms occur on every page.

Rewritten links allow human visitors to browse other pages captured by the web archive, providing a seamless experience. Sometimes rewriting these links has unintended consequences. For example, in Fig. 3 the text "This page has not been archived here" is not part of the original content. Because the playback engine often generates these links at render time, using a standard crawler to gather content from mementos becomes costly. A crawler may not realize that it has already captured a URI-M's content because the playback engine generates new links when it renders each memento.

Web servers, including web archive playback engines, must present *current* HTTP headers to browsers. If a web archive presents a memento's original HTTP headers to a web browser, the browser may behave unexpectedly, incorrectly following redirects or applying incorrect caching policies. For some projects machine actors require the original HTTP headers from the time of capture.

---

[1] https://webarchive.nla.gov.au/awa/20160511214903/http://pandora.nla.gov.au/pan/157302/20160512-0748/www.charroa.org.au/index.html.

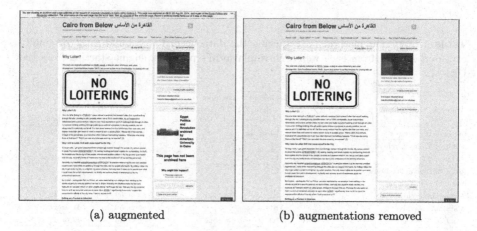

(a) augmented   (b) augmentations removed

Fig. 3. A comparison of an augmented Archive-It memento from the collection *Egypt Politics and Revolution* with its augmentations removed. Note the absence of the banner and iframes linking back to the collection under "Like Us on Facebook".

3 Related Work

Discovering raw memento content has been discussed and addressed in different ways. Many researchers [7,12,13,49] have added the `id_` **modifier** to a URI-M (e.g., changing https://web.archive.org/web/20230322172644/https://xkcd.com/ to https://web.archive.org/web/20230322172644id_/https://xkcd.com/) to acquire raw content, but, as we show in Sect. 4, this is not supported by all web archives. As part of a 2016 content drift study on scholarly references [29], Jones et al. required the raw memento content of almost 700,000 mementos. They documented the challenges with [28] scraping content from several web archives, including the Internet Archive's Wayback Machine, Public Record of Northern Ireland, and WebCite. These challenges led to further proposals by Jones et al. [30] to address the issue using HTTP `Link` header relations. These ideas were later improved upon by Van de Sompel et al. [48] with a concept that applied the HTTP `Prefer` header [45]. As far as we know, these header concepts have not been adopted by web archives, but did inspire solutions for aggregating their holdings [34].

4 Acquiring the Originally Captured Content

We reviewed web archives in the Memento Aggregator Configuration's Archive List [47]. Table 1 shows the different techniques needed to find the information needed to re-synthesize a memento. We did not include web archives that were unreachable or were experiencing technical issues at the time of our review. Most methods require consulting the HTTP headers in a memento's response, as shown in Fig. 1. Some methods (**h2, c1**) require adding the `id_` modifier to

Table 1. Different methods of acquiring the data needed to rebuild a the originally captured content from each web archive platform's playback engine starting from the URI-M.

Web Archive Platform	Methods to Acquire			
	Original HTTP Headers	Original Content	Original URL (URI-R)	Memento-Datetime
Archive-It	h1 or h2	c1	u1 or u2	d1 or d2
Archive.Today (archive.is)	?	c3	u1	d1
Arquivo.pt	h2	c1	u1 or u2	d1 or d2
Bibliothèque et Archives nationale du Québec	?	c1	u2	d2
Canadian Archive	h1	c1	u1 or u2	d1 or d2
Catalonia Archive	h1	c1	u1 or u2	d1 or d2
Conifer	h3	c2	u2 or u3	d2 or d3
Hrvatski Arhiv Weba (Croatian Web Archive)	h1	c1	u1 or u2	d1 or d2
Icelandic Web Archive	h2	c1	u1 or u2	d1 or d2
Internet Archive Wayback Machine	h1 or h2	c1	u1 or u2	d1 or d2
Library of Congress	h1	c1	u1 or u2	d1 or d2
National Diet Library in Japan	?	?	u1	d1
National Records of Scotland	h2	c1	u1 or u2	d1 or d2
perma.cc	w1	w1	u1 or w1	d1 or w1
Slovenian Archive	?	c1	u2	d2
Stanford Web Archive	h2	c1	u1 or u2	d1 or d2
Trove	h3	c2	u2	d2 or d3
UK National Archives Web Archive/ UK Goverment Web Archive	h2	c1	u1 or u2	d1 or d2
UK Parliament Web Archive	h1	c1	u1 or u2	d1 or d2
UKWA	h2	c1	u1 or u2	d1 or d2
Webarchiv	h1	c1	u1 or u2	d1 or d2
York University Archive	h1	c1	u1 or u2	d1 or d2

Key:
? = we could not determine how to acquire this data
h1 = request given URI-M and parse x-archive-orig-* headers, as seen in Fig. 1
h2 = h1, but with id_ modifier added to URI-M [16,37]
h3 = h2, but with special URI-M altered with a different domain [10]
c1 = request special URI-M altered to add id_ URI-M modifier [16,37]
c2 = c1, but with special URI-M altered with a different domain [10]
c3 = request special URL containing raw content
u1 = request given URI-M and parse Memento Protocol Link header
u2 = parse URI-M with custom regular expression to extract URI-R
u3 = u1, but with special URI-M altered with a different domain
and added mp_ modifier [10,37]
d1 = request given URI-M and parse Memento Protocol Memento-Datetime header
d2 = parse URI-M with custom regular expression to extract Memento-Datetime
d3 = d1, but with special URI-M altered with different domain
and added mp_ modifier [10,37]
w1 = special URL for downloading WARC with this information.

the existing URI-M to acquire the desired information. Others (**h3, c2**) require the additional step of changing the URI-M's domain name. Still others (**u3, d3**) require changing the domain name *and* adding the `mp_` modifier to the existing URI-M. Perma.cc provides what we are looking for when acquiring big data. Method **w1** provides a special URL for downloading a WARC. If the actor adds `?type=warc_download` to the end of the URI-M, they can download a WARC file containing the originally captured data. Perma.cc can provide this because a URI-M on their platform does not contain its URI-R or Memento-Datetime.

When crawling web archives to discover additional URI-Ms, we want to avoid crawling rewritten links. Thus, one can save URI-Rs to the frontier rather than rewritten URI-Ms. Klein et al. [35] applied this method when automatically building topical collections from general web archives. Aturban et al. [6] similarly used URI-Rs when creating a dataset of 16,627 mementos from 17 different web archives. They scraped the linked URI-Rs from each raw memento and discovered potential linked URI-Ms by requesting each URI-R's TimeMap. Similar techniques are applied in the DSA tool Hypercane [31,32]. These workarounds are necessary for machine actors due to the rewritten links.

5   Discussion and Conclusions

Web archives have adopted many standards for interoperability, such as WARC and the Memento Protocol. Some conventions, such as the `id_` URI-M modifier and `x-archive-orig-` HTTP response headers, exist for acquiring specific information. These standards and conventions allow machine actors to discover and process resources to provide new applications of web archives. In spite of these standards and conventions, machine actors still encounter differences among web archives when re-synthesizing what was originally captured. We reviewed 22 general web archive platforms to note these differences and discovered 13 methods for discovering this information.

Ideally, each would provide the WARC record corresponding to a URI-M. Perma.cc offers the most straightforward access to a memento's WARC record, but a URI-independent solution is possible using existing standards. A change to web archive playback software could help machine actors. The HTTP protocol already supports a header that allows actors to specify the desired file format of the response [11]. For web pages, a browser often sends the `Accept: text/html` request header to request an HTML file. A machine actor could issue `Accept: application/warc` [20] along with the URI-M HTTP request. A playback engine would then avoid all augmentation steps and return the WARC record to the actor immediately. To indicate that other formats are available, the playback engine would return `Vary: accept` in the response.

Until such a solution is implemented, big data projects that explore web archives will need to apply the techniques we have documented in this paper. With this information, we hope that future big data projects will find web archives more approachable and accessible.

References

1. Ainsworth, S.G., Alsum, A., SalahEldeen, H., Weigle, M.C., Nelson, M.L.: How much of the web is archived? In: Proceedings of the 11th Annual International ACM/IEEE Joint Conference on Digital Libraries, JCDL 2011, Ottowa, Canada, pp. 133–136. Association for Computing Machinery, New York, NY, USA (2011). https://doi.org/10.1145/1998076.1998100
2. Alam, S., Kelly, M., Weigle, M.C., Nelson, M.L.: A survey of archival replay banners. Technical report, Old Dominion University (2018). https://matkelly.com/papers/2018_wadl_banners.pdf. Presented at 2018 Web Archiving and Digital Libraries Workshop
3. Alam, S., Kelly, M., Weigle, M.C., Nelson, M.L.: Unobtrusive and extensible archival replay banners using custom elements. In: Proceedings of the 18th ACM/IEEE on Joint Conference on Digital Libraries, JCDL 2018, pp. 319–320. Association for Computing Machinery, New York, NY, USA (2018). https://doi.org/10.1145/3197026.3203881
4. AlNoamany, Y.A., Weigle, M.C., Nelson, M.L.: Access patterns for robots and humans in web archives. In: Proceedings of the 13th ACM/IEEE-CS Joint Conference on Digital Libraries, JCDL 2013, Indianapolis, Indiana, USA, pp. 339–348. Association for Computing Machinery, New York, NY, USA (2013). https://doi.org/10.1145/2467696.2467722
5. Arms, W.Y., Aya, S., Dmitriev, P., Kot, B., Mitchell, R., Walle, L.: A research library based on the historical collections of the internet archive. D-Lib Mag. **12** (2006). http://www.dlib.org/dlib/february06/arms/02arms.html
6. Aturban, M., Nelson, M.L., Weigle, M.C., Klein, M., Van de Sompel, H.: Collecting 16K archived web pages from 17 public web archives. Technical report, 1905.03836, Old Dominion University (2019). https://arxiv.org/abs/1905.03836
7. Ayala, B.R., Hitchcock, E., Sun, J.: Using image similarity metrics to measure visual quality in web archives. Technical report, University of Alberta (2019). https://doi.org/10.7939/r3-yh2n-rx10. Presented at the 2019 Web Archiving and Digital Libraries Workshop
8. Ben-David, A.: 2014 not found: a cross-platform approach to retrospective web archiving. Internet Histories **3**(3–4), 316–342 (2019). https://doi.org/10.1080/24701475.2019.1654290
9. Callister, P.D.: Perma.cc and web archival dissonance with copyright law. Legal Ref. Serv. Q. **40**(1), 1–57 (2021). https://doi.org/10.1080/0270319X.2021.1886785
10. Cushman, J., Kreymer, I.: Thinking like a hacker: security considerations for high-fidelity web archives (2017). http://labs.rhizome.org/presentations/security.html
11. Fielding, R., Reschke, J.: RFC 7231: hypertext transfer protocol (HTTP/1.1): semantics and content (2014). https://datatracker.ietf.org/doc/html/rfc7231
12. Grusky, M., Naaman, M., Artzi, Y.: NEWSROOM: a dataset of 1.3 million summaries with diverse extractive strategies. In: Proceedings of the 2018 Conference of the North American Chapter of the Association for Computational Linguistics: Human Language Technologies, Volume 1 (Long Papers), pp. 708–719. Association for Computational Linguistics, New Orleans, Louisiana, June 2018. https://doi.org/10.18653/v1/N18-1065. https://aclanthology.org/N18-1065
13. Gunnam, M.: How I changed over time: a webservice to summarize TimeMaps based on SimHashed HTML content. Masters Thesis, Old Dominion University (2018). https://www.cs.odu.edu/~mweigle/papers/gunnam-ms-proj-18.pdf

14. Hafner, K., Palmer, G.: Skin cancers rise, along with questionable treatments. The New York Times (2017). https://www.nytimes.com/2017/11/20/health/dermatology-skin-cancer.html

15. Holzmann, H., Goel, V., Anand, A.: ArchiveSpark: efficient web archive access, extraction and derivation. In: Proceedings of the 16th ACM/IEEE-CS on Joint Conference on Digital Libraries, pp. 83–92. Newark, New Jersey, USA (2016). https://doi.org/10.1145/2910896.2910902

16. IIPC and contributors: OpenWayback Administrator Manual (2015). https://iipc.github.io/openwayback/2.1.0.RC.1/administrator_manual.html

17. IIPC and contributors: IIPC/OpenWayback: The OpenWayback Development (2021). https://github.com/iipc/openwayback

18. Internet Archive, other contributors: Heritrix (2023). https://github.com/internetarchive/heritrix3

19. Internet Archive and contributors: Brozzler (2023). https://github.com/internetarchive/brozzler

20. ISO/TC46/SC4: ISO28500:2017 Information and documentation - WARC file format (2017). https://www.iso.org/standard/68004.html

21. Jayanetti, H.R., Garg, K., Alam, S., Nelson, M.L., Weigle, M.C.: Robots still outnumber humans in web archives, but less than before. In: Linking Theory and Practice of Digital Libraries, pp. 245–259. Springer, Cham (2022). https://doi.org/10.1007/978-3-031-16802-4_19

22. Jones, K.S.: A statistical interpretation of term specificity and its application in retrieval. J. Documentation **1**, 11–21 (1972). https://doi.org/10.1108/eb026526

23. Jones, S.M.: Improving collection understanding for web archives with storytelling: shining light into dark and stormy archives. Ph.D. thesis, Old Dominion University (2021). https://doi.org/10.25777/zts6-v512

24. Jones, S.M., et al.: The DSA toolkit shines light into dark and stormy archives. Code4Lib J. (2022). https://journal.code4lib.org/articles/16441

25. Jones, S.M., Klein, M., Sompel, H.V., Nelson, M.L., Weigle, M.C.: Interoperability for accessing versions of web resources with the memento protocol. In: The Past Web, pp. 101–126. Springer, Cham (2021). https://doi.org/10.1007/978-3-030-63291-5_9

26. Jones, S.M., Klein, M., Van de Sompel, H.: Robustifying links to combat reference rot. Code4Lib J. (2021). https://journal.code4lib.org/articles/15509

27. Jones, S.M., Klein, M., Weigle, M.C., Nelson, M.L.: Summarizing web archive corpora via social media storytelling by automatically selecting and visualizing exemplars. ACM Trans. Web (2023). https://doi.org/10.1145/3606030

28. Jones, S.M., Shankar, H.: Rules of acquisition for mementos and their content. Technical report, 1602.06223, Los Alamos National Laboratory (2016). https://arxiv.org/abs/1602.06223

29. Jones, S.M., Van de Sompel, H., Shankar, H., Klein, M., Tobin, R., Grover, C.: Scholarly context adrift: three out of four URI references lead to changed content. PLOS ONE **11**(12), 1–32 (2016). https://doi.org/10.1371/journal.pone.0167475

30. Jones, S.M., Van de Sompel, H., Nelson, M.L.: Mementos in the raw (2016). https://ws-dl.blogspot.com/2016/04/2016-04-27-mementos-in-raw.html

31. Jones, S.M., Weigle, M.C., Klein, M., Nelson, M.L.: Hypercane: intelligent sampling for web archive collections. In: 2021 ACM/IEEE Joint Conference on Digital Libraries (JCDL), pp. 316–317. ACM, New York, NY, USA (2021). https://doi.org/10.1109/JCDL52503.2021.00049

32. Jones, S.M., Weigle, M.C., Nelson, M.L.: Hypercane: toolkit for summarizing large collections of archived webpages. ACM SIGWEB Newslett. (Summer), 1–14 (2021). https://doi.org/10.1145/3473044.3473047

33. Kahle, B.: Wayback Machine now has 898,570,440,000 URL's. https://twitter.com/brewster_kahle/status/1225167435399036939 (2020)

34. Kelly, M., Nelson, M.L., Weigle, M.C.: A framework for aggregating private and public web archives. In: Proceedings of the 18th ACM/IEEE on Joint Conference on Digital Libraries, JCDL 2018, Fort Worth, TX, USA, pp. 273–282. Association for Computing Machinery, New York, NY, USA (2018). https://doi.org/10.1145/3197026.3197045

35. Klein, M., Balakireva, L., Van de Sompel, H.: Focused crawl of web archives to build event collections. In: Proceedings of the 2018 ACM Conference on Web Science, pp. 333–342. Amsterdam, Netherlands (2018). https://doi.org/10.1145/3201064.3201085

36. Klein, M., et al.: Scholarly context not found: one in five articles suffers from reference rot. PLOS ONE 9(12), 1–39 (2014). https://doi.org/10.1371/journal.pone.0115253

37. Kreymer, I.: Webrecorder pywb documentation! (2023). https://pywb.readthedocs.io/en/latest/index.html

38. Kreymer, I.: Contributors: Core Python Web Archiving Toolkit (2023). https://github.com/webrecorder/pywb

39. Kreymer, I., contributors: Webrecorder (2023). https://webrecorder.net/

40. Lin, J., Milligan, I., Wiebe, J., Zhou, A.: Warcbase: scalable analytics infrastructure for exploring web archives. J. Comput. Cult. Heritage 10(4), 1–30 (2017). https://doi.org/10.1145/3097570

41. Milligan, I.: History in the Age of Abundance: How the Web Is Transforming Historical Research. McGill-Queen's University Press (2019)

42. Mohr, G., Stack, M., Ranitovic, I., Avery, D., Kimpton, M.: An introduction to Heritrix: an open source archival quality web crawler. In: Proceedings of the 4th International Web Archiving Workshop (IWAW) (2004). https://citeseerx.ist.psu.edu/document?repid=rep1&type=pdf&doi=7d4e01113bdb8958428a64bc07645444c01d062e

43. Ohlheiser, A.: Gothamist and DCist just abruptly shut down. What will happen to their archives? The Washington Post (2017). https://www.washingtonpost.com/news/the-intersect/wp/2017/11/02/gothamist-and-dcist-just-abruptly-shut-down-what-will-happen-to-their-archives/

44. Ruest, N., Lin, J., Milligan, I., Fritz, S.: The archives unleashed project: technology, process, and community to improve scholarly access to web archives. In: Proceedings of the ACM/IEEE Joint Conference on Digital Libraries in 2020, Wuhan, China, pp. 157–166. ACM, New York, NY, USA (2020). https://doi.org/10.1145/3383583.3398513

45. Snell, J.: Prefer Header for HTTP (2014). https://tools.ietf.org/html/rfc7240

46. Van de Sompel, H., Nelson, M., Sanderson, R.: RFC 7089 - HTTP Framework for Time-Based Access to Resource States - Memento (2013). https://tools.ietf.org/html/rfc7089

47. The Memento Project: Memento Aggregator Archive List (2023). http://labs.mementoweb.org/aggregator_config/archivelist.xml

48. Van de Sompel, H., Nelson, M.L., Balakireva, L., Klein, M., Jones, S.M., Shankar, H.: Mementos in the raw, take two (2016). https://ws-dl.blogspot.com/2016/08/2016-08-15-mementos-in-raw-take-two.html

49. Weigle, M.C., Nelson, M.L., Alam, S., Graham, M.: Right HTML, wrong JSON: challenges in replaying archived webpages built with client-side rendering. In: Proceedings of the 2023 ACM/IEEE Joint Conference on Digital Libraries, Santa Fe, NM, USA. ACM, New York, NY, USA (2023). Not yet published, preprint available at https://arxiv.org/abs/2305.01071
50. Weixel, N.: Trump administration changes definition of national stockpile after Kushner remarks (2020). https://thehill.com/homenews/administration/491037-trump-administration-changes-definition-of-national-stockpile-after/

A Comparison of Automated Journal Recommender Systems

Elias Entrup[1]([✉]) [iD], Ralph Ewerth[1,2] [iD], and Anett Hoppe[1,2] [iD]

[1] TIB - Leibniz Information Centre for Science and Technology, Hanover, Germany
elias.entrup@tib.eu
[2] L3S Research Center, Leibniz University Hannover, Hanover, Germany

Abstract. Choosing the right journal for an article can be a challenge. Automated manuscript matching can help authors with the decision by recommending suitable journals based on user-defined criteria. Several approaches for efficient matching have been proposed in the research literature. However, only a few actual recommender systems are available for end users. In this paper, we present an overview of available services and compare their key characteristics such as input values, functionalities, and privacy. We conduct a quantitative analysis of their recommendation results: (a) examining the overlap in the results and pointing out the similarities among them; (b) evaluating their quality with a comparison of their accuracy. Due to the providers' lack of transparency about the used technologies, the results cannot be easily interpreted. This highlights the need for openness about the used algorithms and data sets.

Keywords: Scientific publishing · Recommender systems

1 Introduction

The ever-growing number of journals and requirements by funding agencies make it increasingly difficult for researchers to find journals for their manuscripts. Apart from several publication guides [2,3,26,31], the automated recommendation of journals is an active field of study [23,32,39,41]. An overview is provided in [1]. While recommendation approaches based on e.g. co-author networks [23] exist, the majority relies on semantic similarity of the user input to already published scientific articles. Most of the proposed systems do not run in a production mode available to end users.

Two prior articles compare available journal recommendation services: In [13], seven services are compared for features, and illustrative query results are presented. The analysis includes the services provided by Clarivate, Cofactor (since archived [8]), Edanz, Elsevier, IEEE, JANE, JournalGuide, and Springer. In [22] the seven recommendation services by Edanz, Elsevier, Enago, IEEE, JANE, JournalGuide, and Springer are compared. The usefulness of these services is analysed in comparison to the publication habits of 15 interviewed researchers. None of the above-mentioned research provides a quantitative comparison of journal recommender systems; both only include a subset of the available services and compare them using examples or expert evaluations.

O. Alonso et al. (Eds.): TPDL 2023, LNCS 14241, pp. 230–238, 2023.
https://doi.org/10.1007/978-3-031-43849-3_20

Table 1. List of recommender systems, used abbreviation, the provider, and the scope which describes the subgroup of journals suggested.

Recommender Name	Abbreviation	Provider	Scope
Bibliometric and Semantic Open Access Recommender Network [4]	B!SON	TIB and SLUB	Open Access
Charlesworth Author Services Journal Finder [6]	Charlesworth ASJF	Charlesworth Author Services	All
eContent Pro Journal Finder [9]	eContent Pro JF	eContent Pro	All
Edanz Journal Selector [10]	Edanz JS	Edanz (M3)	All
Elsevier Journal Finder [11]	Elsevier JF	Elsevier	Publisher
Food Science and Technology Abstracts Journal Finder [14]	FSTA JF	FSTA/IFIS	Food/Health
Institute of Electrical and Electronics Engineers Publication Recommender [17]	IEEE PR	IEEE	Publisher
Journal/Author Name Estimator [36]	JANE	The Biosemantics Group	Medicine
Jot [37]	Jot	Townsend Lab	Medicine
Journal Guide [18]	Journal Guide	Research Square	All
MDPI Journal Finder [21]	MDPI JF	MDPI	Publisher
Researcher Journal Finder [24]	Researcher JF	Researcher App	All
Researcher.Life Journal Finder [25]	Researcher.Life JF	Researcher.Life	All
Sage Journal Recommender [28]	Sage JR	Sage Publishing	Publisher
ScienceGate Journal Finder [30]	ScienceGate JF	ScienceGate	Publisher
Springer Journal Suggester [34]	Springer JS	Springer Nature	Publisher
Taylor & Francis Journal Suggester [35]	T&F JS	Taylor & Francis	All
Trinka Journal Finder [38]	Trinka JF	Trinka AI	All
Wiley Journal Finder [40]	Wiley JF	Wiley	Publisher
Web of Science/EndNote Manuscript Matcher [7]	WoS MM	Clarivate	All

In this paper, we analyse the 20 currently available journal recommender systems (as of June 6, 2023). We provide an overview of input options, as well as filter and search features. In contrast to previous work, we perform a quantitative evaluation by measuring the accuracy and the number of overlapping results. As a result, we draw conclusions about how well the services perform and complement each other. The paper is organised as follows: Section 2 describes the services selected for the comparison in this paper. A feature comparison with a description of the scope, input, and filters of the services follows. The quantitative analysis of overlapping results and accuracy is presented in Sect. 3. Section 4 summarises our findings and derives implications for users.

2   Selection and Qualitative Comparison

The recommender services in this study were found using "journal recommender", "manuscript matcher" and "journal finder" as a query for Google and Bing, and evaluating the results on the first three pages. This comparison only considers journal recommendation services that offer a form of automatic manuscript matching. It excludes services that only offer to filter journals. We only consider services that are currently online and that work with automated (not expert) recommendations. The search resulted in 20 recommender systems presented in Table 1. In the following, we will abbreviate their names as indicated.

2.1   Description of Services

As shown in Table 1, seven out of 20 services only deliver results that are part of the publisher providing the tool. Of the rest, one is focused on open access and two on medicine. The Charlesworth ASJF, JANE, Jot, Researcher JF, and Trinka.AI JF include pre-print servers in their results.

Only B!SON and Jot are open-source. B!SON, the Elsevier JF, JANE, Jot, and the WoS MM have been described in research papers. The B!SON recommender uses Elasticsearch, a neural network, and bibliographic coupling to recommend journals [5,12]. The Charlesworth Journal Finder claims that its search is powered by Researcher JF. The results, however, are different. The Elsevier JF uses BM 25 to find one million similar articles and averages the scores for each journal [19]. JANE uses Lucene's MoreLikeThis algorithm to find the 50 most similar articles to the user input [29], sums the scores per journal and normalises them. Jot is based on JANE and adds counting of the journal appearances in a user-provided list of references [15]. The WoS MM averages the results of a Support Vector Machine and a Lucene k-Nearest-Neighbors search [27].

2.2   Search Input

While attributes such as full text [16] or authors [20] have been used in research to suggest journals, most services use title and abstract. Keywords and subject are also used by a few services. B!SON works with references by parsing for DOIs in the text the user enters (copied from the PDF or a structured format like bibtex); Jot expects a bibliography file in the RIS format. The Charlesworth ASJF, Edanz JS, IEEE PR, JANE, and Researcher JF use a single input field for several attributes at once. The ScienceGate JF first suggests several, editable keywords based on the title and abstract which are then used for the recommendations.

2.3   Filtering, Sorting and Other Features

Most services offer filter and sorting options for the score, title, publisher, publication time, open access or journal impact factor. The Charlesworth ASJF, eContentPro JF, Researcher JF, T&F JS, and Wiley JF have few to no filter, or sorting options.

In the following, we will list noteworthy features of the systems: B!SON facilitates the search with an already published article by fetching the inputs via e.g. Crossref. Elsevier JF offers to enter the author's organisation to get personalised publishing options based on existing agreements. It also detects if the input data belong to an article already published by Elsevier. The IEEE PR can filter venues to publish before a specified date and also searches for conferences (not considered in this paper). JANE allows searching for similar articles and authors who published similar work. Jot provides a two-dimensional visualisation with the "prospect" (estimated chance of acceptance) on the X-axis and an impact metric (e.g. CiteScore) on the Y-axis. Journal Guide has a comparison function to create an overview of selected journals from the result list.

2.4 Transparency and Privacy

Only B!SON and Jot are open source, but several recommender systems show which similar articles led to the recommendation of a journal: B!SON, Edanz JS, JANE, Jot, Journal Guide, Researcher.Life JF, Sage JR, and Trinka.AI JF. Most services do not publicise which journals are in their data set and if it is up-to-date. The websites often, at least, indicate the number of journals included.

Both the Journal Guide and JANE have the option to scramble the entered abstract on the client side for privacy. All systems offer an encrypted TLS connection; Jot, however, features an expired certificate at the time of writing.

The majority of recommender systems are free and can be used anonymously. However, the WoS MM and the Trinka.Ai JF only work with an account. Researcher.Life JF requires an account for advanced features such as viewing similar articles. Similarly, the eContent Pro JF requires the name and e-mail address for a mandatory sign-up to their e-mail communications. The T&F JS explicitly states that they store the submitted abstracts and which results the user clicks on. The Trinka.AI JF also stores the input along with the generated results so the user can review them later. There is no option to delete searches. Only B!SON and the Edanz JS promise to not store the user inputs.

3 Quantitative Evaluation

In the following, we perform a quantitative comparison of the accuracy and the overlap of the results. We used smaller article test sets to avoid getting blocked.

3.1 Comparison of Independent Recommender Systems

We test the publisher-independent recommender systems with 50 articles from the only journal we found in all recommenders: "New Biotechnologies" (ISSN 1876-4347). Similarly to research on web search engine results [33], we present the average overlap of the top 15 results based on the ISSNs in Table 2.

Table 2. Comparing the average overlap of results for the publisher-independent recommenders systems

	B!SON	Charlesworth ASJF	eContentPro JF	Edanz JS	FSTA JF	JANE	Jot	Journal Guide	Researcher JF	Researcher.Life JF	ScienceGate JF	Trinka.AI JF	WoS MM
B!SON	15.0	1.5	0.0	1.3	0.5	2.6	2.9	2.0	2.9	2.1	1.9	4.5	2.0
Charlesworth ASJF	1.5	7.0	0.0	1.3	0.6	2.7	3.6	2.8	5.6	1.5	1.7	2.8	2.3
eContentPro JF	0.0	0.0	5.0	0.0	0.0	0.0	0.0	0.0	0.0	0.0	0.0	0.0	0.0
Edanz JF	1.3	1.3	0.0	15.0	0.4	3.6	3.6	1.5	2.7	2.1	2.6	4.2	3.6
FSTA JF	0.5	0.6	0.0	0.4	4.6	0.6	0.6	0.4	0.8	0.6	0.8	0.8	0.6
JANE	2.6	2.7	0.0	3.6	0.6	15.0	8.9	3.3	3.7	2.6	2.3	4.4	3.5
Jot	2.9	3.6	0.0	3.6	0.6	8.9	14.7	4.1	5.0	2.6	2.4	5.1	3.7
Journal Guide	2.0	2.8	0.0	1.5	0.4	3.3	4.1	14.4	3.4	1.8	1.5	2.9	1.9
Researcher JF	2.9	5.6	0.0	2.7	0.8	3.7	5.0	3.4	15.0	2.4	2.9	4.9	4.3
Research.Life JF	2.1	1.5	0.0	2.1	0.6	2.6	2.6	1.8	2.4	14.4	2.4	3.9	2.7
ScienceGate JF	1.9	1.7	0.0	2.6	0.8	2.3	2.4	1.5	2.9	2.4	15.0	4.2	3.5
Trinka.AI JF	4.5	2.8	0.0	4.2	0.8	4.4	5.1	2.9	4.9	3.9	4.2	14.6	4.5
WoS MM	2.0	2.3	0.0	3.6	0.6	3.5	3.7	1.9	4.3	2.7	3.5	4.5	15.0

The Charlesworth ASJF, eContentPro JF, and FSTA JF provide fewer results, the rest of the services usually provide the 15 results that were considered. Some queries did not return any or only few results. The prominent overlap between Charlesworth ASJF and Researcher JF confirms that Charlesworth ASJF's recommendations are based on Researcher JF (see Sect. 2.1). A similar effect can be observed with JANE and Jot. The eContentPro JF and FSTA JF share the least results with the other systems. At least for FSTA JF, this might be caused by its very specific scope. The other systems usually share two to four results, with Trink.AI JF showing the highest overlaps with other services.

3.2 Accuracy

We further test the accuracy (precision) of the recommender systems. To ensure a fair comparison, we test with articles from journals in their data set (i.e. test the Elsevier JF only with Elsevier articles). Each system is tested on 100 articles, coming from 100 different journals to broaden the scope of testing. Articles from this year are excluded so that we can assume that the article should be in the training set. As most systems do not disclose the included journals, we used test queries to identify a list of journals in their data set. We use the API of the scientific database Dimensions[1] to retrieve the corresponding test articles. We also assume that the correct journal is the one where the article was published.

The systems might take other factors into account apart from the semantic match, e.g. possible impact. Having the test articles potentially in the training set is a limitation. Nevertheless, high accuracy can indicate how much the system relies on finding a similar article.

The results are shown in Table 3. As JANE is checking for similar articles [29], the accuracy is high because it will usually find the article in question in its data set. Journal Guide and Springer JS also yield high accuracy. The reason for eContentPro JF's, FSTA JF's, and ScienceGate JF's low accuracies are unclear.

Table 3. Recommender systems and their accuracy considering the first and the first ten results.

Name	Acc@1	Acc@10
B!SON	0.20	0.88
Charlesworth ASJF	0.21	0.77
eContentPro JF	0.03	0.16
Edanz JS	0.16	0.54
Elsevier JF	0.35	0.86
FSTA JF	0.07	0.29
IEEE PR	0.26	0.68
JANE	0.83	0.96
Jot	0.19	0.93
Journal Guide	0.38	0.98
MDPI JF	0.48	0.88
Researcher JF	0.07	0.49
Researcher.Life JF	0.15	0.48
Sage JR	0.17	0.69
Springer JS	0.97	0.98
T&F JS	0.48	0.91
Trinka.AI JF	0.07	0.41
ScienceGate JF	0.10	0.35
Wiley JF	0.19	0.59
WoS MM	0.12	0.48

4 Conclusions

In this paper, we systematically compared 20 journal recommendation services. We found that most of them use the title and abstract to find the best-fitting journal. Apart from publisher-specific services, 13 independent services exist. Many try to inform the user how a match was calculated, but few have published their source code, recommendation approach, or data sources.

We tested the accuracy of the services and to what degree they delivered the same results. The accuracy varies widely with the Acc@10 ranging from 16% to 98%. While for most recommender systems two to four results are shared, a higher overlap validates the shared recommendation approach of some services.

We derive the following advice: (a) Users should look beyond the first suggestion. (b) For the medical domain, Jot provides more features than JANE and can be recommended. (c) For open-access publications, B!SON and Journal Guide can be recommended. B!SON is more transparent but both services have a high accuracy and number of sorting and filter options. (d) Otherwise, Journal Guide or publisher-specific services can be used. Background knowledge is still required for the final decision.

Declaration of Competing Interests. The authors were part of the B!SON project.

---

[1] https://docs.dimensions.ai/dsl/.

References

1. Ajmal, S., Muzammil, M.B.: PVRS: publication venue recommendation system a systematic literature review. In: International Conference on Computing Engineering and Design, ICCED 2019, Singapore, 11–13 April 2019, pp. 1–6. https://doi.org/10.1109/ICCED46541.2019.9161106

2. Babor, T.F., Stenius, K., Pates, R., Miovský, M., O'Reilly, J., Candon, P. (eds.): Publishing Addiction Science: A Guide for the Perplexed. Ubiquity Press (2017). https://www.jstor.org/stable/j.ctv3t5qxw

3. Bahadoran, Z., Mirmiran, P., Kashfi, K., Ghasemi, A.: Scientific publishing in biomedicine: how to choose a journal? Int. J. Endocrinol. Metab. **19**(1), e108417 (2020). https://doi.org/10.5812/ijem.108417

4. B!SON: B!SON - the Open-Access journal recommender. https://service.tib.eu/bison. Accessed 6 June 2023

5. B!SON: How it works (2023). https://service.tib.eu/bison/how. Accessed 2 Feb 2023

6. Charlesworth Author Services: Journal Finder — Find Journals — Charlesworth Author Services, https://www.cwauthors.com/Journal-Finder. Accessed 6 June 2023

7. Clarivate: Web of Science Master Journal List - WoS MJL by Clarivate. https://mjl.clarivate.com/home. Accessed 6 June 2023

8. Cofactor: Journal Selector Tool archived (2021). https://cofactorscience.com/journal-selector-tool-archived. Accessed 2 Feb 2023

9. eContent Pro: Journal Identifier Database. https://www.econtentpro.com/journal-finder. Accessed 6 June 2023

10. Edanz: MY JOURNAL SELECTOR, October 2015. https://www.edanz.com/journal-selector. Accessed 6 June 2023

11. Elsevier: Elsevier® JournalFinder. https://journalfinder.elsevier.com/. Accessed 6 June 2023

12. Entrup, E., et al.: B!SON: a tool for open access journal recommendation. In: Silvello, G., et al. (eds.) International Conference on Theory and Practice of Digital Libraries, TPDL 2022, Padua, Italy, 20–23 September 2022. LNCS, pp. 357–364. Springer, Cham. https://doi.org/10.1007/978-3-031-16802-4_33

13. Forrester, A., Björk, B.C., Tenopir, C.: New web services that help authors choose journals. Learn. Publishing **30**(4), 281–287 (2017). https://doi.org/10.1002/leap.1112. eprint: https://onlinelibrary.wiley.com/doi/pdf/10.1002/leap.1112

14. FSTA: Journal Recommendation Service. http://www.fstajournalfinder.com/#/home/suggest. Accessed 6 June 2023

15. Gaffney, S.G., Townsend, J.P.: Jot: guiding journal selection with suitability metrics. J. Med. Libr. Assoc. **110**(3), 376–380 (2022). https://doi.org/10.5195/jmla.2022.1499

16. Ghosal, T., Chakraborty, A., Sonam, R., Ekbal, A., Saha, S., Bhattacharyya, P.: Incorporating full text and bibliographic features to improve scholarly journal recommendation. In: ACM/IEEE Joint Conference on Digital Libraries, JCDL 2019, Urbana-Champaign, Illinois, 2–6 June 2019, pp. 374–375. Champaign, IL, USA (2019). https://doi.org/10.1109/JCDL.2019.00077

17. IEEE: IEEE Publication Recommender. https://publication-recommender.ieee.org/home. Accessed 6 June 2023

18. JournalGuide: JournalGuide - Home. https://www.journalguide.com/. Accessed 6 June 2023

19. Kang, N., Doornenbal, M.A., Schijvenaars, R.J.: Elsevier journal finder: recommending journals for your paper. In: ACM Conference on Recommender Systems, RecSys 2015, Vienna Austria, 16–20 September 2015, pp. 261–264 (2015). https://doi.org/10.1145/2792838.2799663

20. Klemiński, R., Kazienko, P., Kajdanowicz, T.: Where should I publish? Heterogeneous, networks-based prediction of paper's citation success. J. Informet. **15**(3), 101200 (2021). https://doi.org/10.1016/j.joi.2021.101200

21. MDPI: MDPI — Journal Finder. https://www.mdpi.com/about/journalselector. Accessed 6 June 2023

22. Nam, N.D., Trung, T., Trung, N.T., Thao, T.P.T.: Manuscript matcher: a tool for finding the best journal. In: International Multi-Conference on Complexity, Informatics and Cybernetics, IMCIC 2022, Virtual Event, 8–11 March 2022, pp. 50–55. Virtual Conference (2022). https://doi.org/10.54808/IMCIC2022.01.50

23. Pradhan, T., Pal, S.: A hybrid personalized scholarly venue recommender system integrating social network analysis and contextual similarity. Futur. Gener. Comput. Syst. **110**, 1139–1166 (2020). https://doi.org/10.1016/j.future.2019.11.017

24. Researcher: Researcher — Journal Finder. https://journalfinder.researcher-app.com/. Accessed 6 June 2023

25. Researcher.Life: Researcher. Life Journal Finder: Journal Suggester For Your Manuscript. https://researcher.life/journal. Accessed 6 June 2023

26. Rison, R.A., Shepphird, J.K., Kidd, M.R.: How to choose the best journal for your case report. J. Med. Case Rep. **11**(1), 198 (2017). https://doi.org/10.1186/s13256-017-1351-y

27. Rollins, J., McCusker, M., Carlson, J., Stroll, J.: Manuscript matcher: a content and bibliometrics-based scholarly journal recommendation system. In: Mayr, P., Frommholz, I., Cabanac, G. (eds.) Workshop on Bibliometric-Enhanced Information Retrieval Co-Located with the European Conference on Information Retrieval, BIR@ECIR 2017, Aberdeen, UK, April 9th, 2017. CEUR Workshop Proceedings, vol. 1823, pp. 18–29 (2017). CEUR-WS.org. http://ceur-ws.org/Vol-1823/paper2.pdf

28. Sage: Journal Recommender. https://journal-recommender.sagepub.com/. Accessed 6 June 2023

29. Schuemie, M.J., Kors, J.A.: Jane: suggesting journals, finding experts. Bioinformatics **24**(5), 727–728 (2008). https://doi.org/10.1093/bioinformatics/btn006

30. ScienceGate: Journal Finder — Sciencegate. https://www.sciencegate.app/journal-finder. Accessed 6 June 2023

31. Shokraneh, F., Ilghami, R., Masoomi, R., Amanollahi, A.: How to select a journal to submit and publish your biomedical paper? Bioimpacts **2**(1), 61–68 (2012). https://doi.org/10.5681/bi.2012.008

32. Son, H.T., Tan Phong, H., Dac, N.H.: An efficient approach for paper submission recommendation. In: IEEE Region 10 Conference, TENCON 2020, Osaka, Japan, 16–19 November 2020, pp. 726–731. IEEE, Osaka, Japan (2020). https://doi.org/10.1109/TENCON50793.2020.9293909

33. Spink, A., Jansen, B.J., Blakely, C., Koshman, S.: A study of results overlap and uniqueness among major web search engines. Inf. Process. Manag. **42**(5), 1379–1391 (2006). https://doi.org/10.1016/j.ipm.2005.11.001

34. Springer: Springer Journal Suggester. https://journalsuggester.springer.com/. Accessed 6 June 2023

35. Taylor & Francis: Taylor & Francis Journal Suggester. https://authorservices.taylorandfrancis.com/publishing-your-research/choosing-a-journal/journal-suggester/. Accessed 6 June 2023

36. The Biosemantics Group: Journal / Author Name Estimator. https://jane. biosemantics.org/. Accessed 6 June 2023

37. Townsend Lab: Search. https://jot.publichealth.yale.edu/search. Accessed 6 June 2023

38. Trinka AI: Trinka - Grammar Checker For Academic & Technical Writing. https:// cloud.trinka.ai/journal-finder. Accessed 6 June 2023

39. Vara, N., Mirzabeigi, M., Sotudeh, H., Fakhrahmad, S.M.: Application of k-means clustering algorithm to improve effectiveness of the results recommended by journal recommender system. Scientometrics (2022). https://doi.org/10.1007/s11192-022-04397-4

40. Wiley: Wiley SJF - Search a journal. https://journalfinder.wiley.com/search? type=match. Accessed 6 June 2023

41. ZhengWei, H., JinTao, M., YanNi, Y., Jin, H., Ye, T.: Recommendation method for academic journal submission based on doc2vec and XGBoost. Scientometrics **127**(5), 2381–2394 (2022). https://doi.org/10.1007/s11192-022-04354-1

Making PDFs Accessible for Visually Impaired Users (and Findable for Everybody Else)

Ruben van Heusden[✉][iD], Hazel Ling, Lars Nelissen, and Maarten Marx[✉][iD]

Information Retrieval Lab, Informatics Institute, University of Amsterdam,
Amsterdam, Netherlands
{r.j.vanheusden,maartenmarx}@uva.nl
https://irlab.science.uva.nl

Abstract. We treat documents released under the Dutch Freedom of Information Act as FAIR scientific data and find that they are not findable nor accessible, due to text malformations caused by redaction software. Our aim is to repair these documents. We propose a simple but strong heuristic for detecting wrongly OCRed text segments, and we then repair only these OCR mistakes by prompting a large language model. This makes the documents better findable through full text search, but the repaired PDFs do still not adhere to accessibility standards. Converting them into HTML documents, keeping all essential layout and markup, makes them not only accessible to the visually impaired, but also reduces their size by up to two orders of magnitude. The costs of this way of repairing are roughly one dollar for the 17K pages in our corpus, which is very little compared to the large gains in information quality.

Keywords: Optical Character Recognition · Corpus Curation · Quality Control · Digital Libraries

1 Introduction

The guidelines of the European Union on the re-usability of data stipulate that data released by governments should be reusable [8]. In fact, the guidelines prescribed bear a strong resemblance to the FAIR data principles [17]: released data should be findable, accessible, interoperable and indeed reusable. Findability and accessibilty, in particular for the visually impaired, are greatly hampered by the application of redaction software to documents that the government is obliged to release under the Freedom of Information Act. This redaction software is used to black out text for reasons of privacy, national security, competition, etc., using named entity recognition techniques [5].

Github: https://github.com/irlabamsterdam/accessibilifier

O. Alonso et al. (Eds.): TPDL 2023, LNCS 14241, pp. 239–245, 2023.
https://doi.org/10.1007/978-3-031-43849-3_21

The definition of visual impairment, as specified by the World Wide Web Consortium (W3C), states that someone who is visually impaired is not blind, but whose vision is severely limited, even with the use of glasses or other implements.[1] Visually impaired individuals often use additional software, (e.g. for magnification or speak aloud) which uses the machine readable text in a PDF.

We found that 30% of over 1 million text pages released by the Dutch government does not contain a signle machine readable character, and almost all other pages contain non existing words, most likely caused by OCR errors. Believe it or not, but treating brand new digital born documents as if they originate from the 19th century is common practice in redaction software: scan the document, black out the detected text, and, if one is lucky, make the text on the scan also machine interpretable using optical character recognition (OCR). Of course, this is effective in ensuring that redacted text cannot be brought back [3], but is detrimental from the perspective of information quality. Full text search in these documents will not work well [15], and listening to automatically read aloud documents without machine readable text or text containing sequences of malformed words is not informative nor pleasant.

The research reported in this paper originates in this problem and our wish to repair the damage done to these documents. We do this in three consecutive steps: discover segments of mangled OCRed text using a simple heuristic, repair these segments using a Large Language Model (ChatGPT), and convert the inaccessible PDF into XML containing the repaired text. The converted text then does apply to accessibility standards[2] and as a bonus is typically two orders of magnitude smaller in size [10]. Although it does not need training data, the mangled OCR segment heuristic works well. Only repairing those segments is more efficient, cheaper and helps avoiding false positives. We compare repairing by Tesseract and by ChatGPT, with the latter producing less non-existing words, but having a slightly higher Word Error Rate due to hallucination, besides from being more expensive both in processing time and costs. Both methods are effective in reducing the average length of mangled segments, thus improving accessibility, as shorter segments of mangled words are easier to still understand when hearing them spoken through Text-to-Speech software.

If anything, this work highlights the need for organizations and governments to take accessibility seriously, and to prevent the problems pointed out in this paper by changing their workflow at the source, where mistakes are easier to fix than the reconstruction and correction steps that have to be taken when post-correcting mistakes.

2   Related Work

Techniques for automatic detection of OCR error vary from dictionary lookups and ngram methods to more recent sequence-to-sequence models, as well as unsupervised methods that rely on known-good background corpora [1,2,4,

---

[1] https://www.w3.org/TR/low-vision-needs/.
[2] https://www.iso.org/standard/58625.html.

14]. These researchers typically not only detect bad segments of text, but also propose methods for repairing it, such as using ngram probabilities to replace low-probability ngrams with higher probability ones, or by using a sequence-to-sequence models to 'translate' the incorrect words [1,2]. Recently, a pipeline that combines much of the aforementioned techniques has been presented for OCR error detection in the Dutch language [6]. The system, named *QuPipe*, combines dictionary lookup, trigrams, garbage detection, language detection and statistics on word and document level to detect errors in historical Dutch news articles.

A work that is conceptually close to ours is that of Schaefer & Neudecker [13], who also employ a two-step detection and correction pipeline for OCR post-correction on historical documents. In their work they train a character-level LSTM to detect OCR mistakes in the input text and repair them using a trained sequence-to-sequence model. However, since we do not have ground truth data, we cannot train an LSTM model to detect bad segments, and instead use an unsupervised method. We do however follow their reasoning in opting for a high precision detector model. Turró [16] mentions that the most accessible form of a PDF contains tags that define the structural elements of the PDF. A way to create these structural tags from a PDF is to use *pdfthtml*, a tool that is included in the *poppler* package and that outputs information regarding the fonts and positions of the text.

3   Method

3.1   Data

For the evaluation of our approach we use the cleanest part of the 1 million page corpus of Dutch Freedom of Information Act (Woo in Dutch) [12] documents [9]. This part consists of 4K decision letters (17K pages) coming from Dutch ministries written in 2020–2022 by legally trained civil servants. These documents are digital born, carefully drafted and edited and hence virtually error free, and with a simple layout and markup.The machine readable text from the PDFs is extracted with `pdftotext`, part of the Xpdf suite of PDF tools.

3.2   Mangled OCR Detection and Repair

Detection of segments of mangled text goes as follows. We use a word list consisting of the OpenTaal list[3], combined with the vocabulary extracted from the Dutch subcorpus of the ParlaMint project [7]. This corpus contains the manual transcriptions of parliamentary debates, and is of very high quality, thus also virtually error free and contains words that are roughly in the same genre as the decision letters. The combined word list contains 650K words, with 410K in the intersection of both lists, 300K exclusive to the TaalUnie list, and 130K exclusive to the parliamentary vocabulary.

---

[3] https://github.com/OpenTaal/opentaal-wordlist

We define *N-mangled segments* as maximal sequences of Out-Of-Vocabulary (OOV) tokens, which may contain subsequences of In-Vocabulary words of at most length N. Mangled segments must start and end with an OOV token. We call tokens in mangled segments MTTs (short for Mangled Text Tokens). Note that an MTT can be both an Out-Of- or an In-Vocabulary token. We experimented with the value of N and found $N = 3$ to yield the most natural "mangled segments". In the rest of the paper this $N = 3$ is fixed. In the sentence, "H1erb1j w1l **ik u graag** leten wetn dat uw verzoek is geweigerd." the mangled segment is underlined and it contains a bold triple of 3 In-Vocabulary Dutch words. In the second step, we repair the OCR mistakes in the detected segments. We compare three strategies. As a strong baseline we OCR the complete text again with Tesseract 5.0 configured for Dutch. We detect mangled segments in both the original text and in the output of Tesseract and send these segments to ChatGPT to be corrected. We use the *gpt-3.5-turbo* model instance trough the OpenAI API. We have experimented with different prompts, with the best performing one being the following:

> Correct the spelling mistakes in the following Dutch text delimited by triple backticks and remove the triple backticks afterwards. Leave the correct words untouched.

We then insert the corrected segments back into the original text, and perform mangled segment detection again.

3.3 Document Transformation

In order to make the Woo documents more accessible, the PDFs are converted to the more accessible XML format. In fact we convert to Markdown, which is trivially convertable back and forth to XML. Using the *pdftohtml* tool[4], the text, along with layout information, is transformed from PDF into XML, preserving headings, paragraphs and reading order. In turn the XML is then converted into Markdown format. The converter primarily focuses on the position, font size, and font style of a specific piece of text. Based on these characteristics, it determines whether it is a heading, paragraph, or emphasis. For example, by analyzing the differences in font sizes of the headings, the order of nested headings, and thus the reading order, is determined. Hyperlinks and emphasis from the PDF are effectively captured using the 'pdftohtml' library and are directly transferred. The alt text for images is generated using the LAVIS image captioning library from Salesforce[5].

3.4 Evaluation

To evaluate the performance of the correction methods for the mangled segments, the mangled segments of 10 documents (totalling 227 segments and 672 words)

---

[4] https://linux.die.net/man/1/pdftohtml.
[5] https://github.com/salesforce/LAVIS.

were extracted and corrected with all three methods, and the Word Error Rate (WER) [11] was calculated by visually comparing the original text in the PDF with the corrected segment. We also noted whether a mistake was the result of a hallucination, or an OCR error.

To evaluate the *pdftomarkdown* conversion tool, we randomly selected 20 PDF documents from the corpus. The converted documents were then compared to the original documents based on information retention. For each document, the presence of errors in the converted file was examined for each tag.

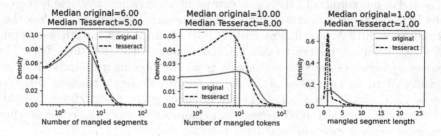

Fig. 1. Comparison between the original text and Tesseract for the number and length of mangled segments, and the number of MTTs (N=17,613 pages).

4 Results

4.1 OCR Correction

Figure 1 displays the effect on the mangled segments when correcting OCR mistakes using Tesseract. The distribution of the number of mangled segments remains roughly the same, but both the number of MTTs and the length of the mangled segments decreases significantly. Roughly 70% percent of the mangled segments after correction by Tesseract were contained within mangled segments in the original text. This indicates that most of the time Tesseract shortens mangled segments, and often drastically.

Table 1 shows that all three correction strategies greatly reduce the number of MTTs in the original text as well as the number and the length of the mangled segments per page. Although Tesseract removes many

Table 1. Comparison of the Tesseract, ChatGPT and Tesseract+ChatGPT correction strategies, with the statistics averaged over pages.(N=17,613) ChatGPT corrections were performed on a random sample of 100 pages due to processing times.

Method	Number of MTTs	Number of Mangled Segments	Mangled Segment Length
original	41.98	9.54	4.4
original+ChatGPT	15.42	4.17	3.7
Tesseract	20.15	7.87	2.5
Tesseract+ChatGPT	14.42	5.27	2.7

244   R. van Heusden et al.

OCR errors, applying ChatGPT on mangled segments remaining in Tesseract's output further reduces the mean number of MTTs and the number of mangled segments.

The WER of the text corrected by ChatGPT, Tesseract, and first Tessearct and then ChapGPT was 11, 7 and 3%, respectively (N = 672 words). Mistakes made by Tesseract are always out-of-vocabulary terms. With ChatGPT however, half of its mistakes are vocabulary terms, thus harder to spot, and sometimes leading to confusing text.

Costs. For our corpus of 17K pages, extracting the machine readable text from the PDF using `pdftotext` and detecting the mangled segments takes less than 2 min on a 2019 Macbook Pro with 16 GB of RAM and an 8th generation i5 CPU. Running Tesseract takes 5 h and running ChatGPT takes 50 h. The monetary expenses are very reasonable given the large increase in information quality. With an hour price of 2.5 dollar cent at Amazon[6], running Tesseract costs 12.5 cents. The costs for ChatGPT based on the pricing from OpenAI[7] of 0.2 dollar cents per 1000 tokens then comes to 80 cents (based on sending mangled segments with in total 400K tokens).

4.2 Accessibility Improvement

The 20 documents used for testing the conversion to HTML contained 184 heading and 593 paragraph elements, which were correctly converted with an accuracy of 0.84 and 0.67 respectively. In the final HTML versions, the documents were roughly 156 times smaller than the original PDF file when compressed with gzip.

5 Conclusion

Findability and accessibility of PDF documents which have been severely damaged by redaction software can be greatly improved using simple out-of-the-box technology like Tesseract and ChatGPT. Converting the PDFs to markdown or HTML, and thereby making layout elements like headings, paragraphs and lists explicit can be done with good accuracy and as a bonus drastically reduces the size of documents. A point of attention should be given to the manner in which ChatGPT repairs OCR mistakes. Whereas mistakes made by Tesseract are easy to spot because they are most often non-existing words, ChatGPT's mistakes are often In-Vocabulary words which on careless reading could be mistaken as correct. As we deal with official governmental documents such mistakes could be worse than "normal OCR mangling". As an example, in our manual evaluation we found that the original term "verkregen" (obtained) was OCRed as "verkragan" which ChatGPT replaced by "verkrachten" (to rape).

---

[6] https://aws.amazon.com/ec2/pricing/on-demand/.
[7] https://openai.com/pricing.

Acknowledgements. This research was supported in part by the Netherlands Organization for Scientific Research (NWO) through the ACCESS project grant CISC.CC.016.

References

1. Ahmed, F., Luca, E.W.D., Nürnberger, A.: Revised N-gram based automatic spelling correction tool to improve retrieval effectiveness. Polibits **40**, 39–48 (2009)
2. Amrhein, C., Clematide, S.: Supervised OCR error detection and correction using statistical and neural machine translation methods. J. Lang. Technol. Comput. Linguist. (JLCL) **33**(1), 49–76 (2018)
3. Bland, M., Iyer, A., Levchenko, K.: Story beyond the eye: glyph positions break PDF text redaction. arXiv preprint arXiv:2206.02285 (2022)
4. Booth, C., Shoemaker, R., Gaizauskas, R.: A language modelling approach to quality assessment of OCR'ed historical text. In: Proceedings of the Thirteenth Language Resources and Evaluation Conference (LREC), pp. 5859–5864 (2022)
5. Data protection commission: redacting documents and records (2021). https://www.dataprotection.ie/sites/default/files/uploads/2021-08/Redacting/%20Documents/%20and/%20Records.pd
6. Cuper, M.: Examining a multi layered approach for classification of OCR quality without ground truth. Digit. Humanit. Benelux J. **43** (2022)
7. Erjavec, T., et al.: The Parlamint corpora of parliamentary proceedings. Lang. Resour. Eval. 415–448 (2022)
8. European commission: a European strategy for data. Technical Report (2020). https://eur-lex.europa.eu/legal-content/EN/TXT/?uri=CELEX:52020DC0066
9. Marx, M.: Woogle dump. Technical Report, DANS (2023), https://doi.org/10.17026/dans-zau-e3rk
10. Marx, M., Gielissen, T.: Digital weight watching: reconstruction of scanned documents. Int. J. Doc. Anal. Recognit. (IJDAR) **14**, 229–239 (2011)
11. McCowan, I.A., et al.: On the Use of Information Retrieval Measures for Speech Recognition Evaluation. Technical Report, IDIAP (2004)
12. Rijksoverheid: wet open Overheid (woo) (2023). https://www.rijksoverheid.nl/onderwerpen/wet-open-overheid-woo
13. Schaefer, R., Neudecker, C.: A two-step approach for automatic OCR postcorrection. In: Proceedings of the 4th Joint SIGHUM Workshop on Computational Linguistics for Cultural Heritage, Social Sciences, Humanities and Literature, pp. 52–57 (2020)
14. Strange, C., McNamara, D., Wodak, J., Wood, I.: Mining for the meanings of a murder: the impact of OCR quality on the use of digitized historical newspapers. Digit. Hum. Q. **8**, 16 p. (2014)
15. Traub, M.C., Samar, T., Van Ossenbruggen, J., Hardman, L.: Impact of crowdsourcing OCR improvements on retrievability bias. In: Proceedings of the 18th ACM/IEEE on Joint Conference on Digital Libraries, pp. 29–36 (2018)
16. Turró, M.R.: Are pdf documents accessible? Inf. Technol. Librar. **27**(3), 25–43 (2008). https://doi.org/10.6017/ital.v27i3.3246, https://ejournals.bc.edu/index.php/ital/article/view/3246
17. Wilkinson, M.D., et al.: The FAIR guiding principles for scientific data management and stewardship. Sci. Data **3**(1), 1–9 (2016)

Knowledge Creation

Multi-view Graph-Based Text Representations for Imbalanced Classification

Ola Karajeh[(✉)] [iD], Ismini Lourentzou[iD], and Edward A. Fox[iD]

Department of Computer Science, Virginia Tech, Blacksburg, VA 24061, USA
okarajeh@vt.edu

Abstract. Text classification is a fundamental task in natural language processing, notably in the context of digital libraries, where it is essential for organizing and retrieving large numbers of documents in diverse collections, especially when tackling issues with inherent class imbalance. Sequence-based models can successfully capture semantics in local consecutive text sequences. On the other hand, graph-based models can preserve global co-occurrences that capture non-consecutive and long-distance semantics. A text representation approach that combines local and global information can enhance performance in practical class imbalance text classification scenarios. Yet, multi-view graph-based text representations have received limited attention. In this work, we introduce **M**ulti-view **M**inority **C**lass **T**ext **G**raph **C**onvolutional **N**etwork (MMCT-GCN), a transductive multi-view text classification model that captures textual graph representations for the minority class, along with sequence-based text representations. Experiments show that MMCT-GCN variants outperform baseline models on multiple text collections.

Keywords: Graph Convolutional Networks · Text Classification · Imbalanced Data

1 Introduction

Text classification is a fundamental natural language processing (NLP) task with practical applications, *e.g.*, question answering [25], sentiment analysis [12,38], spam detection [22,56], and news categorization [2]. In the digital library world, where efficient organization and retrieval of textual information are vital, substantial work has addressed designing and evaluating document, paragraph, or sentence classification models [23,27,40]. Often, the task of creating meaningful text representations is a precursor to text classification. Typical approaches in digital libraries include two important steps: feature engineering that includes handcrafted features (*e.g.*, bag-of-words and n-grams [24,55]) and representation learning methods with recurrent, convolutional, or graph-based models, *e.g.*, CNNs, LSTMs, and Graph Neural Networks (GNNs) [26,33,45].

In practice, many tasks within the digital library domain are intrinsically imbalanced, with data originating from skewed distributions, in which minor-

O. Alonso et al. (Eds.): TPDL 2023, LNCS 14241, pp. 249–264, 2023.
https://doi.org/10.1007/978-3-031-43849-3_22

ity classes are underrepresented whereas majority classes are overrepresented. Various methods – *e.g.*, sampling, weighting, and data augmentation – have been well-studied but mostly rely on ad-hoc heuristics rather than encoding useful representations that are robust to data imbalance [35,49], often leading to marginal improvements in extreme imbalance settings. Multi-view methods that can exploit complementary information could alleviate these challenges [31]. Specifically for imbalanced data text classification, structured semantic global text representations, in conjunction with local n-gram or sequence-based ones, can aid in improving learning efficiency and performance. Intuitively, graph-based methods can aid in the design of structured global representations of text.

In this work, we propose Multi-view Minority Class Text Graph Convolutional Network (MMCT-GCN), a multi-view text classification model that combines minority-class graph-based text representations encoding global word co-occurrences among minority samples, along with tra-ditional local sequence-based meth-ods operating on the full data dis-tribution. Specifically, we construct a graph for the minority class sam-ples, such that there exist heteroge-neous nodes representing words and data samples (data instances, *e.g.*, a sentence, a document, or a text phrase). Word-to-word edges define the relationships between words, while sample-to-word edges relate words and data samples. Experimen-

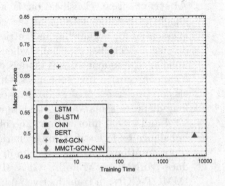

Fig. 1. Macro F1-score vs. training time (seconds) for all models evaluated on the HEART ATTACK dataset (*x*-axis in logarithmic scale). Overall, we observe that MMCT-GCN optimizes the trade-off between performance and training time.

tal results on three benchmark text classification datasets, comparing against six baselines and under various severe class imbalance ratios, demonstrate the efficacy of our proposed method. Figure 1 shows that our model performs bet-ter than all compared baselines, including n-gram representations (*e.g.*, CNNs), contextualized models (BERT), and existing graph-based convolutional network text representations (Text-GCN). Our source code is available at https://github.com/okarajeh/MMCTGCN.

Our contributions can be summarized as follows:

(1) We investigate extreme class-imbalance text classification, considering how multi-view learning can improve learning efficiency and performance. To the best of our knowledge, we are the first to formalize this research problem using graph-based text representations.

(2) We introduce Multi-view Minority Class Text Graph Convolutional Network (**MMCT-GCN**), a model that incorporates global co-occurrence features for the minority class into text classification architectures, to amplify the classifier's ability to correctly predict minority class samples.

(3) To validate the efficacy of our proposed method, we conduct extensive experiments on three benchmark datasets and show that MMCT-GCN outperforms all state-of-the-art baselines in a variety of settings.

2   Related Work

2.1   Imbalanced Classification

Long-tailed data distributions or class imbalance occur frequently in nature. Thus, there has been much research on handling class imbalance. Methodologies proposed in the literature include assigning weights to individual training examples, custom loss functions, data re-sampling, or data augmentation (that generates synthetic training examples to improve robustness). Custom loss functions typically re-adjust class weights when computing the loss, adding more emphasis on minority class samples, and can be considered as reweighting mechanisms. Common loss functions include Weighted Cross-Entropy (WCE) [11], Focal loss [32], Dice loss [21,29,43,53], combinations thereof [1], *etc.* However, these methods often lead to marginal improvements in text classification [30].

Another category of methods for handling class imbalance is data sampling which aims to produce balanced versions of the data, *e.g.*, either by undersampling or oversampling. One of the drawbacks of undersampling is the inherent information loss [4,18]. On the other hand, oversampling techniques are based on randomly duplicating minority class samples [16]. Such strategies, however, may lead to overfitting and misclassification [4,18]. As for data augmentation, these techniques are based on manipulating existing data samples in order to generate new ones. Augmentation methods may operate on the input space, *e.g.*, directly augment the text, or the feature space, *e.g.*, perturbing the embeddings to create variations. A limitation of leveraging such methods for text data is that examples are created based on the feature representations of the training instances. This results in less interpretable models, as generated minority examples don't map to real representative data points. Recently proposed textual data augmentation methods might overcome this bottleneck, allowing for better control of the data distribution. But in most cases, data augmentation methods are ad-hoc in nature and rely on heuristics. Hence, designers are uncertain as to which method will work the best for a specific domain and downstream task, and so employ randomized trial-and-error search strategies that aim to find the best set of data augmentation operations.

2.2   Graph Neural Networks

Many deep learning models achieved great success in learning data represented in Euclidean space (*e.g.*, text, images, and videos). However, in many cases, data is generated from non-Euclidean spaces, *e.g.*, arbitrary graphs, with rich dependency relationships between nodes. Existing machine learning algorithms and methods for graph data include Graph Neural Networks (GNNs) [57]. Recently, GNNs received increasing attention, opening new directions [5,6]. GNNs have found applications in a variety of machine learning tasks such as node classification and clustering, graph generation and embedding, graph portioning, and link prediction [6]. Additionally, GNNs have been used in scene-graph generation [58], few-shot learning [14], natural language processing [52], or even quantum chemistry [15]. Specifically for NLP tasks, GNNs have been applied to machine translation [3,36], semantic role labeling [37], relation extraction [46], and text classification [7,17,20,54]. Text-GCN [59] adopts Graph Convolutional Networks for text data, where the nodes in the constructed graph are documents and words. Text-GCN is based on building one single heterogeneous graph by using word co-occurrence and word-document relationships, and jointly learning embeddings for words and documents. On the other hand, Text-GTL employs Text-oriented Graph-based Transductive Learning [28] to build text graphs and refine the graph topology. The method is based on constructing non-heterogeneous graphs that can modify a GCN implementation to work well in semi-supervised scenarios. TensorGCN [33] also is used for text classification. Three different types of graphs are constructed (*i.e.*, semantic, syntactic, and sequential). Two kinds of propagation rules are utilized (*i.e.*, intra-graph and inter-graph). Nevertheless, these methods have not targeted class imbalance.

2.3   Graph-Based Methods for Class Imbalance

A few recent works [34,49,50,60] propose GNN-based methods to solve class-imbalanced tasks in various applications, evaluated on benchmark graph datasets on citation networks, bio-chemical graphs, and social networks. The first of these [34] introduces a graph-based fraud detection (opinion and financial) model. This work involves three main steps: (i) selecting a balanced sample of nodes and edges to generate a sub-graph that could be used for training, (ii) undersampling of neighbors of the majority class and oversampling of neighbors of the minority class to construct a neighborhood sampler, and (iii) aggregating all information from the chosen neighbor samples. On the other hand, a Dual Regularized Graph Convolutional Network (DR-GCN) [49] was proposed for multi-class imbalanced graph data. By leveraging conditioned adversarial training, the first regularization term ensures that each class is equally represented. The second regularization incorporates latent distribution alignment to ensure that minority and majority classes are learned in a balanced manner. GraphSMOTE [60] adopts synthetic minority oversampling for learning on graphs. In particular, this method utilizes an edge predictor to connect existing and new samples reliably. Also, an intermediate embedding space was utilized for interpolation, where the dimensionality of node attributes is reduced. BoostingGNN [50] is based on an ensemble model that uses several GNNs as primary classifiers and assigns higher weights to misclassified samples during training. Nevertheless, all aforementioned methods are designed with graph datasets in mind (*e.g.*, Cora and Citeseer) and have not been adapted to textual data, let alone with extreme class imbalance.

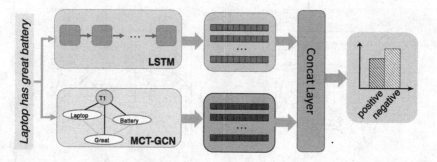

Fig. 2. Model overview. MMCT-GCN is based on a multi-view representation fusion of graphical representations for the minority class and text-based feature representations (*e.g.*, LSTM-based in this pictorial example). The concat layer represents the concatenation of the respective features.

3   Methodology

3.1   Problem Formulation

We propose MMCT-GCN, a multi-view model to tackle extreme class imbalance for text classification via a textual graph-based representation. We construct a text graph convolutional network [59] for only the minority class and combine learned structured text representations with other representations commonly used in the text classification literature. MMCT-GCN contains complementary information that can be utilized during the learning process to generate more discriminative features for minority classes. The proposed method is illustrated in Fig. 2.

3.2   Text-Based Representations

We are given a set of labeled instances $\mathcal{X} = \{(x_i, y_i)\}_{i=1}^{N}$, where x_i is a training example with $y_i \in \mathcal{Y}$ its corresponding label. Without loss of generality, we assume that $\mathcal{Y} = \{0, 1\}$, and denote the number of positive examples as N_1 and the number of negative examples as N_0, with $N_1 \ll N_0$ and $n = N_1 + N_0$. Thus, the marginal class distribution of $\mathcal{X}$ is skewed. Given this class-imbalanced dataset, the goal is to jointly learn a feature encoder $g(\cdot) \colon \mathcal{X} \to \mathbb{R}^d$ that maps data points to a d-dimensional embedding space, and a classifier $f(\cdot) \colon \mathbb{R}^d \to \mathcal{Y}$ where f is such that $f \circ g \colon \mathcal{X} \to \mathcal{Y}$. The design of g depends on the task at hand. Typical choices for text include recurrent, convolutional, or attention-based models, which can be followed by densely connected layers. Independently of model choice, we can denote the penultimate layer (last hidden layer before the classifier output) as $H^{(g)}$, and the corresponding hidden layer representations for all data as $H_{\mathcal{X}} \in \mathbb{R}^{n \times d}$, where d is the number of features. While text-based representations capture local semantics of consecutive word sequences, they tend to ignore global (non-consecutive) word co-occurrence information with long-distance and cross-document dependencies [42,59].

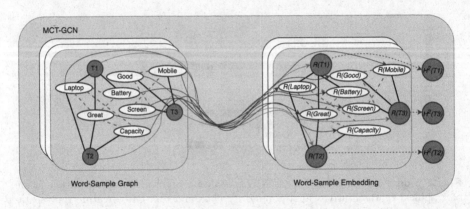

Fig. 3. Overview of MMCT-GCN graph construction. Red circle nodes represent data samples (*e.g.*, here, text sentences T1, T2, and T3), while ellipses represent word nodes (7 words in this pictorial example). Dark black edges represent sentence-word edges and dashed blue edges connect word nodes. A word-sentence embedding represents the embedding values of each node. Thus, R(T1) represents the graph embedding values of T1 that are generated by GCN. H^2 represents the graph hidden layer representation for a sentence that can be aggregated to create the MMCT-GCN graph. (Color figure online)

3.3   Graph-Based Representations

Formally, a minority graph is denoted by $\mathcal{G}_{min} = (\mathcal{V}_{min}, \mathcal{E}_{min})$, where $\mathcal{V}_{min}$ is the set of N_1 nodes (as mentioned, N_1 is the cardinality for the minority class) and E_{min} is the set of edges, all for the minority class. Let A_{min} be the adjacency matrix of $\mathcal{G}_{min}$ and D_{min} the degree matrix. We assume that every node v_{min} is connected to itself, *i.e.*, $(v_{min}, v_{min}) \in \mathcal{E}_{min}$ and diagonal adjacency matrix entries $A_{min}(i, i) = 1, \forall i = 1, \ldots, N_1$ due to self-loops. The feature matrix is denoted by $X_{min} \in R^{N_1 \times m}$, containing all minority class nodes and their corresponding feature vectors, *i.e.*, $x_{min}^{(i)} \in R^m$, where m is the dimension of the feature vectors and $x_{min}^{(i)}$ is the feature vector of node $v_{min}^{(i)}$. In the corresponding GCN, the hidden representation for the first GCN layer can be generated by

$$H_{min}^{(1)} = \sigma \left(\hat{A}_{min} X_{min} W_{min}^0 \right), \tag{1}$$

where $H_{min}^{(1)} \in R^{N_1 \times d_1}$, d_1 is the number of dimensions of feature vectors in the first layer, $\hat{A}_{min} = D_{min}^{-1/2} A_{min} D_{min}^{-1/2}$ is the symmetric normalized adjacency matrix, $W_{min}^0 \in R^{m \times d_1}$ is the initial weight matrix, and σ is the activation function. Generally, the hidden representation $H_{min}^{(j+1)}$ for layer $(j + 1)$ can be calculated by

$$H_{min}^{(j+1)} = \sigma \left(\hat{A}_{min} H_{min}^{(j)} W_{min}^j \right). \tag{2}$$

3.4   Text Graph Construction

Figure 3 presents the proposed graph construction method. We construct a textual heterogeneous undirected graph-based weighted representation created from minority class samples. Two versions of nodes represent words and data instances (*e.g.*, sentences for sentence-level classification, or tweets in the case of Twitter data), respectively. Node representations are initialized as one-hot vectors for words and sentences. The embeddings for words and sentences are learned jointly, as supervised by the known class labels for samples. There are two types of edges: word-to-word edge, which is based on word co-occurrence in the whole corpus, and sample-to-word edge, which is based on word occurrence in data instances (data samples). Inspired by [59], we use term frequency-inverse document frequency (TF-IDF) weights [44] for the sample-to-word edge, where term frequency represents the number of times a word appears in a data instance (sample), and inverse document frequency gives more weight to rarely occurring words. In contrast, point-wise mutual information (PMI) [9] is utilized to calculate the weight of the word-to-word edge, since it is a measure commonly used for word association.

3.5   Minority Class Text GCN Model

After building the textual graph for the minority class, we feed our graphical representation of the text data to a two-layer GCN model (termed MCT-GCN) to produce a graph hidden representation U_{min}; see Eq. (3):

$$U_{min} = \hat{A}_{min} \text{ReLU} \left(\hat{A}_{min} X_{min} W^0_{min} \right) W^1_{min}, \tag{3}$$

where W^0_{min}, W^1_{min} are learned weight matrices, and $\hat{A}_{min}$ is the symmetric normalized adjacency matrix. Here $U_{min} \in R^{N_1 \times \tilde{d}}$, $\tilde{d}$-dimensional graph-based hidden layer representations for N_1 minority samples. Note that MCT-GCN is transductive, similar to prior works on graph representations for text [59]. That means the test samples without labels for both the minority and majority classes are included in building the MCT-GCN graph.

Finally, our multi-view classifier (MMCT-GCN) combines the graph-based and text-based representations to perform text classification. More formally, the concatenation of the graph hidden representations and the text-based representations are fed to a softmax classifier:

$$\hat{Y} = \text{softmax}(W^2[\tilde{U}_\mathcal{X} \ H_\mathcal{X}]), \tag{4}$$

where W^2 is the learned weight matrix, and $H_\mathcal{X}$ designates text-based representations (see Sect. 3.2). Here $\tilde{U}_\mathcal{X}$ denotes the graph-based features for minority class samples $U_{min} \in \mathbb{R}^{N_1 \times \tilde{d}}$ combined with the all-zero vectors for majority class samples $O \in \mathbb{R}^{N_0 \times d'}$ as follows:

$$\tilde{U}_\mathcal{X} = \begin{bmatrix} U_{min} \in \mathbb{R}^{N_1 \times \tilde{d}} \\ O_{maj} \in \mathbb{R}^{N_0 \times d'} \end{bmatrix} \tag{5}$$

Table 1. Summary of dataset statistics. For each dataset, we present the total number of examples (# Examples), the number of examples that are used for training (# Train) and testing (# Test), and how many examples come from the minority (# Minority) and majority (# Majority) classes. In addition, we report the number of unique tokens in the vocabulary (# Tokens) and the average text length (Length). Here, Imbalance Ratio (IR) = 6.45%.

Dataset	# Examples	# Majority	# Minority	# Train	# Test	# Tokens	Length
Movie Review	5,675	5,331 (94%)	344 (6%)	4,540	1,135	7,212	10.59
Heart Attack	5,992	5,629 (94%)	363 (6%)	4,793	1,199	7,672	9.32
COVID-19	4,369	4,104 (94%)	265 (6%)	3,495	874	4,358	13.88

such that $\left|\tilde{U}_\mathcal{X}\right| = |H_\mathcal{X}|$. We train MMCT-GCN and all compared baselines with weighted cross-entropy over all training samples.

$$\mathcal{L}_{WCE} = -\frac{1}{n} \sum_{i=1}^{n} w_i \sum_{c=1}^{|\mathcal{Y}|} y_{ic} \log\left(\hat{y}_{ic}\right), \tag{6}$$

where $y_{ic} = \mathbb{1}\left[y_i = c\right]$ is the one-hot vector representation of the ground-truth label for example x_i. Further, $\hat{y}_{ic}$ is the model estimated class probability for class c for the respective example. Importance weights w_i are typically inversely proportional to the number of examples per class [11].

4   Experiments

We evaluate MMCT-GCN on a variety of benchmark datasets for text classification and compare with several baselines. Specifically, we design experiments under various extreme imbalance scenarios to determine whether MMCT-GCN achieves superior performance over text classification baselines trained with weighted cross-entropy or other custom loss functions designed for class imbalance tasks. Although our method is applicable to various settings, we restrict our analysis to binary text classification. Further, we present extensive comparisons of model architectures, loss functions, and imbalance ratios. In the results discussed, the Imbalance Ratio (IR), *i.e.*, the proportion of minority class samples to the number of majority class samples, is kept at $\sim 6.45\%$ across all datasets. Later, we vary IR and underlying loss functions.

4.1   Experimental Settings

Datasets. Experiments are conducted on three text classification datasets. MOVIE REVIEW is a binary sentence-level sentiment classification dataset [41]. We make use of a version that contains a balanced corpus with 5,331 examples per class label [59]. We construct a new imbalanced dataset with size 5,675 that includes all of the negative examples, plus 344 examples drawn randomly from the positive examples, thus having 94% of the data distribution being *negative* and 6% *positive*. HEART ATTACK is a Twitter medical classification dataset, with tweets classified as containing medical conditions (posts indicating a user having a heart attack) or not. This dataset consists of 5, 992 ground-truth tweets classified as either *informational* (6%) or *non-informational* (94%). COVID-19 is based on CoAID [10], a large-scale healthcare misinformation dataset related to COVID-19, including news articles and claims along with tweets and user replies. We make use of tweets that were collected in May and July of 2020 with *ClaimFake* and *ClaimReal* class labels. To be consistent with the rest of the datasets, we randomly select 4, 369 tweets, with 94% as *ClaimReal* and 6% as *ClaimFake*. Data statistics are summarized in Table 1.

Baselines. We compare the proposed MMCT-GCN model (recall Sect. 3, which covers its variants) with several state-of-the-art methods for text classification: **LSTM** [19] and **Bi-LSTM** [48]: recurrent (bi-directional) models that are widely used for text classification, capturing sequence information in both directions, where the text representation is the last hidden state of the model. **CNN** [51]: a convolutional neural model that uses consecutive convolutional layers that increase the receptive field of an area, thus producing locally discriminative features. **CNN-MC** [8,39]: a multichannel CNN model with multiple kernel sizes [26], capturing n-gram text features. **BERT** [13]: a contextualized attention-based model fine-tuned on our downstream text classification task. **Text-GCN** [59]: a text graph convolutional network in which the corpus is represented by a heterogeneous graph of words and documents. **Text-Level-GNN** [20]: a method of constructing graphs for each input text instead of a single graph for the whole corpus.

We also compare several variants of our proposed method, including **MMCT-GCN-LSTM**: our proposed graph-based text representation used in conjunction with an LSTM-based sequence text representation. **MMCT-GCN-CNN**: our proposed graph-based text representation used in conjunction with a CNN-based local text representation. **MT-GCN-CNN**: Multi-view Text-GCN-CNN, a modified version of our proposed method that builds the graph on both minority and majority classes, and then trains the GCN. The combined graph-based text representation is used in conjunction with a CNN-based local text representation. **MMCT-GCN-CNN-MC**: a combination of the proposed graph-based text representation with the multi-channel CNN-based n-gram representations to construct the final text classifier.

4.2   Experimental Results

Table 2 presents the F1-score for the minority classes, overall macro F1-score, and AUC performance for all datasets. The results are averaged over three trials. In general, we observe that CNN-based models perform better than LSTM-based models. This can be attributed to the nature of the benchmark datasets (*i.e.*, Twitter and reviews) that contain relatively short text. Generally, we notice that

Table 2. Minority class F1-score, Macro F1-score, and AUC. For all metrics, higher is better. Mean and standard deviation reported over 3 independent trials.

	MOVIE REVIEW			HEART ATTACK			COVID-19		
	Minority F1	Macro F1	AUC	Minority F1	Macro F1	AUC	Minority F1	Macro F1	AUC
BERT	0.125±0.01	0.302±0.21	0.537±0.01	0.066±0.07	0.493±0.01	0.519±0.03	0.306±0.05	0.583±0.05	0.798±0.02
Text-GCN	0.167±0.01	0.539±0.00	0.573±0.01	0.406±0.01	0.677±0.00	0.738±0.00	0.478±0.01	0.707±0.01	0.893±0.00
Text-Level-GNN	0.103±0.03	0.522±0.02	0.524±0.02	0.410±0.05	0.679±0.03	0.724±0.00	0.759±0.04	0.872±0.02	0.874±0.00
LSTM	0.093±0.01	0.526±0.01	0.521±0.01	0.521±0.00	0.747±0.00	0.723±0.02	0.907±0.00	0.951±0.00	0.942±0.01
Bi-LSTM	0.121±0.03	0.540±0.01	0.533±0.01	0.488±0.09	0.725±0.06	0.746±0.01	0.872±0.04	0.932±0.02	0.919±0.01
MMCT-GCN-LSTM	0.211± 0.01	0.568±0.01	**0.604±0.04**	0.534±0.01	0.755±0.01	0.723±0.01	0.937±0.02	0.967±0.01	0.959±0.01
CNN	0.133±0.01	0.548±0.01	0.537±0.01	0.593±0.01	0.786±0.01	0.738±0.02	0.967±0.02	0.983±0.01	0.986±0.02
MMCT-GCN-CNN	**0.222±0.05**	**0.578±0.04**	0.596±0.02	**0.616±0.03**	**0.798±0.02**	**0.765±0.02**	0.977±0.01	0.988±0.00	0.989±0.01
MT-GCN-CNN	0.172±0.05	0.564±0.02	0.555±0.02	0.597±0.01	0.788±0.00	0.753±0.02	0.967±0.02	0.983±0.01	0.986±0.01
CNN-MC	0.145±0.02	0.554±0.01	0.541±0.01	0.513±0.00	0.743±0.00	0.721±0.01	0.994±0.01	0.997±0.00	**1.000±0.00**
MMCT-GCN-CNN-MC	0.204±0.01	0.571±0.01	0.588±0.02	0.541±0.02	0.758±0.01	0.723±0.00	**1.000±0.00**	**1.000±0.00**	**1.000±0.00**

our proposed model MMCT-GCN outperforms all baselines across all benchmarks.

For MOVIE REVIEW, MMCT-GCN-LSTM obtains the highest F1-score for the *minority* class compared to other LSTM-based baselines (LSTM and Bi-LSTM). Performance improvements range from 9% to 11.8% whereas the improvement in overall F1-score and AUC ranges from 2.8% to 4.2% and 7.1% to 8.3%, respectively. This indicates that our proposed model can create discriminative features for the minority class that can increase classification performance. In addition, MMCT-GCN-CNN outperforms CNN with 8.9% improvement in F1-score for minority class samples, 3% improvement in overall F1-score, and 5.9% improvement in AUC. Similarly, MMCT-GCN-CNN-MC outperforms CNN-MC with 5.9%, 1.7%, and 4.7% improvement in F1-score for the minority class, overall F1-score, and AUC, respectively.

For the HEART ATTACK dataset, our proposed models (*i.e.*, MMCT-GCN-LSTM, MMCT-GCN-CNN, and MMCT-GCN-CNN-MC) outperform all other baselines in terms of both F1-score for the minority class and overall F1-score. Compared to other LSTM-based models, MMCT-GCN-LSTM achieves 1.3% − 4.6% F1 improvement for the minority class and 0.8% − 3% increase in overall F1. Comparing across CNN models, MMCT-GCN-CNN obtains 2.3% and 1.2% improvement in F1-score for the minority class and overall, respectively. For MMCT-GCN-CNN-MC, the performance gains w.r.t. CNN-MC are 2.8% for the minority class and 1.5% in terms of overall classification performance. For AUC, MMCT-GCN-CNN gains 1.9% w.r.t. the best performing baseline.

For the COVID-19 dataset, our proposed model variations MMCT-GCN-LSTM, MMCT-GCN-CNN, and MMCT-GCN-CNN-MC obtain the highest F1-score values for the minority class compared to their peer baselines. Similarly, all of them outperform all other baselines in terms of overall F1-score. MMCT-GCN-LSTM achieves 3%–6.5% improvement in F1-score for the minority class, 1.6%–3.5% overall F1 improvement, and 1.7%–4% improvement in AUC compared to LSTM-based baselines. Comparing across CNN models, MMCT-GCN-CNN obtains 1%, 0.5%, and 0.3% improvement in F1-score for the minority class, overall F1, and AUC, respectively. MMCT-GCN-CNN-MC outperforms the CNN-MC model with 0.6% improvement in F1-score for the minority class

Table 3. Text classification performance (Macro F1-score) on MOVIE REVIEW dataset with varying data imbalance ratio (IR).

IR	BERT	Text-GCN	LSTM	Bi-LSTM	MMCT-GCN-LSTM	CNN	MMCT-GCN-CNN	CNN-MC	MMCT-GCN-CNN-MC
0.01	0.050	0.486	0.496	0.496	**0.530**	0.496	0.495	0.496	0.495
0.06	0.064	0.558	0.518	0.534	0.577	0.565	**0.617**	0.544	0.577
0.07	0.344	0.561	0.569	0.555	**0.585**	0.532	0.555	0.553	0.574
0.25	0.308	0.607	0.631	0.617	0.639	0.594	0.604	0.589	**0.643**
0.50	0.249	0.596	0.615	0.642	**0.673**	0.607	0.618	0.595	0.632
0.75	0.249	0.582	0.624	0.623	**0.670**	0.600	0.622	0.628	0.666
1.00	0.447	0.551	0.603	0.602	**0.632**	0.556	0.596	0.581	0.616

and 0.3% improvement in overall F1-score. For AUC, MMCT-GCN-CNN-MC obtains the same value as the peer baseline. In total, for this dataset, MMCT-GCN-CNN-MC obtains the best performance compared to the other baselines.

We note that our experimental setting is evaluating models on extreme imbalance scenarios. While Text-GCN and Text-Level-GNN have been found to work well on balanced datasets, they perform less well for highly imbalanced tasks. In general, textual graph methods tend to overfit the majority class, thus generating less discriminative embeddings for minority classes. In other words, the majority class nodes dominate during the node embedding learning process. For all datasets, BERT obtains the worst performance, since it is pre-trained on large out-of-domain data.

As we can see, the best-performing models are incorporating global co-occurrence features for the minority class into traditional text classification architectures, to amplify the classifier's ability to correctly predict minority class samples on the three datasets. For MT-GCN-CNN, that is built on combining both minority and majority samples on a common graph, we see that for the MOVIE REVIEW and HEART ATTACK datasets, these models perform well in terms of minority F1-score, overall F1, and AUC, but still cannot reach the performance of MMCT-GCN-CNN. Our analysis demonstrates the strength of our proposed method in class imbalanced tasks.

Overall, we notice that results varied across the three datasets based on task difficulty. For example, for the COVID-19 dataset, model performance is generally high since the dataset has more discriminative words for the minority class (*claimFake*), such as "myth", "flu", and "alcohol". In contrast, the HEART ATTACK dataset has more common frequently-occurring phrases in both categories (*informational* and *non-informational*), such as "mini heart-attack", "like heart-attack", and "gave me heart-attack". Since MOVIE REVIEW contains review-specific language, where most users utilize similar semantic patterns whether describing *positive* or *negative* reviews, the extreme class imbalance makes this a more challenging task as compared to the rest.

Influence of Imbalance Ratio. For robustness evaluation of our proposed model, we study the performance with respect to different imbalance ratios (IRs). As shown in Table 3, we conducted experiments on the MOVIE REVIEW dataset with IR $= \{0.01, 0.06, 0.07, 0.25, 0.50, 0.75, 1.00\}$. For example, when IR $= 0.01$, there exist 10 minority class samples for every 1000 majority class samples, *i.e.*, there exists extreme class imbalance in the data. Results are based on a single trial. We observe that MMCT-GCN-LSTM and MMCT-GCN-CNN perform well w.r.t. varying low IRs. In particular, MMCT-GCN variations achieve consistent performance improvements in terms of overall F1-score across all IRs, which proves the effectiveness of our proposed multi-view text representation method for challenging class imbalance scenarios, as well as more balanced scenarios.

Table 4. Macro F1-score comparison on MOVIE REVIEW of different custom loss functions that handle class-imbalance. Mean and standard deviation reported over 3 independent trials.

Loss	BERT	Text-GCN	LSTM	Bi-LSTM	MMCT-GCN-LSTM	CNN	MMCT-GCN-CNN	CNN-MC	MMCT-GCN-CNN-MC
WCE (Default)	0.302 ± 0.21	0.539 ± 0.00	0.526 ± 0.01	0.540 ± 0.01	0.568 ± 0.01	0.548 ± 0.01	**0.578 ± 0.04**	0.554 ± 0.01	0.571 ± 0.01
Focal Loss	0.106 ± 0.02	0.511 ± 0.01	0.531 ± 0.02	0.553 ± 0.02	**0.574 ± 0.01**	0.550 ± 0.01	0.554 ± 0.05	0.543 ± 0.00	0.566 ± 0.02
Tversky	0.485 ± 0.00	0.489 ± 0.01	0.485 ± 0.00	0.485 ± 0.00	0.498 ± 0.02	0.485 ± 0.00	0.543 ± 0.05	0.484 ± 0.00	**0.561 ± 0.03**

Custom Loss Functions. We also incorporate commonly used custom loss functions, to evaluate the classification performance when well-established methods, specifically designed for handling class imbalance, are combined with the proposed multi-view approach. Table 4 presents results when models are trained with Weighted Cross-Entropy (WCE), Focal loss, and Tversky loss functions [11,32,47] on the MOVIE REVIEW dataset. Tuning the loss parameters, we set $\gamma = 0.2$ for Focal loss and $\alpha = 0.5$ and $\beta = 0.5$ for Tversky loss. Across all the experimental settings, MMCT-GCN variations yield consistent improvements over baselines. We find that F1 improvements range from 2.1% to 7.2% w.r.t. the best performing baseline, demonstrating the efficacy of the proposed method.

5   Conclusion and Future Work

In real-world scenarios, data distributions are often highly skewed, resulting in extreme class-imbalanced problems. Due to high inter-dependency between nodes, such issues are exacerbated when using simple GNN-based text classification models, where it is likely that graph-based learned representations for the minority classes will be less discriminative and representative of the minority class distribution. To alleviate these challenges, this work introduces MMCT-GCN, a multi-view representation learning model that incorporates graph-based textual representations for the minority class into text-based classification architectures. From extensive experiments on three benchmark datasets, including varying the imbalance ratio and the underlying loss functions, we observe that MMCT-GCN outperforms all compared baselines, and consistently improves recall for the minority class, leading to increased F1 scores. In the future, we hope to extend our evaluation to semi-supervised text classification. We also plan to explore our approach in other digital library settings.

References

1. Abraham, N., Khan, N.M.: A novel focal Tversky loss function with improved attention u-net for lesion segmentation. In: 2019 IEEE 16th International Symposium on Biomedical Imaging (ISBI 2019), pp. 683–687. IEEE (2019)
2. Antonellis, I., Bouras, C., Poulopoulos, V.: Personalized news categorization through scalable text classification. In: Zhou, X., Li, J., Shen, H.T., Kitsuregawa, M., Zhang, Y. (eds.) APWeb 2006. LNCS, vol. 3841, pp. 391–401. Springer, Heidelberg (2006). https://doi.org/10.1007/11610113_35
3. Bastings, J., Titov, I., Aziz, W., Marcheggiani, D., Sima'an, K.: Graph convolutional encoders for syntax-aware neural machine translation. arXiv preprint arXiv:1704.04675 (2017)
4. Batista, G.E., Prati, R.C., Monard, M.C.: A study of the behavior of several methods for balancing machine learning training data. ACM SIGKDD Explor. Newsl. **6**(1), 20–29 (2004)
5. Battaglia, P.W., et al.: Relational inductive biases, deep learning, and graph networks. arXiv preprint arXiv:1806.01261 (2018)
6. Cai, H., Zheng, V.W., Chang, K.C.C.: A comprehensive survey of graph embedding: problems, techniques, and applications. IEEE Trans. Knowl. Data Eng. **30**(9), 1616–1637 (2018)
7. Chen, J., Zhang, B., Xu, Y., Wang, M.: TextRGNN: residual graph neural networks for text classification. arXiv preprint arXiv:2112.15060 (2021)
8. Chen, Y.: Convolutional Neural Network for Sentence Classification. Master's thesis, University of Waterloo (2015)
9. Church, K., Hanks, P.: Word association norms, mutual information, and lexicography. Comput. Linguist. **16**(1), 22–29 (1990)
10. Cui, L., Lee, D.: CoAID: COVID-19 healthcare misinformation dataset. arXiv preprint arXiv:2006.00885 (2020)
11. Cui, Y., Jia, M., Lin, T.Y., Song, Y., Belongie, S.: Class-balanced loss based on effective number of samples. In: Proceedings of the IEEE/CVF Conference on Computer Vision and Pattern Recognition, pp. 9268–9277 (2019)
12. Dawei, W., Alfred, R., Obit, J.H., On, C.K.: A literature review on text classification and sentiment analysis approaches. In: Alfred, R., Iida, H., Haviluddin, H., Anthony, P. (eds.) Computational Science and Technology. LNEE, vol. 724, pp. 305–323. Springer, Singapore (2021). https://doi.org/10.1007/978-981-33-4069-5_26
13. Devlin, J., Chang, M.W., Lee, K., Toutanova, K.: BERT: pre-training of deep bidirectional transformers for language understanding. arXiv preprint arXiv:1810.04805 (2018)
14. Garcia, V., Bruna, J.: Few-shot learning with graph neural networks. arXiv preprint arXiv:1711.04043 (2017)
15. Gilmer, J., Schoenholz, S.S., Riley, P.F., Vinyals, O., Dahl, G.E.: Neural message passing for quantum chemistry. In: International Conference on Machine Learning, pp. 1263–1272. PMLR (2017)
16. He, H., Garcia, E.A.: Learning from imbalanced data. IEEE Trans. Knowl. Data Eng. **21**(9), 1263–1284 (2009)
17. Henaff, M., Bruna, J., LeCun, Y.: Deep convolutional networks on graph-structured data. arXiv preprint arXiv:1506.05163 (2015)
18. Ho, Y., Wookey, S.: The real-world-weight cross-entropy loss function: modeling the costs of mislabeling. IEEE Access **8**, 4806–4813 (2019)

19. Hochreiter, S., Schmidhuber, J.: Long short-term memory. Neural Comput. **9**(8), 1735–1780 (1997)
20. Huang, L., Ma, D., Li, S., Zhang, X., Wang, H.: Text level graph neural network for text classification. arXiv preprint arXiv:1910.02356 (2019)
21. Jadon, S.: A survey of loss functions for semantic segmentation. In: 2020 IEEE Conference on Computational Intelligence in Bioinformatics and Computational Biology (CIBCB), pp. 1–7. IEEE (2020)
22. Jindal, N., Liu, B.: Review spam detection. In: Proceedings of the 16th International Conference on World Wide Web, pp. 1189–1190 (2007)
23. Joulin, A., Grave, E., Bojanowski, P., Mikolov, T.: Bag of tricks for efficient text classification. arXiv preprint arXiv:1607.01759 (2016)
24. Jurafsky, D., Martin, J.H.: Speech and Language Processing: an Introduction to Natural Language Processing, Computational Linguistics, and Speech Recognition. Pearson Prentice Hall, Hoboken (2009)
25. Keskar, N.S., McCann, B., Xiong, C., Socher, R.: Unifying question answering, text classification, and regression via span extraction. arXiv preprint arXiv:1904.09286 (2019)
26. Kim, Y.: Convolutional neural networks for sentence classification. In: Proceedings of the 2014 Conference on Empirical Methods in Natural Language Processing (EMNLP), pp. 1746–1751. Association for Computational Linguistics (2014)
27. Kowsari, K., Jafari Meimandi, K., Heidarysafa, M., Mendu, S., Barnes, L., Brown, D.: Text classification algorithms: a survey. Information **10**(4), 150 (2019)
28. Li, C., Peng, X., Peng, H., Li, J., Wang, L.: TextGTL: graph-based transductive learning for semi-supervised text classification via structure-sensitive interpolation. In: IJCAI. ijcai. org (2021)
29. Li, X., Sun, X., Meng, Y., Liang, J., Wu, F., Li, J.: Dice loss for data-imbalanced NLP tasks. arXiv preprint arXiv:1911.02855 (2019)
30. Li, X., Sun, X., Meng, Y., Liang, J., Wu, F., Li, J.: Dice loss for data-imbalanced NLP tasks. In: Proceedings of the 58th Annual Meeting of the Association for Computational Linguistics, pp. 465–476 (2020)
31. Li, Y., Yang, M., Zhang, Z.: A survey of multi-view representation learning. IEEE Trans. Knowl. Data Eng. **31**(10), 1863–1883 (2018)
32. Lin, T.Y., Goyal, P., Girshick, R., He, K., Dollár, P.: Focal loss for dense object detection. In: Proceedings of the IEEE International Conference on Computer Vision, pp. 2980–2988 (2017)
33. Liu, X., You, X., Zhang, X., Wu, J., Lv, P.: Tensor graph convolutional networks for text classification. In: Proceedings of the AAAI Conference on Artificial Intelligence, vol. 34, pp. 8409–8416 (2020)
34. Liu, Y., et al.: Pick and choose: a GNN-based imbalanced learning approach for fraud detection. In: Proceedings of the Web Conference 2021, pp. 3168–3177 (2021)
35. Ma, J.: Segmentation loss odyssey. arXiv preprint arXiv:2005.13449 (2020)
36. Marcheggiani, D., Bastings, J., Titov, I.: Exploiting semantics in neural machine translation with graph convolutional networks. arXiv preprint arXiv:1804.08313 (2018)
37. Marcheggiani, D., Titov, I.: Encoding sentences with graph convolutional networks for semantic role labeling. arXiv preprint arXiv:1703.04826 (2017)
38. Melville, P., Gryc, W., Lawrence, R.D.: Sentiment analysis of blogs by combining lexical knowledge with text classification. In: Proceedings of the 15th ACM SIGKDD International Conference on Knowledge Discovery and Data Mining, pp. 1275–1284 (2009)

39. Meng, Y., Shen, J., Zhang, C., Han, J.: Weakly-supervised neural text classification. In: Proceedings of the 27th ACM International Conference on Information and Knowledge Management, pp. 983–992 (2018)
40. Minaee, S., Kalchbrenner, N., Cambria, E., Nikzad, N., Chenaghlu, M., Gao, J.: Deep learning-based text classification: a comprehensive review. ACM Comput. Surv. (CSUR) **54**(3), 1–40 (2021)
41. Pang, B., Lee, L.: Seeing stars: exploiting class relationships for sentiment categorization with respect to rating scales. arXiv preprint cs/0506075 (2005)
42. Peng, H., et al.: Large-scale hierarchical text classification with recursively regularized deep graph-CNN. In: Proceedings of the World Wide Web Conference, pp. 1063–1072 (2018)
43. Rahnama, J., Hüllermeier, E.: Learning Tversky similarity. In: Lesot, M.-J., et al. (eds.) IPMU 2020. CCIS, vol. 1238, pp. 269–280. Springer, Cham (2020). https://doi.org/10.1007/978-3-030-50143-3_21
44. Ramos, J., et al.: Using TF-IDF to determine word relevance in document queries. In: Proceedings of the First Instructional Conference on Machine Learning, vol. 242, pp. 29–48. Citeseer (2003)
45. Sachan, D.S., Zaheer, M., Salakhutdinov, R.: Revisiting LSTM networks for semi-supervised text classification via mixed objective function. In: Proceedings of the AAAI Conference on Artificial Intelligence, vol. 33, pp. 6940–6948 (2019)
46. Sahu, S.K., Thomas, D., Chiu, B., Sengupta, N., Mahdy, M.: Relation extraction with self-determined graph convolutional network. In: Proceedings of the 29th ACM International Conference on Information & Knowledge Management, pp. 2205–2208 (2020)
47. Salehi, S.S.M., Erdogmus, D., Gholipour, A.: Tversky loss function for image segmentation using 3d fully convolutional deep networks. In: Wang, Q., Shi, Y., Suk, H.-I., Suzuki, K. (eds.) MLMI 2017. LNCS, vol. 10541, pp. 379–387. Springer, Cham (2017). https://doi.org/10.1007/978-3-319-67389-9_44
48. Schuster, M., Paliwal, K.K.: Bidirectional recurrent neural networks. IEEE Trans. Sig. Process. **45**(11), 2673–2681 (1997)
49. Shi, M., Tang, Y., Zhu, X., Wilson, D., Liu, J.: Multi-class imbalanced graph convolutional network learning. In: Proceedings of the Twenty-Ninth International Joint Conference on Artificial Intelligence (IJCAI-20) (2020)
50. Shi, S., Qiao, K., Yang, S., Wang, L., Chen, J., Yan, B.: Boosting-GNN: boosting algorithm for graph networks on imbalanced node classification. Front. Neurorobot. **15**, 154 (2021)
51. Simonyan, K., Zisserman, A.: Very deep convolutional networks for large-scale image recognition. arXiv preprint arXiv:1409.1556 (2014)
52. Song, L., Zhang, Y., Wang, Z., Gildea, D.: A graph-to-sequence model for AMR-to-text generation. arXiv preprint arXiv:1805.02473 (2018)
53. Sudre, C.H., Li, W., Vercauteren, T., Ourselin, S., Jorge Cardoso, M.: Generalised dice overlap as a deep learning loss function for highly unbalanced segmentations. In: Cardoso, M.J., et al. (eds.) DLMIA/ML-CDS -2017. LNCS, vol. 10553, pp. 240–248. Springer, Cham (2017). https://doi.org/10.1007/978-3-319-67558-9_28
54. Wang, K., Han, S.C., Poon, J.: InducT-GCN: inductive graph convolutional networks for text classification. arXiv preprint arXiv:2206.00265 (2022)
55. Wang, S.I., Manning, C.D.: Baselines and bigrams: simple, good sentiment and topic classification. In: Proceedings of the 50th Annual Meeting of the Association for Computational Linguistics (Volume 2: Short Papers), pp. 90–94 (2012)

56. Wu, T., Liu, S., Zhang, J., Xiang, Y.: Twitter spam detection based on deep learning. In: Proceedings of the Australasian Computer Science Week Multiconference, pp. 1–8 (2017)
57. Wu, Z., Pan, S., Chen, F., Long, G., Zhang, C., Philip, S.Y.: A comprehensive survey on graph neural networks. IEEE Trans. Neural Netw. Learn. Syst. **32**(1), 4–24 (2020)
58. Xu, D., Zhu, Y., Choy, C.B., Fei-Fei, L.: Scene graph generation by iterative message passing. In: Proceedings of the IEEE Conference on Computer Vision and Pattern Recognition, pp. 5410–5419 (2017)
59. Yao, L., Mao, C., Luo, Y.: Graph Convolutional networks for text classification. In: Proceedings of the AAAI Conference on Artificial Intelligence. vol. 33, pp. 7370–7377 (2019)
60. Zhao, T., Zhang, X., Wang, S.: GraphSMOTE: imbalanced node classification on graphs with graph neural networks. In: Proceedings of the 14th ACM International Conference on Web Search and Data Mining, pp. 833–841 (2021)

Large Synthetic Data from the arχiv for OCR Post Correction of Historic Scientific Articles

J. P. Naiman[1]([✉])(ORCID), Morgan G. Cosillo[1](ORCID), Peter K. G. Williams[2](ORCID), and Alyssa Goodman[2](ORCID)

[1] School of Information Sciences, University of Illinois, Urbana-Champaign 61820, USA
{jnaiman,mcosil2}@illinois.edu
[2] Harvard-Smithsonian Center for Astrophysics, Cambridge 02138, USA
{pwilliams,agoodman}@cfa.harvard.edu

Abstract. Historical scientific articles often require Optical Character Recognition (OCR) to transform scanned documents into machine-readable text, a process that often produces errors. We present a pipeline for the generation of a synthetic ground truth/OCR dataset to correct the OCR results of the astrophysics literature holdings of the NASA Astrophysics Data System (ADS). By mining the arχiv we create, to the authors' knowledge, the largest scientific synthetic ground truth/OCR post correction dataset of 203,354,393 character pairs. Baseline models trained with this dataset find the mean improvement in character and word error rates of 7.71% and 18.82% for historical OCR text, respectively. Interactive dashboards to explore the dataset are available online: https://readingtimemachine.github.io/projects/1-ocr-groundtruth-may2023, and data and code, are hosted on GitHub: https://github.com/ReadingTimeMachine/ocr_post_correction.

Keywords: scholarly document processing · optical character recognition · astronomy

1 Introduction

The ability to digitally store and parse scientific literature is vital to ensure access and proliferation of scientific ideas [28,40,44]. While digital storage is supported for much of contemporary scientific literature, the text of many historical documents is "trapped" within scanned pages of paper journals and theses.

Recently, various deep learning methods have been employed to extract page objects (e.g., figures) from scans [10,11,20,32]. An obstacle to the extraction of information from historical articles is the accuracy of these extracted materials. This is especially of concern for any text objects which contain the bulk of the information in an article. A typical solution is to extract text with Optical Character Recognition (OCR) engines [48]. However, the generated text is often noisy which is not only an issue for comprehension by humans and screen readers [41], but also can affect "downstream" natural language processing tasks such as

O. Alonso et al. (Eds.): TPDL 2023, LNCS 14241, pp. 265–274, 2023.
https://doi.org/10.1007/978-3-031-43849-3_23

topic modeling, sentence segmentation and named entity recognition [12], often times causing significant errors in these processes [47].

Here, we discuss a new method for addressing OCR noise in the context of the extraction of text from a subset of ~56k articles from the pre-digital holdings of the Astrophysics Data System (ADS)[1] from ~1850–1997 [29]. While our ultimate goal is to correct all historical text within the ADS holdings, our initial focus is on the correction of "plain text" in the main portions of articles (i.e., not text within tables or captions). Our method relies on generating synthetic data from mining the arχiv source files (LaTeX/TeX files which compile to PDFs [49]) for "post correction" models which are applied to previously extracted OCR text.

Post correction methods are vital to the extraction of text from the historical holdings of ADS as only a small portion of the articles can be mined with PDF-parsing software [29,30]. Additionally, in many large historical corpora it is not computationally feasible to re-OCR holdings each time an OCR engine is upgraded [51], making post correction the only option to reduce errors.

While the work presented here focuses on the literature of the "big-data" science of astronomy and astrophysics [42,46], our methods of synthetic data generation can be generalized to other scientific fields. To aid in future generalizability, we use the open-source OCR engine Tesseract [43] and provide all code in Python. Because the dataset is large we provide interactive visualizations to assist any user of our resource in their investigation of the dataset.

2 OCR Noise Reduction Techniques and Mining the arχiv

OCR noise is prevalent in the majority of OCR datasets used in the fields of digital humanities and cultural analytics [19]. OCR errors do not follow patterns of typical misspellings, thus their correction generally relies on different tools than spell-checking software [31]. OCR post correction, a method of error mitigation, in which OCR'd text is de-noised, is a field covering a wide range of digitization applications [36] and models have historically taken several forms [53]. More recently, deep learning models have been developed to tackle post correction [27] which typically make use of sequence-to-sequence models [26,34,50].

These deep learning methods require large training datasets, making their testing predominately completed with well known OCR post correction datasets from the community [13,16,37]. As manual annotations can be time consuming at scale [27,45], synthetic datasets are often used [24,25,52]. In particular, mining the arχiv is a popular method to generate synthetic machine learning training datasets [24,25,33]. Given the variety of journals represented in the arχiv database, its mining represents a vital opportunity to create domain-specific synthetic data [21,22,35], which is necessary as models trained on one type of document will often fail on documents dissimilar to the training data [15].

---

[1] https://ui.adsabs.harvard.edu/.

3 Methods

In what follows, we make use of two decades of the oldest articles available through the arχiv Bulk Downloads [1] (1991–2011) for a total of 712,975 articles.

3.1 Compiling the Astrophysics arχiv Bulk Downloads

Once downloaded, all article files are checked for corrupt decompression formats and a main TeX file (those containing \documentclass or \documentstyle) for a total of 318,033 articles. To construct an "astronomy article" list, class/style commands are parsed with regex and those which denote typical astrophysical journal names (e.g., "aastex", "apj", "mn") are kept. These names correspond to the three journals which have the most complete scanned historical corpus (The Astrophysical Journal, Astronomy & Astrophysics, and Monthly Notices of the Royal Astronomical Society) [14]. This results in a total of 65,132 articles.

This set of ∼65k files are tested for PDF-compilation errors for a total of 26,578 successfully compiled astronomy articles. The main sources of error are missing files (e.g., missing figure files) and an inability to distinguish which TeX file in a directory is the main article document.

3.2 Segmentation of TeX Documents

Many parsers exist for TeX files with output formats such as plain text (e.g., opendetex [6]), XML (e.g., LaTeXML [17], unarXive [39]) or document trees (e.g., TeXSoup [8]). With all methods, this parsing tends to be non-trivial [38]. As the documents are compiled once marking modifications are applied to the TeX to track synthetic ground truth (SGT) locations, any parser must account for errors that could occur in the compilation process. Additionally, checks for incorrect splitting of TeX source into trees are required. This excludes "off the shelf" parsers which only run a subset of these checks[2]. Thus this work makes use of a custom-built TeX parser.

Figure 1 diagrams the segmentation process which uses regex to break TeX files into document trees. A raw TeX document ("Raw LaTeX" snippet shown in upper left gray panel) is parsed to find the locations of special characters denoting commands, variables, and environments ("Splits with regex" blue upper middle panel). A hierarchy is then constructed with checks for closing and opening statements of commands (closing {}) inline math formulas (paired $'s) and environments (\begin, \end) and stored in a tree ("Tree" purple upper right panel). Commands which reside within plain text sentences such as inline math, citations, and references ("\ref{}" commands) are stored with special tags.

---

[2] For example, following the process in Sect. 3.3, TeXSoup finds errors in only 46.2 % of files, while our method finds errors in 70.4 %.

3.3 Marking the "Ground Truth" Words in LaTeX and OCR'ing Pages

Many methods for marking TeX documents to generate synthetic data for page objects (e.g., figures) modify the LaTeX to add bounding boxes in specific colors around objects and use image processing techniques to extract object locations after the PDF is rendered [24,25]. Rendered PDFs can potentially be mined for SGT text, however, this can lead to errors in the extracted SGT text [25].

To avoid SGT-text parsing errors, this work adopts a different approach by modifying the TeX source documents with markers denoting every word, inline equation, citation, and reference using the tikzmark [9] package as shown within the green outlined "Marked LaTeX" box of Fig. 1. Inline math, citations, and references are included as they are frequently interspersed with the plain text.

After storing the locations of each SGT object ("Tree" purple box in Fig. 1), all text within the "plain text" sections are split into words using white space and starting (ending) \tikzmark commands are placed at the word/citation/reference/inline math start (end). Once the TeX document is compiled, the marks are stored in the auxilary (.aux) file produced during compilation which is then parsed to match each word to its location on the final, rendered PDF page. At this stage, documents which contain the \input command are ignored as these can include text external to the document being parsed.

Once the marked files are compiled, each page of each article is OCR'd with Tesseract, following methods used with articles from the historical holdings of the ADS [29,30]. Examples of these bounding boxes and words are shown in the orange "OCR with boxes" panel of Fig. 1.

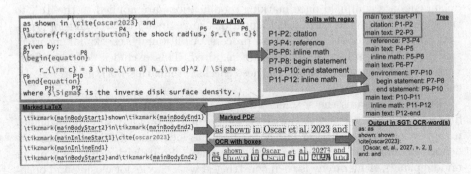

Fig. 1. Diagram of TeX parsed into its attributes ("Raw LaTeX", "Splits with regex"), and the tree structure built from the positions of these splits within the document ("Tree"), as outlined in Sect. 3.2. TeX is then marked with the tikzmark package and OCR'd (section from three top lines in "Tree" shown in "Marked LaTeX", Sect. 3.3). Once the TeX is compiled into a PDF, the auxiliary files are parsed to locate the SGT word locations on the rendered PDF page ("Marked PDF", Sect. 3.4), OCR words are collected ("OCR with boxes"), and SGT-OCR boxes are aligned ("Output data SGT: OCR-word(s)", Sect. 3.4). See text for more details.

3.4   The OCR-SGT Alignment Algorithm and Dataset Characteristics

The final step in creating our SGT - OCR dataset is to align the OCR and SGT words. In what follows, "element" is defined as a plain text word, inline math formula, citation, or reference. Our alignment routine is as follows:

- Step 1: Locations of the bottom left and right bounds of each marked element are found from the .aux files. These locations are shown as solid magenta lines in the magenta "Marked PDF" panel of Fig. 1.
- Step 2: As tikzmark gives only the lower y-position of each element, a bounding box is created by assuming 11pt font for each element (11pt font is an average value, font size is not always specified explicitly in the TeX file), shown by the dashed magenta lines in the "Marked PDF" panel of Fig. 1.
- Step 3: If the bounding box is found to span more than one line, the SGT element is assumed to be hyphenated and each part is marked as a separate word. Alignment operates page-by-page, therefore hyphenated elements which span multiple pages are ignored.
- Step 4: The "raw" SGT element is extracted from the source TeX.
- Step 5: All OCR bounding boxes which overlap with a SGT box are associated with that SGT element. If an OCR bounding box is associated with more than one SGT element, the OCR element is associated with the SGT element with which it has the largest intersection-over-union (IOU).
- Step 6: All OCR elements associated with a SGT element are ordered by increasing horizontal position and combined into a single OCR element for that SGT element. This is shown by the data structure in the yellow "Output in SGT: OCR-words" box of Fig. 1.
- Step 7: SGT word "type" is stored along with SGT word (plain text, inline math, citation, reference and whether the word is hyphenated).
- Step 8: Elements are ordered by tikzmarks and aligned with edit distance operations [5]. spaCY [18] is used to tokenize aligned pages as sentences [7].

While the majority of articles are aligned without error, Tesseract errors are possible on single pages. From this corpus of 7,850 articles which contain successfully aligned pages, our algorithm produces a total of 71,735 pages of 1,527,118 SGT/OCR sentence pairs which contain a total of 203,354,393 character pairs.

The relationships between SGT and OCR aligned characters closely follow other popular datasets with the majority of Levenshtein edit distance [23] operations in our dataset (other datasets) being replacements ∼61.5% (∼40–60%), followed by deletions ∼19.6% (∼10–18%) and insertions ∼18.9% (∼5–24%) [31].

Interactive versions of large confusion matrices for alphabetic characters, digits, punctuation marks and frequent words are hosted on this project's webpage[3].

4   Post Correction Model Baseline Tests

To test the post correction effectiveness of our dataset we train a baseline transformer model – byt5 [50] – with the dataset. This model is effective for datasets

---

[3] https://readingtimemachine.github.io/projects/1-ocr-groundtruth-may2023.

such as ours which contain many out-of-vocabulary OCR words [27]. The model's initial training uses 100k aligned sentences for training, and 5k in the validation and test datasets. Here, transfer learning from the byt5/google-small model on HuggingFace [3] is used, and, for all models, training occurs on a NVIDIA V100 for ∼87000 iterations over ∼24 h, in which the model converges.

The entry above the first thick line of Table 1 ("byt5,words") shows the ability of the model to correct only the parts of each aligned SGT-OCR text which have been tagged as plain text in the test datasets. Here, byt5 improves the character error rate (CER) by 67.35 % and the word error rate (WER) by 60.18 %.

While the focus of this work is on correcting the plain text within our corpus, historical ADS articles also contain inline math and citations. Here, we simplify the problem by testing the accuracy of the model on *detecting* these elements in the text. To proceed, we modify the input and output text by marking these environments with characters that do not appear in the plain text corpus. For example, we replace each instance of a SGT or post corrected OCR inline math formula with a single character ($) and determine how often these characters align in the SGT and predicted OCR. The "byt5,full,fixed" row in Table 1 lists the results of this "fixed" model, trained on 500k "fixed" sentences (10k in the validation and test sets). Here, the CER and WER improvements have both increased to their highest rates of 85.51 % and 84.44 %, respectively.

To test the model's accuracy on pre-digital OCR, we apply the "byt5,full,fixed" model to 202 hand-annotated sentences from the main text of articles in the historical ADS corpus [10,29,30,32]. When applied to this dataset, the mean improvement, $\langle I \rangle$, in CER and WER from correction with the fixed-byt5 model (i.e. "byt5,full,fixed" for the arχiv data) are 7.71 % and 18.82%, respectively, as shown in the "historical,full,fixed" row of Table 1. While the improvements in CER and WER are more modest than the improvement in the arχiv dataset, they are nonetheless significantly larger than those from a generic post correction model [4] ($\langle I \rangle_{CER}$=−2499.35 %, $\langle I \rangle_{WER}$=−499.26 %) or from when byt5 is trained on the words from the historical dataset alone ($\langle I \rangle_{CER}$=−443.18 %, $\langle I \rangle_{WER}$=−209.74 %), both of which result in a large *negative* improvement.

Table 1. Mean CER and WER in percent for original datasets, $\langle B \rangle$, after post correction with listed models, $\langle A \rangle$, and the improvement percent, $\langle I \rangle$. Also shown are the percent of test instances with improvement ($\langle A \rangle < \langle B \rangle$) as "% Improved". All calculations use the arχiv dataset except for the last row which uses the historical dataset.

Model	CER in %				WER in %			
	$\langle B \rangle$	$\langle A \rangle$	$\langle I \rangle$	% Improved	$\langle B \rangle$	$\langle A \rangle$	$\langle I \rangle$	% Improved
byt5, words	5.50	2.37	67.35	93.00	15.34	6.46	60.18	90.38
byt5, full, fixed	12.53	2.47	85.51	98.22	19.81	3.84	84.44	99.24
historical, full, fixed	5.53	3.94	7.71	82.67	8.98	8.20	18.82	82.67

5 Current Limitations and Future Work

While the full dataset cannot be shared directly (arχiv administrators, Private communication), we share a subset of our aligned sentences along with analysis notebooks in GitHub[4]. We are currently working with the arχiv to make a larger portion of the dataset available to the public.

LaTeX source from ∼1990–2010 is known to be difficult to compile due to updates in TeX compilation software [2] which, in part, lead to the drop of the initial ∼65k astronomy articles to ∼7k. Partnership with the arχiv to support more documents, along with adding support for a wider range of documents (e.g., those with the \input command) will increase the dataset size.

While the accuracy of the "byt5,full,fixed" model applied to the historical dataset ("historical,full,fixed") is lower overall, because there is no associated TeX with these historical documents, some ambiguity in the "ground truth" is expected (e.g., the phrase "$\le$90%" can be written as $\le$90\%, $\le$ 90$\%$ or $\le$ 90\%$ and the meaning of the phrase is unchanged). Post correction with consideration for these nuances is relegated to future work.

Finally, a larger historical dataset would undeniably enhance our post correction accuracy. A discussion of the methods used to generate a larger manual dataset is relegated to future work.

Acknowledgments. This work is supported by a NASA Astrophysics Data Analysis Program Grant (20-ADAP20-0225).

References

1. arχiv bulk downloads. https://info.arxiv.org/help/bulk_data_s3.html. Accessed 05 March 2022
2. arχiv hiring and needs. https://info.arxiv.org/hiring/. Accessed 17 July 2023
3. Huggingface byt5-small. https://huggingface.co/google/byt5-small. Accessed 25 Mar 2023
4. Huggingface yelpfeast/byt5-base-english-ocr-correction. https://huggingface.co/yelpfeast/byt5-base-english-ocr-correction. Accessed 20 July 2023
5. The levenshtein package. https://github.com/maxbachmann/Levenshtein. Accessed 29 May 2023
6. Opendetex. https://github.com/pkubowicz/opendetex. Accessed 29 May 2023
7. The spacy sentence tokenizer. https://spacy.io/api/sentencizer. Accessed 29 May 2023
8. Texsoup. https://github.com/alvinwan/TexSoup. Accessed 30 Oct 2022
9. The tikzmark package. https://texdoc.org/serve/tikzmark/0. Accessed 29 May 2023
10. Accomazzi, A., et al.: Improved functionality and curation support in the ADS. In: American Astronomical Society Meeting Abstracts #225. American Astronomical Society Meeting Abstracts, vol. 225, pp. 336–355, January 2015

---

[4] https://github.com/ReadingTimeMachine/ocr_post_correction.

11. Ahuja, A., Devera, A., Fox, E.A.: Parsing electronic theses and dissertations using object detection. In: Proceedings of the first Workshop on Information Extraction from Scientific Publications, pp. 121–130. Association for Computational Linguistics, November 2022. https://aclanthology.org/2022.wiesp-1.14

12. Boros, E., Nguyen, N.K., Lejeune, G., Doucet, A.: Assessing the impact of OCR noise on multilingual event detection over digitised documents. Int. J. Digit. Librar. 1–26 (2022). https://doi.org/10.1007/s00799-022-00325-2

13. Chiron, G., Doucet, A., Coustaty, M., Moreux, J.P.: ICDAR2017 2017 competition on post-OCR text correction. In: 2017 14th IAPR International Conference on Document Analysis and Recognition (ICDAR), vol. 01, pp. 1423–1428 (2017). https://doi.org/10.1109/ICDAR.2017.232

14. Eichhorn, G., Accomazzi, A., Grant, C.S., Kurtz, M.J., Rey Bacaicoa, V., Murray, S.S.: New data and search features in the NASA ADS abstract service, p. 1298, March 2002. https://ui.adsabs.harvard.edu/abs/2002LPI....33.1298E, Conference Name: Lunar and Planetary Science Conference ADS Bibcode: 2002LPI....33.1298E

15. Etter, D., Rawls, S., Carpenter, C., Sell, G.: A synthetic recipe for OCR. In: 2019 International Conference on Document Analysis and Recognition (ICDAR), pp. 864–869. IEEE, Sydney, Australia, September 2019. https://doi.org/10.1109/ICDAR.2019.00143

16. Evershed, J., Fitch, K.: Correcting noisy OCR: context beats confusion. In: Proceedings of the First International Conference on Digital Access to Textual Cultural Heritage, DATeCH 2014, pp. 45–51. Association for Computing Machinery, New York, NY, USA (2014). https://doi.org/10.1145/2595188.2595200

17. Ginev, D., Miller, B.R.: LaTeXML 2012 - a year of LaTeXML. In: Carette, J., Aspinall, D., Lange, C., Sojka, P., Windsteiger, W. (eds.) CICM 2013. LNCS (LNAI), vol. 7961, pp. 335–338. Springer, Heidelberg (2013). https://doi.org/10.1007/978-3-642-39320-4_24

18. Honnibal, M., Montani, I.: spaCy 2: natural language understanding with bloom embeddings, convolutional neural networks and incremental parsing. To appear 7(1), 411–420 (2017)

19. Jiang, M., et al.: The gutenberg-hathitrust parallel corpus: a real-world dataset for noise investigation in uncorrected OCR texts. In: iConference 2021 (Poster) (2021)

20. Kahu, S.Y.: Figure Extraction from Scanned Electronic Theses and Dissertations. Master's thesis, Virginia Tech (2020)

21. Krishnan, P., Jawahar, C.: Generating synthetic data for text recognition. arXiv preprint arXiv:1608.04224 (2016)

22. Le, T.A., Baydin, A.G., Zinkov, R., Wood, F.: Using synthetic data to train neural networks is model-based reasoning. In: 2017 International Joint Conference on Neural Networks (IJCNN), pp. 3514–3521. IEEE (2017)

23. Levenshtein, V.I.: Binary codes capable of correcting deletions, insertions and reversals. Soviet Phys. Doklady 10, 707 (1966)

24. Li, M., Cui, L., Huang, S., Wei, F., Zhou, M., Li, Z.: TableBank: a benchmark dataset for table detection and recognition, July 2020. http://arxiv.org/abs/1903.01949, arXiv:1903.01949 [cs]

25. Li, M., et al.: DocBank: a benchmark dataset for document layout analysis. In: Proceedings of the 28th International Conference on Computational Linguistics, pp. 949–960 (2020)

26. Liu, Y., et al.: Multilingual denoising pre-training for neural machine translation. Trans. Assoc. Comput. Linguist. 8, 726–742 (2020). https://doi.org/10.1162/tacl_a_00343

27. Maheshwari, A., Singh, N., Krishna, A., Ramakrishnan, G.: A Benchmark and dataset for Post-OCR text correction in Sanskrit, November 2022. https://doi.org/10.48550/arXiv.2211.07980, arXiv:2211.07980 [cs]
28. Mayernik, M.S., Hart, D.L., Maull, K.E., Weber, N.M.: Assessing and tracing the outcomes and impact of research infrastructures. J. Assoc. Inf. Sci. Technol. **68**(6), 1341–1359 (2017). https://doi.org/10.1002/asi.23721
29. Naiman, J.P., Williams, P.K., Goodman, A.: The digitization of historical astrophysical literature with highly localized figures and figure captions. Int. J. Digit. Librar. 1–21 (2023). https://doi.org/10.1007/s00799-023-00350-9
30. Naiman, J.P., Williams, P.K.G., Goodman, A.: Figure and figure caption extraction for mixed raster and vector PDFs: digitization of astronomical literature with OCR features. In: Silvello, G., et al. Linking Theory and Practice of Digital Libraries. TPDL 2022. Lecture Notes in Computer Science, vol. 13541, pp 52–67. Springer, Cham (2022). https://doi.org/10.1007/978-3-031-16802-4_5
31. Nguyen, T.T.H., Jatowt, A., Coustaty, M., Nguyen, N.V., Doucet, A.: Deep statistical analysis of OCR errors for effective post-OCR processing. In: 2019 ACM/IEEE Joint Conference on Digital Libraries (JCDL), pp. 29–38, June 2019. https://doi.org/10.1109/JCDL.2019.00015
32. Pepe, A., Goodman, A., Muench, A.: The ADS all-sky survey. In: Ballester, P., Egret, D., Lorente, N.P.F. (eds.) Astronomical Data Analysis Software and Systems XXI. Astronomical Society of the Pacific Conference Series, vol. 461, p. 275, September 2012
33. Pfahler, L., Morik, K.: Self-supervised pretraining of graph neural network for the retrieval of related mathematical expressions in scientific articles, August 2022. http://arxiv.org/abs/2209.00446, arXiv:2209.00446 [cs]
34. Ramirez-Orta, J.A., Xamena, E., Maguitman, A., Milios, E., Soto, A.J.: Post-OCR document correction with large ensembles of character sequence-to-sequence models. In: Proceedings of the AAAI Conference on Artificial Intelligence, vol. 36, pp. 11192–11199 (2022)
35. Ren, X., Chen, K., Sun, J.: A CNN based scene Chinese text recognition algorithm with synthetic data engine. arXiv e-prints arXiv:1604.01891, https://doi.org/10.48550/arXiv.1604.01891, April 2016
36. Rigaud, C., Doucet, A., Coustaty, M., Moreux, J.P.: ICDAR 2019 competition on post-OCR text correction (2019)
37. Rigaud, C., Doucet, A., Coustaty, M., Moreux, J.P.: ICDAR 2019 competition on post-OCR text correction. In: 2019 International Conference on Document Analysis and Recognition (ICDAR), pp. 1588–1593 (2019). https://doi.org/10.1109/ICDAR.2019.00255
38. Saier, T., Färber, M.: Bibliometric-enhanced arxiv: a data set for paper-based and citation-based tasks. In: BIR@ ECIR, pp. 14–26 (2019)
39. Saier, T., Krause, J., Färber, M.: unarXive 2022: all arXiv publications preprocessed for NLP, including structured full-text and citation network. arXiv e-prints arXiv:2303.14957, https://doi.org/10.48550/arXiv.2303.14957. March 2023
40. Sandy, H.M., et al.: Making a case for open research: implications for reproducibility and transparency. Proc. Assoc. Inf. Sci. Technol. **54**(1), 583–586 (2017). https://doi.org/10.1002/pra2.2017.14505401079
41. Schmitt-Koopmann, F.M., Huang, E.M., Darvishy, A.: Accessible PDFs: applying artificial intelligence for automated remediation of STEM PDFs. In: Proceedings of the 24th International ACM SIGACCESS Conference on Computers and Accessibility, ASSETS 2022, pp. 1–6. Association for Computing Machinery, New York, NY, USA, October 2022. https://doi.org/10.1145/3517428.3550407

42. Smith, L., Arcand, K., Smith, R., Bookbinder, J., Smith, J.: Capturing the many faces of an exploded star: communicating complex and evolving astronomical data. JCOM J. Sci. Commun. **16**, 16050202 (2017). https://doi.org/10.22323/2.16050202

43. Smith, R.: An overview of the tesseract OCR engine. In: Proceedings of the Ninth International Conference on Document Analysis and Recognition, vol. 02, ICDAR 2007, pp. 629–633. IEEE Computer Society, USA (2007)

44. Sohmen, L., Charbonnier, J., Blümel, I., Wartena, C., Heller, L.: Figures in scientific open access publications. In: Méndez, E., Crestani, F., Ribeiro, C., David, G., Lopes, J.C. (eds.) TPDL 2018. LNCS, vol. 11057, pp. 220–226. Springer, Cham (2018). https://doi.org/10.1007/978-3-030-00066-0_19

45. Springmann, U., Reul, C., Dipper, S., Baiter, J.: Ground truth for training OCR engines on historical documents in German fraktur and early modern Latin. J. Lang. Technol. Comput. Linguist. **33**(1), 97–114 (2018)

46. Stephens, Z.D., et al.: Big data: astronomical or Genomical? PLOS Biol. **13**(7), 1–11 (2015). https://doi.org/10.1371/journal.pbio.1002195

47. Strien, D., Beelen, K., Coll Ardanuy, M., Hosseini, K., Mcgillivray, B., Colavizza, G.: Assessing the impact of OCR quality on downstream NLP tasks. SCITEPRESS-Sci. Technol. Publ., February 2020. https://doi.org/10.5220/0009169004840496

48. Tafti, A.P., Baghaie, A., Assefi, M., Arabnia, H.R., Yu, Z., Peissig, P.: OCR as a service: an experimental evaluation of google docs OCR, tesseract, ABBYY FineReader, and Transym. In: Bebis, G., et al. (eds.) ISVC 2016. LNCS, vol. 10072, pp. 735–746. Springer, Cham (2016). https://doi.org/10.1007/978-3-319-50835-1_66

49. Urban, M.: An introduction to LATEX. TEX users group (1986)

50. Xue, L., et al.: ByT5: towards a token-free future with pre-trained byte-to-byte models. Trans. Assoc. Comput. Linguist. **10**, 291–306 (2022). https://doi.org/10.1162/tacl_a_00461

51. Zaytsev, A.: Hathitrust and a mission for accessibility. J. Electron. **18**(3) (2015)

52. Zharikov, I., Nikitin, F., Vasiliev, I., Dokholyan, V.: DDI-100: dataset for text detection and recognition. In: Proceedings of the 2020 4th International Symposium on Computer Science and Intelligent Control, pp. 1–5, November 2020. https://doi.org/10.1145/3440084.3441192, arXiv:1912.11658 [cs]

53. Zhu, W., Liu, Y., Hao, L.: A novel OCR approach based on document layout analysis and text block classification. In: 2016 12th International Conference on Computational Intelligence and Security (CIS), pp. 91–94, December 2016. https://doi.org/10.1109/CIS.2016.0029

Human-Computer Interaction

From Textual to Visual Image Searching: User Experience of Advanced Image Search Tool

Elina Late[1][✉] [iD], Hille Ruotsalainen[1] [iD], Mert Seker[1] [iD], Jenni Raitoharju[2] [iD], Anssi Männistö[1] [iD], and Sanna Kumpulainen[1] [iD]

[1] Tampere University, Kalevantie 4, 33100 Tampere, Finland
elina.late@tuni.fi
[2] University of Jyväskylä, Seminaarinkatu 15, 40014 Jyväskylä, Finland

Abstract. This paper reports findings from a study focusing on user experience of image search tool utilizing content-based image retrieval methods. Previous studies have indicated challenges in textual image search especially in the historical domain. As a part of the project, a prototype tool was created for searching digitized historical images based on their visual contents to provide support for user needs identified in earlier studies. The tool was tested by 15 participants who evaluated their user experience with User Experience Scale and by verbal feedback. Our results indicate that participants derived benefits from the search capabilities provided by the tool, which went beyond relying on textual image descriptions. However, problems occurred, for example, in evaluating the search results and in user skills. Results also emphasize the value of intellectually produced metadata for image searching and use. Therefore, future developments should focus on creating hybrid systems supporting both textual and visual image searching.

Keywords: Content-based image retrieval · image archive · user experience

1 Introduction

Historical photographs form an important part of our cultural heritage capturing how the world looked like in the past. During the recent decades efforts have been put in digitizing photograph archives to make the contents available for various users. Indeed, digital image archives have become popular sources of historical information, for example, for scholars, information specialists, amateurs, and for the general public. For example, images are important primary sources for academic historians, and they are used for verification, documentation, or corroboration [1]. Although many digitized collections are openly available, access is often difficult because of the lack or incompleteness of image metadata [2, 3]. However, textual metadata is vital since images are mostly searched using textual queries [2, 4]. Yet, creating metadata manually is resource-consuming and challenging as the same image may have varying interpretations depending on the user's viewpoint. Also, previous experiences have demonstrated that information needs in humanities research can be highly diverse, making it difficult to create a single unified metadata scheme. Therefore, flexible systems are needed [5].

O. Alonso et al. (Eds.): TPDL 2023, LNCS 14241, pp. 277–283, 2023.
https://doi.org/10.1007/978-3-031-43849-3_24

Content-based image retrieval methods (CBIR) have been proposed as a solution to the problem. These methods enable the recognition of people, objects, events, and landscapes within images, all without relying on textual metadata. Another valuable application of CBIR is reverse image search, which allows users to find images by uploading a sample image as a query [6]. Novel methods are already widely available in commercial image search engines, but cultural heritage collections often lack such functionalities because of limited resources in their maintenance and development. As some studies have shown, users are longing for new image search possibilities [7] others have argued that users have conflicting attitudes and needs for automatic methods [8]. In general, users value possibilities for searching conceptual attributes by querying and browsing [9]. However, image use varies according to the user's task and profession [2, 10]. Nevertheless, there is a gap in research in this respect and we do not yet know how the users of historical photograph archives benefit from the recent developments in the automatic query.

This paper aims to fill this gap in knowledge by evaluating the user experience of an image search tool based on CBIR. As a part of our research project, a prototype tool was created for advanced image searching utilizing computer vision methods and machine learning models to identify searchable contents from the images. Our test collection included historical photographs from the Second World War many of which lack original metadata. The prototype was tested by 15 users and user experience was measured using User Engagement Scale [11]. Additionally, user experiences were collected from verbal feedback during and after users tested the prototype.

Our research questions are:

RQ1. How satisfied are users with the advanced image search tool?

RQ2. What benefits and barriers do users see in content-based image retrieval?

Next, we will introduce our research setting with the description of the prototype tool and the data collection and analysis. Finally, we present the findings followed by discussion and conclusions.

2   Research Setting

2.1   Advanced Image Search Tool

Advanced Image Search Tool (AIST) [13] was developed for improved access to digitized photographs. We tested AIST on photographs captured during the Second World War in Finland. The original collection (FWPA, sa-kuva.fi) provided by the Finnish Defense Forces contains in total almost 160.000 photographs captured by photographers who served in Information Company troops in 1939–1945. The search is based on textual metadata of the images that were mostly created during the wartime by the photographers. However, metadata is partly missing because of the chaotic times during the photography. For our sample collection, we selected 23 800 images including 3800 images without any kind of original metadata or captions.

Based on the information collected during our previous studies [2, 7, 9], AIST was designed to provide an easy-to-use implementation for many aspects of Automatic Image Contact Extraction [6] by applying different computer vision methods and machine learning models trained on large publicly available datasets. AIST enables conducting search tasks by a graphical user interface and the tool is publicly available at GitHub [13]. AIST allows various automatic content-based search types ranging from low-level features, such as color distribution, to higher-level semantic information, such as environment or objects, using search options. As image archive users have emphasized the importance of analyzing people and objects from the images [7], several AIST search features are also related to people: their amount, age, gender, facial expression, and gaze direction. It is possible also to use images and text for querying. Different combinations of search features can be freely used.

2.2 Data Collection and Analysis

We invited in total 15 participants to test the prototype in May-June 2022. The participants were recruited partially from the previous interviews and partially through the contacts of the research group. The participants were either experienced users (N = 8) of the original collection (researchers, museum curators, journalists, war history enthusiasts) or novices (history students N = 7). The tests were audio and video recorded and the participants' consents were collected. One test session took on average 45 min.

The tests were conducted remotely via Zoom connection. The prototype was installed on the computer of the researcher and the participants used it via Zoom with "Ask for Remote Control" option. The users were asked to conduct five predefined tasks with AIST. The search tasks were formulated based on the actual searches that emerged in the previously collected interviews. This procedure followed the guidelines by Borlund [14]. The predefined tasks were used to ensure that all the participants were exposed to the different functionalities of the system. After completing the search tasks the respondents were asked to answer a short post-test questionnaire, which was based on the UES short form [11] to measure the user engagement in four factors. The scale consists of 12 statements evaluated with a five-point Likert scale; Strongly disagree, disagree, neither agree nor disagree, agree, strongly agree. We translated the UES into Finnish. We also added one question from the UES long form [11] to measure utilitarian achievement (UA) by asking to evaluate the success of the search task with the system. After completing the survey, the respondents were asked informally how they felt about using AIST and whether it would be useful for themselves.

We analyzed the data using SPSS and Atlas.ti. First, we created five computed variables to evaluate the user experience (FA, PU, AE, RW and UES total, see Fig. 1). Because some of the questions were negative and some positive, the scores were reversed if needed. UA was analyzed separately. We studied the correlations between UA and UES variables using Pearson bivariate correlation. Second, we uploaded the discussion transcripts into Atlas.ti where verbal expressions of user experiences were identified and coded. Quotes were further coded according to the categories used in UES scale (FA, PU, AE and RW). Analyses were done by one researcher, but the codings were discussed in detail with another researcher in several rounds during the analyses process to reach a consensus.

3 Results

The image search tool gained an overall good evaluation by the test users with the user experience scale resulting an average 3.8 with 5 being the highest value. The scores of the four subscales varied (Fig. 1).

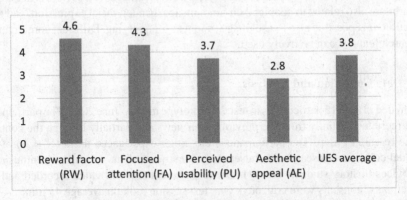

Fig. 1. Mean scores from the 4 UES items and the UES score

Out of the five measures, the **Reward Factor** was scored the highest (mean 4.6). RW consists of three items measuring the experiences of success and reward when using the system. The scores show the users found the experience interesting. In their verbal feedback, the participants discussed the future possibilities of the tool and visioned the tool being even more rewarding for bigger collections. The participants described the tool as supportive, enabling them to overcome the shortcomings of the image metadata and access the images beyond the textual descriptions. They found the tool showing the full potential of the collection providing also more opportunities for research use such as data analysis.

Focused attention (FA) was measured with three items focusing on users' experiences absorbed in the interaction and losing track of time. The mean score for FA was 4.3. In their verbal comments, the users expressed feelings of happiness, excitement, and fun. These feelings were raised by discovering new photographs from the collection and realizing the potential of new methods for retrieving the images.

Perceived usability measured the negative affections experienced as a result of the interaction with the system and the degree of control. The mean score received for PU was 3.7. In the verbal feedback, various problems were brought up, many of them relating to unsuccessful searches and the lack of possibilities to evaluate the search results. Some users talked about the "black box" effect as they did not understand how the system produced the results. When collecting images used as research data, scholars had a need to understand what the search was based on. Searching images by visual contents demanded a new approach also from the users and users hoped for more support and guidance from the system for making the searches. They did not know, for example, what words they should use for querying. Many participants agreed that the old and the new systems should be integrated to allow users to utilize the best features from both approaches (original metadata and content-based searching). Furthermore, users reminded that providing access to the images does not necessarily remove all the problems in using them. For example, using an image for illustrating a book requires trustworthy contextual information about the image. The tool cannot derive this information solely based on the image analyses alone.

Aesthetic appeal factor measures the attractiveness and visual appeal of the interface with three items. The mean score for AE was the lowest compared with other factors totaling 2.8. Indeed, in their verbal comments, users agreed that the visual appearance of the prototype was not aesthetically pleasing but at the same time adding that their expectations for not-for-profit services were not similar as for systems by big corporations. However, participants brought up that the visual design should support the user better, for example by selecting colors guiding the use.

Additionally, we asked if the users were able to find the images they were searching for with the system (UA). More than one fourth (26.7%) agreed and 60% partly agreed with the statement. The UA factor correlated significantly only with the PU factor (r = .577, p = .024). The users successful with searching had fewer negative experiences compared with those experiencing a lower rate of success.

4 Discussion and Conclusions

The aim of our study was to analyze user experiences on a CBIR tool. As CBIR methods have been seen as a solution for problems of lacking metadata for textual searching of historical images, there is a lack of recent studies of the usefulness of such systems for the actual users [7, 8]. As a part of our project, a prototype tool was created for searching images from historical image collections to provide support for user needs identified in earlier studies [2, 7, 9]. The tool was tested by 15 participants who evaluated their user experience. Our results indicate participants having high expectations for the tool but experiencing some difficulties when using it.

Our first research question was: How satisfied are users with the advanced image search tool? Overall, the study participants were very satisfied with the image search tool when evaluated by the UES. The aesthetic appeal of the tool was scored the lowest, although the users did not have high expectations for the prototype looks and the aesthetic appeal was not prioritized in the development. However, more studies with larger samples are needed to cover the variety of CBIR based tools to provide more reliable results of the user experience. Also, comparative studies on different user groups are needed as Beaudoin [8] observed differences in user needs. Nevertheless, this study provides a good starting point for future research.

Secondly, we asked: What benefits and barriers do users see in the content-based image retrieval? Our results show that CBIR has much to offer for searching the contents from historical image collections with limited metadata. Most participants were excited about the possibilities of the novel methods and described such tools as being the "future". With the prototype tool the participants could already find images they had not found before from the collection. Indeed, earlier studies have showed that users desire CBIR methods and experience the lack and incompleteness of metadata as a major barrier to accessing the images [7]. CBIR systems may be helpful also for searching known items as before this has been frustrating for users lacking information of the specific image [2]. Another benefit of CBIR is overcoming the limitations caused by the language of the captions [12].

However, for professional use AIST should be further developed, evaluated and documented. Users value and expect transparency in use, ability to evaluate search results and clear guidelines for use. CBIR based tools demand new approaches also from the users. Before users have tried to imagine what words, the original photographer may have used for describing the image [7], but with the CBIR they need to learn to think about the contents of the image and how the tool might interpret them. Thus, future research should focus on search behaviors in real-life activities to find ways to support the information seekers with AI tools. Additionally, user training is needed.

Although new functionalities were appreciated, users want to also keep the features of the original search tool. Because, for example, the location, time and name of the photographer are among the most important access points for images [7], automatic metadata creation cannot totally·replace the original metadata. Original captions also have their own value for image use in addition to accessing them [1, 2]. Historians place significant importance on the trustworthiness associated with reputational institutions, such as archives, and the provenance of photographs when utilizing them for their research. They value original descriptive information, including captions, keywords, subject headings, the original medium of the photographs, and even details like the image size [1]. Our participants also reminded us that providing access to the images does not solve all the problems in using them. Many images lack metadata that is crucial for interpreting the contents. When gathering research data, scholars need information, for example, about the aboutness of data, characteristics of data, metadata, and secondary information about data [15] that CBIR is unable to produce. More metadata could be produced intellectually by crowdsourcing, i.e., allowing users to annotate contents directly and integrate knowledge from different sources into the collection.

Therefore, new features and search possibilities should be built on top of existing systems or earlier functionalities should be integrated with the new ones to create hybrid systems [8]. Different metadata types could be provided as layers on top of the original metadata and let the users decide which to use. Developing cultural heritage collections requires both financial and intellectual resources to ensure the continuation of the digital curation [16]. Collecting real-life user experiences and use practices of digital tools is crucial in future research to ensure their evidence-based development.

Acknowledgements. We thank all the research participants for their valuable contributions. This work was conducted in IPALIA project supported by the Intelligent Society Profiling Action funded by Academy of Finland. Research was partly funded by the Academy of Finland grant number 351247.

References

1. Chassanoff, A.M.: Historians' experiences using digitized archival photographs as evidence. Am. Arch. **81**(1), 135–164 (2018). https://doi.org/10.17723/0360-9081-81.1.135
2. Late, E., Ruotsalainen, H., Kumpulainen, S.: Searching images from open photograph archive. Search tactics and faced barriers in historical research. Int. J. Dig. Libr. (2023)
3. Roberts, H.E.: A picture is worth a thousand words: Art indexing in electronic databases. J. Am. Soc. Inform. Sci. Technol. **52**(11), 911–916 (2001). https://doi.org/10.1002/asi.1145
4. Cho, H., Pham, M., Leonard, K.N., Urban, A.C.: A systematic literature review on image information needs and behaviors. J. Doc. **78**(2), 207–227 (2022). https://doi.org/10.1108/JD-10-2020-0172
5. Lund, H., Bogers, T., Larsen, B., Lykke, M.: CHAOS: user-driven development of a metadata scheme for radio broadcast archives. In: Proceedings of the iConference 2013, pp. 990–994 (2013). https://doi.org/10.9776/13510
6. Männistö, A., Seker, M., Iosifidis, A., Raitoharju, J.: Automatic Image Content Extraction: Operationalizing Machine Learning in Humanistic Photographic Studies of Large Visual Archives. arXiv:2204.02149 (2022)
7. Late, E., Ruotsalainen, H., Kumpulainen, S.: In a perfect world. exploring the desires and realities for digitized historical image archives. Accepted for publication in the Proceedings of the ASIST Conference. Wiley, London (2023)
8. Beaudoin, J.: Content-based image retrieval methods and professional image users. J. Am. Soc. Inf. Sci. **67**(2), 350–365 (2016). https://doi.org/10.1002/asi.23387
9. Kumpulainen, S., Ruotsalainen, H.: Searching wartime photograph archive for serious leisure purposes. In International Conference on Theory and Practice of Digital Libraries, pp. 81–92. Springer, Italy (2022). https://doi.org/10.1007/978-3-031-16802-4_7
10. Beaudoin, J.: A framework of image use among archaeologists, architects, art historians and artists. J. Doc. **70**(1), 119–147 (2014). https://doi.org/10.1108/JD-12-2012-0157
11. O'Brien, H.L., Cairns, P., Hall, M.: A practical approach to measuring user engagement with the refined user engagement scale (UES) and new UES short form. Int. J. Hum Comput Stud. **112**, 28–39 (2018). https://doi.org/10.1016/j.ijhcs.2018.01.004
12. Menard, E., Khashman, N.: Image retrieval behaviours: users are leading the way to a new bilingual search interface. Library Hi Tech **32**(1), 50–68 (2014). https://doi.org/10.1108/LHT-06-2013-0067
13. GITHUB. https://github.com/mertseker-dev/advanced_image_search_tool
14. Borlund, P.: A study of the use of simulated work task situations in interactive information retrieval evaluations. J. Doc. **72**(3), 394–413 (2016). https://doi.org/10.1108/JD-06-2015-0068
15. Korkeamäki, L., Keskustalo, H., Kumpulainen, S.: Task information types related to data gathering in media studies. J. Doc. **78**(7), 528–545 (2022). https://doi.org/10.1108/JD-04-2022-0082
16. Barbuti, N.: From digital cultural heritage to digital culture: evolution in digital humanities. In: Proceedings of the 1st International Conference on Digital Tools and Uses Congress (DTUC 2018). Association for Computing Machinery, New York, Article 21, pp. 1–3 (2018)

Ranking for Learning: Studying Users' Perceptions of Relevance, Understandability, and Engagement

Yasin Ghafourian[1,2]([⊠]) [ID], Allan Hanbury[2] [ID], and Petr Knoth[3] [ID]

[1] The Research Studios Austria FG, Vienna 1090, Austria
yasin.ghafourian@researchstudio.at
[2] Technische Universität Wien, Vienna 1040, Austria
[3] Knowledge Media Institute, The Open University, Milton Keynes, UK

Abstract. General-purpose search engines are frequently used to retrieve content for learning. However, their ranking strategies are typically optimised for relevance, which means that they do not take into account other criteria important in the learning context, such as the understandability and the degree of engagement of the retrieved resources. We have conducted a user study to assess the extent to which ranking algorithms used by a popular search engine satisfy the expectations of users who are learning by searching. We study the relationships between users' perceptions of topical relevance, engagement, and understandability for retrieved documents with respect to their ranks. While we observe that the perceived user-assigned rank is strongly associated with all dimensions of relevance under study, specifically engagement ($\rho = 0.89$), understandability ($\rho = 0.58$) and topical relevance ($\rho = 0.88$), the relationship between SERP ranks and user-assigned ranks appears unstable, indicating that learners are not necessarily always served well by general-purpose search engines.

Keywords: Information Retrieval · Search as Learning · Background Knowledge · Relevance · Understandability · Engagement

1 Introduction

Search engines have become vital tools for students and researchers [2,3,17], offering access to vast academic libraries and up-to-date research, and there is a growing trend of using web searches as a means of acquiring new knowledge [6,10]. Search engine users interested in learning may have diverse levels of background knowledge in a topic. However, search engines overlook this variation and assume that users' queries adequately represent their information needs [14]. The reason is that search engines are optimised for topical relevance even though relevance is a multidimensional concept consisting of other perspectives such as understandability, novelty, utility, reliability, etc. as well [8,16,19,25].

O. Alonso et al. (Eds.): TPDL 2023, LNCS 14241, pp. 284–291, 2023.
https://doi.org/10.1007/978-3-031-43849-3_25

Additionally, user context such as the user's knowledge state, perceptions, etc., also influence how users interpret the relevance of available online resources [15].

If search engines considered users' background knowledge, they could provide learning resources that match their needs, saving time and effort by avoiding lengthy searches and useless documents. The relationship between user contexts related to knowledge, such as knowledge gain [10,26], knowledge state [27], and the evaluation of information retrieval (IR) systems considering users' cognition and knowledge [4,9,11,24] have been examined from different perspectives in the literature. Previous studies have also highlighted the importance of the users' knowledge dimension [1,5] in creating and evaluating information needs, its effect on user behaviour, and the choice of web pages to read [7,12,23].

In this paper, we are building on top of the existing research by conducting an exploratory study to investigate in more detail how users' background knowledge affects their perception of relevance along three dimensions of relevance in the context of learning. We seek to answer the following research question:

Research Question: To what degree do users find the specific order of web pages provided on a Search Engine's Results page (SERP) suitable for learning?

Our methodology is based on a survey design and proceeds by first collecting data focused on participants' preferences for learning about a topic based on a set of web pages from the topic. We asked the participants to re-rank the web pages and at the same time label them along 3 dimensions of relevance: 1) topical relevance, 2) understandability, and 3) engagement.

To the best of our knowledge, our research is the first study that employs explicit individual re-rankings and relevance feedback along three dimensions to look into how users with varying levels of topic-specific knowledge exhibit differences in their perceived understandability, relevance, and engagement towards SERP web pages and how these differences are reflected in different ranking preferences compared to an algorithm's ranking.

The rest of the paper is structured as follows: Sect. 2 outlines our methodology, including a description of how our study is formulated, and how the data is collected. In Sect. 3, we present our findings after processing and analysing the collected data. Section 4 reflects on the study and concludes the paper.

2   Methodology

Our methodology employs a survey design to gather explicit relevance feedback from online participants' preferences for learning about a specific topic. To ensure the success and accuracy of our experiments, we had initiated a pilot study with a group of 14 Ph.D. students to identify any areas that required revision and confirm the effectiveness of our research methods. Subsequently, we launched the revised survey with a larger sample of participants.

We selected a set of four topics for our research, and for each topic, following the established method in the literature [6,10,20,26], we prepared a multichoice question knowledge test with 10 questions using available online quizzes in a survey to assess the participants' current knowledge on that topic (Urgo et al.

[22] summarises various types of knowledge assessment used in the literature).
Before the quiz, participants were also asked to self-assess their topical knowledge
on a 5-point Likert scale. The topics have been chosen in a way that maintains
a balance between being specific enough to be informative and not too narrow
to limit their relevance to the general population. The topics are: 1) Covid-19,
2) World War 2, 3) Financial Literacy, and 4) Theory of General Relativity.
Subsequently, we sampled 10 web pages from the web for each of the topics. The
participants were then instructed to re-rank the given web pages in descending
order of how suitable they found the web pages for learning about the topic.
Pages were presented as clickable links with randomized order for each user to
mitigate user rank selection bias [18] (AKA trust bias [13]). Simultaneously, they
were asked to provide three labels for each web page on a 5/7 point Likert scale:
1) topical relevance, 2) understandability, and 3) level of engagement offered
by the web page meaning its motivational value for learning about the topic.
The decision to limit the number of web pages to 10 in our study was based on
insights gained from the pilot study, as it was found to be the largest number of
articles that users could effectively sort within the available time.

We recruited participants from Prolific[1], specifically selecting those with a
high level of English proficiency from continental Europe and the UK. A total of
207 participants were included, each topic having 50–56 exclusive participants.

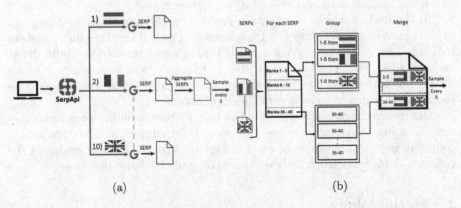

Fig. 1. An overview of our sampling approach to collect web pages for re-ranking and
labeling. (a) Collecting SERPs from different locations. (b) Merging SERPs.

To find topic-related web pages, we used keywords and phrases from knowledge tests to form a representative query for the topic. We selected the top
10 phrases and keywords with the highest TF-IDF score [21] calculated against
Wikipedia dump[2] as a background corpus. To sample web pages, we used Google

---

[1] https://www.prolific.co/.
[2] https://dumps.wikimedia.org/enwiki/20221220.

as the search engine and SerpAPI[3] as the tool to retrieve results in a machine-readable format (In our case XML). To ensure consistent search engine results pages (SERPs) among survey participants, we submitted each query 10 times at 10-minute intervals from various locations in our participant pool. The 10 SERPs obtained per query were merged on the page level with 5 links per page. Finally, a webpage was sampled from each page on the merged SERP, resulting in a total of 10 web pages. Higher weighting was given to pages appearing in multiple SERPs and having higher ranks. We excluded links to books, PDFs, and video links to focus on multimedia web pages consisting primarily of textual content. The sampling approach is depicted in Fig. 1.

3   Results

3.1   Participants' Demographics, Self-declared Vs Demonstrated Knowledge

Table 1 provides an overview of the participants who participated in each of the four topics, including their demographic distribution, the average declared knowledge on the topic, and the average score obtained after taking the knowledge test. The participants were well-balanced in terms of their gender across the four topics. Most participants were in the age group 25–44.

Table 1. An overview of participants' demographics and characteristics. The average declared knowledge is reported using a 5-point Likert scale and the attained average knowledge test scores are mapped to the same scale to allow comparison.

Topic Name	Number of Participants	Time Spent on the Survey (Minutes)		Gender Distribution			Age Distribution					Average Declared Knowledge (1–5)	Average Knowledge Test Score	Difference between Declared Knowledge Score and Test Score
		Mean	Standard Deviation	Female	Male	Other	18–24	25–34	35–44	45–54	55+			
World War 2	56	21.25	10.37	44%	56%	0%	5%	51%	22%	15%	7%	3.4	3.48 (62%)	0.08
Financial Literacy	51	22.10	10.12	45%	55%	0%	12%	27%	37%	20%	4%	3.1	3.20 (55%)	0.10
Covid-19	50	18.8	7.41	58%	40%	2%	12%	52%	18%	14%	4%	3.82	2.84 (46%)	0.98
Theory of General Relativity	50	26.62	14.12	44%	54%	2%	4%	38%	28%	24%	6%	2.26	2.32 (33%)	0.06

3.2   SERP Rank vs User-Assigned Rank

We evaluated the alignment between user-assigned ranks and SERP ranks by comparing the average assigned rank for each web page with its corresponding SERP rank. The relationship between the two ranks varied significantly across the four topics (Fig. 2). We found low-moderate positive correlations for two

---

[3] https://serpapi.com.

topics where users were more knowledgeable (WW2 & Finance) but strong negative and no correlations for the other two topics. This result was surprising, and it suggests two possible explanations: (1) Search engines may not reliably retrieve the most suitable documents for learners' needs across different topics. (2) Learners with limited knowledge of a topic may struggle to evaluate and rank documents appropriately. Both phenomena could contribute to this outcome.

3.3 Engagement, Topical Relevance, and Understandability as a Function of User-Assigned Rank

We conducted an analysis of the Likert-scale labels that the participants assigned to each of the web pages for topical relevance, engagement, and understandability. We wanted to understand to what extent they are associated with the user-assigned ranks. This is important as it will help us to understand the extent to which these dimensions of relevance should be taken into account when building, and potentially personalising, search engine for learners.

As these labels were assessed using a Likert scale, we converted the indicated perceptions into numeric values. To facilitate a comparison between ranks and these labels, we converted the Likert scale values so that a lower value indicated a higher preference. For example, "Very Engaging" in the engagement label was assigned the value of 1, while "Not Engaging at all" received the value of 5. Figure 3, reports on the relationship between the average user-assigned rank of the web pages and the average-assigned value for engagement, topical relevance,

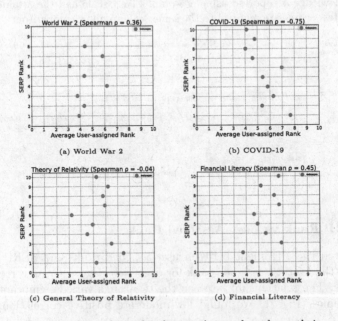

(a) World War 2

(b) COVID-19

(c) General Theory of Relativity

(d) Financial Literacy

Fig. 2. Comparative scatter plots of web pages' actual rank vs their average user-assigned rank across the four analysed topics.

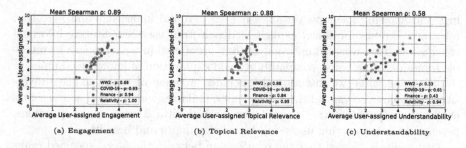

Fig. 3. Spearman correlations between average rankings and average values of (a) engagement, (b) relevance, and (c) understandability of web pages across four topics.

and understandability. We observe that user-assigned rank is strongly correlated with engagement ($\rho = 0.89$) and topical relevance ($\rho = 0.88$) while also medium-strongly correlated with understandability ($\rho = 0.58$). This confirms that both engagement and understandability, are two characteristics of retrieved content that are important to learners as well as topical relevance.

Furthermore, we noticed that in topics "World War 2" and "Financial Literacy", the average user-assigned ranks have a weaker correlation with average user-assigned understandability value compared to engagement and topical relevance. This observation suggests that in topics where our users were more knowledgeable, the understandability of the texts played a relatively less important role compared to perceived topical relevance and engagement. Additionally, we noted a higher correlation between the average assigned rank and the perceived understandability of web pages for the two topics where users possessed a lower average knowledge level, namely "General Theory of Relativity" and "COVID-19," compared to the other two topics. This implies that for topics that users know less about, the understandability of the web pages becomes a more crucial factor to be considered by search engines. Reflecting on the alignments observed between user ranks and SERP ranks across all topics, our data suggest that the original SERP ranking may not have adequately accounted for the understandability of web pages, as an increased emphasis on understandability in users' specified rankings leads to decreased agreement with the SERP ranking. The findings of this analysis highlight the role of perceived engagement, understandability, and topical relevance as factors that determine users' preferred rankings.

4   Discussion and Conclusion

In this paper, we explored in more detail how search engine users perceive the relevance of the SERP results rankings along different dimensions when viewing the results for learning purposes. We have conducted a user study in which we asked online users to re-rank a set of web pages from SERP and asked them to provide labels for these web pages along three dimensions of relevance as well.

Our work has a notable strength in its unique approach of organizing web pages for all participants within each topic, ensuring comparability of rankings and allowing focus on variables like background knowledge and perceived relevance. We also obtained explicit feedback from users, facilitating informed conclusions. However, a limitation is that users couldn't participate in multiple topics, limiting result comparability and exploration of knowledge influence. Additionally, while we intentionally included a range of topics to have diversity, the topics also vary in their complexity, making generalisation across topics challenging. Furthermore, our evaluation relied on a limited set of questions, potentially not capturing users' full knowledge depth and breadth.

Our analysis showed that the relationship between the users' specified ranks and the SERP ranks ranges from low-moderate to strongly correlated, suggesting that delivered search engine ranks were found on average unsuitable by users for learning. Moreover, our findings showed that along with topical relevance, engagement, and understandability are also other aspects of the web pages that are significant to learners having moderate-strong correlations with user ranks.

Acknowledgements. This work was supported by the EU Horizon 2020 ITN/ETN on Domain Specific Systems for Information Extraction and Retrieval - DoSSIER (H2020-EU.1.3.1., ID: 860721).

References

1. Anderson, L.W., Bloom, B.S., et al.: A Taxonomy for Learning, Teaching, and Assessing: a Revision of Bloom's Taxonomy of Educational Objectives. Longman, London (2001)
2. Apuke, O.D., Iyendo, T.O.: University students' usage of the internet resources for research and learning: forms of access and perceptions of utility. Heliyon 4(12), e01052 (2018)
3. Sure, Y., Domingue, J. (eds.): ESWC 2006. LNCS, vol. 4011. Springer, Heidelberg (2006). https://doi.org/10.1007/11762256
4. Bailey, P., et al.: User task understanding: a web search engine perspective. In: NII Shonan Meeting on Whole-Session Evaluation of Interactive Information Retrieval Systems, Kanagawa, Japan (2012)
5. Bloom, B.: Taxonomy of educational objectives, handbook i: The Cognitive Domain. New York: David Mckay Co Inc. as cited in file. D:/bloom. html (1956)
6. Câmara, A., Roy, N., Maxwell, D., Hauff, C.: Searching to learn with instructional scaffolding. In: Proceedings of the 2021 Conference on Human Information Interaction and Retrieval, pp. 209–218 (2021)
7. Cole, M.J., Zhang, X., Liu, C., Belkin, N.J., Gwizdka, J.: Knowledge effects on document selection in search results pages. In: Proceedings of the 34th International ACM SIGIR Conference on Research and Development in Information Retrieval, pp. 1219–1220 (2011)
8. Cosijn, E., Ingwersen, P.: Dimensions of relevance. Inf. Process. Manage. 36(4), 533–550 (2000)
9. El Zein, D., da Costa Pereira, C.: User's knowledge and information needs in information retrieval evaluation. In: Proceedings of the 30th ACM Conference on User Modeling, Adaptation and Personalization, pp. 170–178 (2022)
10. Gadiraju, U., Yu, R., Dietze, S., Holtz, P.: Analyzing knowledge gain of users in informational search sessions on the web. In: Proceedings of the 2018 Conference on Human Information Interaction & Retrieval, pp. 2–11 (2018)

11. Ghafourian, Y., Knoth, P., Hanbury, A.: Information retrieval evaluation in knowledge acquisition tasks. In: Proceedings of the Third Workshop on Evaluation of Personalisation in Information Retrieval (WEPIR) @ CHIIR, pp. 88–95 (2021)
12. Jansen, B.J., Booth, D., Smith, B.: Using the taxonomy of cognitive learning to model online searching. Inf. Process. Manage. **45**(6), 643–663 (2009)
13. Joachims, T., Granka, L., Pan, B., Hembrooke, H., Radlinski, F., Gay, G.: Evaluating the accuracy of implicit feedback from clicks and query reformulations in web search. ACM Trans. Inf. Syst. (TOIS) **25**(2), 7-es (2007)
14. Kelly, D., Belkin, N.J.: A user modeling system for personalized interaction and tailored retrieval in interactive IR. Proc. Am. Soc. Inf. Sci. Technol. **39**(1), 316–325 (2002)
15. Liu, J., Liu, C., Belkin, N.J.: Personalization in text information retrieval: a survey. J. Assoc. Inf. Sci. Technol. **71**(3), 349–369 (2020)
16. Mao, J., et al.: When does relevance mean usefulness and user satisfaction in web search? In: Proceedings of the 39th International ACM SIGIR conference on Research and Development in Information Retrieval, pp. 463–472 (2016)
17. Marchionini, G.: Exploratory search: from finding to understanding. Commun. ACM **49**(4), 41–46 (2006)
18. Pan, B., Hembrooke, H., Joachims, T., Lorigo, L., Gay, G., Granka, L.: In google we trust: users' decisions on rank, position, and relevance. J. Comput.-Mediated Commun. **12**(3), 801–823 (2007)
19. Pasi, G.: Contextual search: issues and challenges. In: Holzinger, A., Simonic, K.-M. (eds.) USAB 2011. LNCS, vol. 7058, pp. 23–30. Springer, Heidelberg (2011). https://doi.org/10.1007/978-3-642-25364-5_3
20. Roy, N., Moraes, F., Hauff, C.: Exploring users' learning gains within search sessions. In: Proceedings of the 2020 Conference on Human Information Interaction and Retrieval, pp. 432–436 (2020)
21. Salton, G., Buckley, C.: Term-weighting approaches in automatic text retrieval. Inf. Process. Manage. **24**(5), 513–523 (1988)
22. Urgo, K., Arguello, J.: Learning assessments in search-as-learning: a survey of prior work and opportunities for future research. Inf. Process. Manage. **59**(2), 102821 (2022)
23. Vakkari, P.: Searching as learning: a systematization based on literature. J. Inf. Sci. **42**(1), 7–18 (2016)
24. Vakkari, P., Völske, M., Potthast, M., Hagen, M., Stein, B.: Modeling the usefulness of search results as measured by information use. Inf. Process. Manage. **56**(3), 879–894 (2019)
25. Xu, Y., Chen, Z.: Relevance judgment: what do information users consider beyond topicality? J. Am. Soc. Inf. Sci. Technol. **57**(7), 961–973 (2006)
26. Yu, R., Gadiraju, U., Holtz, P., Rokicki, M., Kemkes, P., Dietze, S.: Predicting user knowledge gain in informational search sessions. In: The 41st International ACM SIGIR Conference on Research & Development in Information Retrieval, pp. 75–84 (2018)
27. Yu, R., Tang, R., Rokicki, M., Gadiraju, U., Dietze, S.: Topic-independent modeling of user knowledge in informational search sessions. Inf. Retrieval J. **24**(3), 240–268 (2021). https://doi.org/10.1007/s10791-021-09391-7

Digital Humanities

Image Modification Modeled
as a Storytelling Process

Ergun Akleman[1] , Filipe Castro[2] , and Richard Furuta[1(✉)]

[1] Texas A&M University, College Station, TX 77843, USA
{akleman,furuta}@tamu.edu
[2] Universidade de Coimbra, Center for Functional Ecology, Coimbra, Portugal
luis.castro@uc.pt
https://cfe.uc.pt/

Abstract. Digital libraries have focused on change to images from the perspectives of prevention and reversal. Since change is a required component of scholarship, we seek to adding the modeling of change to support its characterization. In this paper we discuss change to images in traditional media and propose a formal model of that change. The subject calls for a kaleidoscopic approach as tracking changes in images is an interesting exercise in storytelling, both when one looks at deliberately changing them with a purpose and at tracking past changes.

Keywords: Image modification · Storytelling perspective · Modeling instead of managing change

1 Introduction

The holdings of a library—books, photos, paintings, and so forth—are snapshots taken from the evolution of their creators' intellectual activity. At times, they represent the culmination of the activity (e.g., a book whose author moves to other topics once it has been sent to the publisher). In others, they are a waypoint in a continuing process. The holdings themselves—the artifacts—may be static or they themselves may continue to change (e.g., [12]). However, in a traditional library, the permanence of the holdings' substrate (e.g., paper) tends to lead to the view that the content of the objects is fixed.

In digital libraries, the impermanence of the digital substrate has led to substantial efforts to provide more long-lived storage (e.g., LOCKSS [16]), to save the state of information over time (e.g., the Internet Archive [13]), and to detect the change and resurrect earlier content (see, e.g., [9] and [21]). It is relevant to note, though, that even when library objects are fixed, they continue to be staged along the progression of intellectual activity—e.g., copyright law protects specific collections of *words* but not *ideas* [5], although the questions about how copyright affects digital creativity are significant [10].

Understanding the progression of development of an artifact and how it evolves into another requires a new focus on modeling change. Further, change cannot be interpreted in a vacuum; we also must recognize the need to incorporate the "intent" of the change in the analysis of the change (or of multiple, conflicting, intentions). We focus on images in our initial work, as they require a more complex representation than linear text. In this paper, we first begin by turning our attention to the ways in which images have been transformed over time. We recognize that many contexts surround image transformation, which can be viewed as different "narratives" or "stories," which can be separated from the actual changes. This allows us to propose a formal model for image change. Finally, we discuss briefly some of the uses and implications of the model.

2   Images

Images are seldom static. They exist in a time arrow and are experienced in different ways as time passes. Painters regularly produce preparatory studies and often modify the original paintings. In 1888 and 1889, van Gogh painted five different versions of his famous "Sunflowers." He is not alone. Edvard Munch painted four versions of "The Scream," and on another note, in 1958 Pablo Picasso painted 58 studies of Diego Velazquez's famous 1656 painting "Las Meninas".

Fig. 1. The seven sunflower pictures painted by Vincent van Gogh in Arles, France between 1888 and 1889. It is ordered left to right based on the time order. The first one is in a private collection, the second one was destroyed during World War II. The rest of them are in the Neue Pinakothek Museum in Munich, the National Gallery in London, the Philadelphia Museum of Art, the van Gogh Museum, in Amsterdam, and the Seiji Togo Memorial Sompo Japan Museum of Art, in Tokyo.

Like Picasso, painters sometimes reproduce the work of other painters. But the mere process of reproducing images is a form of transformation, as the process of digitizing an image will introduce distortions. For example, digital images circulating on the Internet are often cropped and have different aspect ratios and colors.

Another type of modification, less common, are fakes. These are images painted or modeled in the style of a known artist. They have sometimes been used to cheat gullible buyers, but they are interesting on a different level because they are produced in the style of a particular artist and raise a number of questions associated with what makes an artist's style. A history of fake images will certainly include wrongly attributed works of art.

It is important to distinguish between modifications and fakes because modifications range from the simplest cropping of part of an image, to Banksy's ironic remake of Millet's "Des glaneuses," or to Stalin's suppression of figures in official pictures. Modeling the relationships among images' sources will secure the integrity of the process and ensure that the resulting findings are trustworthy and reliable.

There are laws and regulations that apply to the use, change, and re-use of images [5]. Copyright laws forbid a wide range of reproductions and changes of original images, but we argue that these rules are not always fair or productive. Developing a model that tracks changes seems to us a better strategy than the blanket prohibitions imposed by copyright laws, and we believe that it opens a wide range of possibilities for both artistic and scholarly work. Modifying an image may reinforce its meaning or change it in ways that can serve an intellectual purpose.

By transforming an image, we risk losing important context and thereby erasing or distorting the historical record. As Johanna Drucker writes, "When images are dissociated from their historical or cultural contexts, the ability to misrepresent, misuse, and abuse them grows exponentially" ([7] p. 98). Still, there are interesting alterations, such as albums about Hergé's hero Tintin, which changed markedly between reprints. The story "L'Ile Noire" was re-written and partially re-drawn by another cartoonist, Bob de Moor, who had a better grasp on Scotland—the place where the action takes place—than Hergé [22].

Modifications can be considered good or bad depending on the context within which they are interpreted. Our approach will distinguish between mechanism and policy. We will separate the process of change and the change in content. For instance, ships represented in the backgrounds of paintings are often copied from stock images and to establish a genealogy for images and their symbolic value. Maritime archaeologist Kotaro Yamafune (2012) demonstrated that the Portuguese naus represented in the famous Namban Screens were copied from a small collection of books offered by Pope Gregory XIII in 1582 to the Japanese Christian embassy to Rome, the Tensho Embassy [27].

Repurposing is a way to provide different viewpoints from which to interpret what we know. Examples range from the correction of perspective to changes in the environment, such as redressing the people represented, or emphasizing secondary characters. Another application of purposeful modification is pointing out hidden symbology and relating it to the cultural and social contexts where an image was produced, its archetypes and ambivalence.

3   Narrative Structures for Images

We propose a storytelling-centered methodology based on Forster's categorization of narrative structures over events into two levels: (1) Story: A chronological sequence of events (2) Plot: A causal and logical structure which connects events [8]. To represent image modifications we view every image as an event. From this view, a story over images always exists. For instance, images in archives are time-stamped by providing evidence for originals. Consider our earlier van Gogh example; there are several originals, all painted from an original idea and there is no physical connection between the originals. However, they are created at different times and these times are known by creating a story for them.

Outside the archives there is no original, and images are rarely fixed. They have stories since temporal information exists. Images are fluid and change with time. In many ways, each restored version is an interpretation of the original and can be the source of other modifications. Painters make successive studies or revisit a subject of a particular subject. Changed versions can become icons, like Banksy's "Cigarette Break." Stories cannot have cycles in the representation of things: broken statues or sculptures can be repaired, but the result is no longer the original, ancestral form.

Although the story is a common narrative form for images, the plots rarely exist since to construct a plot we need a causal and logical structure [18] that can connect the images [1,15]. To develop a plot there is a need for something beyond temporal information. We need to reconstruct a causal and logical structure that connects images. This requires a formal structure. This causal information can provide an answer to the six journalism questions in the form of what, why, when, where, who, and how about the change, or "What is the modification?", "Why was the modification made?", "When was the modification made?", "Where was the modification made?", "Who made the modification?", and "How was the modification made?". Since answers to these questions may not exist, we do not require an answer to each of them to classify a structure as a plot, but we need to identify a casual correspondence between two images: one as an original and another as its modification. Note that the modified image must always have a larger time stamp and the original image can still be a modification of another image. Now, we are ready to describe a mathematical model to describe a plot structure among images.

4   A Mathematical Model for Plot Structure Among Images

A story structure for images should be simple, consisting of a disconnected set of elements. Each image can have additional information to a time stamp. However, there should be no casual connection between the images. A set of images can be considered as a set of disconnected vertices. Regardless of how much information we have about each one of them, we cannot form any connection between any two of them. A good example of the story of images is seven paintings shown in Fig. 1. We know when there were created, where, who made them, and where are they now. On the other hand, we have no information to construct any causal connection between them.

Now, let us consider existing historical knowledge about these paintings. Art historians know that van Gogh painted the number five by copying the number three of Fig. 1 [3]. He also copied the number four to paint numbers six and seven. If we draw an arrow between these originals and their modifications, we

Fig. 2. Vincent van Gogh's sunflowers reorganized as a plot, with a causality relation between them. Note that just adding arrows made it clear that there are actually four distinct paintings. There is a copy of the third one (fifth) and two copies of the fourth one (sixth and seventh).

obtain the structure shown in Fig. 2. We can classify them into four distinct paintings with modifications.

If we consider arrows as directed edges and each painting as a vertex, this structure becomes a graph consisting of disconnected pieces. Each of the disconnected pieces must be a directed acyclic graph (DAG) [23,25] since it cannot have a loop. These directed acyclic graphs will not necessarily be trees, since a modification can have more than a single parent. Good examples of multiple parental images come from academic painters of the 19th century who used multiple photographs to create paintings as collages of images [6,28]. This formalization of using directed acyclic graphs is also in sync with causality theory, which essentially builds upon DAG structures [17]. The directed edges carry the information about the modifications answering six journalism questions. For instance, consider the directed edge connecting image six and image seven in Fig. 2. Six was extended on all sides at a later time. It is generally thought that the first owner, Émile Schuffenecker, made the extension [3]. Similar pieces of information, along with disagreement among experts, should be included in the directed edges.

Directed acyclic graphs allow the representation of the successive nature of images, in which each vertex can be a new version and each directed edge is a relation between versions. Directed acyclic graphs also allow us to trace the evolution of an image. We can use two directed acyclic graphs, one showing the evolution from the original to the present versions; and one in the form of a DAG, establishing a genealogy of every image. In this case, if we view the two edges in opposing directions, as an undirected edge, the combined structure will be a cyclic graph [25].

The creation of directed acyclic graphs is essentially a forensic activity. Each modification is perceived and experienced differently and may be considered an enrichment or a simplification of a story as if we were trying to analyze a collage. These directed acyclic graphs connecting related images help to analyze arcs of intention, such as changing a narrative by deleting a political enemy from a picture [20]. This is important today, since current graphics tools made it easy to modify photographs [2]. People routinely manipulate images to create fake narratives [24]. The directed acyclic graph structure can provide context and help to identify and characterize such fake narratives by creating a meta-narrative.

5   Discussion, Future Work, and Conclusions

This paper proposes a theoretical model to represent changes in images. Applying graph theory will allow analysis and characterization of changes within the context provided by "story lines". Although our examples have presented the organization of image change as a single directed graph, there are multiple and independent contexts for the interpretation of image change. In developing our model we have taken inspiration from the concept of separation of mechanism and policy, as introduced in operating system design [11,14,26]. Our model represents a *mechanism* that can be used to reflect different and potentially conflicting interpretations for the causes of change (i.e., different *policies*). In a sense, this is analogous to Propp's reduction of Russian fairy tales to a compact set of twenty-five basic functions [19].

Given the structure provided by the model, a second layer of analysis could focus on the socio-cultural environment where images change. The forensic side of this methodology will help us establish chronologies, and to interpret the changes in relation to the time and place where they were modified. Although we cannot specify intent, we can try to make sense of the changes and what we know about the contexts where they happened. We propose to develop models that can shed some light on changes in images. On another level, with a large enough sample of images, it may be possible to develop theories to analyze certain types of images. Perspective is a good code that can be broken and understood. Lines of force, the use of golden ratios, composition lines such as the horizon, vertical lines, volumes, and colors, or light and shadow. Inconsistencies are part of a work of art because they create tensions.

Walter Benjamin [4] argued that the traditional value of an original work of art was based on its uniqueness and authenticity, and that the mechanical reproduction of images radically changed their meaning and value. For Benjamin mechanical reproduction could help disseminate revolutionary ideas and promote action, making the dissemination of art a weapon of the proletariat and a democratic instrument to question the status quo and empower the masses [4].[1] For us, the availability of images on media like the Internet opens a world of creativity and a plethora of applications of modifications of images with even more potential to empower the masses.

A first, and critical step in interpreting and understanding the effect of changes to images is to be able to represent the changes in a formal, consistent, neutral, and analyzable model. This promises to provide us with the basis to work towards understanding the various motivations behind the changes as well as their varying effects.

---

[1] It is also interesting to analyze how Walter Benjamin could view the concept NFTs [4] and how DAGs can be used to classify and organize digital artworks.

References

1. Akleman, E., Franchi, S., Kaleci, D., Mandell, L., Yamauchi, T., Akleman, D.: A theoretical framework to represent narrative structures for visual storytelling. In: Proceedings of Bridges 2015: Mathematics, Music, Art, Architecture, Culture, pp. 129–136 (2015)
2. Avidan, S., Shamir, A.: Seam carving for content-aware image resizing. In: ACM SIGGRAPH 2007 Papers, pp. 10-es (2007)
3. Bailey, M.: The Sunflowers are Mine: The Story of Van Gogh's Masterpiece. White Lion Publishing, London (2019)
4. Benjamin, W.: The Work of Art in the Age of Mechanical Reproduction. Penguin, UK (2008)
5. Boyle, J.: The Public Domain: Enclosing the Commons of the Mind. Yale University Press, New Haven (2008)
6. Çakmak, G.: The panoramic studium in nineteenth-century history painting: Paul delaroche and jean-léon gérôme. In: Mobility and Fantasy in Visual Culture, pp. 69–79. Routledge (2014)
7. Drucker, J.: Humanities approaches to graphical display. Digit. Humanit. Q. **5**(1) (2011)
8. Forster, E.M.: Aspects of the Novel. Harcourt, Brace, San Diego (1927)
9. Francisco-Revilla, L., Shipman, F., Furuta, R., Karadkar, U., Arora, A.: Managing change on the web. In: Proceedings of the First ACM/IEEE-CS Joint Conference on Digital Libraries, pp. 66–76 (2001)
10. Garnett, J., Meiselas, S.: On the Rights of Molotov Man. Harper's Magazine, New York (2007)
11. Hansen, P.B.: The evolution of operating systems. In: Hansen, P.B. (ed.) Classic Operating Systems: From Batch Processing to Distributed Systems. Springer, New York (2001). https://doi.org/10.1007/978-1-4757-3510-9_1
12. Jackson, H.J.: Marginalia: Readers Writing in Books. Yale University Press, New Haven (2001)
13. Jaffe, E., Kirkpatrick, S.: Architecture of the internet archive. In: Proceedings of SYSTOR 2009: The Israeli Experimental Systems Conference. SYSTOR '09. Association for Computing Machinery, New York (2009). https://doi.org/10.1145/1534530.1534545
14. Levin, R., Cohen, E., Corwin, W., Pollack, F., Wulf, W.: Policy/mechanism separation in hydra. In: Proceedings of the Fifth ACM Symposium on Operating Systems Principles, pp. 132–140 (1975)
15. Liu, Y., Akleman, E., Chen, J.: Never-ending storytelling with discrete-time Markov processes. In: Proceedings of Bridges 2012: Mathematics, Music, Art, Architecture, Culture, pp. 85–92 (2012)
16. Maniatis, P., Roussopoulos, M., Giuli, T.J., Rosenthal, D.S.H., Baker, M.: The LOCKSS peer-to-peer digital preservation system. ACM Trans. Comput. Syst. **23**(1), 2–50 (2005). https://doi.org/10.1145/1047915.1047917
17. Pearl, J.: Causal diagrams for empirical research. Biometrika **82**(4), 669–688 (1995)
18. Pearl, J.: Causality. University Press, Cambridge (2009)
19. Propp, V.: Morphology of the Folktale, second edn. University of Texas Press, Austin (1928, 1968)
20. Skopin, D.: Photography and Political Repressions in Stalin's Russia: Defacing the Enemy. Routledge, Milton Park (2022)

21. de Sompel, H.V., Nelson, M., Sanderson, R.: HTTP framework for time-based access to resource states - memento. RFC 7089 (2013). https://doi.org/10.17487/RFC7089, https://www.rfc-editor.org/info/rfc7089

22. Thompson, H.: Tintin: Hergé and His Creation. Hachette UK, Paris (2011)

23. Thulasiraman, K., Swamy, M.N.: Graphs: Theory and Algorithms. John Wiley & Sons, Hoboken (2011)

24. Vosoughi, S., Roy, D., Aral, S.: The spread of true and false news online. Science **359**(6380), 1146–1151 (2018)

25. Weisstein, E.W.: Acyclic graph (2023). https://mathworld.wolfram.com/AcyclicGraph.html

26. Wulf, W., et al.: Hydra: the kernel of a multiprocessor operating system. Commun. ACM **17**(6), 337–345 (1974)

27. Yamafune, K.: Portuguese Ships on Japanese Namban Screens. Ph.D. thesis, Texas A & M University (2012)

28. Zalewski, L.M.: The Golden Age of French Academic Painting in America, pp. 1867–1893. City University of New York, New York (2009)

From ISAD(G) to Linked Data Archival Descriptions

Inês Koch(✉) ⓘ, Catarina Pires(✉) ⓘ, Carla Teixeira Lopes(✉) ⓘ,
Cristina Ribeiro(✉) ⓘ, and Sérgio Nunes(✉) ⓘ

INESC TEC and Faculty of Engineering, University of Porto, Porto, Portugal
{ines.koch,catarina.o.pires}@inesctec.pt, {ctl,mcr,ssn}@fe.up.pt

Abstract. Archives preserve materials that allow us to understand and interpret the past and think about the future. With the evolution of the information society, archives must take advantage of technological innovations and adapt to changes in the kind and volume of the information created. Semantic Web representations are appropriate for structuring archival data and linking them to external sources, allowing versatile access by multiple applications. ArchOnto is a new Linked Data Model based on CIDOC CRM to describe archival objects. ArchOnto combines specific aspects of archiving with the CIDOC CRM standard. In this work, we analyze the ArchOnto representation of a set of archival records from the Portuguese National Archives and compare it to their CIDOC CRM representation. As a result of ArchOnto's representation, we observe an increase in the number of classes used, from 20 in CIDOC CRM to 28 in ArchOnto, and in the number of properties, from 25 in CIDOC CRM to 28 in ArchOnto. This growth stems from the refinement of object types and their relationships, favouring the use of controlled vocabularies. ArchOnto provides higher readability for the information in archival records, keeping it in line with current standards.

Keywords: Archival Description · CIDOC CRM · ArchOnto

1 Introduction

Archives play a central role in understanding and interpreting the past. They are a resource from which we reflect and attempt to revisit what has already transpired [11]. The content of public archives is part of humanity's knowledge heritage for present and future generations. It is essential to safeguard and ensure the continued accessibility of archives [10]. As the information society moves forward, archives face new challenges, among which is the increase in the amount of information produced, specifically information from the digital world. Most documents today are created electronically [7].

The change in information access habits increased the need for digitally available archives. However, access is only one requirement when people explore an extensive collection, such as public archives. Archives should also follow the other FAIR Principles [15], which include findability, interoperability, and reusability.

O. Alonso et al. (Eds.): TPDL 2023, LNCS 14241, pp. 303–309, 2023.
https://doi.org/10.1007/978-3-031-43849-3_27

This work aims to analyze the representation of existing archival records in the Portuguese National Archives using ArchOnto. ArchOnto is a modular ontology developed within the scope of the EPISA Project that introduces a set of specific classes and properties.

To understand the impact of using a Linked Data Model to represent archival records, we compare the representations of a sample of documents in CIDOC CRM and ArchOnto. The impact is measured in terms of applicability in archives.

2   Background

The Portuguese National Archives curate a unique collection of historical and contemporary objects accumulated since the 9th century, distributed among the various institutions that compose the archives. The National Archives comprise two national archives and 16 regional archives at the district level. It curates over 3,5 million records described through a combination of the various standards for archival description developed by the International Council on Archives (ICA), namely the ISAD(G) – General International Standard Archival Description [3], and the ISAAR(CPF) – International Standard Archival Authority Record for Corporate Bodies, Persons and Families [4].

Among the assets held by this institution are a large number of Fonds, which are organized in groups, namely Central and Local Administration; Collections; Companies; Judicial; Monastics; Notaries; Parish; and Personal. Collections include records from previous political systems; records from contemporary, ecclesiastical, monastic, and conventual institutions; records of archives of individuals, families, associations, companies, commissions, and congresses; and records of photographic archives [8].

In the archival domain, efforts have been made to develop a data model to represent the archival assets. ICA is developing the RiC-CM (Records in Context Conceptual Model) and RiC-O (RiC-Ontology) to illustrate archival concepts, considering the main descriptive entities [5]. As this model was still preliminary when this work started, CIDOC CRM emerged as the model to use.

The CIDOC Conceptual Reference Model (CRM) is a formal ontology developed in the scope of museums by the International Committee for Documentation (CIDOC) of the International Council of Museums (ICOM). It intends to facilitate the integration, mediation and interchange of heterogeneous cultural heritage information and similar information from other domains [2]. It is under active development by the CIDOC CRM Special Interest Group. It is the only ontology in the Cultural Heritage domain accepted as an ISO standard (ISO 21127:2014) [6]. It has events as a central concept and provides a detailed description of people, places, and periods [1].

ArchOnto [8,9] is a modular ontology developed in the scope of the EPISA Project. Its classes and properties capture concepts that contribute to specific aspects of an archival organization. The ontology also specializes CIDOC CRM to include controlled vocabularies used in the archives. It comprises five ontologies that can be imported whenever needed — CIDOC CRM, N-ary, DataObject,

Link2DataObject, and ISAD Ontology. A prefix identifies each ontology according to Semantic Web best practices.

The CIDOC CRM is the base ontology of ArchOnto and provides the concepts and properties to capture archival records' essential features, e.g., event, date, location, person, and group. N-ary systematically represents non-binary associations, i.e., those that connect more than two individuals. This ontology is based on the CIDOC's early proposal for representing tuples with an arity higher than two. DataObject is an ontology created to handle literal values and their validation. The goal is that each individual with a representation as a simple type, such as a date or a string, is validated against the corresponding DataObject class. Link2DataObject connects DataObject to CIDOC CRM.

Finally, to ensure the integrity of information when migrating data from the legacy description to ArchOnto, the ISAD Ontology was created to represent the entire description expressed with the elements of the ISAD(G) standard. This allows the structured contents in the Linked Data to be validated against the information in the original ISAD(G) record.

3   Linked Data Representation

A sample of archival documents from the Portuguese National Archives was selected to understand and discuss the applicability of ArchOnto and CIDOC CRM in the archival context. The selected sample [13] contains 1,318 records, including Groups of Fonds that stand out among those existing in this National Archive. Among the records represented, 102 relate to the Decentralized Central Administration (*"Registo de Passaportes Deferidos"* about passports from 1914 to 1918), and 1,216 are related to parish records (*"Registos de Baptismo"* about baptisms from 1644 to 1911). This sample considers one series, 16 installation units, and 1,301 items.

The *Baptismo* and *Passaportes* datasets [13] were automatically represented in CIDOC CRM from their ISAD(G) description. The translation is based on rules that map the archival descriptive information to the CIDOC CRM representation semantically [12]. Additionally, the translated information was subject to some refinements to correspond to the same CIDOC CRM version used in ArchOnto. The migration from CIDOC CRM to ArchOnto also followed an automatic approach. The two data models were aligned based on the ontologies, identifying the differences and developing SPARQL Update queries for the required transformations. The result is a valid ArchOnto representation [14].

4   Results and Discussion

We could identify and quantify the classes and properties used in each representation of the selected archival records in CIDOC CRM and ArchOnto. Table 1 show an excerpt[1] of the results obtained when representing all the documents

---

[1] Due to space limitations, we could only place the Top-5 from 2 of the 4 tables. The remaining tables are available in the *Statistics* folder of the dataset in [14].

that are part of the series *Registos de Baptismo* and *Registo de Passaportes Deferidos* in CIDOC CRM and ArchOnto. For each class, we include the number of individuals and, for each property, the number of assertions that use it.

Table 1. Top 5 Classes and Properties in *Registos de Baptismo.*

Ontology	Class	CIDOC	ArchOnto	Ontology	Property	CIDOC	ArchOnto
CIDOC	E52 Time-Span	4,927	4,927	CIDOC	P1 is identified by	12,404	16,134
CIDOC	E21 Person	3,782	3,782	CIDOC	P2 has type	11,035	10,878
CIDOC	E67 Birth	3,367	3,367	Link2DataObject	L2DO has value	0	5,236
CIDOC	E41 Appellation	1,203	2,801	CIDOC	P4 has time-span	3,730	3,730
CIDOC	E53 Place	2,539	2,539	CIDOC	P98 brought into life	3,367	3,367

By CIDOC we mean CIDOC CRM. Full Tables are available in the *Statistics* folder of the dataset in [14].

An automatic and systematic method was used to obtain the results presented in the tables. The results were obtained using a 2-step script. The first step consists of importing the baptism dataset using Apache Jena[2], namely its RDF API, to load the dataset file into a model. In the second step, we count the occurrences of classes and properties and export them to a file in tabular form.

The *Registo de Baptismo* and *Registo de Passaportes Deferidos* representations offer similar results, and the same conclusions can be drawn. As the *Passaportes* dataset is smaller when compared to the *Baptismo* dataset, the results discussed are based on the latter (see Table 1).

Taking into account their specificity, we verified that the ArchOnto representation uses, in total, eight more classes and three more properties than the representation in CIDOC CRM. From a more general perspective, regarding the number of statements in each representation, CIDOC CRM has 151,950 statements, whereas ArchOnto has 160,611 statements, an increase of 6%. Observing the representation of records in the sample, it was possible to see an increase in the number of classes (+16%) and properties (+13%) used in ArchOnto, relative to CIDOC CRM.

Considering the data in the tables, we can see that several classes were used the same number of times. This is the case with generic classes such as *E52 Time-Span*, *E21 Person*, and *E67 Birth*. However, when archival records are represented using ArchOnto, there is a 40% increase in the number of classes used: from 20 classes in CIDOC CRM to 28 in ArchOnto.

Due to its more specific nature, ArchOnto allows a more detailed categorization of concepts related to the archival domain. These concepts consider the existing controlled vocabularies in this area of cultural heritage. Thus, the use of the *E55 Type* class decreased by 21%, going from 24 in the CIDOC CRM representation to 19 in ArchOnto. This results from using eight classes in ArchOnto that allow types specific to archival concepts rather than the more generic CIDOC CRM classes. This is the case with *ARE1 Level of Description* (for the archival hierarchical structure), *ARE2 Formal Title* and *ARE3 Supplied Title* (for titles), and *ARE5 Identifier Type*, *ARE6 Date Type*, *ARE8 Role*

---

[2] https://jena.apache.org.

Type, ARE9 Date Certainty and *ARE14 Place Type* (for more specific types). Most of these classes are subclasses of *E55 Type*, making them a specialization. Among these are the *ARE1 Level of Description, ARE5 Identifier Type, ARE6 Date Type, ARE8 Role Type, ARE9 Date Certainty* and *ARE14 Place Type*. On the other hand, the classes *ARE2 Formal Title* and *ARE3 Supplied Title* are subclasses of *E35 Title*, as the concept of *Title* is also present in CIDOC CRM.

Considering these classes, there is a decrease in the use of classes and properties used to represent the type of a title through a ternary relationship, which happens in the CIDOC CRM representation. With this, in the ArchOnto representation, the *E35 Title* class is no longer used, as well as the *PC102 has title*. Instead, the *ARE2 Formal Title* and *ARE3 Supplied Title* classes appear. Associated with these classes, properties used also differ, with a decrease in the use of *P01 has domain, P02 has range*, and *P102.1 has type*. Although these properties are present in CIDOC CRM, they are organized in the N-ary ontology in ArchOnto. They are therefore used in the same circumstances but taken from a different ontology.

In CIDOC CRM, the classes *E59 Primitive Value* and *E61 Time Primitive* represent time primitives, but information regarding their temporal extent is missing. In ArchOnto, on the other hand, it is possible to distinguish between an instant and a time interval with *DOE10 Instant* and *DOE11 Interval* classes, respectively. This means that the way dates are represented differs, and the classes and properties used are no longer those used in the CIDOC CRM representation. As a result, there is a decrease in the use of these classes and an increase in the expression through the DataObject ontology.

Furthermore, CIDOC CRM does not establish a sufficient distinction between literal values, whereas, in ArchOnto, it is also possible to differentiate strings with the help of DataObject. This is visible in the complete comparison of the left side of Table 1 with the *DOE8 String* and *DOE17 Person Name* classes, where people's names are separate from other strings.

The class that stood out the most was *E41 Appellation*, with an increase of 33%, from 1,203 occurrences in CIDOC CRM to 2,801 in ArchOnto. This happened since, in CIDOC CRM, the literal values were not considered an appellation, contrary to ArchOnto, particularly with DataObject.

As the number of classes increases, there is a subsequent increase in the number of properties used, as seen in the complete comparison of the right-side Table 1. There was an increase of approximately 12% in the present sample when represented in ArchOnto.

With the previously mentioned ArchOnto's temporal extent capabilities, it is possible to define a start and end date time for a time interval (*DOE11 Interval*) with *DOP6 start date value* and *DOP2 end date value* properties, respectively, and, for a time instant, to determine the timestamp associated with the *DOP8 timestamp* property.

The validation of all existing literal values in the ArchOnto representation resulted in an increase (+30%) in the use of the properties *P1 is identified by* and the emergence of the use of the *L2DO has value*, a property that makes the connection of CIDOC CRM to the DataObject ontology.

To preserve the integrity of the original descriptions, the ISAD Ontology contains the property *ISAD18 has note*, where the description referring to the ISAD(G) notes is present. This property corresponds to the CIDOC CRM property *P3 has note*, used for informal notes. It is used in ArchOnto to make sure existing information from archival descriptions is kept throughout the migration.

5   Conclusions

CIDOC CRM is one of the most mature ontologies regarding the representation of cultural objects in Linked Data. Based on events, this model can represent several concepts essential to heritage, such as people, places, and dates. However, the model showed limitations in representing critical elements in archival records. With the use of CIDOC CRM in the archives, it was possible to observe that very distinct concepts had to be mapped to the same class. The most obvious case was *E55 Type*. The examples made it clear that, in ArchOnto, it is possible to distinguish the various "types" with classes that enable the use of specific controlled vocabularies. Therefore, ArchOnto provides a more straightforward application of Linked Data in the archival domain.

With the migration of a collection of real-world records to CIDOC CRM and ArchOnto, it was possible to verify that the more specific "types" provide an appropriate range of classes and properties to be used. ArchOnto also added the validation of simple types using the DataObject ontology.

Representations in ArchOnto provide easier access to individuals associated with the specific types. In CIDOC CRM, this would require following extra relationships. For example, to retrieve all people's names, in ArchOnto, it is only necessary to search for individuals of type *DOE17 Person Name*. In contrast, in CIDOC CRM, we need to search for individuals whose type is *E21 Person* and then follow the respective link to arrive at that person's name.

We found that the records migrated from ISAD(G) considered in this work had a very similar structure, making the results less expressive than expected. However, the values obtained allowed us to conclude that ArchOnto provides greater granularity than CIDOC CRM alone. We conclude that ArchOnto is more expressive than CIDOC CRM, as it supersets the latter and generally favours the use of more specific classes and properties.

In the future, we plan to expand this study by considering a more diverse set of archival records to verify whether other description elements can be extracted at a more specific level. It will be interesting, for example, to extract statistics related to a single document or documents according to their description level.

Acknowledgements. National Funds finance this work through the Portuguese funding agency, FCT – Fundação para a Ciência e a Tecnologia within project DSAIPA/DS/0023/2018. Inês Koch is also financed by National Funds through the Portuguese funding agency, FCT, within the research grant 2020.08755.BD.

References

1. Bruseker, G., Carboni, N., Guillem, A.: Cultural heritage data management: the role of formal ontology and CIDOC CRM. In: Vincent, M.L., López-Menchero Bendicho, V.M., Ioannides, M., Levy, T.E. (eds.) Heritage and Archaeology in the Digital Age. QMHSS, pp. 93–131. Springer, Cham (2017). https://doi.org/10.1007/978-3-319-65370-9_6
2. ICOM/CIDOC CRM special interest group: definition of the CIDOC conceptual reference Model. ICOM, 7.1.2 edn. (2022)
3. International Council on Archives: ISAD(G): General International Standard Archival Description - 2nd edn. International Council on Archives (2000)
4. International Council on Archives: ISAAR (CPF): International Standard Archival Authority Record for Corporate Bodies, Persons and Families, 2nd edn. International Council on Archives (2004)
5. International Council on Archives Expert Group on Archival Description: Records in Context - Conceptual Model. International Council on Archives (2021)
6. ISO Central Secretary: Information and documentation - A reference ontology for the interchange of cultural heritage information. Standard ISO 21127:2014, International Organization for Standardization (2014), https://www.iso.org/standard/57832.html
7. Kampffmeyer, U.: Document life-cycle management for the European public sector industry white papers. In: Proceedings of the DLM-Forum, pp. 52–63 (2002)
8. Koch, I., Lopes, C.T., Ribeiro, C.: Moving from ISAD(G) to a CIDOC CRM based linked data model in the Portuguese archives. J. Comput. Cult. Heritage (JOCCH) (2023)
9. Koch, I., Ribeiro, C., Teixeira Lopes, C.: ArchOnto, a CIDOC-CRM-based linked data model for the Portuguese archives. In: Hall, M., Merčun, T., Risse, T., Duchateau, F. (eds.) TPDL 2020. LNCS, vol. 12246, pp. 133–146. Springer, Cham (2020). https://doi.org/10.1007/978-3-030-54956-5_10
10. Liikanen, U.: The memory of the information society. In: Proceedings of the DLM-Forum, pp. 21–26 (2002)
11. Lyons, B.: Writing archives/crafting order: a critique on the longstanding archival practices of arrangement and description (2009)
12. Melo, D., Rodrigues, I.P., Varagnolo, D.: A strategy for archives metadata representation on CIDOC-CRM and knowledge discovery. Semant. Web 1, 1–32 (2022). https://doi.org/10.3233/sw-222798
13. Melo, D., Rodrigues, I.P., Varagnolo, D.: CIDOC-CRM ontology representation of the Portuguese archival description unit obtained from the semantic migration process of DigitArq. Dataset, INESC TEC (2022). https://doi.org/10.25747/BSW1-TQ51
14. Pires, C., Koch, I., Nunes, S.: ArchOnto ontology representation of Portuguese archival description units (baptism records and passports). Dataset, INESC TEC (2023). https://doi.org/10.25747/x78e-1a27
15. Wilkinson, M.D., et al.: The FAIR guiding principles for scientific data management and stewardship. Sci. Data 3, 1–9 (2016). https://doi.org/10.1038/sdata.2016.18

Detection of Redacted Text in Legal Documents

Ruben van Heusden[(✉)][iD], Aron de Ruijter, Roderick Majoor,
and Maarten Marx[(✉)][iD]

Information Retrieval Lab, Informatics Institute, University of Amsterdam,
Amsterdam, Netherlands
{r.j.vanheusden,maartenmarx}@uva.nl
https://www.irlab.science.uva.nl

Abstract. We present a technique for automatically detecting redacted text in legal documents, using a combination of Optical Character Recognition (OCR) and morphological operations from the Computer Vision domain, allowing us to detect a wide variety of different types of redaction blocks with little to no training data. As this is a segmentation task, we evaluate our technique using the Panoptic Quality methodology, with the algorithm obtaining F1 scores of 0.79, 0.86 and 0.76 on black, colored and outlined redaction blocks respectively, and an F1 score of 0.62 for gray blocks. The total running time of the algorithm is two seconds on average measured on a thousand pages from a government supplier, with roughly 98% of this time being used by Tesseract and the conversion from PDF to PNG, and 2% by the detection algorithm. Detecting text redaction at scale thus is feasible, allowing a more or less objective measurement of this practice.The redacted text detection code and the manually labelled dataset created for evaluation is released via Github.

Keywords: Text Redaction · Image Segmentation · Panoptic Quality

1 Introduction

Redacted text is text that has been made unreadable or has been covered up. This can be due to privacy and legal reasons, or because the text reflects the opinion of an employee, or because of commercial conflicts that might arise from the publication of the data [5]. Multiple countries have *Freedom of Information* acts that require governmental bodies to release documents upon the request of civilians [7,13]. This has resulted in multiple commercial text redaction tools in use by governments to speed up the very time-consuming manual redaction process. The form of redacted text varies, from (traditional) completely black filling to gray bars to completely white pieces, and even manual crossing out with a pen, see Fig. 1. A tool as Zylab [14] has a white with black border option, as several scandals have given the blacked out version a bad connotation and the

---

Github: https://github.com/irlabamsterdam/TPDLTextRedaction
Demo: https://lakdetector.wooverheid.nl.

white fill with black borders is more 'social-media friendly' and less aggressive-looking.

The task of automatic recognition of redacted text has not yet been described as such in the literature. It is briefly mentioned by Bland et al. [2], as part of their algorithm to de-redact text from legal documents. Their detection step is based on the location of characters in a PDF document, but this approach does not work on scanned-in documents, where this information is not present.

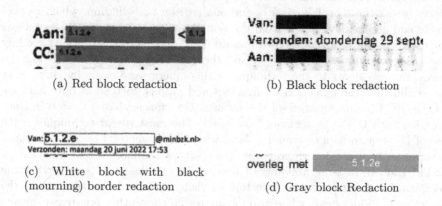

(a) Red block redaction

(b) Black block redaction

(c) White block with black (mourning) border redaction

(d) Gray block Redaction

Fig. 1. Examples of the four most common types of text redaction blocks. Codes like 5.1.2.e inserted in the redacted regions indicate the legal article used to redact the particular piece of text.

The main problem of redacted text detection is to ensure high recall, while avoiding picking up logo's, images, layout structures and other noise from the page [2]. This problem is complicated by the fact that there is a large variety of different types of text redaction, as described above. The task can be seen as the complement of document-image segmentation, in which the goal is to detect the text present in an image of a document [3].

We present an unsupervised approach for detecting redacted text blocks by using Tesseract to detect and remove regular/unredacted text from the image, after which we use morphological operations to remove text missed by Tesseract, similar to the approach used by Bloomberg [3]. Finally we filter out shapes that are too big or too small, or that are taller than they are wide, reducing the amount of false positives. This approach needs no external training data (except for Tesseract, which has been trained on large amounts of text), and is not limited to detecting black or gray blocks, but can also detect blocks with outlines, and colored blocks.

By being able to automatically detect redacted text with a high confidence we can gather statistics on how much text has been redacted in a corpus of released documents, e.g., the distribution of the redacted character ratio per page. These then can be compared across different governmental bodies.

Our algorithm performs well on black, colored and outlined redaction blocks, with F1 (PQ's recognition quality) scores of 0.79 and 0.86 and 0.76 respectively. Recall for gray blocks is hard, resulting in a somewhat lower F1 of 0.69. The overall F1 measured on 1.530 items is 0.77.

2　Related Work

Bloomberg [3] presents a method for segmenting an image into text and non-text pieces, using the morphological operations *erosion* and *dilation*, which respectively add and remove pixels from the boundaries of objects. These operations are useful, as they can be used to remove noise from an image, by first eroding the image to remove noise pixels, and then dilating the image to re-add the edges. Improvements to the technique of Bloomberg were made by Bukhari et al. to allow for the detection of drawings and graphs, instead of only halftone images [4]. The current state-of-the-art uses Transformer based models in combination with CNNs to segment images [1]. The most recent techniques make use of large quantities of training data, whereas our method is rule-based and requires no training data (except for Tesseract, as the most recent model is an LSTM trained on large amounts of textual data). This task is somewhat the complement of our task: the detection of visible text and non text versus the detection of hidden text, while also having to filter out other non-text elements such as figures and logos.

Redacted text detection is used by Bland et al. [2] as part of their method for breaking text-redaction schemes, where they develop the X-Ray Tool[1] for detecting improper text redaction. Their detection method relies on information on the location of text within a document, and detecting the existence of multiple spaces between characters. If these spaces are coloured then it is assumed that a block of redacted text is present. One of the major downsides of this approach is that it relies on knowing the position of characters on the page, something that is not present in scanned documents. At least for the Dutch redacted text landscape, scanning and then again OCR-ing documents is the predominant technique used by text-redaction tools. We thus need a method that works on scanned documents.

3　Method

3.1　Dataset

Our manually labelled dataset consists of 170 pages with 1.530 redacted text blocks from decision letters originating from Dutch ministeries written in 2020–2022, originally published at https://open.overheid.nl and now available as a curated dataset at the Dutch scientific Data repository DANS [11]. The set is split into the 4 redaction types from Fig. 1. The support column in Table 1 specifies the number of examples per type. Redacted regions were annotated using

---

[1] https://free.law/projects/x-ray.

VGG Image Annotator [6] by two annotaters, each specializing in a redacting type, with no data being annotated twice.

If there were humanly visible gaps between redaction blocks these were annotated as separate blocks. Horizontally touching blocks on separate lines were annotated as one block when the touching region was longer than the non touching one.

3.2 Algorithm for Detecting Redacted Text

Figure 2 shows the main steps of the algorithm with the output for each step. The algorithm consists of 5 main steps, namely text detection, text removal, image thresholding, contour detection, and a final contour filtering step to remove False Positives usually coming from images and logos. For the precise details of the algorithm together with examples of output for each step, we refer to the Github repository. We now briefly describe the five steps.

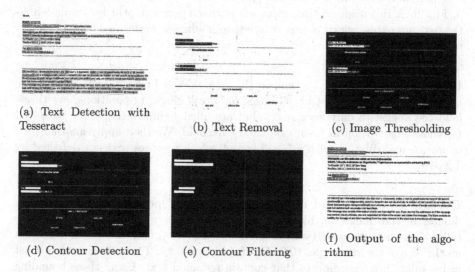

(a) Text Detection with Tesseract

(b) Text Removal

(c) Image Thresholding

(d) Contour Detection

(e) Contour Filtering

(f) Output of the algorithm

Fig. 2. The steps in the redacted block detection algorithm shown on an example with a gray redacted text containing the valediction of a letter (name, function, phone and email have been redacted).

Preprocessing. In preparation for the text detection by Tesseract, three preprocessing steps are applied to increase the quality of the image for Optical Character Recognition (OCR), following Patil et al. [12]. First, the image is converted to grayscale, after which dilation and erosion are applied to remove noise. Finally, bilateral blur with a 5 by 5 kernel is used to further remove noise while maintaining sharp edges, as proposed by Kumar [10].

For the preparation of the image used for the contour detection, erosion and dilation are applied to connect text redaction areas that are only separated by a few pixels, but that should be considered one redacted block. We apply erosion and dilation with a horizontal 1×3 and a vertical 3×1 kernel. We opted for this small kernel size as it allows us to connect lines of borders of redacted blocks while keeping the rest of the page mostly un-distorted. A larger kernel would connect edges of more bounding boxes, but at the price of more false positives. After the dilation and erosion, a bilateral blur with a kernel size of 5 by 5 is used to remove noise from the image.

Text Detection and Removal. Tesseract (Version 5) [8] is run to obtain bounding boxes of the text on a page. Because the documents are primarily in Dutch, both the Dutch and English language files are used with Tesseract. Using the confidence scores returned by Tesseract, all text with a confidence score of 65 or higher is removed, to avoid accidentally removing redaction blocks. The text is removed by filling the detected text contours with white, as can be seen in Fig. 2b A downside of this approach is that there can still be words left in the text after this, which is why image thresholding is performed to remove this text.

Image Thresholding. To remove the text missed by Tesseract, we use the approach from Bukhari et al. [4] based on morphological operations. We threshold the image, to only keep parts that are filled significantly, where we opted for Otsu binarization in favor of a fixed threshold. We then apply another pass of erosion and dilation with a 5×5 kernel, which removes text not detected by Tesseract.

Contour Detection and Filtering. Here we use OpenCV to detect the coordinates of the remaining blocks in the image. We remove rectangles that are taller than they are wide (such as images, logos etc.), and also put a minimum on the size of the rectangle, (0.025% of the page size). The output is thus a list of bounding box coordinates that contain redacted text. Using these bounding boxes we estimate the total number of characters that have been redacted by using heuristics based on the used font size, and the total portion of the page that has been redacted in terms of characters.

3.3 Evaluation Metrics

As text redaction is a segmentation task, we use the *Panoptic Quality (PQ)* metric [9] for evaluation. In this approach, a pair of gold standard and predicted redaction block is considered a True Positive if their IoU, measured in pixels, is strictly larger than .5 (i.e., the overlapping region is strictly larger than the concatenation of the (in our case usually two) non overlapping regions). The Segmentation Quality (SQ) then is the mean IoU over the True Positives; the

Recognition Quality (RQ) is the F1 score and PQ is simply RQ weighted by SQ. We aggregated the scores over all pages, in essence viewing the entire dataset as one large image. We compute precision and recall using the same set of true positives.

4   Results

Table 1 contains the evaluation of our algorithm, grouped by type of redaction. There is little variation in the segmentation quality SQ and it is high. Thus if the overlap is large enough ($IoU > .5$), segmentation goes very well. The recognition quality RQ or F1 score on the other hand does vary a lot, from .86 for colored blocks to .69 for (light)gray blocks. The precision and recall columns somewhat explain these scores: the high F1 score for colored blocks is due to a strong recall with a good precision; for the other 3 types, recall is much lower, and also lower than precision. The algorithm has the most difficulty picking up the (light)gray blocks.

Looking into these errors we found that the False Negatives are mostly due because the legal codes (like 5.1.2.e) within the boundary boxes get recognized as text, which causes part of the redaction block to be removed from the image. The thickness of the border also plays a part, as in some cases the line is too thin and gets removed by the contour filtering step. A similar explanation holds for the gray colored redacted text blocks: often the text within the blocks gets recognized, and the

Table 1. Panoptic quality metrics for our redacted text detection method grouped by the type of redaction. The support column contains the number of redacted text segments used in the evaluation.

	SQ	RQ/F1	PQ	Precision	Recall	Support
color	0.89	0.86	0.77	0.84	0.89	247
black	0.92	0.79	0.73	0.85	0.75	371
border	0.93	0.76	0.71	0.85	0.69	264
gray	0.90	0.69	0.62	0.77	0.63	468
All	0.91	0.77	0.70	0.82	0.72	1.530

entire block gets removed by the text removal step. If we changed the thresholding step after the text removal to a fixed threshold instead of the Otsu variation, the results improved for the gray type, but decreased slightly for the other types. On a 2019 Macbook Pro with 16 GB of RAM and an 8th generation i5 CPU our algorithm takes just over 2 s per page on average. Of this, 88% is used by Tesseract, 10% by the PDF to PNG conversion, and just 2% by our detection and pre- and post-processing.

5   Conclusion

We presented an algorithm for automatically detecting a wide range of different redaction types using Tesseract and simple morphological operations. We evaluated the algorithm using the Panoptic Quality method and found that the algorithm performs best on redaction blocks that are black, colored or have a mourning border, and that it does not perform well on blocks that are (light)gray.

As a possible improvement of the algorithm, a pre-classification can be done on the type of redaction block (or this information might already be present, given that some suppliers use one type exclusively), after which the algorithm can be fine-tuned for a specific class, by changing for example the threshold parameters in the contour detection step.

Acknowledgements. This research was supported in part by the Netherlands Organization for Scientific Research (NWO) through the ACCESS project grant CISC.CC.016.

References

1. Biswas, S., Banerjee, A., Lladós, J., Pal, U.: DocSegTr: an instance-level end-to-end document image segmentation transformer. arXiv preprint arXiv:2201.11438 (2022)
2. Bland, M., Iyer, A., Levchenko, K.: Story beyond the eye: glyph positions break PDF text redaction. arXiv preprint arXiv:2206.02285 (2022)
3. Bloomberg, D.S.: Multiresolution morphological approach to document image analysis. In: Proceedings of the International Conference on Document Analysis and Recognition (ICDAR), Saint-Malo, France (1991)
4. Bukhari, S.S., Shafait, F., Breuel, T.M.: Improved document image segmentation algorithm using multiresolution morphology. In: Document Recognition and Retrieval XVIII, vol. 7874, pp. 109–116. SPIE (2011)
5. Data Protection Commission: Redacting Documents and Records (2021). https://www.dataprotection.ie/sites/default/files/uploads/2021-08/Redacting/%20Documents/%20and/%20Records.pd
6. Dutta, A., Zisserman, A.: The via annotation software for images, audio and video. In: Proceedings of the 27th ACM International Conference on Multimedia (ICM), pp. 2276–2279 (2019)
7. United States Government: Freedom of information act (2023). https://www.foia.gov
8. Kay, A.: Tesseract: an open-source optical character recognition engine. Linux J. **2007**(159), 2 (2007)
9. Kirillov, A., He, K., Girshick, R., Rother, C., Dollár, P.: Panoptic segmentation. In: Proceedings of the IEEE/CVF Conference on Computer Vision and Pattern Recognition (CCVPR), pp. 9404–9413 (2019)
10. Kumar, B.S.: Image denoising based on Gaussian/Bilateral filter and its method noise thresholding. Sig. Image Video Process. **7**(6), 1159–1172 (2013)
11. Marx, M.: Woogle dump. Technical report, DANS (2023). https://doi.org/10.17026/dans-zau-e3rk
12. Patil, S., et al.: Enhancing optical character recognition on images with mixed text using semantic segmentation. J. Sens. Actuator Netw. **11**(4), 63 (2022)
13. Rijksoverheid: Wet Open Overheid (woo) (2023). https://www.rijksoverheid.nl/onderwerpen/wet-open-overheid-woo
14. Zylab: The Zylab ediscovery Platform (2023). https://www.zylab.com

The First Tile for the Digital Onomastic Repertoire of the French Medieval Romance: Problems and Perspectives

Marta Milazzo[1]([✉]) [iD] and Giorgio Maria Di Nunzio[2] [iD]

[1] Department of Linguistic and Literary Studies, University of Padua, Padua, Italy
marta.milazzo@phd.unipd.it
[2] Department of Information Engineering, University of Padua, Padua, Italy
giorgiomaria.dinunzio@unipd.it

Abstract. This contribution provides an account of the design experience of a digital onomastic repertoire for the French medieval romance (12th-15th centuries). Given the large amount of data to analyze (more than 250 texts), the research project has been conceived as modular and integrable. After discussing the main methodological problems faced, especially in terms of knowledge organization, the achieved results are described: the onomastic portal on the old French *Roman d'Alexandre*, a first tile for a larger digital repertoire.

Keywords: Onomastics · Digital Philology · Knowledge Organization

1 Introduction

In recent years, Romance philology – the discipline that studies neo-Latin languages and literature – has started to benefit from technological innovations: critical editions, lexicons, databases, even thematic portals (like PARLI [1] or AtLiVe [2]), have enriched the field of Digital Humanities. This increase has opened up new research paths. However, the possibilities offered by digital resources remain still largely unexplored. One of the areas that could benefit most from an interdisciplinary approach that includes Computer Science is medieval literary onomastics, which is "the study of names in literary texts (with 'literary' defined as broadly as possible)" [3]. In fact, medieval onomastic research is characterized by a marked interdisciplinary nature, as stated by Francesco Carapezza [4]: the proper name is a *locus criticus* of the text but is also the story of a destiny (*nomen omen*). Therefore, it is not surprising to note that since the beginning of the 20th century, numerous medieval onomastic repertoires have been produced: the reference is to Alfred Franklin [5], Ernest Langlois [6], and Louis-Fernand Flutre [7]. However, these praiseworthy repertoires appear today susceptible to updating. In addition to the increase of new editions and bibliographies, it is also worth rethinking the practical principles on which these repertoires were built. In this sense, digital data processing and a redesign of the data organization would make it possible to extend analyses to larger corpora: where the philological-textual competence clearly remains manual responsibility of the

O. Alonso et al. (Eds.): TPDL 2023, LNCS 14241, pp. 317–323, 2023.
https://doi.org/10.1007/978-3-031-43849-3_29

humanities scholar, a collaboration of a computer science scholar would make it possible to better collect, represent, and interpret large quantities of correlated data [8, 9]. In the lights of virtuous projects such as the REMLT [10] and DINAM [11] the objective of our research is the preparation of a digital onomastic repertoire for the medieval French romance. Our tool is not intended as an update of previous repertoires but as a digitally native work.

The paper is organized as follows: Sect. 2 describes the preliminary work carried out to define the general framework of the research, justify the methodological choices and conceive the best knowledge organization for our purposes; in Sect. 3, we present the preliminary results obtained by the design and implementation of the tool on a specific case study; in Sect. 4, we present our final remarks and future works.

2 A Methodology for Designing a Digital Onomastic Repertoire

Our goal is to find an innovative methodology for the creation of a digital onomastic repertoire that supports the scholar in the analysis and creation and management of the textual content. We divided our work into two parts: (1) a preliminary analysis to understand the requirements and challenges of such methodology by means of a large corpus of known studies; (2) the design and implementation of a prototype for managing onomastic repertoires.

2.1 A Study of Previous Literature of Old French Romances

The first part of the proposed methodology consists in assembling the corpus: the old French romances corpus (12th-15th century). This operation required significant efforts since medieval literature does not have precise textual genres. Based on critical bibliography ([12–16]), approximately 250 romances were identified and, for each one, a reference edition was chosen (see footnote 3 for the online documentation). The research was then limited to anthroponymy alone. The corpus provided a large onomastic material: at least 20,000 proper names (the estimation, approximative, was made from existing indexes).

The second part of the methodology involves the scanning of the text from each edition, including the *apparatus* of variants. The variant readings constitute important data since proper names are subject to different and relevant spellings and forms. Approximately 120,000 scans were acquired and this material underwent optical character recognition.[1]

The third part of the methodology consists in searching for anthroponyms. For this part, we take advantage of a typographic element: all proper names are written with a capital letter. The editor of medieval texts faces numerous problems with anthroponyms: in manuscripts they are not capitalized; furthermore, a proper name may be a fixed combination of common names (the *Lady of the Lake*, the *Black Knight*). For this reason, although not entirely satisfactory, the capital letter criterion provided the most economical solution for filtering out common names from a large corpus. All (single) words and

---

[1] https://pdf.abbyy.com/

combinations of two or more words starting with a capital letter can be automatically extracted with regular expressions, while the philological task would be to manually isolate the true anthroponyms and his variants, regroup and interpret them.

2.2 Methodological and Technical Challenges

In this section, we want to highlight some theoretical and technical issues of the proposed methodology that emerged during the preliminary work on the initial dataset.

First, the paratextual nature of a critical edition poses problems for an off-the-shelf OCR tool due to the presence of numerous "noisy elements", such as *apparatus* foot-notes, manuscript sigla, line numbers, etc. Ensuring the correspondence between the attestation of an anthroponym in the critical edition and the page or line number where the anthroponym appears proved to be a rather complex task.

Secondly, the plurality of spellings of the same name poses some challenges regarding how to validate these spellings (a true variant or an OCR mistake?) and how to relate these variants to the same character. Is the *king Baudins* in a certain romance the same character as the *king Gaudins* or the *king Condrins*, also in the same text? Are these different spellings of the same name or three different characters? The romance is unclear on this matter. Similarly, many characters appear in multiple texts, and it is not easy to determine if they are, each time, the same character. The panorama is even more complicated due to the changing nature of medieval names and the conventions of the literary genre, where names tend to repeat, resulting in many cases of homonymy. It is evident that the lemmatization of nominal forms into onomastic entries associated with characters and the description and interpretation of the latter remain entirely a detailed manual task, to be conducted only through careful reading and knowledge of the text.

2.3 Requirements for a Digital Onomastics Web Application

Besides the methodological and technical challenges, we collected with the experts in this field the functionalities that a digital tool of this kind should have in order to facilitate their work. These functionalities can be categorized into two main groups: searching for romances and searching for proper names.

Searching for romances is basically a filter on metadata about the romance itself: title, dating, author, localization; subject matter, geography; form; editions. Filters can be added together so that users can search according to typological and chronological intersections, for example: Arthurian romances (by selecting subject matter: Arthurian), in verse (by selecting form: verse), in the 12th century (by selecting dating). Conversely, it is also possible to select and investigate categories and abstractions: for example, searching for all the names of characters located in "Africa" or all the names of characters belonging to the category "Saracen".

Searching for proper names corresponds to an exploration of a specific spelling. The interface should return the onomastic entries where that spelling is attested. By selecting the chosen onomastic entry, the user can access the data that describes the character corresponding to the searched name, specifying, if possible, the character's category (i.e., "Saracen", "king", "giant") and their geographical origin (i.e., "Africa",

"Brittany", "Constantinople"). It is also possible to analyze all the spellings and variants assumed by the lemmatized onomastic form.

3 The *Roman d'Alexandre*: A Case Study

In this section, we describe the design and implementation of the first prototype of a tool that allows users to follow the process of extraction and semi-automatic curation of data in an integrated and harmonized way. In order to implement such a prototype for an accurate digital onomastic repertoire, we selected a portion of the corpus: the *Roman d'Alexandre*, an extraordinary and renowned textual constellation. Despite its importance, there exists only one, troublesome, edition of the *Alexandre* [17], moreover, incomplete with an *Index nominum*. This is the main reason why we chose a corpus as significant as the *Alexandre* as a prototype for the digital onomastic repertoire. The whole corpus consists of 532 pages with 28,827 verses that have already been scanned and OCRed. There are also 265 additional pages with variants and notes to different branches that are still under analysis.

3.1 A Pipeline from Image Scans to Text

We opted for the R programming language and a particular set of packages that allow a fully fledged management of the conversion process from the digitized documents to the text analysis, including the rapid prototyping of the Web application [18].

In Fig. 1 (top), we show an example of a page of the texts of the corpus and how we intend to process it according to the regular disposition of the content. There are five main areas of interest: the title of the book, the number of the page, the text, the number of each verse, the notes. In order to process each scan and transform it into usable text, we designed the following pipeline with the corresponding packages[2]: (1) **pdftools** to render each scanned page of the digitized text; (2) **png** and **magick** to work with the bitmap version on the scan in order to get the geometry of the page and the spaces of the different areas of interest; (3) **tesseract** to produce the OCR version of the page; (4) **tidyverse** to clean, manage, and extract the text of interest; (5) **shiny** to create the Web application for the management and curation of the data.[3]

3.2 From Text to Data Enrichment

Once the text is OCRed and the geometry for the page is detected, it is possible to go to the next step of the process which is the alignment and enrichment of textual data in order to have the correct information properly stored and reusable for further analysis.

In Fig. 1 (bottom), we show a portion of the window of the preliminary Web application that allows the user to see the process of text extraction through three panels. On the left side we have the original scan, in the center, the OCRed text (with some noise

---

[2] https://cran.r-project.org/web/packages/name_of_package/Substitute **name_of_package** with the name indicated in points 1–5 of the list.

[3] Source code of the application available at https://github.com/gmdn/TPDL2023.

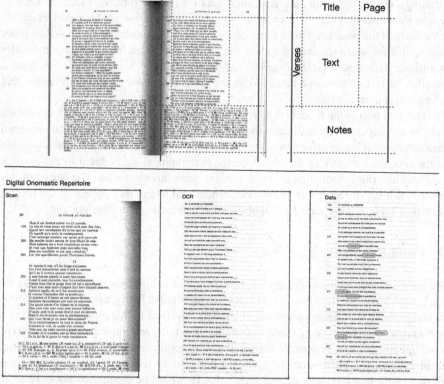

Fig. 1. (Top) An example of the organization of a text in the Roman d'Alexandre corpus. On the left side of the figure, we highlighted the (right) page of a book (red line) and the different parts of the text (dashed blue line). On the left side of the figure, the meaning of the different parts of the text that we need to process. (Bottom) A screenshot of the Web application during the process of the conversion of the pdf (right) to OCRed text (center) to structured data (right). (Color figure online)

Table 1. Example of enriched data for the character Abiene appearing in different parts (i.e., Book 1 (B1), page 45 (P45), Verse 143 (V143)).

Character	Role/Category	Spelling	Occurrence
Abiene	King of Naples	*Abiene*	B1.P45.V143
Abiene	King of Naples	*Abiierne*	B1.P51.V221
Abiene	King of Naples	*Anerne*	B2.P5.V81
Abilon	King of Lerie	*Abilon*	B2.P12.V119
Abilon	King of Lerie	*Abiron*	B3.P42.V421

cleaning), on the right side, the structured data (in tabular format). From the OCRed text to the structured data, it is required a manual intervention of the expert to decide what parts of the page need to be retained (or corrected). Highlighted with yellow ovals (not visible for space reasons), we show the proper names that have been automatically identified: *Aristotes, Aristote, Emenedus, France, Tholomers*. In this case, we have a possible variant of the same name, *Aristotes* vs *Aristote*, and an additional name that refers to a country, France.

The next step of the process requires the manual validation curation of the extracted data by the experts. The application will allow the user to interact with the extracted data by adding relevant information for each proper name (link to variants already found in the text, the category of the character, the geographical area related to the context, etc.) and link this information to other relevant items already found. The output of this process is a list of records of all the occurrences and where they appear in the text, as shown in Table 1. This part of the application is currently under development.

4   Final Remarks

We have described a methodology for the creation of a digital onomastic repertoire for the French Medieval Romance divided into two main parts: firstly, a preliminary analysis to comprehend the requirements and challenges involved in this methodology using a substantial corpus of existing studies; secondly, designing and implementing a prototype to efficiently manage onomastic repertoires. The application will offer functionalities to investigate the intertextual fortune of a name or to inquire about representations of time and places. In perspective, such a device would be configured not only as an onomastic dictionary but as a true atlas of the ancient French medieval romance, useful for a better understanding of that textual genre, the novel, which still represents our privileged literary expression.

Acknowledgments. This work is part of the initiatives of the Center for Studies in Computational Terminology (CENTRICO) of the University of Padua and in the research directions of the Italian Common Language Resources and Technology Infrastructure CLARIN-IT.

References

1. Prosopographic Atlas of Medieval Romance Literatures (PARLI). https://parli.seai.uniroma1.it/content/about-atlas
2. Atlas of the Literature of Medieval Veneto (AtLiVe). https://atlive.disll.unipd.it/public/frontend
3. The Journal of Literary Onomastics. https://soar.suny.edu/handle/20.500.12648/1972
4. Carapezza, F., (ed.): Il nome proprio nella letteratura romanza medievale = «InVerbis, Lingue Letterature Culture», 2 (2018)
5. Franklin, A.: Dictionnaire des noms, surnoms et pseudonymes latins de l'histoire littéraire du Moyen Age (1100–1530). Firmin Didot, Paris (1875)
6. Langlois, E.: Table des noms propres compris dans les Chansons de geste. Bouillon, Paris (1904)

7. Flutre, L.-F.: Table des noms propres avec toutes leurs variantes figurant dans les romans du Moyen Age, C.E.S.C.M, Poitiers (1962)

8. Bates, M.J.: The design of databases and other information resources for humanities scholars: the getty online searching project report no. 4. Online and CD-Rom Rev. **18**(6), 331–340 (1994). https://doi.org/10.1108/eb024508

9. Golub, K., Liu, Y.H.: Information and Knowledge Organisation in Digital Humanities: Global Perspectives. Routledge, London (2021). https://doi.org/10.4324/9781003131816

10. Repertorium van Eigennamen in Middelnederlandse Literaire teksten (REMLT). http://bouwstoffen.kantl.be/remlt/)

11. Diccionario de nombres del ciclo amadisiano (DINAM). https://dinam.unizar.es/

12. Frappier, J., Grimm, R.R. (eds.): Le roman jusqu'à la fin du XIIIe siècle, 2 voll., in J. Frappier et al. (eds.), Grundriss der Romanischen Literaturen des Mittelalters, Heidelberg, C. Winter (1978, 1984)

13. Woledge, B.: Bibliographie des romans et des nouvelles françaises antérieurs à 1500, Droz, Genève (1954); Supplement 1954–1973, Droz, Genève (1975)

14. Colombo Timelli, M., Ferrari, B., Schoysman, A., Suard, F. (eds.): Nouveau Répertoire des mises en proses (XIV-XVI siècles). Garnier, Paris (2014)

15. Archives Littéraires du Moyen- Âge (Arlima). https://www.arlima.net/index.html

16. Dictionnaire Étimologique de l'Ancien Français, Bibliographie en ligne (DEAFBiblEl), Möhren F. (ed.). https://alma.hadw-bw.de/deafbibl/fr/

17. Armstrong et al. (eds.): The Medieval French "Roman d'Alexandre", 7 voll. Princeton UP, Princeton (1937–1976)

18. Del Fante, D., Di Nunzio, G.M.: Correzione dell'OCR per Corpus-assisted Discourse Studies: un caso di studio su vecchi quotidiani. Umanistica Digitale **5**(11), 99–124 (2021). https://doi.org/10.6092/issn.2532-8816/13689

Digital Cultural Heritage

Fostering Access to Cultural Heritage Knowledge: Iterative Design for the Visit of Historical Monuments

Adrien Fallot(✉) ⓘ, Aurélien Bénel ⓘ, and Ines Di Loreto ⓘ

Laboratory "Computer Science and Digital Society" (LIST3N), team "Technologies pour la coopération, l'interaction et les connaissances dans les collectifs" (Tech-CICO), Troyes University of Technology, 12 rue Marie Curie, 42060, 10004 Troyes, CS, France
{adrien.fallot,aurelien.benel,ines.di_loreto}@utt.fr

Abstract. Following the trend towards open data, various cultural organisations offer information about their collections. However, these knowledge bases are not used to accompany a visit to historical monuments. We think that a possible explanation for this observation lies in the distinction between availability and accessibility of the knowledge offered: although these knowledge bases make this knowledge available, it is difficult for non-experts to make use of it and make it their own. Rather than a semantic approach to visiting based on description, we advocate an active and semiotic approach based on comparison. We have identified four challenges in applying this approach to church stained-glass windows. The first two challenges are to link the physical space of the building and the stained glass with the documentary space so that visitors can move between the two. Visitors also need to understand and use 'reading keys' to match a representation with its subject. Visitors should afterward finally be able to use their knowledge and skills on other visits. Through interviews and observations, we have iteratively designed paper and digital prototypes to meet these challenges.

Keywords: cultural heritage · user study · knowledge organisation system · user experience

1 Introduction

Traces of the evolution of societies can be found in cultural heritage, including art, industry, architecture, traditions, stories, etc. [1]. By studying these traces, we can understand the past in order to better anticipate the future. However, if not made available to the public as a common good, the knowledge gained from these studies may be lost [2]. Nowadays, through the Web, many platforms, both private and public, make this knowledge available. The modelling of the available knowledge can take two opposed forms. The first approach is based on a high degree of genericity (sometimes at the cost of a certain impoverishment) and allows the constitution of global databases. The second, based on a high degree of malleability of the infrastructure, allows a "specific" approach adapted to local contexts. In both cases, these knowledge bases aim to provide a better understanding of cultural heritage.

O. Alonso et al. (Eds.): TPDL 2023, LNCS 14241, pp. 327–340, 2023.
https://doi.org/10.1007/978-3-031-43849-3_30

The objective of providing a better understanding of the cultural heritage is shared by the cultural heritage visit tools. It is therefore logical to find more or less the same two approaches described in the previous paragraph: the reuse of global databases[1] or, on the contrary, the site-specific visit[2]. As most stained-glass windows are located outside museums, they are one of the most striking examples of this dual approach. A visiting tool must have a generic approach to cover all the places where they can be seen[3]. But there is also a need for local "specifying" to understand each individual stained-glass window [3]. In this article we propose an "in-between" approach (between genericity and specificity) using an "expert knowledge bank". The approach has been applied in the city of Troyes, a historical city in the east of France. The aim of this approach is to facilitate access to knowledge in a generic way when visiting several sites, while maintaining the "specificity" that one could have by using a support designed for a specific site.

This article is divided into three sections. The next section shows how knowledge bases can be used to create new knowledge and skills from cultural heritage. We will then see how this approach can be applied to the visit of stained-glass windows in Troyes. Section three discusses the design rationale of a hybrid visit tool for this area. In the final section, we will discuss the feedback received from the visitors and thus the resulting design choices that seem most relevant to keep for future work. We will also discuss the current limitations of this hybrid design.

2 Accessing Cultural Heritage Through Knowledge Bases

2.1 Cultural Heritage Knowledge Bases

Following the trend towards open data, various organisations are making cultural heritage knowledge available on the web [4]. Public institutions are opening up national inventories[4]. These digitised collections are mainly used by professionals, experts or hobbyists to find information, confirm hypotheses or illustrate articles [5]. Major museums also offer scans and information about their collections[5]. This opening not only makes the unexhibited parts of their collections visible, but also attracts new visitors who will be able to prepare their visit [6]. Private actors are collecting, arranging and offering virtual exhibitions to present cultural heritage knowledge to the general public[6].

These knowledge bases are mostly used *ex situ* (i.e., at a distance from the consulted works). However, these knowledge bases can also be relevant during a visit *in situ*, in front of the consulted pieces. For example, describing a work of art by the painting

---

[1] For instance, *Pokemon Go* (2016) and *Harry Potter Wizards Unite* (2019) from Niantic.

[2] For instance, phone games from Troyes Champagne Tourisme (https://jeux-de-piste.troyeslac hampagne.com) and applications from Explor Games (https://www.explorgames.com).

[3] 9000 m^2 of stained-glass windows spread over 6,004 km^2 in 211 communes in the Aube department.

[4] For instance, *Europeana* (https://www.europeana.eu) from the European Commission and *POP* (https://www.pop.culture.gouv.fr) from the French Ministry of Culture.

[5] For instance, *Collections* (https://collections.louvre.fr) from the Musée du Louvre and *Rijksstudio* (https://www.rijksmuseum.nl/en/rijksstudio) from the Rijksmuseum.

[6] For example, *Arts & Culture* (https://artsandculture.google.com) from Google.

technique used is relevant both *ex-situ* and *in situ*. However, as far as we know, there are no knowledge bases accompanying a visit *in situ*, nor users hijacking existing ones. One possible explanation lies in the distinction between availability and accessibility of the knowledge offered: although these knowledge bases make this knowledge available, it is difficult for non-experts to make use of it and make it their own [7]. In fact, the accessibility of knowledge can be questioned in the context of autonomous use by the general public.

2.2 From Knowledge to Knowing

Accessibility to knowledge inside these knowledge bases is not only a problem of openness or even ergonomics. There is also the problem of how users of these knowledge bases "interrogate the work to reveal its semantic richness and make it understandable" [7]. This problem questions the very place of knowledge in the process of understanding. As John Dewey wrote, knowledge is only the product of inquiry after a problem has been solved [8]. In the case of cultural heritage, as in a reading situation, the meaning does not come from the text, but from the reflective attitude of the visitor [9]. Her knowledge can evolve to include new information based on her observations.

It would be wrong, however, to ignore the role that the organisation of displayed information plays in the construction of meaning. As Verón and his colleagues wrote, "exhibiting is not simply giving access to a meaning that would, in all autonomy, be proper to what is exhibited; exhibiting is always and inevitably proposing, from what is shown, a particular meaning" [10]. But if, as we saw earlier, meaning is constructed by the visitor, and is specific to him, the designer can only hope to assist, or at best guide, the construction of that meaning. In order to answer this challenge of individuality, Ioannis Kanellos proposes to adapt the information offered to each visitor by means of "navigation modes" and "points of view" [7]. Each "point of view" represents a different aspect of the work (e.g., technical, contextual, aesthetic, interpretation, etc.), while each "navigation mode" is a different sequence between these aspects (e.g., discovery, study, deepening, etc.). These "points of view" and "navigation modes" allow the user to compare works of art to identify their common semantic features [11]. These successive comparisons force the user-visitor to question the current state of her knowledge by adding new singular elements.

2.3 Knowing by Interacting with Information

These successive comparisons are made on the basis of information relevant to the user-visitor's questions. She extracts new knowledge from this information and from her experience [12]. This reflective stance is part of a long line of so-called "learning by doing" approaches. Popularised by authors such as Dewey and Peirce, these approaches encourage the active participation of learners. Experiential learning is one of its applications. Based on the reflective observation of a concrete experience, the learner will propose a conceptual abstraction that she will implement in an active experiment [13].

Games are a good example of creating new knowledge through experience. In order to understand the systems that govern the game environment, the player must test her assumptions about how these systems work in each unfamiliar situation and then compare the results [14, 15]. Through these cycles of "successive challenges", the player understands more and more about the systems that govern the game and the way to achieve her goals [8, 15]. By proposing role-playing situations, game designers can make it easier to see the consequences of these actions on oneself, others and the environment, thus allowing reflective observation [16, 17] and can put the player in the position of an expert (e.g., taking part in a collaborative inventory and interacting with peers [18]). However, if the playful part takes precedence over or is too different from the reflective part, the game will not be able to accompany the reflective stance [19, 20].

2.4 Knowing Outside Museums

As the backbone of the mission to disseminate cultural goods to as many people as possible, museums are a privileged place for transmission and learning [21]. In a museum context, external factors that affect an impact on learning (such as temperature, lighting or geographical extent) are relatively controlled [22, 23]. In addition, the place is designed to contain written materials to help visitors orient themselves and understand the works [24].

Outside museums, however, there are constraints inherent in the places visited that limit control over these external factors. We can categorise these constraints into four different types: geographical, functional, legal or physical. The first is found in large places, such as cities, or where elements of particular interest are scattered over an area. Functional constraints are found in places that are also used for other than cultural purposes, such as institutional buildings that receive visitors. Legal constraints limit what can be done, for example in a protected natural area. Physical constraints are inherent to this type of visit. Unlike in a museum, where scenography plays a special role, it is difficult or impossible to control it outside museums.

3 Iterative Design for Visiting Historical Monuments

In the previous section we saw how it is possible to use the information contained in knowledge bases during a visit. In this section we will see how we have iteratively designed paper or digital prototypes to implement this idea of accompanying a visit to a stained-glass historical monument.

The majority of stained-glass windows are found in religious buildings. These buildings combine all four of the above constraints. The geographical constraint, due to their dispersion and the quantity of artworks involved3. The functional constraint stems from their dual purpose, both religious and cultural [3, 25]. The majority of these buildings are classified as historical monuments, which legally restricts any modification [26]. Last but not least, visiting buildings limits the control and possible changes of the environment (such as visibility, luminosity, temperature, order of stained-glass windows).

3.1 Methodology: Between Theorising, Designing and Observing

Research on human interaction with tools needs to take into account that the user adapts to the tool and at the same time adapts the tool to her practices. This type of study therefore requires a regular exchange between theoretical models, artefact designs and observations [27]. Inspired by the practice of redesigning museum panels, we undertook design cycles to identify elements of friction with visitors [24]. These were addressed through iterative adaptation of our documents. These cycles consist of on-site permanencies interspersed with minor adaptations (superficial changes such as spelling mistakes, minor omissions, sentence or vocabulary clarifications) and redesign (major changes to content, presentation, activity order).

We structured our experiment through five design cycles. The first four cycles took place in the church of Saint-Jean-au-Marché in Troyes. During these cycles, we offered church visitors to use our documents during their visit[7]. The visit was followed by a short interview to collect their feelings and remarks. In the last cycle, to limit the influence of personal motivation to visit the church, we tested our documents in the context of a course dedicated to the discovery of stained glass[8]. During three hours, the students visited three buildings similar to the church of Saint-Jean-au-Marché. During these visits we shadowed the groups and also conducted short interviews after the visits.

In this first experiment, our aim was to explore how we could design an active approach to the visit. Based on learning-by-doing approaches and some game design elements, we designed our supports to understand how visitors could create new knowledge through experience. Later, we replaced some of our paper prototypes with digital ones, laying the groundwork for content reuse between sites. We chose a qualitative approach in order to go beyond trends, to cope with each visitor's point of view, even rare ones [28]. Singular experiences help us to identify unforeseen design challenges and address them iteratively in the next cycle. In the first cycles, our aim was to design, test and improve our paper prototypes. Between cycles, we labelled interview transcripts. We associated situations, difficulties and design choices until saturation [29]. This approach allows us to describe a situation in detail and better understand difficulties (e.g., if a visitor cannot identify a figure, it is either because they do not understand the artwork, they cannot identify certain parts of it, or they do not understand the story of the figure). In the last cycle we extended our approach to several buildings in order to observe the challenges of multiple visits.

3.2 Design Challenges to Enhance Historical Monument Visits

The information used for the design of our prototypes comes from an inventory created by the CNRS[9], the *Corpus Vitrearum* [29]. This inventory contains technical information (size, materials, etc.) and iconographic information (story, character, etc.). This information describes the stained-glass window, but it does not explain it. In order to make these stained-glass windows accessible, we had to overcome four design challenges. Firstly, to enable visitors to match the information in the documents with the corresponding part of the stained-glass windows, and secondly, to enable visitors to associate the information

---

[7] Our documents were used by 19 visitor groups (from 1 to 4 people). In the verbatims below, each group is identified in chronological order.

[8] The students divided themselves into 8 groups (from 3 or 4 people). In the verbatims below, each student is identified by a unique number.

[9] Centre National de la Recherche Scientifique (National Center for Scientific Research).

in the documents with the corresponding part. Once they have found the right part of the stained-glass window, visitors need to understand and use 'reading keys' to match an image to the right subject. Visitors should then be able to use their knowledge and skills on other visits. To meet these challenges, we decided to design three different types of documents: an index, thematic itineraries and a notebook. This choice allows us to offer different types of visits and to introduce visitors to the use of an inventory. The index presents each stained-glass window and allows free consultation. The itineraries guide the visitor through a specific topic. The notebook accompanies the visitor so that she can take notes.

Linking the Physical Space with the Documentary Space. As mentioned earlier, there were a number of constraints that made it difficult to make physical changes to the building (e.g., with a descriptive plaque). However, when using tools, visitors need to know which stained glass is explained by the information they read or hear.

In order to create a clear link between the physical space and the documentary space, we have chosen to retain the "system established by the Corpus Vitrearum. All the stained-glass windows on the south side of the building have an even number, while those on the north side have an odd number. The hundred represents the floor (0 to 99 for the ground floor, 100 to 199 for the first floor, etc.). This standardised identification is used throughout Europe. First, to understand which approach would facilitate the use of standardised identification, we compared two presentations: by stained-glass windows (see Fig. 1A) or by topic (see Fig. 1B). Later we added a front cover to the index to explain the standardized identification of stained-glass windows (see Fig. 1C). To encourage visitors to use this identification, we added exploration steps to the itineraries. These steps require the visitor to move towards a particular stained-glass window. A large map was also added to the notebook and index cover to assist these exploration steps. In previous cycles we observed that the organisation and size of the index did not seem appropriate for a visit:

"It's very good to use, but it's not practical to have them in numerical order. I always have to think and make sure I'm on the right page. I'd have to put them in order of visit." (Visitor #11).

To overcome these problems and make it easier to add new buildings, in the fifth cycle we modified the interface of an existing digital knowledge base [30, 31]. We added a map with the standardized identification scheme and photograph of each stained-glass window (see Fig. 1D).

Associating Information to the Corresponding Part of the Stained-Glass Windows. Although often described as "comic strips" from ancient times, stained-glass windows are complex works of art to understand. In addition to iconographic knowledge, many stained-glass windows use specific narrative techniques. In order to explain a stained-glass window, our tool must be able to refer to a specific part of it.

To identify the part of a stained-glass window, we have chosen to use the architectural vocabulary of a window. This vocabulary can be applied to any window and is easier to use than the standardised identification established by the Corpus Vitrearum. We added a location attribute to each source in the stained-glass window (see Fig. 2A). To identify this location, we used architectural vocabulary and placed a diagram on the

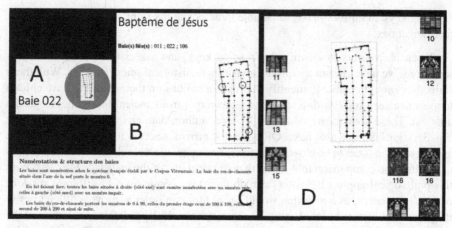

Fig. 1. Linking between the physical and the documentary space (A. stained glass window approach; B. thematic approach; C. explanation of the standardized identification; D. map with thumbnail and number). (Documents excerpts and software screenshot)

cover page to explain it (see Fig. 2C). In itineraries, we have also included photographs with captions to illustrate some of the topics (see Fig. 2D). We also added some of the practical activities related to finding an element in a stained-glass window (finding the order of a story, finding a character in the building, etc.) (see Fig. 2B). In the fifth cycle, the digital prototype contains both entries describing the whole stained glass window and entries describing its details. To find the appropriate page, the user-visitor has to compare the actual stained-glass window with a photograph (see Fig. 2E).

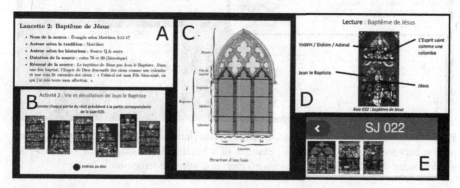

Fig. 2. Associating information to the corresponding glass panes (A. description of a topic with location in title; B. example of activity; C. diagram of architectural vocabulary; D. example of captioned photographs; E. example of fragments of the same stained-glass window). (Documents excerpts and software screenshot)

Matching Subjects and Representations. While some stained-glass windows are easy to understand (e.g., the Crucifixion or the Last Supper), others may be difficult to understand. With large knowledge bases, similar subjects can easily be confused without clear "reading keys". Our tool needs to be able to associate the right subjects with the right representations.

To enable visitors to identify the 'reading keys' and associate subjects and representations, we have chosen to introduce visitors to historical sciences skills. With these skills they should be able to identify the representations on their own. We have chosen to associate each topic with a source (e.g., excerpts from ancient texts, encyclopaedia articles). These sources are described by title, author, date and a brief summary (see Fig. 3A). Each source also has a QR code that provides access to the full text. For the ancient texts, in order to be closer to historical sciences, we have chosen to direct visitors to a translation comparison tool rather than to select one of the texts (see Fig. 3B). With this philological approach, visitors can do their own comparison of different versions of the same source, as a historian would. In addition, in order to move a little closer to the practice of historical scholarship, we have systematically indicated the author of the source, according to tradition and according to historians (see Fig. 3A). We have also added a heading to each stained-glass window, indicating the date, the author and the techniques used (see Fig. 3C). These changes were made in response to visitors who were more interested in the technical aspect than the religious one:

"It is also important to have the date of the work" (Visitor #7).

Moving on to the fifth cycle and the numerical index, each stained-glass window is described by tags divided into two points of view ('history of religion' and 'history of art') (see Fig. 3D).

Fig. 3. Matching subjects and representations. (A. description of a topic; B. example of a comparison between two ancient texts; C. example of a heading; D. description of a stained-glass window in the digital index). (Documents excerpts and software screenshot)

Remobilisation of Knowledge and Skills. As shown in a previous article, most stained-glass windows mediation tools in Troyes represent singular, non-reusable knowledge [32]. Unfortunately, given the geographical constraints outlined above, it is not possible to cover every stained-glass window. In order to include the uncovered windows, the knowledge must be reusable. Reusable knowledge also empowered visitors by giving them 'reading keys' to use on each subsequent visit.

In order to make knowledge reusable, we have chosen to use a thematic approach (the topics are applicable to several stained-glass windows) rather than a singular description (applicable to a single stained-glass window). In addition, the standardised identification and architectural vocabulary presented earlier, can be reused in other buildings and in other existing mediation tools[10]. We organised the itineraries into reading steps (see Fig. 4B) and practising steps (see Fig. 4C).

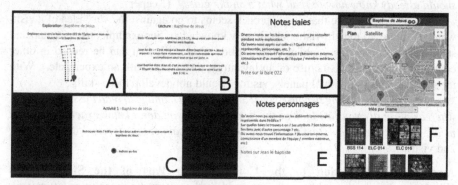

Fig. 4. Remobilisation of knowledge and skills (A-B-C example of sequence "Exploring (A) - > Reading (B) -> Practising (C)"; D. notes by stained-glass windows; E. notes by character; F. thematic research). (Documents excerpts and software screenshot)

We then restructured them into a series of "Exploring - > Reading - > Practising" sequences (see Fig. 4A–C). Reading steps presents information related to the topic (the story of a saint, the representation of a story, etc.). Practising steps allows visitors to develop their skills by using the information they have already seen (identifying a story, finding a character in the building, etc.). To encourage visitors to identify the important aspects of a topic, they can take notes (see Fig. 4D–E). In the index, stained-glass windows with similar topics have been added to the header of each page to facilitate comparison. In the fifth cycle, the use of a digital index allows all the stained-glass windows in a topic to be displayed simultaneously, also facilitating comparisons (see Fig. 4F).

4 Discussion

In this section, we discuss the results obtained for the four design challenges presented above. We will compare them with other approaches. In the final section, we discuss the limitations of our current study.

4.1 Open Problems to Enhance Historical Monument Visits

Linking the Physical Space with the Documentary Space. As one visitor asked, *"Why not add a little text to each stained glass?"* (Visitor #8). In addition to the constraints

---

[10] For instance "Minois, D., 2012. Les vitraux de Troyes: XIIe-XVIIe siècle." and "Rivale, L., Dohrmann, N., Lloza, B., 2016. Les Triomphes de Pétrarque.".

on physical changes to the building, other respondents did not want to see a place of worship turned into a museum with the use of explanatory panels:

"[…] panels are too much like a museum. Not because I don't want to read, but out of respect for believers who don't necessarily want to be in a museum." (Visitor #17).

"A lot of people ask me why there aren't any explanatory panels, but this isn't a museum. I've already suggested the idea to the priest, but he didn't like it. The faithful should already know how to read what's on the glass." (Keeper).

However, we believe that this approach seems to go against the very idea of a visit, which is supposed to help visitors build new knowledge. For example, using a map and standardised numbering enables visitors to develop skills that can be reused in other contexts (subsequent visits, use of an inventory, discussion with an expert, etc.). With the installation of individual panels, visitors would not develop these skills:

"It's really interesting because you learn more, you manage to read the stained glass, whereas normally you just look at the drawings, but you don't know exactly what they mean. After a while you start to see the donors, the saints, the stories." (Student #17, 2nd visit).

Associating Information to the Corresponding Part of the Stained-Glass Windows. Another possible approach could be the automatic recognition of stained-glass windows. For example, this approach was chosen for an application for the stained-glass windows of Sainte-Chapelle. Judging by the comments on the application shops, it seems to be appreciated and awaited (28 comments out of 38[11,12]). It makes it much easier to find information by associating it with the right work. However, this approach also seems to go against the construction of new knowledge. In fact, such an application delivers the information and leaves the user as a spectator of the cultural work. They are never helped to develop new skills. Some users of the Sainte-Chapelle stained-glass windows application explicitly criticise this fact:

"The free version provides only the names of the stained-glass windows. No explanation of the stained-glass windows, which does not empower the curious visitor." (Google store user, April 2018)11.

"Where is the explanation of the scenes shown? The techniques used? The history of this great place? I expected more from a national monument." (Apple store user, October 2017)12.

Matching Subjects and Representations. To help the visitor-user understand the key elements of a subject, we have proposed semiotic approaches based on comparison (of ancient texts and stained-glass windows) and semantic approaches based on description (of a stained-glass window and a subject). On one hand, a comparative approach comes closer to art historian's practise. On the other hand, the comparison with ancient texts has been little used (4 accesses by 2 groups out of 17 with the index). The use of QR codes and the number of documents seem to be the main factors. In view of this observation, it seems to us that the problem does not lie in the comparative approach, but in its form. During the thematic itineraries, visitors are also encouraged to compare representations

---

[11] Https://play.google.com/store/apps/details?id=com.cmn.vitrauxsaintechapelle

[12] https://apps.apple.com/fr/app/vitraux-sainte-chapelle/id1117906282?see-all=reviews.

of the same subject in order to identify the "reading keys" to understanding it. To identify these keys, visitors have to compare their initial knowledge with each new stained-glass window they consult. Visitors seem to have appreciated this approach, which involves "successive comparisons" of their knowledge:

"We really discovered the attributes of the patron saints as we went along. So now when you see a patron, you know that you're going to look behind them and you know that you recognise this or that attribute and so you're able to recognise them. And I think it's much more enjoyable because you immediately understand the scene you're looking at." (Student #13, 3rd visit).

Remobilisation of Knowledge and Skills. During the design phase, we noticed the benefits of a visit structured into sequences of "Exploring -> Reading - > Practicing". Based on that, we believe it is possible to automate the creation of itineraries using bricks with different levels of difficulty. Reusing the same brick in different itineraries and buildings could make it easier for visitors to reuse previously acquired knowledge. However, interested visitors have indicated that they get bored with repeating the same topic:

"It was good because we revisited things we learned […] in the previous church, but it's the same saints and we could have learned more about new saints" (Student #6, 3rd visit).

We also noticed that note-taking during the visit did not seem to correspond to a visit of a historical monument. Only 6 out of 9 notebooks were used for note-taking and the other 10 groups refused the notebook. The main reasons seem to be the temperature, the amount of space and the lack of interest in this activity. In order to allow the visitor-user to keep a record and build up their own collection of stained-glass windows, the addition of "favourites" could be considered. However, this feature is a far cry from note-taking, where visitors need to formulate their knowledge. The ability to share on social networks could encourage this formulation.

4.2 Limits of Our Study

As we have seen in the previous section, there was a short-term re-mobilisation of skills when the activities were carried out. However, further research would be needed on the medium- and long-term retention of knowledge. Furthermore, during the last cycle we tested our documents in the context of a course on stained glass discovery. Although it is a "natural" setting since students volunteered for this course, once the visit started, they had no option to stop if they found it uninteresting. In addition, our experiments were conducted in a very specific visiting context (stained-glass windows in a French historic monument) and can therefore only provide potential clues for other contexts.

5 Conclusion and Future Works

In this article we have discussed the challenges in the design of visitor tools for historical monuments, especially churches. Although many open knowledge bases exist, the accessibility of knowledge can be questioned. It is not just a question of openness or even ergonomics. It's about the very way in which users are able to develop their knowledge and skills from the information that is available in these databases. We advocate an active approach to visiting. Where visitors gain understanding by using information to create and remobilise knowledge and skills. To bring visitors closer to the practices of an expert, we have iteratively designed our prototypes to meet four challenges. The first two challenges are to link the physical space of the building and the works to the documentary space, so that visitors can move between the two. Visitors also need to understand and use 'reading keys' to match an image to the correct subject. Visitors should then be able to use their knowledge and skills on other visits. Our active approach, seems to be appreciated by visitors and helps them to re-mobilise their skills in the short term. Finally, we have discussed other possible approaches. However, the issues raised in this article remain open in other visitor contexts.

To take this further, we want to continue to offer semiotic approaches based on comparison rather than semantic approaches based on description and classification. We want to create itineraries that compare the stained-glass windows of different buildings in order to decipher the keys to reading a topic. We also want to explore the limitations of semantic and semiotic approaches. A stained-glass window, like any other work of art, was created in a specific historical context. So even if the stories remain the same, we can question the relevance of linking or comparing very different contexts.

Acknowledgments. This work was funded by the Conseil départemental de l'Aube. The authors would also like to thank the volunteers who visited churches with our documents.

References

1. Vecco, M.: A definition of cultural heritage: from the tangible to the intangible. J. Cult. Herit. **11**, 321–324 (2010). https://doi.org/10.1016/j.culher.2010.01.006
2. Edson, M.P.: Fire and frost: the virtues of treating museums, libraries and archives as commons. In: Patterns of Commoning. Commons Strategy Group and Off the Common Press, Amherst, Massachusetts (2015)
3. Smørvik, K.K.: Why enter the church on holiday? tourist encounters with the Basilica of Santa Maria in Trastevere, Rome. J. Heritage Tourism **16**, 337–348 (2021). https://doi.org/10.1080/1743873X.2020.1807557
4. Mathis, R.: L'Open Data culturel. Documentaliste-Sciences de l'Information **51**, 56–67 (2014). https://doi.org/10.3917/docsi.512.0056
5. Clough, P., Hill, T., Paramita, M.L., Goodale, P.: Europeana: what users search for and why. In: Kamps, J., Tsakonas, G., Manolopoulos, Y., Iliadis, L., Karydis, I. (eds.) Research and Advanced Technology for Digital Libraries. TPDL 2017. Lecture Notes in Computer Science, vol. 10450. Springer, Cham (2017). https://doi.org/10.1007/978-3-319-67008-9_17
6. Walsh, D., Hall, M., Clough, P., Foster, J.: The ghost in the museum website: investigating the general public's interactions with museum websites. In: Kamps, J., Tsakonas, G., Manolopoulos, Y., Iliadis, L., Karydis, I. (eds.) Research and Advanced Technology for Digital Libraries. TPDL 2017. Lecture Notes in Computer Science, vol. 10450. Springer, Cham (2017). https://doi.org/10.1007/978-3-319-67008-9_34
7. Kanellos, I.: Les musées virtuels et la question de la lecture : pour une muséologie numérique centrée sur le visiteur. Revue des Interactions Humaines Médiatisées (RIHM) = Journal of Human Mediated Interactions **10**, 3–33 (2009)

8. Hildebrand, D.: John Dewey. In: Zalta, E.N. (éd.) The Stanford Encyclopedia of Philosophy. Metaphysics Research Lab, Stanford University (2021)
9. Denis, S.: Nous sommes tous des poissons : les stratégies de lecture des visiteurs d'exposition (1995). https://bibliotheque-archives.canada.ca:443/eng/services/services-librar ies/theses/Pages/item.aspx?idNumber=46529972
10. Verón, E., Levasseur, M., Barbier-Bouvet, J.-F.: Ethnographie de l'exposition: l'espace, le corps et le sens. BPI : Centre Georges Pompidou, Paris (1991)
11. Rousseaux, F.: La collection, un lieu privilégié pour penser ensemble singularité et synthèse. EspacesTemps.net Revue électronique des sciences humaines et sociales (2006)
12. Rowley, J.: The wisdom hierarchy: representations of the DIKW hierarchy. J. Inf. Sci. **33**, 163–180 (2007). https://doi.org/10.1177/0165551506070706
13. Kolb, D.A.: Experiential Learning: Experience as the Source of Learning and Development. FT Press (2014)
14. Gee, J.P.: What video games have to teach us about learning and literacy. Comput. Entertain. **1**, 20 (2003). https://doi.org/10.1145/950566.950595
15. Koster, R.: Theory of Fun for Game Design. O'Reilly Media, Incorporated (2005)
16. Mannsverk, S.J., Di Loreto, I., Divitini, M.: Flooded: a location-based game for promoting citizens' preparedness to flooding situations. In: De Gloria, A. (ed.) Games and Learning Alliance, pp. 90–103. Springer International Publishing, Cham (2014)
17. Sanchez, E., et al..: Geome et son Compagnon Digital : un dispositif permettant la mise en place de visites muséales ludiques. In: 10e Conférence sur les Environnements Informatiques pour l'Apprentissage Humain, pp. 405–408. Marie Lefevre, Christine Michel, Fribourg, France (2021)
18. Gicquel, P.Y., Hamon, L., Plaut, F., George, S.: Albiziapp: a gamified tool dedicated to tree mapping. In: Liapis, A., Yannakakis, G., Gentile, M., Ninaus, M. (eds.) Games and Learning Alliance. GALA 2019. Lecture Notes in Computer Science, vol. 11899. Springer, Cham (2019). https://doi.org/10.1007/978-3-030-34350-7_28
19. Su, C.-H., Cheng, C.-H.: A mobile gamification learning system for improving the learning motivation and achievements: a mobile gamification learning system. J. Comput. Assist. Learn. **31**, 268–286 (2015). https://doi.org/10.1111/jcal.12088
20. Pellon, G., et al..: Les cahiers du LLL – N°8 : Jouer pour apprendre dans l'enseignement supérieur ? LLL, Presses universitaires de Louvain (2020)
21. Falk, J., Dierking, L.: The Museum Experience Revisited. Left Coast Press Inc, Walnut Creek, Calif (2013)
22. Bitgood, S., Patterson, D.: Principles of exhibit design. Visitor Behav. **2**, 4–6 (1987)
23. Falk, J., Storksdieck, M.: Using the contextual model of learning to understand visitor learning from a science center exhibition. Sci. Educ. **89**, 744–778 (2005). https://doi.org/10.1002/sce. 20078
24. Poli, M.-S.: Le texte au musée : une approche sémiotique. L'Harmattan, Paris Budapest Torino (2002)
25. Bideci, M., Albayrak, T.: Motivations of the Russian and German tourists visiting pilgrimage site of Saint Nicholas Church. Tourism Manag. Perspect. **18**, 10–13 (2016). https://doi.org/ 10.1016/j.tmp.2015.12.022
26. République française: Article L621-9 du Code du patrimoine. (2016)
27. Mackay, W.E., Fayard, A.-L.: HCI, natural science and design: a framework for triangulation across disciplines. In: Proceedings of the Conference on Designing Interactive Systems Processes, Practices, Methods, and Techniques - DIS 1997, pp. 223–234. ACM Press, Amsterdam (1997)
28. Adolph, S., Hall, W., Kruchten, P.: Using grounded theory to study the experience of software development. Empir. Softw. Eng. **16**, 487–513 (2011). https://doi.org/10.1007/s10664-010- 9152-6

29. Inventaire général des monuments et des richesses artistiques de la France: Les vitraux de Champagne-Ardenne. Éditions du Centre National de la Recherche Scientifique., Paris (1992)

30. Bénel, A.: Archives numériques et construction du sens ou «Comment échapper au Web sémantique ?». La Gazette des Archives **245**, 163–177 (2017). https://doi.org/10.3406/gazar.2017.5524

31. Bénel, A.: Document numérique : L'informatique en quête d'un corps. La Gazette des Archives **45** (2021)

32. Fallot, A., Bénel, A., Di Loreto, I.: Cadre de conception et de rétro-conception de dispositifs de visite autonome. Présenté à H2PTM 23 octobre 18 (2023)

Persistent Identifier Usage by Cultural Heritage Institutions: A Study on the Europeana.eu Dataset

Nuno Freire[1]([ENVELOPE]) [iD], Hugo Manguinhas[1], Antoine Isaac[1,2] [iD], and Valentine Charles[1] [iD]

[1] Europeana Foundation, The Hague, The Netherlands
{nuno.freire,hugo.manguinhas,antoine.isaac,
valentine.charles}@europeana.eu
[2] Vrije Universiteit Amsterdam, Amsterdam, The Netherlands

Abstract. To inform future decisions regarding the use of persistent identifiers (PID) in the common European data space for cultural heritage, we have analysed the usage of PIDs in the metadata that cultural heritage institutions deliver to Europeana. Focusing on the identification of cultural heritage objects and their digital representations, we present statistics on the usage of 5 PID schemes: Archival Resource Key (ARK), Digital Object Identifier (DOI), HANDLE, Persistent URL (PURL), and Uniform Resource Name (URN). We found that 13% of the Europeana records contain a PID and that ARK and HANDLE are most frequently used. We have also analysed the uniqueness of the existing PIDs and identified some data quality issues.

Keywords: persistent identifiers · cultural heritage · Europeana · Archival Resource Key · Digital Object Identifier · HANDLE · Persistent URL · Uniform Resource Name

1 Introduction

The importance of persistent identification has long since been recognized in cultural heritage (CH). For example, national libraries in several countries use the National Bibliography Number (NBN), an identification system for publications, which predates modern Persistent Identifier (PID) schemes. Over the past years, several PID schemes have been adopted in CH and academia. To inform future decisions regarding the use of PIDs in the common European data space for cultural heritage [1], we have analysed the usage of PIDs in the metadata that CH institutions (CHIs) deliver to Europeana, focusing on identification of CH objects and their digital representations, reliability of the PIDs, and data quality issues.

2 Related Work

Several efforts have researched persistent identification in cultural heritage in recent years. In [2], McKenna & Fokke present PIDs requirements and recommendations in CH, and Koster has conducted a comprehensive analysis of PIDs for CH applications [3],

O. Alonso et al. (Eds.): TPDL 2023, LNCS 14241, pp. 341–348, 2023.
https://doi.org/10.1007/978-3-031-43849-3_31

highlighting the (dis)advantages of current PID infrastructures and practices. Europeana also carried some work when it prototyped a PID resolution service [4].

Quantitative data on current PID usage in CHIs is not available at global or even European levels, but a 2020 survey conducted by the Heritage PIDs project in the UK found that more than 75% of the respondents were aware of PIDs, and more than 50% of the CHIs used them [5, 6]. Our work aims to better quantify and characterise the usage of PIDs (and different PID schemes) by CHIs in Europe by analysing actual metadata published in one of the largest CH data aggregations - Europeana.

Finally, the persistence of PIDs has been thoroughly investigated, e.g., by Klein & Balakireva for DOI identifiers, which are highly relevant in the scholarly domain [7]. The authors concluded that persistence of DOIs is not warranted: many become inconsistent after some time. In our study, we have not investigated the persistence of PIDs, but we identified other reliability issues.

3   Design of the Study

To meet our goal, we processed the metadata that CHIs deliver to Europeana, using a dump of the Europeana dataset[1] from February 2023. Although CHIs may use PIDs for identifying several types of entities[2], for this study our interest is on the identification of CH objects ("CHOs" in the Europeana Data Model - EDM [8]) and their digital representations ("web resources" in EDM). This means that we exclude PIDs used for, e.g., concepts or persons that appear as the subject or creator of a CHO.

All identifiers of CHOs and web resources in the dataset were checked for a PID. Based on our knowledge of the dataset and on an ad-hoc search across the values of the EDM elements that may contain PIDs, we decided to investigate the usage of five PID schemes. Table 1 lists them and describes how their usage was checked. We detected PIDs expressed either as HTTP(S) URIs (taking into account that some schemes allow using different resolver hosts) or compact URIs (cf. Column 3 of Table 1).

We checked the presence of a PID in four EDM elements. In EDM, a PID in the dc:identifier of an ore:Proxy identifies a CHO, while a PID in edm:isShownBy, edm:isShownAt and edm:hasView properties identifies a web resource. Notwithstanding possible data quality issues (see Sect. 4), the semantics of these properties also enables us to make hypotheses on whether PIDs resolve to web pages giving access to digital representations (useful for browsing), or directly to media files (useful for re-use by other services, e.g., web portals like europeana.eu).

We have also analysed the prefixes of some of the PID schemes. Those identify registration authorities and namespaces and can give a good indication of the reliability of the PIDs. Last, we investigated the uniqueness of PIDs, checking for the cases where more than one CHO or web resource has the same PID in Europeana.

---

[1] Obtained via https://pro.europeana.eu/page/harvesting-and-downloads#downloads.

[2] ARK identifiers, for example, have been assigned to bibliographic records, persons, organisations, vocabulary terms, archeological artefacts, etc. [9].

Table 1. The detection methods applied in this investigation for the five PID schemes.

PID scheme	Detection methods	Examples in HTTP(S) URI and compact URI forms
Archival Resource Key (ARK)	HTTP(S) URI has a path that starts with '/ark:'; URI start with 'ark:'	https://n2t.net/ark:/12148/btv1b8 449691v/f29 ark:12148/btv1b8449691v/f29
Digital Object Identifier (DOI)	HTTP(S) URI has host 'doi.org' or 'dx.doi.org'; URI starts with 'doi:'	http://doi.org/10.2298/BG2013 0206SPEHAR doi:10.2298/BG20130206SP EHAR
HANDLE	HTTP(S) URI has a host that starts with 'handle.' or contains '.handle.'; URI start with 'hdl:'	http://hdl.handle.net/10062/5516 hdl:10062/5516
Persistent URL (PURL)	HTTP(S) URI has a host that starts with 'purl.' or contains '.purl.'	http://www.purl.org/yoolib/inha/ 10136
Uniform Resource Name (URN)	HTTP(S) URI has a path that starts with '/urn:'; URI start with 'urn:'	http://urn.fi/URN:NBN:fi-fd2 010-00003198 URN:NBN:fi-fd2010-00003198

4 Results

This section presents statistics on PID usage in general and for individual schemes, and reports on the (non-)uniqueness of PIDs and other data quality issues. A more complete version of these results is available at [10].

General PID Usage Statistics. 7,387,012 Europeana records (13% of the 56,743,557 records in the dataset) have at least one PID. Table 2 indicates the proportion of Europeana records that an individual PID scheme appears in and their representation counting all PIDs that appear in Europeana. Note that it is common for records to contain more than one PID - sometimes from different PID Schemes - since CHOs and web resources may - and should! - be referenced using different PIDs, and dc:identifier is a repeatable property in EDM. ARK and HANDLE are the most frequently used schemes, with ARK occurring in more records but HANDLE having the highest number of PIDs overall (this is further explained in Sect. 4).

Table 3 shows the metadata properties where PIDs are used. Edm:hasView contains the most PIDs, followed by edm:isShownAt, dc:identifier (of the CHO) and edm:isShownBy. The EDM semantics allow the values of edm:hasView - which is repeatable, thus contributing to its ranking first - to refer to either (1) web pages giving access to a digital object or (2) media files directly. PIDs in edm:isShownBy shall resolve directly to media files and those in edm:isShownAt and CHOs' dc:identifier to web pages that give access to the digital object. Our results thus hint that a majority of the PIDs resolve to web pages rather than to media files.

Table 2. Distribution of PID schemes.

PID scheme	Use in nr. records	% of statements with PIDs
ARK	3,176,131 (43.0%)	6,664,671 (35.5%)
HANDLE	2,051,327 (27.8%)	9,369,773 (49.9%)
URN	1,482,709 (20.1%)	1,768,135 (9.4%)
DOI	549,298 (7.4%)	551,634 (2.9%)
PURL	275,196 (3.7%)	409,677 (2.2%)

Table 3. Distribution of PIDs across properties.

Properties	Total statements with PIDs
edm:hasView	6,841,900
edm:isShownAt	5,795,176
dc:identifier	4,613,432
edm:isShownBy	1,513,382
Total	**18,763,890**

Individual PID Schemes Statistics. Table 4 presents the distribution of individual PID schemes across properties. A very small percentage of ARKs are used in edm:isShowBy (1.7%), which indicates that ARKs typically resolve to an access webpage. But we cannot draw general conclusions here since the ARKs in Europeana originate from only four Name Assigning Authorities (see Table 5), and one of them (the National Library of France) is by far the largest source.

The HANDLE PID scheme comes second in number of records using it, but it has the highest number of total PIDs because it is used very often in the repeatable edm:hasView. 74 distinct HANDLE prefixes are present (Table 6 shows the most frequently used)[3]: more Europeana providers are using HANDLE than ARK. One should highlight that two of the prefixes (20 and 21) are Multi-Primary Administrators (MPAs) of the DONA Foundation, therefore these identifiers should be reliably persistent.

URN comes third and is used differently from ARKs and HANDLES; URNs are indeed mostly used for identifying CHOs (dc:identifier). 6 URN Namespace Identifiers (NID) are present, but the NID for the National Bibliography Number (NBN) is the most used (70% of the existing URNs). Within NBN, we found 14 country codes, 5 having over a thousand PIDs: Germany, Norway, Finland, Croatia and Slovakia. A closer look at URN namespaces raises concerns of the general reliability of URNs. Three of the NIDs

---

[3] See full list at [10]. Note that DOIs are also based on the HANDLE system (prefix '10') but given their prominence, we decided to analyse them separately.

Table 4. Distribution of all PID schemes across properties.

Property	ARK	Handle	URN	DOI	PURL
dc:identifier	2,150,108 (32.3%)	1,334,324 (14.2%)	1,031,407 (58.3%)	77,136 (14.0%)	20,457 (5.0%)
edm:isShownAt	3,024,583 (45.4%)	1,871,274 (20.0%)	379,304 (21.5%)	474,461 (86.0%)	45,554 (11.1%)
edm:isShownBy	115,423 (1.7%)	800,572 (8.5%)	357,326 (20.2%)	35 (0.0%)	240,026 (58.6%)
edm:hasView	1,374,557 (20.6%)	5,363,603 (57.2%)	98 (0.0%)	2 (0.0%)	103,640 (25.3%)

are not registered in IANA[4] (see Table 7), some URNs omit the NID and some NBN URNs have invalid country codes (for example, 'nbn:imp272'). Further investigation is required to determine which URNs ensure persistent resolution services.

DOIs, although very well-known in academia, are infrequent in Europeana. They almost always resolve to web pages, but in a few cases, they resolve to media (typically, to a PDF file).

PURL is the least used PID Scheme. It is mainly used to identify web resources, only in some cases the CHO. There are five PURL services in use (see Table 8), one of them being the widely known purl.org.

Table 5. ARK Name Assigning Authorities.

NAAN	Authority	Count
12148	National Library of France	6,395,780
73189	Data Archiving and Networked Services	200,103
81055	British Library	64,831
86084	Blavatnik Archive Foundation	3,954

Uniqueness of the Persistent Identifiers. Uniqueness of identifiers is strongly desirable for Europeana objects and their digital representations, which are expected to be distinct. We have checked whether more than one record shares the same PID, after normalising the PIDs that can be expressed in different forms (HTTP(S) URI or compact URI) and be attached to different resolvers.

There are 385,796 cases where more than one record shares the same PID, and this occurs for all PID Schemes (Table 9). The large majority of non-unique PIDs are

---

[4] Cf. The IANA URN NID registry: https://www.iana.org/assignments/urn-namespaces/urn-namespaces.xhtml.

Table 6. Mostly used HANDLE prefixes.

Prefix	Count
10648	5,302,114
11088	1,003,623
10934	679,048
10891	348,611
10622	321,454

Table 7. URN Namespace Identifiers.

NID	Count	Registered in IANA?
nbn	1,254,620	Yes
repox.ist.utl.pt	197,832	No
rs	46,691	No
imss	9,219	No
isbn	4,866	Yes
issn	64	Yes

Table 8. PURL domain names.

Domain	Count
purl.ox.ac.uk	333,269
purl.org	41,018
purl.pt	35,061
purl.sgmf.gov.pt	328
purl.access.gpo.gov	1

shared by only two records, but there are cases where a PID is shared by many records, sometimes more than 5 (Table 10). The most extreme cases happen when a PID assigned to a periodic publication or collection is used for all the individual issues/objects in the group, resulting in hundreds of records with the same PID.

There are also cases that are actually valid because the same PID appears in records about the same CHO aggregated via different data aggregation routes.

Data Quality Issues. Most of the shared PID cases above. Come from a PID being attributed to a CHO while it identifies a collection or a serial, which can be seen as a data quality issue.

Table 9. Number of cases, per PID scheme, with more than one record with the same PID.

PID scheme	Count
ARK	222,493
HANDLE	143,646
URN	11,905
DOI	7,711
PURL	41
Total	**385,796**

Table 10. Number of occurrences of the same PID.

Number of records with the same PID	Number of cases
2	320,301
3	31,909
4	20,458
5	8,565
More than 5	4,563

We have also detected that some providers unintentionally use PID schemes in their identifiers. Some HANDLE prefixes are not valid, e.g., '123456789'). It appears that some digital library systems have built-in support for automatically outputting HANDLE identifiers in the metadata. The data providers may have neglected to deactivate or configure this functionality properly. A similar case was found for URNs. Where providers did not configure the namespace identifier used by a particular repository system ('repox.ist.utl.pt'). In the same vein, we found a few trivial typos[5].

Finally, we have detected uses of PIDs that do not fit EDM semantics. Especially, some PIDs in edm:isShownBy resolve to a web page, while this property should point directly to media files. This issue is not specific to PID values and has been detected earlier by the Europeana Data Quality Committee[6].

5 Conclusion

This study confirms that PIDs are already being used by CHIs to a small but significant extent (13% of the records in Europeana contain one). Our analysis raises some concerns regarding the reliability of these PIDs. While ARK, HANDLE and DOI are supported

---

[5] E.g. 'hdl:10622/COLL00467–10' instead of 'hdl:10622/COLL00467.10'; 'URN:URN:NBN:SI:doc-DU27Q92N' instead of 'URN:NBN:SI:doc-DU27Q92N' (for 333,284 PIDs!).

[6] https://pro.europeana.eu/project/data-quality-committee#problem-patterns.

by reliable persistence policies and resolution systems, it is unclear which URNs and PURLs have an underlying persistence policy. We have also identified data quality problems, such as invalid namespaces and assignment of PIDs to CHOs while they identify collections or serials.

Overall, this study indicates that the usage of PIDs still needs to increase and mature, so that they can fully benefit the common European data space for cultural heritage and its applications. It also brings concrete elements that can be used to refine data governance policies and data quality reporting that are crucial to such data spaces, especially regarding the adoption of the FAIR principles (PIDs without persistence policy or with non-registered prefixes are less commendable). Some of our efforts have already fed into the work of the Europeana Data Quality Committee[7]. In future work we would like to investigate methods for determining which PIDs are reliably persistent, e.g., exploiting IANA registration status and perhaps connecting to past studies on persistence. We also want to better detect data quality problems related to PIDs, especially (1) invalid non-unique PIDs and (2) usage of EDM elements with PIDs that refer to types of digital resources not expected in these elements.

References

1. European Commission: Commission recommendation of 10.11.2021 on a common European data space for cultural heritage. European Commission (2021). https://digital-strategy.ec.eur opa.eu/en/news/commission-proposes-common-european-data-space-cultural-heritage
2. Gordon McKenna, G., Fokke, C.: D 2.2 state of the art report on persistent identifier standards and management tools. Project Linked Heritage (2013). https://www.linkedheritage.eu/get File.php?id=556
3. Koster, L.: Persistent identifiers for heritage objects. Code4Lib J. (47) (2020)
4. Svensson, L.G.: Universal access to cultural heritage material: the Europeana resolution discovery service for persistent identifiers. In: International Conference on Dublin Core and Metadata Applications, pp. 184–185 (2010). https://dcpapers.dublincore.org/pubs/article/view/1008
5. Kotarski, R., et al.: PIDs as IRO Infrastructure-Early Findings (2020). https://doi.org/10.23636/1214
6. Kotarski, R., Madden, F.: Persistent identifiers as IRO infrastructure: survey data. British Lib. (2020). https://doi.org/10.23636/1210
7. Klein, M., Balakireva, L.: An extended analysis of the persistence of persistent identifiers of the scholarly web. Int. J. Digit. Libr. 23, 5–17 (2022). https://doi.org/10.1007/s00799-021-003 15-w
8. Europeana Foundation: Definition of the Europeana Data Model v5.2.8. (2017). http://pro.europeana.eu/edm-documentation
9. Kunze, J.: ARK identifiers FAQ (2021). Accessed 5 June 2023. https://wiki.lyrasis.org/dis play/ARKs/ARK+Identifiers+FAQ#ARKIdentifiersFAQ-ARKedThingsWhatkindsofthing sareARKsassignedto?
10. Freire, N., Manguinhas, H., Isaac, A., Charles, V.: Inventory of persistent identifiers for cultural heritage objects and web resources provided to Europeana. Technical report (2023). https://doi.org/10.5281/zenodo.8169237

---

[7] https://pro.europeana.eu/post/help-us-to-make-cultural-heritage-data-more-persistent.

Real Experienced Needs for Accessible and Inclusive Cultural Heritage - First Results in MuseIT

Elena Maceviciute(✉) 📧 and Nasrine Olson 📧

Swedish School of Library and Information Science, University of Borås, 50190 Borås, Sweden
elena.maceviciute@hb.se

Abstract. The aim of this paper is to present an overview of the preliminary findings in an ongoing study conducted in MuseIT – a Horizon Europe project (Oct. 2022 – Sept. 2025) – proposing technologies facilitating and widening access to cultural assets in an 'inclusive way'. The paper reports the results of a literature review and the first ideation workshop conducted in January 2023. The workshop participants represented cultural institutions and their users, and/or consumers and producers of cultural assets, with a focus on people with disabilities. The findings show that the digital environment is greatly appreciated by participants with disabilities for both communication with others and for self-expression. Cultural institutions are aware of the variety of needs, including the need for collaborative development of services accessible to all. However, there is a perception gap between the two. To address these, there is a need to involve people with disabilities – who are experts on such needs based on lived experiences – in the design of tools and services aimed at meeting their needs. Furthermore, there is a need for improved understanding of disability and diversity of needs, in projects involved in developing technological systems to facilitate and broaden accessibility.

Keywords: Accessible cultural assets · digital cultural heritage · people with disabilities · need for cultural inclusion · MuseIT

1 Introduction

Extensive scholarly publications explore the relationship between information, digital technologies, their design, and societal implications [1–4] highlighting the biassed embedded intentions which reinforce inequalities that privilege some members of the society and exclude others. According to a report by the WHO "[a]n estimated 1.3 billion people experience significant disability. This represents 16% of the world's population, or 1 in 6 of us" [5]. The *UN's Universal Declaration of Human Rights* [6] proclaims human rights for all people, including people with disabilities to receive information (article 19) and to "***participate in the cultural life***" (article-27). The *Convention on the Rights of Persons with Disabilities* (CRPD) [7] proclaims the rights of *all persons with disabilities "to take part on an equal basis with others in **cultural life**"* and have access to places for cultural services, such as museums and libraries. Appropriate measures

O. Alonso et al. (Eds.): TPDL 2023, LNCS 14241, pp. 349–356, 2023.
https://doi.org/10.1007/978-3-031-43849-3_32

shall be taken "*to enable persons with disabilities to have the opportunity to **develop and utilise their creative, artistic and intellectual potential**, not only for their own benefit, but also for the enrichment of society*" (Article-30). In practice, however, the extent of accessibility still remains limited for those with disabilities [8] and many requirements remain unfulfilled [e.g., 9]. To address some of the shortcomings, the EU-funded MuseIT project proposes novel technologies for alternative expressions and layered multisensory representations (including visual, audio, text-based, kinetic 3D/4D, and haptic representations). These innovations enrich the experiences of all, while enabling those with disabilities to engage with cultural assets, with agency and based on their individual needs and preferences. The idea is to include all people of all abilities. While a technological project, MuseIT addresses a major social issue and encourages a rethinking of cultural heritage (CH) as a first-person experience for all people.

Based on this background, the MuseIT project addresses three main challenges:

(a) **Extending accessibility of cultural assets**: This is done by developing *multisensory representations* (e.g., representation of the same object in text, sound, haptic, 3D etc.) and *alternative expressions* (e.g., a musical piece as an interpretation of a painting) to enable engagement by the public regardless of functional or sensory impairments, based on their own needs and preferences. These layered representations are then brought together in an integrated interactive way in an immersive user experience (AR/VR, haptic) environment.

(b) **Broadening engagement with cultural assets and cultural co-creation**: There are many impediments to the creative production of cultural assets, e.g., barriers in mobility excluding co-presence in the same physical space, lack of accessible tools and technologies for co-creation from distance. MuseIT proposes *an accessible platform for co-creation and performance of music from a distance with zero latency*, which will incorporate tools for intricate emotional communications between the performers to compensate for lack of co-presence and to enable collaborative performances from distance. Co-creation and co-performance of music from distance through online platforms remains a major challenge due to latency issues. The MuseIT zero-latency platform will therefore address this challenge for music co-creation and performance..

(c) **Extending methodologies for inclusive preservation of CH**: These methodologies improve access to the preserved material and enable storage of layered multisensory representations in an integrated way, including means of storing and preserving new modalities such as *haptic information*.

MuseIT brings together information science, museology, and policy studies with computer science (including ML, NLP, AR, VR), engineering, haptics and more to develop cutting-edge technologies for an interactive and multisensory engagement with cultural assets. MuseIT aims to address real experienced needs and, therefore, involves participants from two main user groups: a) people with disabilities seeking engagement with CH and involvement in cultural activities, and b) representatives of cultural institutions. The project uses extensive participatory elements to define design priorities and carry out related decisions. Users play a central role in explorative activities of the project as *co-researchers*, *co-designers* and *co-creators*.

The aim of this paper is to present an overview of the preliminary results from ongoing studies in MuseIT seeking to: (i) explore and better understand real experienced needs and expectations of the two user groups, and (ii) provide insights on the specific user requirements and constraints to orient the technical development of the project and to create a shared understanding of the user needs. The results presented here are based on a literature review and the first ideation workshop conducted in January, 2023.

2 Literature Review

Scholarly publications on the needs or experiences related to digital cultural heritage or cultural activities by people with disabilities remain limited. A search in the Web of Science database using the query *"cultural participation* AND *people with disabilit*"* from 2010 returned 293 items. Excluding items on medicine and nursing left 233 articles mainly dealing with cultural participation in physical spaces and only some related to digital cultural participation. For this review we have used 23 articles that on closer inspection either discuss both digital and physical cultural participation needs or needs for digital CH of people with disabilities.

Leahy and Ferri [10] have conducted a narrative review of existing literature to identify barriers and facilitators to cultural participation of people with disabilities. This review has a view of disability that is shared by the MuseIT, in which, disability is seen as a social construct (rather than a medical condition) brought about by social, environmental, and attitudinal barriers. The 'people first' language convention ('persons/people with disabilities') is adopted.

The view of culture presented in that review involves multiple dimensions: *"culture as possibility for personal expression (creation), culture as enjoyment of other people's creation (consumption), and culture as the qualifications or skills needed to create, or competence and knowledge needed to build a critical opinion or make cultural choices"* [10, p. 69]. The authors identify five social barriers to the general access to cultural participation: 1) lack of effective/adequate legislation, policies, and legal standards; 2) lack of funding and/or of adequate services; 3) negative attitudes; 4) lack of accessibility; 5) lack of consultation with, and involvement of, persons with disabilities in cultural organisations. These barriers relate to some general types of needs visible in other previous research:

A holistic approach is needed that includes physical access to CH institutions with inclusive, multi-sensory signage, and includes individuals with disabilities in all aspects and events [11]. Accessibility to digital content should cater to individuals with sensory disabilities, ID, dementia, and various cognitive impairments [12, 13]. It is crucial to portray people with disabilities as equal citizens in art and culture and increase staff awareness of varying disability needs [10]. Shifting focus from therapeutic art benefits to understanding professional artists with disabilities' needs is essential [14]. Life satisfaction issues due to solitary leisure require support for leisure participation [15–17], with a focus on self-management, personal growth, and community responsibility [18, 19]. Implementing multiple sign languages, readable print, user-friendly interfaces, and accessibility information about cultural events is necessary [20–23].

Cultural heritage institutions are recognising these needs and interested in implementing accessibility features to their digital collections and provision of digital tools to enhance the participation of people with disabilities. The rise of interest in multisensory museum experiences prompted the re-evaluation of physical access to museums' collections [24] and acquired new meanings during the Covid-19 pandemic when the need for immersive exhibitions in museums became evident [25]. It becomes imperative that new ways of experiencing CH are inclusive from the start and it is not just a side effect for people with disabilities [26]. Audio-descriptions, accessible virtual and video tours attract visitors who could no longer attend CH institutions and places in person [27].

The accessibility of CH for all should be approached from two directions - accessible CH and accessible ICTs [28]. Cultural heritage professionals are responsible for creating a message that needs transmission in an accessible way. Digital tools and means can help in communicating cultural value and enhancing access to inaccessible heritage to all using universal design "*seeking maximum flexibility in order to adapt the solutions to the greatest number of possible needs*" [28, p. 72]. Buono et al. [29] have reflected on the accessibility and multisensory issues as fundamental tools for transferring multilevel knowledge between physical and digital placing the user at the centre of experience.

Cultural heritage institutions involve people with disabilities in their projects on various levels to increase the inclusion and cohesion in the respective communities. Most of these projects report positive outcomes for all participants, however, it is not a straightforward process with the same outcome for everyone. A study of the collaboration of people with Parkinson disease in Second Life indicated an increase in cultural capital [30] and a research of digital divide in reading and creating comic books with peers [31] found that different workshops had different effects on people with different disabilities because of particular experiences related to social environment. Cecilia [27, p. 2] notes that "*the process to overcome exclusion and to create equality of access practices in museums is ongoing and it requires deep changes at institutional levels.*" This could be said of other CH institutions as well.

3   The First Ideation Workshop and Its Results

The first participatory activity in MuseIT was organised as an ideation workshop, in which the participants could share their views on the existing possibilities available for people with disabilities to interact with digital cultural assets and participate in online cultural activities. The participants with disability were reached through broad networks already established in MuseIT and by publication of invitations online in related forums and on the project website. Participants with disabilities including musicians and cultural workers responded. The types of disabilities were not registered per participant but ranged over physical, sensory, and cognitive disabilities. The participants with disabilities indicated that they could only participate online.

The representatives of cultural institutions answered the invitation on the project website, arrived at the meeting place in Paris and participated on site.

Two techniques were prepared to engage the participants in sharing their ideas: 1) stimulation of the discussion with regard to personal and professional experiences through using post-its, and 2) focus group on the following topics: using digital CH and/or cultural participation (personal experiences or professional solutions), their benefits and limitations, suggesting fruitful ways of inclusion.

The workshop consisted of two parts. First, the participants were introduced to the haptic tools created by a project partner organisation, Actronika, namely, a tablet user interface with haptic feedback, devices that enabled haptic experiences such as a cup that emulated the sensation of holding a cup that is being filled or a cup filled with fizzy drink, and Skinetic vest which enables a large set of haptic sensations, such as rain, being struck, etc. (https://www.skinetic.actronika.com/).

Second, the participants were split into three groups for further activity: one online group (six participants), and two on site groups (five participants in each). Each group had two moderators and several observers. The moderators' role was to stimulate the discussion. The observers took notes of what was happening in the group and how the discussion was developing. One observer in the online group monitored the chat. The online session was recorded after having received the agreement of all participants. The quotes in the results are taken from the notes and recordings.

Most of the **participants with disabilities** praised digital communication tools and the Internet enhancing their life choices and enriching experiences. They emphasised the opening of a rich world of *"connections with other people from home"*, overcoming mobility barriers that some of them face. One indicated surprise by the *"rich possibilities to engage in music with others"*. The participants mentioned tools, such as Everdrive, digital games allowing one to make music in a "Cottage". Different apps and the use of tablets allowing people to use their body to play an instrument, or Soundbeam were seen as positive developments in the music world.

The respondents also pointed out the shortcomings of the technologies that limit their use by people with disabilities. One of them reported that *"the size of the iPad is too small and the screen too cluttered by various apps"* and called for the possibility to *"use digital instruments without complex movements"*, also having bigger devices. This could help people with spasticity who cannot aim their movements precisely. The attempt of creating music and transferring it to Gameboy and YouTube as a new version of the song, was an example of the need to use easy file transfer and create spaces for musical expression. Some developments were pointed out as desired breakthrough technologies for the future, e.g., representing music by colour stream and pictures by sounds and haptic interfaces, affordable home recording studios for people with disabilities. They drew attention to the fact *"that many people with disabilities do not have high quality equipment, but work with simple telephones or laptops"* and that *"accessibility is a financial"* concept. This is often forgotten in designing accessible technologies.

One participant pointed out that, during Covid-19 pandemics, there were many initiatives to create digital access to museums and exhibitions, but they were not aimed at people with disabilities. Accessibility was considered as *"a fringe benefit. Why would they not involve people with disabilities from the start?"* Another one had pointed out earlier in the discussion that *"many disabled people are experts in computers and their use, they should be moved to leading positions,"* *"sitting at the design tables from the very beginning so that they can make things accessible from the very beginning"* and not *"episodically through focus groups."* These ideas were seconded by others suggesting that *"differently disabled people feel differently"* and people in wheelchairs or with white canes should meet providers of services to explain what they do not like; their help in designing the services is not only desirable but necessary.

Most of the ***representatives of the cultural institutions*** indicated awareness of diversity among visitors with disabilities, and people in general. Different people may have different "*levels of disability: light–heavy*", thus digital environments should be adjusted to meet all needs, for example, "*working environments for the slightly deaf or not well seeing*". All users of cultural assets have agency in making decisions and need a possibility of various choices, especially, between physical and digital options: a virtual guided tour, synchronous with the one taking place in, e.g., a museum or an asynchronous visit through a digital device.

Choices for people with diverse sensory preferences should be available both online and in physical spaces: "*For persons with hearing disorders – haptic solutions, visualising music by changing colours.*" "*Devices that appeal to the sense of smell, such as the Chronograph in Nantes. Immersive.*" "*We use recordings of cicadas in front of a painting by Cézanne and smells of particular plants for an immersive experience.*" The choice of active participation or passive observation is necessary for some, e.g., those with autism or anxiety, as well as choice of language and control of communication.

The participants from cultural institutions were concerned about meeting the requirements of Web Content Accessibility Guidelines (WCAG): accessibility plug-ins for websites, magnifying and light contrast/white balance tools, screen readers, fonts for visually impaired or dyslexic, easy read options, and "*alt-text on images on all editorial material…*".

The ***final part of the workshop*** brought the participants in all three groups together. They were asked to express their experience of participating in the workshop where they provided useful comments. An important issue raised by an online participant was an underlying perspective of ableism seeping through the conversation in her particular group, indicating the need for improved moderation. This was a lesson learned leading to a review of (a) the planning of future events, (b) instructions provided for session moderation, and (c) the contents of previously planned and upcoming internal learning workshops.

4 Concluding Part

Based on the literature review and the ideation workshop we can conclude that participants with disabilities value the digital environment for communication and self-expression, their needs influenced by personal biographies and societal contexts. Their involvement in designing digital cultural environments is crucial for respect, power sharing, and decision making. Cultural heritage institutions approach the issue in a different way from the perceived needs of their users and organisational requirements. They have pioneered a range of digital inclusion tools, but the opportunities for further refinement and inclusion of the carriers of the perceived needs is imperative in the process of creation of their services. Successful collaboration, co-research, and co-creation demand clear information, better interaction modes, and increased researcher awareness. Plans are underway within MuseIT to enhance future study design and quality based on preliminary study insights.

Acknowledgments. We would like to thank all the workshop participants who generously shared their lived experiences with us. Thanks also to our colleagues, the workshop moderators Maud

Ntonga, Corinne Szteinsznaider, Nigel Osborne and Patricia Alessandrini and colleagues involved in note taking, Andrea Scharnhorst, Moa Johansson, Vyacheslav Tykhonov and Sándor Darányi, and all the other members of the MuseIt project who contributed to and or were involved with the organisations of the workshop. Gratitudes are also due to IRCAM for hosting us for this event. Both authors gratefully acknowledge the grant from EU for the project MuseIT (Grant agreement 101061441). Views and opinions expressed are, however, those of the author(s) only, for which neither the colleagues mentioned, European Union or the MuseIT project can be held responsible.

References

1. Bijker, W.E., Hughes, T.P., Pinch, T.: The Social Construction of Technological Systems: New Directions in the Sociology and History of Technology. The MIT Press, Cambridge (2012)
2. Noble, S.U.: Algorithms of Oppression: How Search Engines Reinforce Racism. New York University Press, New York (2018)
3. O'Neil, C.: Weapons of Math Destruction: How Big Data Increases Inequality and Threatens Democracy. Crown, New York (2016)
4. Wolf, C.T.: Invisible women: data bias in a world designed for men by Caroline Criado Perez (review). Inf. Cult. **54**(3), 400–402 (2019)
5. World Health Organization (2023). https://www.who.int/news-room/fact-sheets/detail/disabi lity-and-health#:~:text=Key%20facts,1%20in%206%20of%20us. Accessed 10 June 2023
6. UN: Universal declaration of human rights. https://www.un.org/en/about-us/universal-declar ation-of-human-rights. Accessed 12 June 2023
7. UN: Convention on the rights of persons with disabilities (2006). https://www.ohchr. org/en/instruments-mechanisms/instruments/convention-rights-persons-disabilities#:~: text=The%20purpose%20of%20the%20present,respect%20for%20their%20inherent%20d ignity. Accessed 11 June 2023
8. Fu, H., Cord, L., McClain-Nhlapo, C.: A billion people experience disabilities worldwide – where is the data? World Bank Blogs (2019). https://blogs.worldbank.org/opendata/billion-people-experience-disabilities-worldwide-so-wheres-data. Accessed 11 June 2023
9. Chen, H.-X., Chou, W.H.: Exploratory design research for the blind and visually impaired visitor in exhibitions. Des. J. **23**(3), 395–417 (2020). https://doi.org/10.1080/14606925.2020. 1744257
10. Leahy, A., Ferri, D.: Barriers and facilitators to cultural participation by people with disabilities: a narrative literature review. Scand. J. Disabil. Res. **24**(1), 68–81 (2022)
11. Eardley, A.F., Mineiro, C., Neves, J., Ride, J.: Redefining access: embracing multimodality, memorability and shared experience in museums. Curator: Mus. J. **59**(3), 263–286 (2016). https://doi.org/10.1111/cura.12163
12. Seale, J., Garcia Carrizosa, H., Rix, J., Sheehy, K., Hayhoe, S.: A participatory approach to the evaluation of participatory museum research projects. Int. J. Res. Method Educ. **44**(1) (2021). https://doi.org/10.1080/1743727X.2019.1706468
13. Renel, W.: Sonic accessibility: increasing social equity through the inclusive design of sound in museums and heritage sites. Curator: Mus. J. **62**(3), 377–402 (2019). https://doi.org/10. 1111/cura.12311
14. Richards, M., Lawthom, R., Runswick-Cole, K.: Community-based arts research for people with learning disabilities: challenging misconceptions about learning disabilities. Disabil. Soc. **34**(2), 204–227 (2019). https://doi.org/10.1080/09687599.2018.1522243
15. Pagan, R.: Leisure activities and loneliness among people with disabilities. In: Lubowiecki-Vikuk, A., de Sousa, B.M.B., Đerčan, B.M., Leal Filho, W. (eds.) Handbook of Sustainable Development and Leisure Services. WSS, pp. 67–83. Springer, Cham (2021). https://doi.org/ 10.1007/978-3-030-59820-4_5

16. Pagán, R.: How do leisure activities impact on life satisfaction? Evidence for German people with disabilities. Appl. Res. Qual. Life **10**(4), 557–572 (2015). https://doi.org/10.1007/s11 482-014-9333-3

17. Shandra, C.L.: Disability and patterns of leisure participation across the life course. J. Gerontol. Ser. B Psychol. Sci. Soc. Sci. **76**(4), 801–809 (2021). https://doi.org/10.1093/geronb/gba a065

18. Doistua, J., Lazcano, I., Madariaga, A.: Self-managed leisure, satisfaction, and benefits perceived by disabled youth in northern Spain. Front. Psychol. **11**, 716 (2020). https://doi.org/ 10.3389/fpsyg.2020.00716

19. Labbé, D., Miller, W.C., Ng, R.: Participating more, participating better: health benefits of adaptive leisure for people with disabilities. Disabil. Health J. **12**(2), 287–295 (2019). https:// doi.org/10.1016/j.dhjo.2018.11.007

20. Constantinou, V., Loizides, F., Ioannou, A.: A personal tour of cultural heritage for deaf museum visitors. In: Ioannides, M., Fink, E., Moropoulou, A., Hagedorn-Saupe, M., Fresa, A., Liestøl, G., Rajcic, V., Grussenmeyer, P. (eds.) EuroMed 2016. LNCS, vol. 10059, pp. 214–221. Springer, Cham (2016). https://doi.org/10.1007/978-3-319-48974-2_24

21. Kosmas, P., Galanakis, G., Constantinou, V., Drossis, G., Christofi, M., Klironomos, I., Zaphiris, P., Antona, M., Stephanidis, C.: Enhancing accessibility in cultural heritage environments: considerations for social computing. Univ. Access Inf. Soc. **19**(2), 471–482 (2019). https://doi.org/10.1007/s10209-019-00651-4

22. Sorce, S., Gentile, V., Oliveto, D., Barraco, R., Malizia, A., Gentile, A.: Exploring usability and accessibility of avatar-based touchless gestural interfaces for autistic people. In: Schmidt, A., et al. (eds.) Proceedings of PerDis18: The 7th ACM International Symposium on Pervasive Displays, Munich, Germany, pp. 6–8. ACM (2018). (Art. no. 30). https://doi.org/10.1145/320 5873.3210705

23. De Luca, V., et al.: Virtual reality and spatial augmented reality for social inclusion: the "Includiamoci" project. Information **14**(1), 38 (2023). https://doi.org/10.3390/info14010038

24. Classen, C.: The Museum of the Senses: Experiencing Art and Collections. Bloomsbury Academic, London (2016)

25. Gianini, T., Bowen, J.P.: Museums and digital culture: from reality to digitality in the age of COVID-19. Heritage **5**(1), 192–214 (2022). https://doi.org/10.3390/heritage5010011

26. Sørmoen, O., Arenghi, A., Garofolo, I.: Accessibility as a Key Enabling Knowledge for Enhancement of Cultural Heritage. Franco Angeli, Milan (2016)

27. Cecilia, R.R.: COVID-19 pandemic: threat or opportunity for blind and partially sighted museum visitors? J. Conserv. Mus. Stud. **19**(1), 1–8 (2021). https://doi.org/10.5334/jcms.200

28. Arenghi, A., Agostiano, M.: Cultural heritage and disability: can ICT be the 'missing piece' to face cultural heritage accessibility problems? In: Gaggi, O., Manzoni, P., Palazzi, C., Bujari, A., Marquez-Barja, J.M. (eds.) GOODTECHS 2016. LNICSSITE, vol. 195, pp. 70–77. Springer, Cham (2017). https://doi.org/10.1007/978-3-319-61949-1_8

29. Buono, M., Capece, S., Scognamiglio, C.: Multisensory fruition between cultural heritage and digital transformation. In: Martins, N., Brandão, D., Paiva, F. (eds). Perspectives on Design and Digital Communication III. SSDI, vol. 24, pp. 329–355. Springer, Cham (2022). https:// doi.org/10.1007/978-3-031-06809-6_21

30. Davis, D.Z., Boellstorff, T.: Compulsive creativity: virtual worlds, disability, and digital capital. Int. J. Commun. **10**, 2096–2118 (2016). https://ijoc.org/index.php/ijoc/article/view/5099/ 1639

31. Maceviciute, E., Wilson, T., Manzuch, Z.: Assessing the graphic questionnaire used in digital literacy training. Issues Inf. Sci. Inf. Technol. **16**, 113–126 (2019). https://doi.org/10.28945/ 4301

Author Index

O. Alonso et al. (Eds.): TPDL 2023, LNCS 14241, pp. 357–358, 2023.
https://doi.org/10.1007/978-3-031-43849-3